AUSCHWITZ

THE NAZIS & THE 'FINAL SOLUTION'

In memory of 1.1 million men,
women and children
who died at Auschwitz

AUSCHWITZ

THE NAZIS & THE 'FINAL SOLUTION'

LAURENCE REES

TED SMART

This book is published to accompany *Auschwitz*,
first broadcast on BBC2 in 2005
Written and produced by Laurence Rees

Published by BBC Books, BBC Worldwide Ltd,
Woodlands, 80 Wood Lane, London W12 0TT

First published 2005

This edition produced for The Book People Ltd,
Hall Wood Avenue, Haydock, St Helens WA11 9UL

ISBN 0 563 52267 4

Commissioning editor: Sally Potter
Project editor: Martin Redfern
Copy editor: Esther Jagger
Designer: Ann Burnham
Picture researcher: Joanne King
Production controller: Christopher Tinker

Set in Sabon by BBC Books
Printed and bound in Great Britain by CPI Bath
Colour origination by Butler & Tanner Ltd

Contents

INTRODUCTION 6

CHAPTER 1
SURPRISING BEGINNINGS 19

CHAPTER 2
ORDERS AND INITIATIVES 73

CHAPTER 3
FACTORIES OF DEATH 121

CHAPTER 4
CORRUPTION 174

CHAPTER 5
FRENZIED KILLING 224

CHAPTER 6
LIBERATION AND RETRIBUTION 263

NOTES 303

ACKNOWLEDGEMENTS 312

INDEX 315

PICTURE CREDITS 320

Introduction

There is much in this book that is upsetting, but I still think it is a necessary piece of work. Not just for the obvious reason that surveys[1] still show that there is confusion in the popular consciousness about the true history of Auschwitz, but also because I hope it offers something distinctive.

It is the culmination of 15 years of writing books and making television programmes about the Nazis, and is an attempt to show how one of the worst crimes in history is best understood through the prism of one physical place: Auschwitz. Unlike the history of anti-Semitism, Auschwitz has one certain beginning (the first Polish prisoners arrived on 14 June 1940), and unlike the history of genocide, it has one definite end (the camp was liberated on 27 January 1945). In between these two dates Auschwitz had a complex and surprising history that in many ways mirrored the intricacies of Nazi racial and ethnic policy. It was never conceived as a camp to kill Jews, it was never solely concerned with the 'Final Solution' – though that came to dominate the place – and it was always physically changing, often in response to the constant shifts in fortunes of the German war effort elsewhere. Auschwitz, through its destructive dynamism, was the physical embodiment of the fundamental values of the Nazi state.

The study of Auschwitz also offers us something other than an insight into the Nazis; it gives us the chance to understand how human beings behaved in some of the most extreme conditions in history. From this story there is a great deal we can learn about ourselves.

This is a book based on unique research – around 100 specially conducted interviews with former Nazi perpetrators and survivors from the camp – and draws on hundreds more interviews conducted for my previous work on the Third Reich, many with former members of the Nazi party[2]. The benefit of meeting and questioning survivors and perpetrators is immense. It offers an opportunity for a level of insight that is rarely available from written sources alone. Indeed, although since my school days I had always been interested in this period of history, I can trace my own deep fascination with the Third Reich to one moment during a conversation with a former member of the Nazi party back in 1990. While writing and producing a film about Dr Josef Goebbels, I talked to Wilfred von Oven who, as his personal attaché, had worked closely with the infamous Nazi propaganda minister. After the formal interview, over a cup of tea, I asked this intelligent and charming man: 'If you could sum up your experience of the Third Reich in just one word, what would it be?' As Herr von Oven thought for a moment and considered the question, I guessed his response would make reference to the horrible crimes of the regime – crimes he freely admitted had occurred – and of the damage Nazism had wreaked upon the world. 'Well,' he finally said, 'if I was asked to sum up my experience of the Third Reich in one word, that word would be – Paradise.'

'Paradise'? That didn't coincide with anything I had read in my history books. Nor did it square with the elegant, sophisticated man who sat in front of me, who did not, come to that, look or talk as I had imagined a former Nazi should. But 'Paradise'? How was it possible that he could say such a thing? How could any intelligent person think of the Third Reich and its atrocities in such a way? Indeed, how was it possible that during the twentieth century people from Germany, a cultured nation at the heart of Europe, had ever perpetrated such crimes? Those were the questions that formed in my mind that afternoon all those years ago, and that still sit heavily in my mind today.

In my attempt to answer them I was helped by two accidents of history. The first was that I set out to question former Nazis at exactly the point at which most of them had nothing to lose by speaking openly. Fifteen years earlier, holding down influential jobs and pillars of their communities, they would not have spoken. Today most of them, including the charming Herr von Oven, are dead.

It often took months, in some cases years, to persuade them to allow us to record an interview. We can never know exactly what tipped the balance and made an individual agree to be filmed, but in many cases they clearly felt that, nearing the end of their lives, they wanted to put on record – warts and all – their experiences of these momentous times; they also believed that the BBC would not distort their contribution. I would add that I think only the BBC would have given us the necessary support to pursue this enterprise. The research period for these projects was so long that only a public service broadcaster could have made such a commitment.

The second break I had was that my interest coincided with the fall of the Berlin Wall and the opening up of eastern Europe; and it was not just the archives that suddenly became available for research, but the people as well. I had filmed in the Soviet Union in 1989 under Communism, and back then it was hard to get anyone to speak about their nation's history in anything other than propaganda slogans. Now, suddenly, in the 1990s, it was as if a dam had broken and all the suppressed memories and opinions came tumbling out. In the Baltic states I heard people say how they had welcomed the Nazis as liberators; on the wild steppes of Kalmykia I learnt first hand about Stalin's vindictive deportations of whole ethnic communities; in Siberia I met veterans who had been imprisoned twice – once by Hitler and once by the Soviet dictator; and in a village near Minsk I encountered a woman who had been caught in the middle of the most vicious partisan war in modern history and, on reflection, thought the Red Army partisans were worse than the Nazis. All of these deeply held convictions would have died with the people who held them had Communism not fallen.

I also encountered something more frightening as I travelled around these newly liberated countries, from Lithuania to the Ukraine and from Serbia to Belarus: virulent anti-Semitism. I had expected people to tell me how much they hated the Communists; that seemed only natural now. But to hate Jews? It seemed ludicrous, especially since there were hardly any Jews in the places I was visiting – Hitler and the Nazis had seen to that. Yet the old man in the Baltic states who had helped the Nazis shoot Jews in 1941 still thought he had done the right thing 60 years ago. And even some of those who had fought against the Nazis held wild anti-Semitic beliefs. I remember the question one Ukrainian veteran put to me over lunch. He was a man who had fought bravely for the Ukrainian Nationalist partisans against both the Nazis and the Red Army and been persecuted as result. 'What do you think,' he asked me, 'of the view that there is an international conspiracy of Jewish financiers operating out of New York which is trying to destroy all non-Jewish governments?' I looked at him for a second. Not being Jewish myself, it is always something of a shock to encounter naked anti-Semitism from an unexpected source. 'What do I think of that view?' I replied finally. 'I think it's total garbage.' The old partisan took a sip of vodka. 'Really,' he said. 'That's your opinion. Interesting ...'

What shocked me most of all was that these anti-Semitic views were not just confined to the older generation. I remember the woman at the Lithuanian Airways check-in desk who, after learning the subject of the film we were making, said, 'You're interested in the Jews, are you? Well, just remember this – Marx was a Jew.' Or, also in Lithuania, I recall an army officer in his mid-twenties showing me round the site of the 1941 Jewish massacres at a fort in Kaunas and saying, 'You're missing the big story, you know. The story isn't what we did to the Jews. It's what the Jews did to us.' I do not claim for a moment that everyone – or even the majority – in the eastern European countries I visited subscribes to these views; but that this kind of prejudice is openly expressed at all is disturbing.

All this should be remembered by those people who think that the history in this book is of little relevance today. And it should also be mulled over by those who think that corrosive anti-Semitism was somehow confined to the Nazis or even to Hitler. Indeed, the view that the crime of the extermination of the Jews was somehow imposed by a few mad people upon an unwilling Europe is one of the most dangerous of all. There was nothing 'uniquely exterminatory' – to use the current academic buzzwords – about German society before the Nazis came to power. How could there have been, when many Jews fled from anti-Semitism in eastern Europe in the 1920s to seek sanctuary in Germany?

Yet there is something about the mentality of the Nazis that seems at odds with the perpetrators who flourished in many other totalitarian regimes. That was certainly the conclusion I reached after completing three separate projects on World War II, each a book and television series: first *Nazis: A Warning from History*, then *War of the Century*, an examination of the war between Stalin and Hitler, and finally *Horror in the East*, an attempt to understand the Japanese psyche during the 1930s and World War II. One unplanned consequence of this experience is that it puts me in a unique position as the only person I know of who has met and questioned a significant number of perpetrators from all three of the major wartime totalitarian powers: Germany, Japan and the Soviet Union. Having done so, I can confirm that the Nazi war criminals I met were different.

In the Soviet Union the climate of fear under Stalin was pervasive in a way it never was in Germany under Hitler until the last days of the war. The description one former Soviet air force officer gave me of open meetings in the 1930s, when anyone could be denounced as an 'enemy of the people', still haunts me to this day. No one was safe from the knock at the door at midnight. No matter how well you tried to conform, no matter how many slogans you spouted, such was Stalin's malevolence that nothing you did or said or thought could save you if the spotlight picked you out. But in Nazi Germany, unless you were a member of a specific risk group – the Jews, the Communists, the gypsies, homosexuals, the 'work-shy' and, indeed, anyone who opposed the regime – you could live comparatively free from fear. Despite all the recent academic work that rightly emphasizes how the Gestapo relied hugely upon denunciations from members of the public to do its work,[3] the central truth still holds that the majority of the German population, almost certainly right up until the moment Germany started to lose the war, felt so personally secure and happy that they would have voted to keep Hitler in power if there had been free and fair elections. By contrast, in the Soviet Union not even Stalin's closest, most loyal colleagues ever felt they could sleep securely.

The consequence of this for those who perpetrated crimes at Stalin's behest was that the suffering they inflicted was so arbitrary that they often did not know the reasons for it. For example, the former Soviet secret policeman I met who bundled up Kalmyks and put them on trains to exile in Siberia still did not have a clear idea about what was behind the policy even today. He had one stock response when asked why he had taken part – ironically, it is the one most commonly ascribed to Nazis in popular myth; he said he had been 'acting under orders'. He had committed a crime because he was told to, and knew that if he failed to do so then he would be shot, and he trusted that his bosses knew what they were doing. Which meant, of course, that when Stalin died and Communism fell he was free to move on and leave the past behind. It also shows up Stalin as a cruel, bullying dictator who has many parallels in history, not least in our own time with Saddam Hussein.

Then there were the Japanese war criminals I encountered who committed some of the most appalling atrocities in modern history. In China, Japanese soldiers split open the stomachs of pregnant women and bayoneted the foetuses; they tied up local farmers and used them for target practice; they tortured thousands of innocent people in ways that rival the Gestapo at their worst; and they were pursuing deadly medical experiments long before Dr Mengele and Auschwitz. These were the people who were supposed to be 'inscrutable'. But on examination they turned out to be nothing of the kind. They had grown up in an intensely militaristic society, had been subjected to military training of the most brutal sort, had been told since they were children to worship their Emperor (who was also their commander-in-chief) and lived in a culture that historically elevated the all-too-human desire to conform into a semi-religion. All this was encapsulated by one veteran who told me that when he had been asked to take part in the gang rape of a Chinese woman he saw it less as a sexual act and more as a sign of final acceptance by the group, many of whom had previously bullied him mercilessly. Like the Soviet secret policemen I met, these Japanese veterans attempted to justify their actions almost exclusively with reference to an external source – the regime itself.

Something different appears in the minds of many Nazi war criminals and is encapsulated in this book by the interview with Hans Friedrich who admits, as a member of an SS unit in the East, to having personally shot Jews. Even today, with the Nazi regime long defeated, he is not sorry for what he did. The easy course for him would be to hide behind the 'acting under orders' or 'I was brainwashed by propaganda' excuses, but such is the strength of his own internal conviction that he does not. At the time he personally believed it was right to shoot Jews, and he gives every appearance of still believing it today. It is a loathsome, despicable position – but nonetheless an intriguing one. And the contemporary evidence shows that he is not unique. At Auschwitz, for example, there is not one case in the records of an SS man being prosecuted for refusing to take part in the killings, whilst there is plenty of material showing that the real discipline problem in the camp – from the point of view of the SS leadership – was theft. The ordinary members of the SS thus appear to have agreed with the Nazi leadership that it was right to kill the Jews, but disagreed with Himmler's policy of not letting them individually profit from the crime. And the penalties for an SS man caught stealing could be draconian – almost certainly worse than for simply refusing to take an active part in the killing.

Thus the conclusion I reached, not just from interviews but also from subsequent archival research[4] and discussion with academic researchers, was that there was a greater likelihood of individuals who committed crimes within the Nazi system taking personal responsibility for their actions than war criminals who served Stalin or Hirohito. Of course, that is a generalization and there will be individuals within each regime who do not conform to that type. And all these regimes certainly had much in common – not least a reliance on intense ideological propaganda imposed from above. But as a generalization it appears to hold good, and is all the more curious given the rigid training of the SS and the popular stereotype of German soldiers as automatons. As we shall see, this tendency for individual Nazis who committed crimes to feel more personally in control contributed to the development of both Auschwitz and the 'Final Solution'.

It is worth trying to understand why so many of the former Nazis I have met over the last 15 years appear to find an internal justification for their crimes ('I thought it was the right thing to do') rather than an external one ('I was ordered to do it'). One obvious explanation is that the Nazis carefully built on pre-existing convictions. Anti-Semitism existed in Germany long before Adolf Hitler, and plenty of other people blamed the Jews, falsely, for Germany's defeat in World War I. In fact, the whole of the Nazis' initial political programme in the early 1920s was virtually indistinguishable from those of countless other nationalistic right-wing parties. Hitler brought no originality of political thought; what he brought was originality of leadership. And when the Depression gripped Germany in the early 1930s, millions of Germans voluntarily turned to the Nazis for a solution to the country's ills. No one in the elections of 1932 was forced at gunpoint to vote for the Nazis, and the Nazis went on to gain power within the existing law.

Another clear reason why the belief system amongst so many Nazis was internalized was the work of Dr Josef Goebbels,[5] who was much the most effective propagandist of the twentieth century. In popular myth he is often dismissed as a crude polemicist, infamous for *Der ewige Jude* (*The Eternal Jew*), a notorious film in which shots of Jews were intercut with pictures of rats. But in reality the vast majority of his work was much more sophisticated and much more insidious. It was Hitler who was more keen on obvious hate-filled films like *Der ewige Jude*; Goebbels disliked that rudimentary approach, preferring the much more subtle *Jud Süs*, a drama in which a beautiful 'Aryan' girl was raped by a Jew. Goebbels' own audience research (a science he was obsessed with) revealed that he was right; cinemagoers much preferred to see propaganda films where, as he put it, 'they cannot see the art in it'.

Goebbels believed that it was always preferable to reinforce the existing prejudice of the audience rather than to try to change someone's mind. On those occasions when it was necessary to attempt to alter the views of the German people, his technique was to move 'like a convoy – always at the speed of the slowest vessel'[6] and constantly to reiterate, in subtly different ways, the message he wanted the audience to receive. And in doing so he rarely tried to tell the viewers anything; he showed images and told stories that led ordinary Germans to reach the conclusion he wanted, whilst leaving them thinking they had worked it out for themselves.

During the 1930s Hitler, to Goebbels' approval, did not often try to impose policies on the majority of the population against their wishes. This was a radical regime, of course, but one that preferred the consent of the majority, and relied to a large extent for the dynamism it so desired upon individual initiative coming from below – all of which meant that when it came to the persecution of the Jews the Nazis progressed gingerly. Central though the hatred of the Jews was to Hitler, it was not a policy he overtly pushed in the elections of the early 1930s. He did not hide his anti-Semitism, but he and the Nazis consciously emphasized other policies, such as their desire to 'right the wrongs' of the Versailles treaty, get the unemployed back to work and restore a sense of national pride. In the immediate aftermath of Hitler becoming Chancellor there was an outpouring of violence against the German Jews, orchestrated to a large extent by Nazi stormtroopers. There was also a boycott of Jewish businesses (supported by Goebbels, an ardent anti-Semite), but this only lasted for one day. The Nazi leadership were concerned about public opinion both at home and abroad; in particular they didn't want their anti-Semitism to make Germany a pariah state. Two more anti-Semitic upsurges – one in 1936 with the advent of the Nuremberg Laws withdrawing citizenship from German Jews, and the second in 1938 with the burning of synagogues and the imprisonment of tens of thousands of Jews at the time of Kristallnacht – marked the other significant pre-war moments in the Nazi persecution of the Jews. But overall the pace of Nazi anti-Semitic policy was gradual, and many Jews tried to stick out life in Hitler's Germany during the 1930s. Nazi propaganda against the Jews proceeded (with the exception of fringe fanatics like Julius Streicher and his outrageous anti-Semitic rag *Der Stürmer*) at Goebbels' speed of the slowest vessel in the convoy, with neither of the overtly anti-Semitic films, *Der ewige Jude* or *Jud Süss*, shown until after the war had begun.

This notion that the Nazis proceeded incrementally against the Jews goes against the understandable desire to point to a single moment when one crucial decision was made for the 'Final Solution' and the gas chambers of Auschwitz. But this history is not so easily resolved. The decisions that led to the sophistication of a killing technique that delivered families to their deaths by a railway link which stopped only metres from the crematoria, took years to evolve. The Nazi regime was one that practised what one historian famously called 'cumulative radicalisation',[7] whereby each decision often led to a crisis that led to a still more radical decision. The most obvious example of how events could spiral into catastrophe was the food crisis in the Łódź ghetto in the summer of 1941 – a situation that led one Nazi functionary to ask whether the most 'humane solution might not be to finish off those of the Jews who are not fit for work by means of some quick-working device'.[8] Thus the idea of extermination is offered up out of 'humanity'. It should be remembered, of course, that it was the policies of the Nazi leadership that had created the food crisis in the Łódź ghetto in the first place.

This does not mean that Hitler was not to blame for the crime – he undoubtedly was – but he was responsible in a more sinister way than simply calling his subordinates together on one particular day and forcing the decision upon them. All the leading Nazis knew their Führer prized one quality in policy-making above all others: radicalism. Hitler once said that he wanted his generals to be like 'dogs straining on a leash' (and in this they most often failed him). His love of radicalism, plus his technique of encouraging massive competition within the Nazi leadership often by appointing two people to do more or less the same job, meant that there was intense dynamism in the political and administrative system – plus intense inherent instability. Everyone knew how much Hitler hated the Jews, everyone heard his 1939 speech in the Reichstag during which he predicted the 'extermination' of the European Jews if they 'caused' a world war, and so everyone in the Nazi leadership knew the kind of policy towards the Jews to suggest – the more radical the better.

Hitler was massively preoccupied with one task during World War II: trying to win it. He spent much less time on the Jewish question than on the intricacies of military strategy. His attitude to Jewish policy is likely to have been similar to the instructions he gave to the Gauleiters (regional leaders) of Danzig, West Prussia and the Warthegau when he told them he wanted their areas Germanized, and once they had accomplished the task he promised to ask them 'no questions' about how they had done it. In just such a manner it is not hard to imagine Hitler saying to Himmler in December 1941 that he wanted the Jews 'exterminated' and that he would ask him 'no questions' about how he had achieved the desired result. We cannot know for sure whether the conversation went this way, of course, because during the war Hitler was careful to use Himmler as a buffer between himself and the implementation of the 'Final Solution'. Hitler knew the scale of the crime the Nazis were contemplating and he did not want any document linking him to it. But his fingerprints are everywhere – from his open rhetoric of hatred to the close correlation between Himmler's meetings with Hitler at his East Prussian headquarters and the subsequent radicalization of the persecution and murder of the Jews.

It is hard to convey the excitement that leading Nazis felt at serving a man who dared to dream in such epic terms. Hitler had dreamt of defeating France in weeks – the very country in which the German army had been stuck for years during World War I – and he had succeeded. He had dreamt of conquering the Soviet Union, and in the summer and autumn of 1941 it looked almost certain that he would win. And he dreamt of exterminating the Jews, which in some ways was to prove the easiest task of all.

Hitler's ambitions were certainly on a grand scale – but they were all ultimately destructive, the 'Final Solution' the most conceptually destructive of them all. It is of significance that in 1940 two Nazis who would subsequently become leading figures in the development and implementation of the 'Final Solution' both separately acknowledged that mass murder would go against the 'civilized' values to which even they aspired. Heinrich Himmler wrote that 'physically exterminating a people' was 'fundamentally un-German', and Reinhard Heydrich recorded that 'biological extermination is undignified for the German people as a civilized nation'.[9] But step by step, within the next 18 months, 'physically exterminating a people' was just the policy they would be embracing.

Tracing how Hitler, Himmler, Heydrich and other leading Nazis created both their 'Final Solution' and Auschwitz offers us the chance to see in action a dynamic and radical decision-making process of great complexity. There was no blueprint for the crime imposed from above, nor one devised from below and simply acknowledged from the top. Individual Nazis were not coerced by crude threats to commit murders themselves. No, this was a collective enterprise owned by thousands of people, who made the decision themselves not just to take part but to contribute initiatives in order to solve the problem of how to kill human beings and dispose of their bodies on a scale never attempted before.

As we follow the journey upon which both the Nazis and those whom they persecuted embarked, we also gain a great deal of insight into the human condition. And what we learn is mostly not good. In this history, suffering is almost never redemptive. Although there are, on very rare occasions, extraordinary people who act virtuously, for the most part this is a story of degradation. It is hard not to agree with the verdict of Else Baker, sent to Auschwitz as an eight-year-old, that 'the level of human depravity is unfathomable'. However, if there is a spark of hope, it is in the power of the family as a sustaining force. Heroic acts are committed by those sent to the camps, for the sake of a father, mother, brother, sister or child.

Perhaps above all, though, Auschwitz and the Nazis' 'Final Solution' demonstrate the power of the situation to influence behaviour to a greater extent than we might like to imagine. It is a view confirmed by one of the toughest and bravest survivors of the death camps, Toivi Blatt, who was forced by the Nazis to work in Sobibór and then risked his life to escape: 'People asked me,' he says, '"What did you learn?", and I think I'm only sure of one thing – nobody knows themselves. The nice person on the street, you ask him "Where is North Street?" and he goes with you half a block and shows you, and is nice and kind. That same person in a different situation could be the worst sadist. Nobody knows themselves. All of us could be good people or bad people in these [different] situations. Sometimes when somebody is really nice to me I find myself thinking, "How will he be in Sobibór?"'[10]

What these survivors have taught me (and, if I am honest, I learnt it from the perpetrators as well) is that human behaviour is fragile and unpredictable and often at the mercy of the situation. Every individual still, of course, has a choice as to how to behave; it is just that for many people the situation is a key determinant in that choice. Even those unusual individuals – Adolf Hitler himself, for example – who appear to be masters of their own destiny were to a considerable extent created by their response to previous situations. The Adolf Hitler known to history was substantially formed by the interaction between the pre-war Hitler, who was a worthless drifter, and the events of World War I, which was a global conflict over which he had no control. I know not a single serious scholar of the subject who thinks that Hitler could ever have risen to prominence without the transformation he underwent during that war, and the sense of intense bitterness he felt when Germany lost. Thus we can go further than saying, 'No World War I, no Hitler as German Chancellor', and say, 'No World War I, no individual who ever became the Hitler that history knows'. And whilst, of course, Hitler decided for himself how to behave (and in the process made a series of personal choices that made him utterly deserving of all the obloquy heaped upon him), he was made possible only by that specific historical situation.

However, this history also shows us that if individuals can be buffeted around by the situation, then groups of human beings working together can create better cultures, which in turn can help individuals to behave more virtuously. The story of how the Danes rescued their Jews, and of how they ensured the Jews had a warm welcome when they returned at the end of the war, is a striking example of that. The culture in Denmark of a strong and widely held belief in human rights helped make the majority of individuals behave in a noble way. But one must not be overly romantic about the Danish experience. The Danes too were influenced hugely by situational factors outside their control: the timing of the Nazi attack on the Danish Jews (at a point when the Germans were clearly losing the war); the geography of their country (which allowed for a relatively straightforward escape across a narrow stretch of water to neutral Sweden); and the lack of a concerted effort by the SS to enforce the deportations. Nonetheless, it is reasonable to conclude that one form of partial protection against more atrocities like Auschwitz lies in individuals collectively ensuring the cultural mores of their society are antipathetic to such suffering. The overtly Darwinian ideals of Nazism, which rested on telling every 'Aryan' German he or she was racially superior, created, of course, precisely the reverse effect.

In the end, though, there is a profound sense of sadness around this subject that cannot be reduced. Throughout the time I was working on this project the voices I heard loudest were those of the people whom we could not interview: the 1.1 million human beings who were murdered in Auschwitz, and in particular the more than 200,000 children who perished there and were denied the right to grow up and experience life. One image stuck in my mind from the moment I heard it described. It was of a 'procession'[11] of empty baby carriages – property looted from the dead Jews – pushed out of Auschwitz in rows of five towards the railway station. The prisoner who witnessed the sight said they took an hour to pass by.

The children who arrived at Auschwitz in those baby carriages, together with their mothers, fathers, brothers, sisters, uncles and aunts – all of those who died there – are the ones we should always remember, and this book is dedicated to their memory.

Laurence Rees, London, July 2004

— 1 —

Surprising Beginnings

On 30 April 1940 SS Hauptsturmführer (Captain) Rudolf Hoess achieved a great ambition. At the age of 39, and after six years' service in the SS, he had been appointed commandant of one of the first Nazi concentration camps in the New Reich. On this spring day he arrived to take up his duties in a small town in what had been until eight months previously southwest Poland and was now part of German Upper Silesia. The name of the town in Polish was Oświęcim – in German, Auschwitz.

Although Hoess had been promoted to commandant, the camp he was to command did not yet exist. He had to supervise its construction from a collection of dilapidated and vermin-infested former Polish army barracks, grouped around a horse-breaking yard on the edge of the town. And the surrounding area could scarcely have been more depressing. This land between the Soła and Vistula rivers was flat and drab, the climate damp and unhealthy.

No one on that first day, and that certainly included Rudolph Hoess, could have predicted the camp would, within five years, become the site of the largest mass murder the world has yet seen. The story of the decision-making process that led to this transformation is one of the most shocking in the whole of history and one that offers great insights into the functioning of the Nazi state.

Adolf Hitler, Heinrich Himmler, Reinhard Heydrich, Hermann Goering – all these leading Nazis and more took decisions that led to the extermination of more than a million people at Auschwitz. But a crucial precondition for the crime was also the mentality of more minor functionaries such as Hoess. Without Hoess's leadership through the hitherto uncharted territory of mass murder on this scale, Auschwitz would never have functioned as it did.

To look at, there was little exceptional about Rudolf Hoess. He was of medium height, with regular features and dark hair. He was neither ugly nor strikingly handsome; he simply resembled – in the words of American lawyer Whitney Harris,[1] who interrogated Hoess at Nuremberg – 'a normal person, like a grocery clerk'. Several Polish inmates of Auschwitz confirm this impression, remembering Hoess as quiet and controlled, the kind of person you walk past every day in the street and fail to notice. In appearance, Hoess was thus as far away as it is possible to get from the conventional image of the red-faced, saliva-spitting SS monster, which, of course, makes him all the more terrifying a figure.

As Hoess carried his suitcase into the hotel opposite Auschwitz railway station that would be the SS officers' base until suitable accommodation had been arranged within the camp, he also brought with him the mental baggage of an adult life devoted to the nationalist cause. Like most ardent Nazis, his character and beliefs had been shaped by his reaction to the previous 25 years of German history – the most turbulent the country had ever experienced. Born in the Black Forest in 1900 to Catholic parents, Hoess was affected in his early years by a series of important influences: a domineering father who insisted on obedience; his service in World War I, where he was one of the youngest non-commissioned officers in the German army; his desperate sense of betrayal at the subsequent loss of the war; his service in the paramilitary Freikorps in the early 1920s in an attempt to counter the perceived Communist threat on the boundaries of Germany; and an involvement in violent right-wing politics that led to his imprisonment in 1923.

Many, many other Nazis were forged in a similar crucible. Not least among them was Adolf Hitler. Son of a domineering father,[2] nursing his violent hatred of those whom he felt had lost Germany the war in which he had just fought (and during which, like Hoess, he had been awarded an Iron Cross), Hitler tried to seize power in a violent *Putsch* in exactly the same year as Hoess was elsewhere involved in a politically inspired murder.

For Hitler, Hoess and others on the nationalist right, the most urgent need was to understand why Germany had lost the war and made such a humiliating peace. And in the immediate post-war years they believed they had found the answer. Was it not obvious, they felt, that the Jews had been responsible? They pointed out that Walther Rathenau, who was Jewish, had become Foreign Minister in the new post-war Weimar government. And in 1919 they believed the link between Judaism and the feared creed of Communism had been proved beyond doubt when in Munich a Soviet-style Räterepublik (Councils' Republic) was established briefly in the spring; the majority of the leaders of this Communist-led government had been Jewish.

It did not matter that large numbers of loyal German Jews had fought with bravery (and many had died) during the war. Nor that thousands of German Jews were neither left wing nor Communist. It was much easier for Hitler and his followers to find a scapegoat for Germany's predicament in the German Jews. In the process, the newly formed Nazi party built on years of German anti-Semitism. And from the first its adherents claimed that their hatred of the Jews was motivated not by ignorant prejudice but by scientific fact: 'We fight their [the Jews'] actions as they cause a RACIAL TUBERCULOSIS OF NATIONS,' declares one of the earliest Nazi posters, published in 1920. 'And we are convinced that convalescence can only begin when this bacteria has been removed.'[3] This kind of pseudo-intellectual attack on the Jews had a huge effect on men like Hoess, who professed to despise the primitive, violent, almost pornographic anti-Semitism propagated by another Nazi, Julius Streicher, in his magazine *Der Stürmer*. 'The cause of anti-Semitism is ill-served by the frenzied persecution that was provided by *Der Stürmer*,'[4] wrote Hoess in prison after the defeat of Nazism. His approach was always colder, more 'rational', as he saw it. He claimed to have little quarrel with individual Jews; the problem for him was the 'International world Jewish conspiracy', by which he imagined that Jews secretly held the levers of power and sought to help each other across national boundaries. This was what he believed had led to Germany's defeat in World War I. This was what he felt had to be destroyed: 'As a fanatical National Socialist I was completely convinced that our ideal would gradually be accepted and would prevail all over the world ... Jewish supremacy would therefore be destroyed.'[5]

After his release from prison in 1928 Hoess pursued another of the treasured right-wing nationalist beliefs which, like anti-Semitism, helped define the Nazi movement: love of the land.

Whilst the Jews were hated because for the most part they lived in cities (despised, as Goebbels put it, for their 'asphalt culture'), 'true' Germans never lost their love of nature. It was no accident that Himmler himself had studied agriculture, nor that Auschwitz was eventually to have one incarnation as an agricultural research station.

Hoess joined the Artamans, one of the agricultural communities that flourished in Germany at the time, met the woman who became his wife, and settled down to become a farmer. Then came the moment that changed his life. In June 1934 Himmler, Hitler's chief of police, invited him to give up farming and become a full-time member of the SS, the elite Shutzstaffel that had originally been founded as the Führer's personal bodyguard and, among other duties, was now running the concentration camps.[6] Himmler had known Hoess for some time and liked what he saw. Hoess was an early member of the Nazi party, having joined in November 1922, and held party number 3240.

Hoess had a choice. He was not forced to volunteer – no one was conscripted into the SS. Yet he chose to join. In his autobiography he gives this reason for his decision: 'Because of the likely prospect of swift promotion and the salary that accompanied it, I was convinced that I had to take this step.'[7] This was only half the truth. Not surprisingly, writing after Nazism had been defeated, Hoess omits what must have been for him the most important deciding factor: his emotional state at the time. In 1934 Hoess would have felt he was witnessing the beginning of a new and wonderful world. Hitler had been in power for a year and already the Nazis' internal enemies – the left-wing politicians, the 'work-shy', the anti-socials, the Jews – were being confronted. All over the country Germans not in these specific risk-groups welcomed what they saw. Typical was the reaction of Manfred von Schroeder, a banker's son from Hamburg who joined the Nazi party in 1933: 'Everything was in order again, and clean. There was a feeling of national liberation, a new start ... People said, "Well, this is a revolution; it is an astonishing, peaceful revolution, but it is a revolution."'[8] Hoess now had a chance to be a player in this revolution; a revolution that he had prayed for since the end of World War I. Joining the SS meant status, privilege, excitement and a chance to influence the course of the new Germany. Staying a farmer meant, well, staying a farmer. Is it surprising that Hoess made the choice he did? So he accepted Himmler's invitation and in November 1934 arrived at Dachau in Bavaria to start his service as a concentration camp guard.

In the popular consciousness today, certainly in Britain and America, there exists confusion about the function of the various camps in the Nazi state. Concentration camps like Dachau (which was established in March 1933, less than two months after Adolf Hitler became German Chancellor) were conceptually different from death camps like Treblinka, which were not in existence until the middle of the war. Adding further to the confusion in many people's minds is the complex history of Auschwitz, the most infamous camp of all, which was to evolve into *both* a concentration camp and a death camp. Grasping the importance of the distinction between the two is essential in order to understand how Germans at the time rationalized the existence of places like Dachau during the 1930s. None of the Germans I have filmed – even those who were formerly fanatical Nazis – professed themselves 'enthusiastic' about the existence of the death camps, but many were more than content during the 1930s with the reality of the concentration camps. They had just lived through the nightmare of the Depression and had witnessed how, as they saw it, democracy had failed to prevent the country entering a spiral of decline. The spectre of Communism still existed. In elections held in the early 1930s Germany seemed to be splitting towards the extremes, with large numbers voting for the Communist party. And to a man like Manfred von Schroeder, who hailed the Nazis' 'peaceful revolution' in 1933, there were clear historical parallels that explained the necessity for the existence of the concentration camps: 'To be a French nobleman in the Bastille was not so agreeable, was it? ... There were the concentration camps, but everyone said at that time, "Oh, the English invented them in South Africa with the Boers."'

The first prisoners who entered Dachau in March 1933 were mostly political opponents of the Nazis. Jews were taunted, humiliated and beaten up in those early days, but it was the left-wing politicians[9] of the former regime who were seen as the more immediate threat. And Hoess, when he arrived at Dachau, believed absolutely that these 'true opponents of the state must be securely locked up'.[10] The next three and a half years at Dachau were to play a defining role in shaping his character. For the carefully conceived regime at Dachau, inspired by Theodor Eicke, the first commandant of the camp, was not just brutal; it was designed to break the will of the inmate. Eicke channelled the violence and hatred the Nazis felt towards their enemies into systems and order. Dachau is infamous for the physical sadism practised there: whippings and other beatings were commonplace. Prisoners could be murdered and their death dismissed as 'killed whilst attempting an escape', and a significant minority of those sent to Dachau did die there. But the real power of the regime at Dachau lay less in physical abuse – terrible as it undoubtedly was – and more in mental torture.

The first innovation at Dachau was that, unlike in a normal prison, the inmate had no clue as to how long his sentence was likely to be. Whilst during the 1930s most prisoners in Dachau were released after a stay of about a year, any individual sentence could be shorter or longer depending on the whim of the authorities. There was no end date for the prisoner to focus upon, only the permanent uncertainty of never knowing if freedom would come tomorrow, or next month, or next year. Hoess, who had endured years of imprisonment himself, knew at once the terrible power of this policy: 'The uncertainty of the duration of their imprisonment was something with which they could never come to terms,' he wrote. 'It was this that wore them down and broke even the most steadfast will ... Because of this alone their life in camp was a torment.'[11]

Added to this uncertainty was the way in which the guards could play with the minds of the prisoners. Josef Felder, an SPD (socialist) member of the Reichstag who was one of the earliest inmates of Dachau, remembers – when he was at his lowest point emotionally – how his jailer took a rope and demonstrated the best way to tie a noose so that he could hang himself.[12] Only by exercising enormous self-control and remembering 'I have a family' was he able to resist the suggestion. Inmates were required to keep their barracks and clothes in meticulous order. Regular inspections allowed the SS guards to find fault continually and, if they wished, punish the whole block for imaginary infractions. Everyone in a block could be 'locked down' and ordered to lie silent and motionless in their bunks for days.

At Dachau a system of 'Kapos' was also introduced – something that would be adopted across the whole concentration camp network and subsequently play an important part in the running of Auschwitz. (The term 'Kapo' appears to have derived from the Italian *capo*, meaning 'head'.) The authorities at the camp would appoint one prisoner to be 'Kapo' in each block or work 'commando', and this inmate would have enormous power over his fellow prisoners. Not surprisingly, that power was often abused. Almost more than the SS guards, the Kapos, in moment-to-moment contact with the other prisoners, could use arbitrary behaviour to make life inside the camp intolerable. But the Kapos too were at risk if they failed to please their SS masters. As Himmler put it: 'His [the Kapo's] job is to see that the work gets done ... thus he has to push his men. As soon as we are no longer satisfied with him, he is no longer a Kapo and returns to the other inmates. He knows that they will beat him to death his first night back.'[13]

From the Nazis' point of view camp life was a microcosm of the outside world. 'The idea of struggle is as old as life itself,' Hitler said in a speech as early as 1928. 'In this struggle the stronger, the more able, win, while the less able, the weak, lose. Struggle is the father of all things ... It is not by the principles of humanity that man lives or is able to preserve himself above the animal world, but solely by means of the most brutal struggle.'[14] This quasi-Darwinian attitude, at the very core of Nazism, was evident throughout the administration of the concentration camps. The Kapos, for example, could 'justly' mistreat those in their charge since they had proved themselves superior in life's 'struggle'.

Above all else, Hoess learnt the essential philosophy of the SS while in Dachau. Theodor Eicke had preached one doctrine from the first – hardness: 'Anyone who shows even the slightest vestige of sympathy towards them [prisoners] must immediately vanish from our ranks. I need only hard, totally committed SS men. There is no place amongst us for soft people.'[15] Thus any form of sympathy, any form of compassion was a demonstration of weakness. If an SS man felt these emotions come to him, it was a sign that the enemy had succeeded in deceiving him. Nazi propaganda preached that it was often in the most unlikely places that an enemy might lurk; one of the most widespread pieces of anti-Semitic propaganda aimed at children was a book called *The Poisoned Mushroom*, which warned of the insidious danger of the Jews by using the metaphor of a mushroom that seems attractive on the surface but is in reality poisonous. In just such a way the SS were conditioned to despise their own feelings of concern when, for example, they witnessed the beating of an inmate. They were taught that any lingering feeling of compassion was caused by the trickery of the victim. As 'enemies of the state' these cunning creatures were said to use any method – not least an appeal to the pity of those who held them captive – in an attempt to pursue their malicious goal. The memory of the 'stab in the back', the myth that Jews and Communists had plotted behind the lines to lose Germany World War I, was never far away and fitted perfectly into this vision of a dangerous but concealed enemy.

The only certainty for members of the SS was the fundamental rightness of the orders they were given. If a superior ordered someone to be imprisoned, someone to be executed, then – even if to the individual ordered to carry out the sentence the judgment appeared incomprehensible – the order must be correct. The only protection against the cancer of self-doubt in the face of orders that were not immediately explicable was hardness, which therefore became a cult throughout the SS. 'We must be hard as granite, otherwise the work of our Führer will perish,'[16] said Reinhard Heydrich, the most powerful figure in the SS after Himmler.

In the process of learning how to bury emotions like compassion and pity, Hoess absorbed the sense of brotherhood that was also strong in the SS. Precisely because an SS man knew that he would be called upon to do things that 'weaker' men could not, a powerful *esprit de corps* developed in which the loyalty of one's SS comrades became a vital pillar of support. The crude values of the SS – unquestioning loyalty, hardness, protection of the Reich against the enemy within – became almost a substitute religious creed, a distinct and easily absorbed world-view. 'I was full of gratitude to the SS for the intellectual guidance it gave me,' said Johannes Hassebroeck, commandant of another SS concentration camp. 'We were all thankful. Many of us had been so bewildered before we joined the organization. We did not understand what was happening around us – everything was so mixed up. The SS offered us a series of simple ideas that we could understand, and we believed in them.'[17]

Hoess also learnt at Dachau another significant lesson that would have consequences for Auschwitz. He observed how prisoners were better able to endure their imprisonment because the SS enabled them to work. He remembered his own imprisonment in Leipzig, and how it was only by being allowed to work (he had glued paper bags together) that he had been able to face each day in a more or less positive frame of mind. Now he saw how work played a similar role at Dachau, allowing the prisoners to 'discipline themselves and so enable them to withstand better the demoralizing effect of their imprisonment'.[18] So convinced was Hoess of the palliative effect of work in the concentration camp that he even imported the slogan that had first been used at Dachau – *Arbeit macht frei* (Work brings freedom) – and emblazoned it across the iron gate at the entrance to Auschwitz.

Hoess was a model member of the SS and rose through the ranks at Dachau until in April 1936 he was made Rapportführer, chief assistant to the commandant of the camp. Then, in September 1936, he was promoted to lieutenant and transferred to Sachsenhausen concentration camp, where he remained until his elevation to commandant of the new concentration camp at Auschwitz. This, then, was the man who arrived in southwest Poland in the spring of 1940 – a product of his genetic inheritance, of course, but also someone hugely moulded by the history of the times, with six years' service behind him as a camp guard. He now felt ready to take on his biggest challenge: creating a model concentration camp in the new Nazi empire. In his mind he knew what was expected of him, knew the purpose of the place he was about to construct. His experience at Dachau and Sachsenhausen offered a clear example for him to follow. But his superiors had other plans, and over the next months and years the camp Hoess built at Auschwitz was to develop along a very different path indeed.

At the same time as Hoess was beginning work at Auschwitz, 250 miles to the northwest his boss was doing something extremely unusual – composing a memorandum for the Führer. Heinrich Himmler sat in Berlin and wrote the diffidently entitled 'Some

Thoughts on the Treatment of the Alien Population of the East'. Himmler, one of the most astute power brokers in the Nazi state, knew that it was often unwise to commit thoughts to paper. At the highest level, Nazi policy was frequently formulated verbally. Once his views were on paper Himmler realized that they could be dissected by his rivals and, like any leading Nazi, he had many enemies who were always seeking to seize some of his power for themselves. But the situation in Poland, which the Germans had occupied since the autumn of 1939, was such that he felt he had to make an exception and prepare a written document for Hitler. The document he wrote is one of the most significant in the history of Nazi racial policy, not least because the words Himmler committed to paper were to clarify the context within which the new camp at Auschwitz was to function.

At that moment, in his capacity as Reich Commissar for the Strengthening of German Nationhood, Himmler was involved in the largest and swiftest ethnic reorganization of a country ever contemplated, and the whole process was going badly wrong. Far from bringing order to Poland, a country whose supposed inefficiency the Nazis held in contempt, Himmler and his colleagues had brought only violence and chaos.

There was no dispute amongst the Nazis about their basic attitude to the Poles. It was one of loathing. The question was what to do about it. One of the most important 'problems' the Nazis felt they had to solve related to the Jews of Poland. Unlike in Germany, where Jews represented much less than 1 per cent of the population (around 300,000 in 1940) and where most were assimilated into society, in Poland there were 3 million Jews, the majority of whom lived in their own communities and were often readily identifiable by their beards and other marks of their faith. After Poland was divided up between Germany and the Soviet Union in the immediate aftermath of the outbreak of war (under the terms of the secret part of the Nazi–Soviet non-aggression pact of August 1939), over 2 million Polish Jews were left in the Nazi-occupied zone of the country. What should be their fate?

Another, self-created, problem for the Nazis was finding homes for the hundreds of thousands of ethnic Germans who were currently being shipped to Poland. Under an agreement between

Germany and the Soviet Union, ethnic Germans from the Baltic states, Bessarabia (northern Romania), and other regions now occupied by Stalin were permitted to emigrate to Germany – to 'come home to the Reich' as the slogan went. Obsessed as they were by notions of the racial purity of 'German blood', it was an act of faith for men like Himmler to be able to accommodate all Germans who wanted to return home to their native land. The difficulty was, where should they actually go? Added to this was a third and final issue that the Nazis had to resolve. How should the 18 million Poles now under German control who were not Jewish be treated? How should the country be organized so that they never posed a threat?

Hitler had made a speech in October 1939 which offered some guidelines to those wrestling with these questions of policy. He made it clear that 'the main task is to create a new ethnographic order; i.e. to resettle the nationalities so that in the end better lines of demarcation exist than today'.[19] In practice this meant that German-occupied Poland was to be divided: part of it would be a place where the majority of Poles would live, and part would be incorporated into Germany. The incoming ethnic Germans would then be settled not in the 'Old Reich' but in this 'New Reich'; they would indeed be 'coming home to the Reich' – just not to the Reich they were expecting.

This left the question of the Polish Jews. Until the start of the war Nazi policy towards Jews living under their control had been one of growing official persecution through countless restrictive regulations, interspersed with moments of unofficial (though sanctioned) violent outrage. Hitler's views about the Jews had changed little since the mid-1920s, when in his book *Mein Kampf* he expressed the opinion that it would have been to Germany's advantage during World War I to use 'poison gas' on '10 to 12,000 of these Hebrew destroyers of the nation'. But whilst Hitler clearly hated the Jews and had demonstrably done so since the end of World War I, and may indeed have privately expressed the desire to see them all die, no Nazi blueprint planning their extermination was yet in existence.

Lucille Eichengreen[20] grew up in a Jewish family in Hamburg during the 1930s and remembers all too well the circumstances under which German Jews were forced to live. 'Until 1933 it was a very nice comfortable life,' she says. 'But once Hitler came to power, the children that lived in the same building no longer spoke to us; they threw stones at us and called us names. And we couldn't understand what we had done to deserve this. So the question was always – why? And when we asked at home the answer was pretty much, "It's a passing phase. It'll normalize."' In the mid-1930s the Eichengreens were informed that Jews were no longer permitted to live in their current building. Instead, they were assigned to places called 'Jewish houses' owned partly by Jewish landlords. Their first new apartment was nearly as large as their previous one, but over succeeding years they were forced to move into smaller and smaller accommodation until they finished up in a single furnished room for the entire family. 'I think we more or less accepted it,' says Lucille. 'This was the law, those were the rules, and you could do nothing about it.'

The illusion that Nazi anti-Semitic policy would one day 'normalize' was destroyed by Kristallnacht, which occurred on the night of 9 November 1938. Nazi stormtroopers destroyed Jewish property and rounded up thousands of German Jews in a revenge action motivated by the news that a Jewish student called Herschel Grynszpan had murdered Ernst vom Rath, a German diplomat, in Paris. 'Walking to school we saw the synagogues burning,' says Lucille Eichengreen, 'the glass of Jewish shops broken, merchandise in the streets, and the Germans laughing ... We were so afraid. We thought they would grab us and do I don't know what.'

By the outbreak of war in 1939 Jews could no longer hold German citizenship, marry non-Jews, own businesses or work in certain professions; they could not even hold driving licences. Discrimination by regulation, coupled with the violent outburst of Kristallnacht in which more than 1000 synagogues were destroyed, 400 Jews killed and around 30,000 male Jews imprisoned for months in concentration camps, caused a large number of German Jews to emigrate. By 1939 around 450,000 of them had left the area of the new 'Greater German Reich' (Germany, Austria and the ethnic German Czech lands) – this amounted to more than half the Jews who lived there. The Nazis were pleased; especially since, following the pioneering work of SS Jewish 'expert' Adolf Eichmann in 1938 after the Anschluss (annexation) with Austria, a system had been devised whereby the Jews were robbed of most of their money before they were allowed to leave the country.

But it was initially hard for the Nazis to see how the solution they had evolved to their self-created 'problem' of the German Jews was transferable to Poland. Not only were there now millions of Jews under their control rather than a few hundred thousand, but most were poor, and in the midst of a war where could they be forcibly encouraged to emigrate to? Then, in the autumn of 1939, Adolf Eichmann thought he had the answer: the Jews should be made to emigrate not to another country, but to the least hospitable part of the Nazis' own empire. Moreover, he thought he had found the ideal place – the Lublin district of Poland, around the town of Nisko. This remote area at the far eastern extreme of Nazi territory seemed to him the perfect location for a 'Jewish reservation'. German-occupied Poland would thus be divided into three: a German-settled part, a Polish part and a Jewish part, all set on a neat geographical axis moving from west to east. Eichmann's ambitious plan was agreed, and thousands of Jews from Austria began to be shipped to the area. Conditions were appalling. Little or no preparation was made for their arrival and many died. This was a matter of no concern to the Nazis. Indeed it was something to be encouraged. As Hans Frank, one of the most senior Nazis at work in Poland, put it to his staff in November 1939: 'Don't waste any time on the Jews. It is a joy finally to be able to deal with the Jewish race. The more that die the better.'[21]

However, as Himmler sat composing his memorandum in May 1940 he knew only too well that the internal emigration of Jews to the far east of Poland had been a dismal failure. To a large extent this was because the Nazis were attempting three separate emigrations simultaneously. The incoming ethnic Germans had to be transported to Poland and found somewhere to live. This meant Poles had to be thrown out of their houses and transported elsewhere. At the same time Jews were being transported east into property from which Poles also had to be evicted. It was scarcely a wonder that this all led to chaos and confusion on an epic scale.

By the spring of 1940 Eichmann's Nisko plan had been abandoned and Poland had finally been divided into just two separate categories of territory. There were the districts that had officially become 'German' and were part of the 'New Reich': West Prussia, around Danzig (Gdańsk); the Warthegau, in the west of Poland around Posen (Poznań) and Łódź; and Upper Silesia, around Katowice (the area that included Auschwitz). And then there was the biggest single area of all, called the General Government, encompassing the cities of Warsaw, Kraków and Lublin, which had been designated as living space for the majority of the Poles.

The most pressing problem Himmler faced was providing suitable housing for the hundreds of thousands of incoming ethnic Germans – a difficulty that would in turn impact on the way he thought both Poles and Jews should be dealt with. The case of Irma Eigi[22] and her family illustrates just how ruthlessly the Nazis attempted to solve the seemingly intractable predicament they had manoeuvred themselves into, and also how the population problems fed upon themselves, spiralling away towards crisis. In December 1939 Irma Eigi, a 17-year-old ethnic German from Estonia, found herself, together with the rest of her family, in temporary accommodation in Posen, in what had been Poland and was now the part of Germany known as the Warthegau. They had thought, when they accepted the offer of safe passage 'to the Reich', that they were going to be sent to Germany: 'When we were told we were going to the Warthegau, well, it was quite a shock, I can tell you.' Just before Christmas 1939 a Nazi housing official gave her father keys to a flat that had until hours before belonged to a Polish family. Days later a restaurant was commandeered from its Polish owner so that the newcomers could also have a business to run. The Eigis were appalled: 'We had no inkling of that before it happened ... You can't live with this guilt. But on the other hand, every person has an instinct for self-preservation. What else could we have done? Where were we supposed to go?'

This individual case of expropriation must be multiplied by a factor of more than 100,000 to give an impression of just what was taking place in Poland during this period. The scale of the relocation operation was enormous – within a year and a half around half a million ethnic Germans arrived to be resettled in the new part of the Reich, and hundreds of thousands of Poles were dispossessed in order to make room for them. Many were simply shoved on cattle trucks and taken south to the General

Government, where they were dumped without food or shelter. It is not surprising that Goebbels remarked in his diary in January 1940, 'Himmler is presently shifting populations. Not always successfully.'[23]

All of this still left the question of the Polish Jews. Having discovered that simultaneously attempting to relocate the Jews, the Poles and the ethnic Germans was simply impractical, Himmler embraced another solution; if space was needed for the ethnic Germans – and it clearly was – then the Jews should be forced to live with a good deal less of it. Ghettos were the answer.

Ghettos, which were to become such a striking feature of the Nazi persecution of the Jews in Poland, were never intended to have the life they did. Like so much in the history of Auschwitz and the Nazis' 'Final Solution', they evolved in ways that had not initially been planned. As early as November 1938, when discussing how to deal with the housing issues raised by the eviction of German Jews from their homes, Reinhard Heydrich of the SS had said: 'As for the question of ghettos, I would like to make my position clear right away. From the point of view of the police, I don't think a ghetto, in the form of a completely segregated district where only Jews would live, can be put up. We could not control a ghetto where Jews congregate amid the whole Jewish people. It would remain a hideout for criminals and also for epidemics and the like.'[24]

Nonetheless, now that other avenues seemed, albeit perhaps temporarily, closed to them, the Nazis sought to ghettoize Polish Jews. This was not just a practical measure designed to release more housing (even though Hitler remarked in March 1940 that 'the solution of the Jewish question is a question of space'[25]); it was also motivated by the visceral hatred and fear of Jews that had been at the core of Nazism from the beginning. Ideally, the Nazis believed, the Jews should just be made to 'go away', but if that was not immediately practicable, then, since they – especially Eastern Jews – were believed to be carriers of disease, they should be kept separate from everyone else. The Nazis' intense, physical loathing of Polish Jews was something Estera Frenkiel,[26] a teenage Jewish girl living in Łódź, felt from the first: 'We were used to anti-Semitism ... Polish anti-Semitism was perhaps more financial. But Nazi anti-Semitism was: "Why do you exist? You shouldn't be! You ought to disappear!"'

In February 1940, as deportations of Poles to the General Government proceeded apace, it was announced that the Jews of Łódź were to be 'relocated' to a ghetto area within the city. From the first it was intended that such ghettos should be only a temporary measure, a place in which to incarcerate the Jews before they were deported somewhere else. In April 1940 the Łódź ghetto was sealed and Jews could no longer leave the area without permission from the German authorities. That same month the Reich Security Main Office announced that deportations of Jews to the General Government were to be curtailed. Hans Frank, Hitler's former lawyer who ran the General Government, had been campaigning for months to halt all 'unauthorized' forced emigrations because the situation had become untenable. As Dr Fritz Arlt,[27] head of the Department for Population Affairs in the General Government, later put it: 'The people were thrown out of the trains, whether in the marketplace or on the train station or wherever it was, and nobody cared about it ... We received a phone call from the district officer and he said, "I don't know what to do any more. So and so many hundreds have arrived again. I have neither shelter nor food nor anything."' Frank – no friend of Himmler's – complained to Hermann Goering (who took a keen interest in Poland in his capacity as head of the Economic Four Year Plan) about the deportation policy and the use of the General Government as a 'racial dustbin', and an uneasy truce was arranged, whereby Himmler and Frank would 'agree upon the procedures of future evacuation'.

It was this mess that Himmler tried to address in his memorandum of May 1940. In response he sought to reinforce the division of Poland into German and non-German areas and to define how the Poles and Jews were to be treated. Himmler, in this statement of racial faith, wrote that he wanted the Poles to be turned into a nation of ill-educated slaves and that the General Government should be home to a 'leaderless labouring class'.[28] 'The non-German population of the Eastern territories must not receive any education higher than that of an elementary school,' wrote Himmler. 'The objective of this elementary school must simply be to teach: simple arithmetic up to 500 at the most, how to write one's name, and to teach that it is God's commandment to be obedient to Germans and to be honest, hard-working and well-behaved. I consider it unnecessary to teach reading.'

Alongside this policy of turning Poland into a nation of illiterates was a proactive attempt to 'sift out those with valuable blood and those with worthless blood'. Polish children between the ages of six and ten would be examined, and those who were thought racially acceptable would be snatched from their families and raised in Germany; they would not see their biological parents again. The Nazi policy of stealing children in Poland is a good deal less well known than the extermination of the Jews. But it fits into the same pattern. It demonstrates how seriously a man like Himmler believed in identifying the value of a human being through racial composition. Removing these children was not for him, as it might seem today, some evil eccentricity, but an essential part of his warped world-view. For, from his standpoint, if such children were allowed to remain, then the Poles 'might acquire a leader class from such people of good blood'.

Significantly, Himmler wrote of these children: 'However cruel and tragic each individual case may be, if one rejects the Bolshevik method of physically exterminating a people as fundamentally un-German and impossible, then this method is the mildest and best one.' Though Himmler writes this in the immediate context of the Polish children, it is clear, since he refers to 'physically exterminating a people' as being 'fundamentally un-German', that he must also extend this admonition to other 'peoples' – including the Jews. (Further confirmation of this interpretation is provided by Heydrich's statement in the summer of 1940, directly in the context of the Jews, that: 'Biological extermination is undignified for the German people as a civilized nation.')[29]

In his wide-ranging memorandum Himmler also announced what he wanted the fate of the Jews to be: 'I hope to see the term "Jews" completely eliminated through the possibility of a large-scale emigration of all Jews to Africa or to some other colony.' This return to the previously established policy of emigration was available now because of the wider context of the war. Himmler was counting both on the imminent defeat of France and the consequent swift capitulation of the British, who would then want to sue for a separate peace. With the war over, the Polish Jews could be packed on to ships and removed, possibly to one of the former African colonies of the French.

Far-fetched as the idea of shipping millions of people to Africa seems today, there is no doubt that at the time it was taken seriously by the Nazis. Radical anti-Semites had been suggesting the removal of the Jews to Africa for years, and now the course of the war seemed about to make this solution to the Nazis' Jewish 'problem' possible. Six weeks after Himmler's memo, Franz Rademacher in the German Foreign Office wrote a document that announced the proposed African destination of the Jews – the island of Madagascar.[30] However, it is important to remember that this plan, like all the other wartime solutions to the 'Jewish problem', would have meant widespread death and suffering for the Jews. A Nazi governor of Madagascar would most likely have presided over the gradual elimination of the Jews within a generation or two. The Nazis' 'Final Solution' as we know it would not have occurred, but almost certainly there would still have been another kind of genocide.

Himmler passed his memorandum to Hitler, who read it and told him that in his view it was '*gut und richtig*' ('good and correct'). Significantly, Hitler never wrote down his views on the memo. It was sufficient for Himmler to be armed with the Führer's verbal approval for its contents. In such a way was high policy decided in the Nazi state.

Rudolf Hoess and his embryo concentration camp at Auschwitz were but a small part of this overall picture. Auschwitz was situated in one of the parts of Poland that was to be 'Germanized', and so the immediate future of the camp would be decided to a large extent by its location. The Upper Silesia region had passed between the Poles and the Germans a number of times before, and immediately preceding World War I it had been part of Germany, only to be lost in the Versailles settlement. Now the Nazis wanted to reclaim it for the Reich. But, unlike the other areas to be 'Germanized', Upper Silesia was heavily industrialized, and large parts of it were unsuitable for settlement by the incoming ethnic Germans. This meant that many of the Poles would have to remain as a slave workforce, which in turn meant that a concentration camp was thought particularly necessary in the area in order to subdue the local population. Originally Auschwitz had been conceived as a holding concentration camp – a 'quarantine' camp in Nazi jargon – in which to keep prisoners before they were sent on to other concentration camps in the Reich, but within days it became clear that the camp would function as a place of permanent imprisonment in its own right.

Hoess knew that the war had radicalized everything, including the concentration camps. Although modelled on a place like Dachau, this new camp would have to deal with a more intractable problem than the institutions in the 'Old Reich'. The camp at Auschwitz needed to imprison and terrorize Poles at a time when the whole country was being ethnically reordered and Poland as a nation intellectually and politically destroyed. Thus, even in its first incarnation as a concentration camp, Auschwitz had a proportionately higher death rate than any 'normal' camp in the Reich. Of the 20,000 Poles initially sent to the camp, more than half were dead by the start of 1942.

The first prisoners to arrive at Auschwitz in June 1940 were not Poles but Germans – 30 criminals transferred from Sachsenhausen concentration camp. They would become the first Kapos, the inmates who would act as agents of control between the SS and the Polish prisoners. The sight of these Kapos was the strongest first impression made on many of the Poles who arrived in the initial transports to the camp. 'We thought they were all sailors,' says Roman Trojanowski,[31] who arrived at Auschwitz as a 19-year-old in the summer of 1940. 'They had berets like mariners. And then it turned out they were criminals. All of them were criminals.' 'We arrived and there were German Kapos and they yelled at us and struck us with short batons,' says Wilhelm Brasse,[32] who arrived at about the same time. 'When someone was slow in coming down from the cattle truck he was beaten, or in several instances they were killed on the spot. So I was terrified. Everyone was terrified.'

These earliest Polish prisoners at Auschwitz had been sent to the camp for a variety of reasons: they might be suspected of working in the Polish underground, or be members of a group the Nazis specially targeted, such as priests or the intelligentsia, or simply be someone to whom a German had taken exception. Indeed, many of the first group of Polish prisoners, who arrived at the camp on 14 June 1940, transferred from Tarnów prison, were university students.

The immediate task for these new arrivals was simple – they had to build the camp themselves. 'We used very primitive tools,' recalls Wilhelm Brasse. 'The prisoners had to carry stones. It was very difficult, hard labour. And we were beaten.' But not enough construction materials had been provided to complete the task, so a typical Nazi solution was found – theft. 'I worked at demolishing houses that used to belong to Polish families,' Brasse continues. 'There was an order to take building materials such as bricks, planks and all kinds of other wood. We were surprised the Germans wanted to build so rapidly and they did not have the material.'

The camp quickly developed a culture of theft not just from the local population, but from within the institution itself. 'The German Kapos would send us inmates off and say, "Go and steal cement from another work commando. We don't care about the other guys,"' says Brasse. 'And that is what we did. Planks or cement would be stolen from another commando. In the camp lingo that was called "organizing". But we had to be very careful not to be caught.' Nor was this culture of 'organizing' confined to the inmates. In those early days Hoess too stole what he needed: 'Since I could expect no help from the Inspectorate of Concentration Camps, I had to make do as best I could and help myself. I had to scrounge up cars and trucks and the necessary petrol. I had to drive as far as 100 kilometres to Zakopane and Rabka just to get some kettles for the prisoners' kitchen, and I had to go all the way to the Sudetenland for bed frames and straw sacks ... Whenever I found depots of material that was needed urgently I simply carted it away without worrying about the formalities ... I didn't even know where I could get a hundred metres of barbed wire. So I just had to pilfer the badly needed barbed wire.'[33]

While Hoess was 'organizing' what he considered necessary to make Auschwitz into a 'useful' camp, behind the newly pilfered barbed wire it soon became clear to the Poles that their chances of survival depended chiefly on one factor – which Kapo they worked for. 'I very quickly understood that in the "good" work commandos the prisoners would usually have full, round faces,' says Wilhelm Brasse. 'They behaved differently from the ones who had the hard jobs and looked haggard, like skeletons wearing uniforms. And immediately I would notice that with this Kapo it's better because the prisoners look better.'

Roman Trojanowski struggled under the command of one of the cruellest Kapos, who once punished him for a minor transgression by smashing him in the face and then making him squat for two hours holding a stool in front of him. The harshness of life in this work commando was breaking him. 'I had no strength to run around with wheelbarrows every day,' he says. 'After one hour the wheelbarrow would fall out of your hands. You just fell on the wheelbarrow and you would hurt your leg. I had to save my skin.' Like many inmates before and after him at Auschwitz, Roman Trojanowski knew he had to find a way out of his current work commando or perish.

One morning an announcement was made at roll-call – experienced carpenters were required. So Trojanowski volunteered, and even though he had never been a carpenter in his life he said that he had 'seven years of practice'. But the plan backfired: it was obvious once he began work in the carpentry shop that he could not do the job. 'The Kapo called me, took me to his room and stood there with a big stick. When I saw that stick I felt weak. And he said that for damaging material I'd get twenty-five hits. He told me to bend over and he hit me. He did it especially slow so that I would taste every blow. He was a big guy. He had a heavy hand and it was a heavy stick. I wanted to yell but I bit my lips and I managed not to shout, not even once. And it paid off, because on the fifteenth blow he stopped. "You're behaving nicely," he said, "and so I'll pardon you the last ten." Out of twenty-five blows I got only fifteen; but fifteen sufficed. My arse was in colours from black to violet to yellow for two weeks and I couldn't sit down for a long time.'

Thrown out of the carpentry shop, Trojanowski still sought a job indoors. 'That was decisive,' he says. 'To survive you had to be under a roof.' He spoke to a friend who knew a relatively benign Kapo called Otto Küsel. Together with his friend he approached Küsel, exaggerated the amount of German he knew, and managed to get a job working in the kitchen preparing food for the Germans. 'That's how I saved my life,' he says.

In this struggle for survival within the camp two groups of people were singled out from the moment of their arrival for particularly sadistic treatment: priests and Jews. Although at this stage of its evolution Auschwitz was not a place where large numbers of Jews were sent – the policy of ghettoization was still in full swing – some of the intelligentsia, members of the resistance and political prisoners who were sent to the camp were also Jews. They, together with Polish Catholic priests, were more likely than the other inmates to fall into the hands of the penal commando unit run by one of the most notorious Kapos of all, Ernst Krankemann.

Krankemann arrived at the camp in the second batch of German criminals, transferred from Sachsenhausen on 29 August 1940. Many in the SS disliked him, but he had two powerful SS supporters in Karl Fritzsch, the Lagerführer (camp leader, and Hoess's deputy), and Gerhard Palitzsch, the Rapportführer (commandant's chief assistant). Krankemann, who was enormously fat, would sit on top of the harness of a giant roller that was used for flattening the roll-call square in the centre of the camp. 'First time I saw him,' says Jerzy Bielecki,[34] one of the earliest prisoners to arrive in Auschwitz, 'they were rolling the square between the two blocks, and because it was a very heavy roller the twenty or twenty-five people in the unit were unable to pull it. Krankemann had a whip and would hit them. "Faster, you dogs!" he said.'

Bielecki saw these prisoners forced to work without a break all day levelling the square. As evening fell, one of them collapsed on his knees and could not get up. Then Krankemann ordered the rest of the penal commando to pull the giant roller over their prostrate comrade. 'I had got used to seeing death and beatings,' says Bielecki, 'but what I saw then just made me cold. I just froze.'

Far from being indifferent spectators to this kind of brutality, the SS actively encouraged it. As Wilhelm Brasse and, indeed, all the Auschwitz survivors testify, it was the SS who created the culture of murderous brutality in the camp (and often committed murder themselves). 'Those Kapos that were especially cruel,' says Brasse, 'were given prizes by the SS – an additional portion of soup or bread or cigarettes. I saw it myself. The SS would urge them on. I frequently heard an SS man say, "Beat him well."'

Notwithstanding the appalling brutality prevalent in the camp, Auschwitz was, from the Nazi perspective, still something of a backwater in the maelstrom of the brutal reorganization of Poland. The first sign that all this was to change came in the autumn of 1940. In September, Oswald Pohl, head of the SS Main Administration and Economic Office, inspected the camp and told Hoess to increase its capacity. Pohl believed that the sand and gravel pits nearby meant that the camp could be integrated into the SS-owned German Earth and Stone Works (DESt). Economic considerations had been growing in importance for Himmler and the SS ever since 1937 when, with the concentration camp population in Germany down to 10,000 from over 20,000 in 1933, he had hit on an innovative solution to protect the future of the camps – the SS would go into business.

From the beginning, this was business of an unusual kind. Himmler did not want to form a capitalist enterprise, more a series of companies that would operate according to Nazi philosophical ideas in the service of the state. The concentration camps would provide the raw materials for the new Germany, such as the vast quantities of granite that were needed for Hitler's gigantic new Reich Chancellery in Berlin. In pursuit of this goal, after the Anschluss with Austria in 1938, the SS opened a new concentration camp at Mauthausen specifically to be near a granite quarry. It was thought particularly apt that the opponents of the regime should contribute to its growth. As Albert Speer, Hitler's favourite architect, put it: 'After all, the Jews were already making bricks under the Pharaohs.'[35]

Himmler's enthusiasm for industrial production did not stop at providing building materials for the Reich. He gave his blessing to a whole host of other projects as well. An experimental unit was established to look into natural medicines and new forms of agricultural production (two subjects close to Himmler's heart), and soon the SS were also involved in the production of clothing, vitamin drinks and even porcelain (making figurines of goatherds and other racially suitable subjects). As recent research has shown,[36] the SS managers of many of these enterprises were incompetent, almost comically so, were the subject not so bleak.

No sooner had Pohl demanded that Auschwitz produce sand and gravel for the Nazi state than the camp gained another function. In November 1940 Rudolf Hoess had a meeting with Himmler, and the plans for Auschwitz that Hoess produced during this encounter caught his boss's imagination. Suddenly their shared interest in agriculture forged a bond between them. Hoess recalled

Himmler's new vision for the camp: 'Every necessary agricultural experiment was to be attempted there. Massive laboratories and plant cultivation departments had to be built. Cattle breeding of all types was to become important ... The marshlands were to be drained and developed ... He continued with his talk of agricultural planning even down to the smallest details, and ceased only when his adjutant called his attention to the fact that a very important person had been waiting a long time to see him.'[37]

This meeting between Hoess and Himmler, long eclipsed by the even greater horror that was to develop at Auschwitz, gives an insight into the mentality of the two key figures in the history of the camp. It is too easy, and simply wrong, to dismiss them as 'madmen' motivated by irrational feelings that we can never understand. Here, at this meeting, we can see them as two enthusiasts, almost cranks, who, in the context of war, were able to pursue visions that in peacetime would only be pipe dreams. But as a result of Nazi aggression Himmler, as he sat there poring over the plans of Auschwitz with Hoess, was a man who had already had direct experience of turning his dreams into reality. He had swept his hand across a map and reordered the lives of hundreds of thousands of ethnic Germans and Poles. In the process, he had pronounced judgements in the most sweeping terms imaginable.

It is vital to remember that all the time Himmler was speaking in such grandiloquent terms of his desire for Auschwitz to become a centre of agricultural research, he was doing so in pursuit of a coherent vision – a repulsive vision, of course, but nonetheless a coherent one. At this November 1940 meeting he was enthused by the vision of Silesia as a German agricultural utopia, almost a paradise. Gone would be the tawdry Polish homesteads of the south; in their place would rise solid, well-managed German farms. Hoess and Himmler had been farmers themselves; both had an emotional, almost mystical, attachment to nurturing the land. So the idea that Auschwitz could be developed in a way that could further agricultural knowledge must have been hugely attractive for both of them.

In the pursuit of this sudden enthusiasm it was a matter of little consequence to Himmler that Auschwitz concentration camp was in precisely the wrong place for such an enterprise. Sited at the confluence of the Soła and Vistula rivers, the camp lay in an area notorious for flooding. Nevertheless, from now until the day the camp closed Auschwitz prisoners would labour in pursuit of Himmler's vision, digging ditches, draining ponds, shoring up riverbanks – all because it was much more exciting for the Reichsführer SS to dream a dream than to discuss practicalities. Thousands would die in the process, a thought that would scarcely have flitted across Himmler's mind as he enthusiastically outlined his fantasy in front of his faithful subordinate Rudolf Hoess.

By the end of 1940 Hoess had established many of the basic structures and principles under which the camp would function for the next four years: the Kapos who effectively controlled the prisoners from moment to moment, the absolute brutality of a regime that could inflict punishment arbitrarily, and a pervasive sense within the camp that if an intimate did not learn quickly how to manipulate himself out of a dangerous work commando then he risked a swift and sudden death. But there was one final creation in those early months that symbolized the culture of the camp even more appropriately – Block 11.

From the outside Block 11 (at first called Block 13, then renumbered in 1941) looked like any of the other red-brick, barrack-like buildings that ran in straight rows throughout the camp. But it served a unique purpose – and everyone in the camp knew it. 'I personally was scared to pass by Block 11,' says Józef Paczyński.[38] 'I was really afraid.' Inmates felt this way because Block 11 was a prison within a prison – a place of torture and murder.

Jerzy Bielecki was one of the few who experienced what happened in Block 11 and lived to tell the story. He was sent there because one morning he woke up so sick and exhausted that he felt unable to work. In Auschwitz there was no possibility of asking for a day's rest to recover, so he tried to conceal himself in the camp and hope his absence would not be noticed. To begin with he hid in the latrines, but he knew there was a strong risk of capture if he spent the whole day there, so he left and tried to pretend he was cleaning up around the camp. Unfortunately he was caught by a guard and sent to Block 11 for punishment.

He was led up the stairs to the attic. 'I walked in and the [roof] tiles were hot,' he says. 'It was a beautiful day in August. And there was this stench and I could hear someone moaning, "Jesus, oh Jesus!" It was dark – the only light came through the tiles.' He looked up and saw a man hanging from the roof beam by his hands, which were tied behind his back. 'The SS man brought a stool and said, "Climb on it." I put my hands behind my back and he took a chain and tied them.' Once the SS man had attached him to the beam by a chain he suddenly kicked away the stool. 'I just felt – Jesus Mary – it was terrible pain! I was moaning and he told me, "Shut up, you! You dog! You deserve to suffer!"' Then the SS man left him.

The pain as he hung suspended with his hands and arms pulled behind him was appalling: 'And of course the sweat was pouring down my nose and it's very hot and I'm saying, "Mummy!" And after an hour my shoulders were breaking out from their joints. The other guy wasn't saying anything. Then another SS guard came. He went to the other guy and released him. My eyes were closed. I'd been hanging without a spirit – without a soul. But what reached me was something the SS man was saying. He said, "Just fifteen more minutes."'

Jerzy Bielecki remembers little more until the same SS man returned. '"Lift your legs," he said. But I couldn't do it. He took my legs, put one on the stool and then another one. He let the chain loose and I fell from the stool on to my knees and he helped me. He raised my right hand up and said, "Hold it." But I didn't feel my arms. He said, "This will pass after an hour." And I walked down, barely, with the SS man. He was a very compassionate guard.'

Jerzy Bielecki's story is remarkable for a number of reasons, not least his own personal courage under torture. But perhaps what is most surprising is the contrast between the two SS guards – the one who without warning sadistically kicked away the stool he was standing on, and the 'compassionate' guard who helped him down after the torture was over. It is an important reminder that just as the Kapos could vary widely in temperament, so could the SS. A common theme amongst the reminiscences of camp survivors is that there was no single identikit model of their captors. Crucial to surviving in the camp was the ability to read the different characters, not just of the Kapos but of the SS as well. On such a talent could rest your life.

Even though Jerzy Bielecki emerged crippled from Block 11, he was still fortunate because it was very likely that if you walked up those concrete steps and in through the front door you would never emerge alive. During interrogations the Nazis tortured the inmates of Block 11 in a variety of horrific ways; not just using the back-breaking method of hanging suffered by Bielecki, but also by whipping prisoners, practising water torture, putting needles under their fingernails, searing them with red-hot irons, and pouring petrol over the inmates and setting them alight. The SS at Auschwitz also used their initiative to devise new tortures, as former prisoner Bolesław Zbozień observed when an inmate was brought to the camp hospital from Block 11: 'A favourite method, particularly in wintertime, was holding the prisoner's head on the coke heating stove as a way of extracting testimony. The face would be completely fried ... That man [brought from Block 11 to the hospital] was completely fried and his eyes were burned out, but he could not die ... The Politische Abteilung [Political Department] staff still needed him ... that prisoner died after several days, without ever having lost consciousness.'[39]

In those days Block 11 was the empire of SS Untersturmführer (2nd Lieutenant) Max Grabner, one of the most notorious of the camp personnel. Before joining the SS Grabner had been a cowherd, but now he had the power of life and death over the prisoners in his block. Every week he would 'dust out the bunker', a process that consisted of Grabner and his colleagues deciding the fate of each of the prisoners in Block 11. Some would be left in their cells, others sentenced to 'Penal Report 1' or 'Penal Report 2'. 'Penal Report 1' meant a flogging or some other torture. 'Penal Report 2' meant immediate execution. Those sentenced to death were first taken to the washrooms on the ground floor of Block 11 and ordered to undress. Once naked, they were taken out of a side door into a secluded courtyard. The yard between Block 11 and Block 10 was bricked off from the rest of the camp, the only space between blocks treated in this way. In this courtyard prisoners were murdered. They were taken to the brick wall – known in camp jargon as 'the screen' – furthest from the block entrance with their arms held tight by a Kapo. Once they reached the far wall, a small-calibre gun (used in order to minimize the noise) would be held close against their head by an SS executioner and they would be shot.

But it was not just the inmates of Auschwitz who suffered in Block 11 – this was also the location of the Police Summary Court for the German Kattowitz (the former Polish Katowice) area. Thus it was possible for Poles arrested by the Gestapo to come straight to Block 11 from the outside world without passing through the rest of the camp. One of the judges in such cases was Dr Mildner, an SS Obersturmbannführer (Lieutenant Colonol) and State Councillor. Perry Broad, a member of the SS who worked in Auschwitz, described how the sadistic Mildner liked to conduct his business: 'A youth of sixteen was led into the room. Unbearable hunger had driven him to steal some food from a shop – he therefore fell into the category of "criminal" cases. After reading the death sentence, Mildner slowly put the paper on the table and directed his penetrating gaze at the pale, poorly clad boy standing there at the door. "Have you a mother?" The boy lowered his eyes and replied in a quiet voice: "Yes." "Are you afraid to die?" asked the relentless bull-necked butcher, who seemed to derive a sadistic pleasure from the suffering of his victim. The youth was silent, but his body trembled slightly. "You shall be shot today," said Mildner, trying to give his voice a full, fateful significance. "You would be hanged anyway, some day. You will be dead in an hour."'[40]

According to Broad, Mildner particularly enjoyed talking to women immediately after he had sentenced them to death: 'He would tell them in the most drastic manner about their imminent death by shooting.'

Yet despite the horrors of Block 11, Auschwitz at this stage of its evolution still clung to some of the attributes of a traditional concentration camp such as Dachau. Nothing illustrates more clearly this lack of conceptual difference than the fact that, contrary to popular myth, it was possible in those early months to be incarcerated in Auschwitz, serve time there, and then be released.

Just before Easter 1941 Władysław Bartoszewski,[41] a Polish political prisoner, was in the hospital in Block 20 when two SS men approached him. 'They told me, "Get out!" I didn't get any explanation, didn't know what was happening. It was a shock because there was a change in my situation, and my colleagues around me didn't know what was going to happen. I was terrified.' He soon learnt that he was to be taken to appear before a panel of

German doctors. On the way to see them a Polish doctor, an inmate, whispered to him, 'If they ask you, say you're healthy and that you feel well, because if you say you're sick they won't release you.' Bartoszewski was shocked at the sudden news that he might be able to leave the camp. 'Are they to release me?' he asked the Polish doctors in wonder and excitement; but they just replied 'Shut up!'

One major obstacle now stood in the way of Władysław Bartoszewski's release – his physical state. 'I had great boils on my back, on my hips, on the back of my head and nape of my neck. These Polish doctors put a lot of balm on me and powdered the boils so I'd look a little better. They told me, "Don't fear, they'll not look too closely at you, but you shouldn't say anything, that would be against the rules, because no one is sick here, right?" Then they took me before the German doctor and I didn't even look at him. The Polish doctors were eager and said, "Everything's OK." And the German doctor just bowed his head.'

Having passed this cursory medical examination, Bartoszewski was taken to the camp chancellery where the clothes he was wearing when he entered the camp were returned to him. 'They didn't give me back my golden cross,' he says. 'They kept that as a souvenir.' Then, almost in a parody of a normal prison release, the SS asked if he had any complaints about his stay. 'I was cunning,' he says, 'and I said, "No." They asked: "Are you satisfied with your stay in the camp?" I said, "Yes." And I had to sign a form that I had no complaints and I will not go against the law. I didn't know what law they had in mind because as a Pole I was not interested in German law. Our law was represented by our government in exile in London. But, of course, that was not the conversation I had with these guys.'

Together with three other Poles who were released that day Bartoszewski was escorted by a German guard to Auschwitz railway station and put on a train. As the train pulled away he felt keenly 'those first minutes of freedom'. Ahead of him lay a lengthy journey home, back to his mother in Warsaw. On the train, 'People shook their heads. Some women were wiping their eyes out of compassion. You could see they were moved. They just asked, "Where are you coming from?" We said, "Auschwitz." There was no comment – just a look, just fear.' Eventually, late that night,

Bartoszewski arrived at his mother's flat in Warsaw. 'She was amazed to see me. She threw herself on me and embraced me. From above her I saw this white strand of hair on her head, which was the first change I noticed. She didn't look too well. No one looked very well at that time.'

Altogether several hundred prisoners were released in a similar manner from Auschwitz. No one knows for certain why these individuals were chosen. But in Bartoszewski's case it seems that public pressure might have played a part since the Red Cross and other institutions had been campaigning for his release. That the Nazis were susceptible to international pressure over prisoners at this time is confirmed by the fate of a number of Polish academics arrested in November 1939. Professors at the Jagiellonian University in Kraków were snatched from their lecture rooms as part of the purge of the intelligentsia and imprisoned in a variety of concentration camps, including Dachau. Fourteen months later the surviving academics were released, almost certainly as a result of pressure from the outside world, including representations from the Pope.

Meantime, Auschwitz entered a new and crucial phase of its evolution as another German had a 'vision' that would further affect the development of the camp. Dr Otto Ambros of I.G. Farben, the giant industrial conglomerate, was looking for a suitable site for a synthetic rubber factory in the East. He was only searching for such a location at all because the war had taken a different course from the one anticipated by the Nazi leadership. Just as Himmler had imagined in May 1940 that it was possible the Jews could be transported to Africa because the war would soon be over, so did I.G. Farben imagine at that time that it was unnecessary to pursue the difficult and expensive process of producing synthetic rubber and fuel. Once the war was over – say, at the latest, autumn 1940 – plenty of raw materials would be available from outside the Reich, not least from Germany's own new colonies seized from its enemies.

But now, in November 1940, the war was demonstrably not over. Churchill had refused to make peace and the RAF had repulsed German air attacks during the Battle of Britain. Once again German planners had to react to the unexpected. Indeed, it is a recurring theme of this history that the Nazi leadership constantly has to contend with events they have not properly anticipated. Always they are driven by a sense of enormous ambition and optimism – anything can be accomplished by 'will' alone – and then they are pulled short either by their own lack of planning and foresight, or because their enemy is stronger than their own inflated sense of themselves ever allowed.

At I.G. Farben, expansion plans that had been shelved because of the expected imminent end of the war were now hurriedly dusted off and implemented. Although not a nationalized company, I.G. Farben was nonetheless hugely sympathetic to the needs and desires of the Nazi leadership. The Nazis' Four Year Plan had called for a Buna (synthetic rubber) plant to be built in the East, and now, after much discussion, I.G. Farben agreed to site one in Silesia.[42] Synthetic rubber was produced by taking coal and subjecting it to a process called hydrogenation, which involved passing hydrogen gas over coal at high temperature. Without lime, water and, crucially, coal, no Buna plant could function. A necessary precondition of any site, therefore, was ready access to these essential raw materials. In addition, I.G. Farben insisted on there being a developed transport and housing infrastructure in the area surrounding any proposed plant.

After poring over maps and plans, Otto Ambros believed he had hit upon a suitable site for I.G. Farben's new Buna plant about 3 miles east of the Auschwitz camp. But the proximity of the concentration camp was not a major factor in the initial decision to locate the Buna factory in the Auschwitz area. I.G. Farben was more interested in using the incoming ethnic Germans as workers than in relying solely upon slave labour.

Himmler's attitude to the news that I.G. Farben was interested in coming to Auschwitz can best be described as schizophrenic. As Reichsführer SS, Himmler had doubts about the move. Up to now he had ensured that prisoners in the concentration camp system worked only for SS-run enterprises. The precedent of prisoners working for private industry – with the money for their labour eventually routed to the Nazi state rather than kept entirely in the hands of the SS – was not one Himmler was keen to encourage. Even though the SS would make money selling I.G. Farben gravel, Himmler clearly had more elaborate ambitions for his own SS-run concerns which this arrangement prevented.

However, in his capacity as Reich Commissar for the Strengthening of German Nationhood, Himmler was a good deal less discouraging. He knew about I.G. Farben's need for ethnic Germans and was happy to try to provide them. Finding accommodation for the incoming workforce would not be a problem. The Auschwitz authorities were happy to 'turn out'[43] the Jews and Poles who lived in the town in order to make room for them. In the end the final decision was taken by Goering in his role as head of the Economic Four Year Plan: I.G. Farben would build their factory near to Auschwitz concentration camp and Himmler and the SS were expected to cooperate with them.[44]

This interest from I.G. Farben transformed Auschwitz from a minor camp within the SS system into potentially one of its most important components. Symptomatic of this change in the camp's status was Himmler's decision to make his first visit to the camp on 1 March 1941. In his memoirs and during his interrogation after the war Hoess supplied a detailed account of the visit, during which Himmler gave free reign to his megalomaniacal tendencies. If Himmler's vision of Auschwitz as an agricultural research station had been ambitious in November, his dream in March was positively gargantuan. With his initial doubts about the wisdom of I. G. Farben's presence now firmly set to one side, Himmler breezily announced that the camp would no longer contain 10,000 inmates but be expanded to hold 30,000. The Gauleiter of Upper Silesia, Fritz Bracht, who was accompanying Himmler, raised objections to such a rapid expansion. Another local official chipped in with the received wisdom that the drainage problems of the site remained unresolved. Himmler merely told them that they should consult experts and solve the problem themselves. He summed up the discussion with the words: 'Gentlemen, the camp will be expanded. My reasons for it are far more important than your objections.'[45]

Subservient as he was to Himmler, Hoess felt so strongly about the difficulty of implementing his master's new vision that he waited until only he, Himmler and the Higher SS and Police Leader for the Southeast, Erich von dem Bach-Zelewski, were all alone in the car together and then launched into a litany of complaints. He was short of building materials, he objected, he was short of staff, he was short of time – in fact he was short of everything. Himmler reacted in a predictable way: 'I want to hear no more about difficulties!' he said. 'For an SS officer there are no difficulties! When they come up, it's his job to get rid of them. How you do that is your business, not mine.'

What is significant about this exchange is not so much Himmler's response to Hoess's grumbling, but more that Hoess felt able to talk to the head of the SS in this way at all. In the Soviet system anyone who talked to Stalin or Beria (head of the NKVD secret police and Himmler's nearest equivalent in Moscow) in such a manner risked their life. Strange as it may seem at first sight, the Nazi leadership tolerated much more internal criticism from its supporters than did the Stalinist system. And this is one reason why the Third Reich was the more dynamic of the two political regimes, with functionaries lower down the chain of command free to use their initiative and voice their views. Unlike most of those who committed crimes under Stalin, Hoess was never acting out of fear of terrible retribution if he questioned an order. He had joined the SS because he believed wholeheartedly in the overall Nazi vision, and this meant he felt free to criticize the details of its implementation. He was that most powerful of subordinates, someone who was doing his job not because he was told to, but because he believed that what he was doing was right.

Of course, feeling free to criticize your superior over detail and actually accomplishing anything through such criticism are two different things. And Hoess accomplished nothing by complaining to Himmler: the Reichsführer's vision for the expansion of Auschwitz concentration camp was to be implemented regardless. As Hoess mournfully concluded, 'The Reichsführer was always more interested in hearing positive reports rather than negative ones.'

In the wake of I.G. Farben's decision to build a Buna plant in Auschwitz, Himmler did not confine his grandiose ideas to the camp but expanded his vision to encompass the town and surrounding area. At a planning meeting in Kattowitz on 7 April, his representative announced: 'It is the aim of the Reichsführer to create on this spot an exemplary Eastern settlement, special attention being paid to settling here German men and women who are particularly qualified.'[46] Plans were drawn up for a new German town of Auschwitz to hold 40,000 people, and these plans went hand in hand with the expansion of the nearby concentration camp.

Around this time Hoess also came to recognize the potential usefulness of the relationship with I.G. Farben. The minutes of a meeting held on 27 March 1941[47] between Auschwitz officials and company representatives reveal just how he sought to gain an advantage for the camp. After one of the I.G. Farben engineers asked how many prisoners could be supplied over the coming years, 'Sturmbannführer [Major] Hoess pointed out the difficulties of accommodating a sufficient number of inmates in Auschwitz concentration camp, the main problem being that it is not possible for the construction of accommodation to proceed at full speed.' What was preventing this, Hoess declared, was a lack of raw materials. This was, of course, the same difficulty he had just been haranguing Himmler about and that he had previously attempted to solve himself by travelling the countryside and 'pilfering' barbed wire. Hoess now argued that if I.G. Farben would help to 'speed up the extension of the camp' then 'this would, after all, be in their own interest, because only in this way could the deployment of sufficient prisoners be achieved'. At last Hoess appeared to have found an audience sympathetic to his difficulties, as the gentlemen from I.G. Farben agreed to 'take on the task of finding out whether it is possible to assist the camp'.

During the same meeting I.G. Farben agreed to pay a daily 'all-inclusive' sum of 3 Reichsmark per unskilled worker and 4 Reichsmark per skilled worker, and 'work performance [for each camp prisoner]' was 'estimated as being 75 per cent of that of a normal German worker'. Agreement was also reached on the price I.G. Farben would be charged per cubic metre of gravel dug by camp inmates from the nearby Soła river. Overall, 'the entire negotiations were conducted in cordial harmony. Both sides emphasized their wish to assist each other in every way possible.'

But vast as Himmler's and I.G. Farben's plans for Auschwitz were, they were dwarfed by the far-reaching decisions being made by Nazi strategists back in Berlin. For some months officers of the High Command of the German armed forces had been working on plans for the invasion of the Soviet Union, codenamed Operation Barbarossa. At a meeting at his Bavarian retreat, the Berghof, back in July 1940, Hitler had announced to his military commanders that the best way to bring a swift end to the war was to destroy the Soviet Union. He believed that Britain only stayed in the war in the hope that Stalin would eventually break the non-aggression pact signed with the Nazis in August 1939. If the Germans destroyed the Soviet Union, then, he thought, Britain would make peace and the Nazis would be the undisputed masters of Europe. This single decision would shape the course of the war, indeed the course of the whole history of Europe for the rest of the century. As a result of the invasion, 27 million Soviet citizens would die, greater losses than any nation in history has ever sustained as a consequence of a single conflict. And the war would also provide the context for the implementation of the Nazis' 'Final Solution' – the extermination of the Jews. It is thus impossible to understand the way in which Auschwitz was now to develop without setting the changes at the camp in the context of both the planning for Operation Barbarossa and the course of the war in the summer and autumn of 1941. Indeed, from this point until Hitler committed suicide on 30 April 1945 the progress, or lack of it, of the war in the East would dominate Nazi thinking.

The Nazis believed this was not a war against the 'civilized' nations of the West, but a fight to the death against Judeo-Bolshevik 'subhumans'. As a consequence, Franz Halder, Chief of the Army General Staff, recorded in his diary on 17 March 1941 that in Russia 'force must be used in its most brutal form' and 'The intelligentsia put in by Stalin must be exterminated.' This attitude meant that it was possible for economic planners to come up with a devastating solution to the problem of feeding the German army during its advance into the Soviet Union. A document of 2 May 1941 from the Wehrmacht's central economic agency states that 'the entire German army' would have to 'be fed at the expense of Russia'. The consequence of this was clear: 'Thereby tens of millions of men will undoubtedly starve to death if we take away all we need from the country.'[48] Three weeks later, on 23 May, another even more radical document was produced by the same agency. Entitled 'Political-Economic Guidelines for the Economic Organization East', it states that the goal now was to use Russian resources not just for feeding the German army, but also for supplying Nazi-controlled Europe. As a consequence, 30 million people in the northern part of the Soviet Union might die of starvation.[49]

Recent research has demonstrated that such shocking documents do not represent a thought process that was merely expedient; there existed a strand of intellectual thinking within the Nazi movement that saw such population reduction as economically justified. Working to a theory of 'optimum population size', Nazi economic planners could examine any area and work out, simply from the number of people living there, whether the land would produce a profit or a loss. For example, German economist Helmut Meinhold of the Institute for German Development Work in the East calculated in 1941 that 5.83 million Poles (including old people and children) were 'surplus' to requirements.[50] The existence of this surplus population meant 'an actual erosion of capital'. The people who constituted this excess population were '*Ballastexistenzen*' – a 'waste of space'. At this stage such economists had not followed their own logic through – they were not calling for the physical extermination of these *Ballastexistenzen* in Poland. But these planners did note how Stalin had dealt with similar overpopulation in the Soviet Union. In the Ukraine during the 1930s a policy of deportation of the *kulak* (rich peasant) class and collectivization of the remainder had led to the deaths of around 9 million people.

Such thinking also gave an intellectual underpinning to the civilian deaths that were expected to result from the German invasion of the Soviet Union; to the Nazi planners, the fact that '30 million people' might die of starvation would not only be of immediate benefit to the advancing German army, it would also have a long-term benefit for the German people. Fewer people to feed in the Soviet Union would not only mean that more food could be transported west for the citizens of Munich or Hamburg, it would also facilitate the swift Germanization of the occupied territories. Himmler had already noted that most Polish farms were too small to support a German family and now, he no doubt believed, mass starvation would ease the creation of great German estates in the Soviet Union. Just before the invasion was launched Himmler spoke frankly to his colleagues at a weekend party: 'The purpose of the Russian campaign [is] to decimate the Slavic population by 30 millions.'[51]

The prospect of war against the Soviet Union clearly released the most radical ideas imaginable in the minds of leading Nazis. When Hitler wrote to Mussolini to tell him of his decision to invade the Soviet Union, he confessed that now he felt 'spiritually free'; and that 'spiritual freedom' consisted of the ability to act during this conflict in any way he liked. As Goebbels, Hitler's propaganda chief, wrote in his diary on 16 June 1941: 'The Führer says that we must gain victory, no matter whether we do right or wrong. We have so much to answer for anyhow ...'

It was also clear from this planning stage of the war that the Jews of the Soviet Union were to suffer grievously. In a speech to the Reichstag on 30 January 1939 Hitler had made an explicit connection between any future world war and the elimination of the Jews: 'I want today to be a prophet again: if international finance and Jewry inside and outside Europe should succeed in plunging the nations once more into a world war, the result will be not the Bolshevization of the earth and thereby the victory of Jewry, but the annihilation of the Jewish race in Europe.'[52] Hitler used the term 'Bolshevization' specifically to emphasize the linkage in Nazi racial theory between Communism and Judaism. In his mind the Soviet Union was the home of a Bolshevik–Jewish conspiracy. It mattered not that Stalin himself had clear anti-Semitic tendencies. The Nazi fantasy was that Jews secretly pulled the strings throughout Stalin's empire.

To deal with the perceived threat from the Jews of the Soviet Union, four Einsatzgruppen were formed. Similar operational squads of the Security Service (part of the SS) and Security Police had previously functioned in the wake of both the Anschluss in Austria and the invasion of Poland. Their task, operating just behind the front line, had been to root out 'enemies of the state'. In Poland the Einsatzgruppen had conducted terror operations in which around 15,000 Poles – mostly Jews or members of the intelligentsia – had been killed. That total was to be dwarfed by the actions of the Einsatzgruppen in the Soviet Union.

The murderous effect of these units was, initially, to be out of all proportion to their size. Einsatzgruppe A, attached to Army Group North, was the largest, with a complement of 1000 men. The remaining three (B, C and D), attached to the other army groups, each contained between 600 and 700 soldiers. Just before the invasion the leaders of these Einsatzgruppen were briefed by Heydrich on their tasks. The orders he issued were later compiled in a directive of 2 July 1941, which stated that the Einsatzgruppen were charged with killing Communist politicians, political commissars and 'Jews in the service of the party or the state'. The Nazis' obsession with the link between Judaism and Communism is thus made explicit in Heydrich's directive.

During the early days of the invasion the Einsatzgruppen moved into the Soviet Union behind the German army. Progress was swift, and by 23 June, just one day into the attack, Einsatzgruppe A, under the command of Police General and SS Brigadeführer (Brigadier) Dr Walter Stahlecker, reached Kaunas in Lithuania. Immediately they arrived the Einsatzgruppe incited pogroms against the Jews of the town. Significantly, Heydrich's directive had contained the words: 'No steps will be taken to interfere with any purges that may be initiated by anti-Communist or anti-Jewish elements in the newly occupied territories. On the contrary, these are to be secretly encouraged.' What this instruction demonstrates is that killing 'Jews in the service of the party or the state' constituted the bare minimum that was expected of the Einsatzgruppen. As Stahlecker wrote in a subsequent report: 'The task of the security police was to set these purges in motion and put them on the right track so as to ensure that the liquidation goals that had been set might be achieved in the shortest time.'[53] In Kaunas, Lithuanians who had just been released from prison clubbed Jews to death in the street, under the benign gaze of the Germans. Some of the large crowd that gathered to watch the killings shouted out, 'Beat the Jews!' to encourage the murderers. After the killing was over one of the murderers climbed on top of the bodies, took out an accordion and played the Lithuanian national anthem. This was, no doubt, exactly the kind of action Heydrich wished his men to 'secretly encourage'.

Mostly away from the main towns, the Einsatzgruppen carried out their work of selecting 'Jews in the service of the party or the state' and killing them. In practice, this often meant that all male Jews in a village would be shot. After all, according to Nazi theory, which male Jew in the Soviet Union was not implicitly 'in the service of the party or the state'?

As the Einsatzgruppen and associated SS units carried on killing Soviet Jews, the regular German army too participated in war crimes. Under the infamous Barbarossa decree and commissar order, partisan fighters were shot out of hand, collective reprisals against whole communities were ordered and Soviet political officers – the commissars – were killed even after being captured as prisoners of war. And it was because of the Nazi attitude towards these commissars that Auschwitz was to become involved in the conflict. Under an agreement with the SS, the German army allowed Heydrich's men into the POW camps to weed out any commissars who had slipped through the initial selection of prisoners on the front line. The question then was: where should these commissars be taken? It was clearly not ideal from the Nazi point of view to murder them in front of their comrades, which is why, in July 1941, several hundred commissars who had been found in the ordinary POW camps were shipped to Auschwitz.

From the moment of their arrival these prisoners were treated differently from the other inmates. Incredibly, given the suffering that already existed in the camp, as a group they were treated worse. Jerzy Bielecki heard the sound of their mistreatment before he saw them: 'It was a great yelling and moaning and roaring.' He and a friend made their way towards the gravel pits on the edge of the camp where they saw the Soviet prisoners. 'They were pushing these wheelbarrows full of sand and gravel whilst running,' he says. 'It was very difficult. The planks they pushed the wheelbarrows over were sliding from side to side. It was not normal work; it was a hell that the SS men created for those Soviet prisoners of war.' The Kapos beat the commissars with sticks as they worked, encouraged by the watching SS who yelled, 'Boys! Hit them!' But it was what he saw next that particularly shocked Jerzy Bielecki: 'There were four or five SS men with guns. And those that had a gun from time to time would load it, look down, take aim and then shoot into the gravel pit. Then my friend said, "What is that son of a bitch doing?" And we saw that a Kapo was hitting a dying man with a stick. My friend had army training and he said, "Those are prisoners of war. They have rights!" But they were being killed while working.' In such a manner, during the summer of 1941, the war on the Eastern Front – the war without rules – came to Auschwitz.

The murder of the Soviet commissars was, of course, only a small part of the function of Auschwitz during this period; above all else the camp remained a place to oppress and instill terror into the Polish prisoners. And in striving to make the institution perform that service for the Nazi state, Hoess constantly tried to limit the number of escapes. Only two people attempted to escape in 1940, but that number increased to 17 in 1941 (and was to rise still further, leaping to 173 in 1942, 295 in 1943 and 312 in 1944).[54] Because in the early years the vast majority of the inmates were Poles, and the locals were sympathetic to their cause, once a prisoner had evaded the camp security it was possible to avoid recapture permanently – to vanish into the maelstrom of population movement caused by the ethnic reorganizations. Since many inmates worked away from the camp during the day, it was not even necessary for them to cross the electrified wire that surrounded the camp itself. They needed to surmount only one obstacle, the outside perimeter fence, the so-called *Grosse Postenkette.*

Hoess's policy to prevent these escapes was simple: brutal retribution. If the Nazis could not capture the person who had escaped they would imprison his relatives. They would also select ten prisoners from the block where he had lived and put them to death in a deliberately sadistic way. Roman Trojanowski participated in three separate selections during 1941 after escapes had been detected from his block. 'The Lagerführer and others would look into the eyes of the prisoners and choose,' he says. 'Of course, those who looked worse, those who were the weakest, they were the ones most likely to be chosen. I don't know what I thought about during the selection. I just didn't want to look into his eyes – this could be dangerous. You want to stand straight so that no one will notice you. And when Fritzsch stopped by somebody and pointed his finger, it wasn't certain where he was pointing and your heart would stop.' Trojanowski remembers one selection that epitomized the mentality of Karl Fritzsch, the Lagerführer: 'During such a selection Fritzsch noticed a man who was standing shivering not far from me. He asked him, "Why are you shivering?" And through the translator the man said, "I'm shivering because I'm afraid. I have several small children at home and I want to bring them up, I don't want to die." And Fritzsch answered, "Watch out and see it doesn't happen again, because if it does I'll send you there." And he pointed to the chimney of the crematorium. The man didn't understand, and because of Fritzsch's gesture he stepped forward. And the translator said, "The Lagerführer is not selecting you, go back." But Fritzsch said, "Leave him. If he stepped out, then that is his destiny."'

The selected inmates were taken to the cellars of Block 11 and locked in a cell where they were left to starve to death. It was a slow and agonizing process. Roman Trojanowski learnt that one person he knew was reduced to eating his own shoes after more than a week without food. But during the summer of 1941 the starvation cells were also the site of one of the few events in this history that offer any solace for those who believe in the redemptive possibility of suffering. Maksymilian Kolbe, a Roman Catholic priest from Warsaw, was forced to participate in a selection for the starvation cell after an inmate had apparently escaped from his block. A man standing near him, Franciszek Gajowniczek, was selected by Fritzsch, but he called out that he had a wife and children and wanted to live. Kolbe heard him and volunteered to take his place. Fritzsch agreed, and so Kolbe was thrown into the starvation cell as one of the ten selected. Two weeks later the four who were left alive, including Kolbe, were finally murdered by lethal injection. Kolbe was canonized by the Polish Pope John Paul II in 1982. His story has caused considerable controversy, not least because a magazine he published before his arrest carried anti-Semitic material. What remains unchallengeable, however, is Kolbe's bravery in sacrificing his own life for another.

That same month, July 1941, a series of decisions made thousands of miles away resulted in Auschwitz becoming a still more sinister place. Auschwitz prisoners were about to be murdered by gassing for the first time – but not in the way for which the camp was eventually to become infamous. These inmates were to be killed because they fell victim to the Nazi 'adult euthanasia' programme. This murderous operation had its root in a Führer decree of October 1939, which allowed doctors to select chronically mentally ill or physically disabled patients and kill them. Initially chemical injections were used to murder the disabled, but later bottled carbon monoxide became the preferred method. Gas chambers, designed to look like shower rooms, were built in special killing centres, mostly former mental hospitals. Some months before issuing his October 1939 decree, Hitler had authorized the selection and murder of disabled children. In so doing he was following the bleak logic of his own ultra-Darwinian view of the world. Such children forfeited their lives because they were weak and a drain on German society. And, as a profound believer in racial theory, he was concerned in case these children were able to reproduce themselves once they grew to adulthood.

The decree that extended the euthanasia programme to adults was backdated to 1 September and the start of the war – another sign that the conflict acted as a catalyst to radicalize Nazi thinking. The disabled were, to these fanatical National Socialists, another example of *Ballastexistenzen*, now especially burdensome to a country at war. Dr Pfannmüller, one of the most notorious figures within the adult euthanasia programme, expressed his feelings this way: 'The idea is unbearable to me that the best, the flower of our youth must lose its life at the front in order that the feeble-minded and irresponsible asocial elements can have a secure existence in the asylum.'[55] Not surprisingly, given the mentality of the perpetrators, the selection criteria included not just the severity of the mental or physical illness but also the religious or ethnic background of the patient. Thus Jews in mental hospitals were sent to be gassed without selection, and in the East similar draconian methods were used to clear Polish asylums of patients. Between October 1939 and May 1940 around 10,000 mental patients were killed in West Prussia and the Warthegau, many by the use of a new technique – a gas chamber on wheels. Victims were shoved into a hermetically sealed compartment in the back of a converted van and then asphyxiated by bottled carbon monoxide. Significantly, the living space thus released was used to house the incoming ethnic Germans.

At the start of 1941 the adult euthanasia campaign was extended to concentration camps in an action known as 14f13, and the programme reached Auschwitz on 28 July. 'During evening roll-call it was said that all the sick could leave to be healed,' says Kazimierz Smoleń,[56] then a political prisoner at the camp. 'Some inmates believed it. Everyone had hope. But I wasn't so convinced of the good intentions of the SS.' Neither was Wilhelm Brasse, who listened to his Kapo, a German Communist, describe what he thought the fate of the sick would be: 'He told us that in Sachsenhausen camp he had heard rumours that people are taken from hospitals and that they disappear somewhere.'

Around 500 sick inmates – a combination of volunteers and those selected – were marched out of the camp to a waiting train. 'They were all worn out,' says Kazimierz Smoleń. 'There were no healthy people. It was a march of spectres. At the end of the line were nurses carrying people on stretchers. It was macabre. No one yelled at them or laughed. The sick people were pleased, saying, "Let my wife and children know about me."' Much to the joy of the remaining prisoners, two of the most notorious Kapos were included in the transport, one of them the hated Krankemann. The rumour in the camp was that he had fallen out with his protector, the Lagerführer Fritzsch. Both Kapos, in fulfilment of Himmler's prediction of the fate of Kapos once they had returned to ordinary prison life, were almost certainly murdered on the train before it reached its destination. All the other inmates who left the camp that day died in a gas chamber in a converted mental hospital at Sonnenstein near Danzig. The first Auschwitz prisoners to be gassed were therefore not killed in the camp but transported to Germany, and they were not murdered because they were Jews but because they could no longer work.

The summer of 1941 was not only a crucial time in the development of Auschwitz, it was also a decisive moment in both the course of the war against the Soviet Union and the Nazis' policy towards the Soviet Jews. Superficially, during July the war seemed to be going well, with the Wehrmacht making good progress against the Red Army. As early as 3 July Franz Halder of the German High Command wrote in his diary, 'It is thus probably no overstatement to say that the Russian campaign has been won in the space of two weeks.' Goebbels echoed such thoughts in his own diary on 8 July, writing, 'No one doubts any more that we shall be victorious in Russia.' By mid-July Panzer units were 350 miles inside the Soviet Union, and by the end of the month a Soviet intelligence officer – on the orders of Beria, Himmler's Soviet counterpart – was approaching the Bulgarian ambassador in Moscow to see if he would act as an intermediary with the Germans and sue for peace.[57]

But on the ground the situation was more complex. The policy of starvation, which had been such a central part of the invasion strategy, meant that, for example, Vilnius, the capital of Lithuania, had by the start of July food supplies for only two weeks. And Goering stated clear Nazi policy when he said that the only people who were entitled to be fed by the invading force were those 'performing important tasks for Germany'.[58] There was also the unresolved question of the dependants of those Jewish men who had been shot by the Einsatzgruppen. These women and children, having in most cases lost their breadwinners, were liable to starve especially swiftly; they were certainly not 'performing important tasks for Germany'.

Meanwhile, a crisis over food supply was predicted, not just on the Eastern Front but back in Poland in the Łódź ghetto. In July Rolf-Heinz Hoeppner of the SS wrote to Adolf Eichmann, who was in charge of the section dealing with Jewish affairs in the Reich Security Main Office: 'This winter there is a danger that not all the Jews can be fed any more. One should weigh honestly if the most humane solution might not be to finish off those of the Jews who are not fit for work by means of some quick-working device. At any rate, that would be more pleasant than to let them starve to death.' (It is significant that Hoeppner writes of the potential need to kill those Jews 'not fit to work' – not all the Jews. Increasingly, from the spring of 1941, the Nazis were making a distinction between Jews who were useful to the Germans and those who were not, a distinction that would later become crystallized in the infamous 'selections' of Auschwitz.)

At the end of July Himmler issued orders that were to resolve the question of those Jews who were considered 'useless eaters' by the Nazis, at least as far as the Eastern Front was concerned. He reinforced the Einsatzgruppen with units of the SS cavalry and police battalions. Eventually around 40,000 men would be involved in the killing, a ten-fold increase in the initial complement of the Einsatzgruppen. This massive increase in manpower was for a reason: the policy of killing in the East was to be extended to include Jewish women and children. The order for this action reached different Einsatzgruppe commanders at different times over the next few weeks, often given by Himmler personally as he went on a tour of the killing fields. But by mid-August all the commanders of the murder squads knew of the expansion in their task.

This moment marks a turning point in the killing process. Once women and children were to be shot, the Nazi persecution of the Jews entered an entirely different conceptual phase. Almost all the Nazi anti-Jewish policies during the war so far had been potentially genocidal, and Jewish women and children had already died in the ghettos or during the failed Nisko emigration. But this was different. Now the Nazis had decided to gather together women and children, make them strip, line them up next to an open pit and shoot them. There could be no pretence that a baby was an immediate threat to the German war effort, but a German soldier would now look at that little child and pull the trigger.

Many factors came together at this crucial time to cause the change in policy. One important precondition was, of course, that the Jewish women and children in the Soviet Union now presented a 'problem' for the Nazis – one they had created themselves by a combination of shooting male Jews and instigating a policy of starvation in the East. But that was not the only reason the decision was taken to extend the killing. In July Hitler had announced that he wanted a German 'Garden of Eden' in the East, and by implication there would be no place for the Jews in this new Nazi paradise. (And it can surely be no accident that Himmler ordered the extension of the killing to include women and children after attending several secret one-to-one meetings with Hitler in July; this move would not have occurred without the Führer wishing it so.) With killing units already shooting Jewish men, it must have seemed a logical step from the Nazi ideological perspective to send extra men to the murder squads in order to 'cleanse' this new 'Garden of Eden' completely.

Hans Friedrich[59] was a member of one of the SS infantry units that was sent to the East to reinforce the Einsatzgruppen in the summer of 1941. His SS brigade operated primarily in the Ukraine and he says they met no resistance from the Jews they came to murder. 'They [the Jews] were extremely shocked, utterly frightened and petrified, and you could do what you wanted with them. They had resigned themselves to their fate.' The SS and their Ukrainian collaborators forced the Jews out of their village and made them stand by a 'deep, broad ditch. They had to stand in such a way that when they were shot they would fall into the ditch. That then happened again and again. Someone had to go down into the ditch and check conscientiously whether they were still alive or not, because it never happened that they were all mortally wounded at the first shot. And if somebody wasn't dead and was lying there injured, then he was shot with a pistol.'

Friedrich admits that he himself shot Jews in these pit killings.[60] He claims that he thought of 'nothing' as he saw his victims standing just a few metres in front of him: 'I only thought, "Aim carefully so that you hit." That was my thought. When you've got to the point where you're standing there with a gun ready to shoot ... there's only one thing, a calm hand so that you hit well. Nothing else.' His conscience has never troubled him over the murders he committed; he has never had a bad dream about the subject or woken in the night and questioned what he did.

Documents confirm that Friedrich was a member of the 1st SS Infantry Brigade, which entered the Ukraine on 23 July. Although Friedrich, either because of the distance of time or out of a desire not to incriminate himself further, is not specific about the exact places where he carried out the killings, the records point to his brigade having participated in a number of murders of Jews in several named places. One such action took place in the western Ukraine on 4 August 1941. Over 10,000 Jews from surrounding villages had been forced from their homes and gathered in the town of Ostrog. 'Early in the morning [of 4 August] the cars and lorries came,' says Vasyl Valdeman,[61] then a 12-year-old member of a Jewish family. 'They were armed and came with dogs.' Having surrounded the town, the SS forced thousands of Jews out towards a nearby hamlet where there was an area of sandy soil. 'Everyone understood that we were going to be shot,' says Vasyl Valdeman, 'but it was impossible for the SS to shoot those amounts of people. We arrived there at ten o'clock [in the morning] and everyone was ordered to sit down. It was very hot. There was no food or water; people were just pissing on the ground. It was a very hard time. Somebody said they would rather be shot than sit there in the hot weather. Someone fainted and some people just died of fear itself.'

Oleksiy Mulevych,[62] a non-Jewish villager, saw what happened next. He climbed on to the roof of a nearby barn and witnessed small groups of 50 or 100 Jews being led away from the field and ordered to strip naked. 'They put the Jews on the edge of a pit,' he says, 'and officers told their soldiers to choose a Jew to shoot at ... The Jews were crying and shouting. They felt they saw their death ... Then everyone shot and the Jews fell immediately. The officer then chose strong Jews to throw the bodies into the pit.'

The shootings continued all day. Several thousand Jews – men, women and children – were murdered, but there were simply too many Jews for the SS to kill everyone in this single action. So at nightfall the remainder, including Vasyl Valdeman and his family, were moved back to Ostrog. In this and subsequent actions Vasyl lost his father, grandmother, grandfather, two brothers and two uncles, but together with his mother he managed to escape from the ghetto and was hidden by local villagers for the next three years until the Red Army liberated the Ukraine. 'I don't know about other villages,' he says, 'but people in our village helped Jews very much.' A few days later Oleksiy Mulevych went out to visit the killing fields and saw a gruesome sight: 'The sand was moving. I think there were wounded people who were moving under the sand. I felt sorry. I wanted to help, but then I understood that even if I took someone from the pit I could not cure them.'

'We had dogs at our house,' says Vasyl Valdeman, 'but we never were as cruel to them as the fascists were to us ... I was thinking all the time, "What makes these people so cruel?"' Hans Friedrich has one answer to Vasyl Valdeman's question – hatred: 'If I'm honest I have no empathy [for the Jews]. For the Jews harmed me and my parents so much that I cannot forget.' As a result, Friedrich is 'not sorry' for all the Jews he shot. 'My hatred towards the Jews is too great.' When pressed, he admits that he felt, and still feels, justified in killing the Jews out of 'revenge'.

An understanding of Friedrich's past is crucial in order to comprehend both why he felt able to take part in the killing and why he feels able to defend his actions today. He was born in 1921 in a part of Romania dominated by ethnic Germans. As he grew up he learnt to hate the Jews he and his family encountered. His father was a farmer and the Jews in the locality acted as traders, buying produce and then selling it on at market. Friedrich was told by his parents that the Jews earned too much profit from their business dealings and that he and his family were regularly cheated by them. 'I would like to have seen you,' he adds, 'if you had experienced what we experienced – if you were a farmer and wanted to sell, say, pigs and you couldn't do it. You could only do it via a Jewish trader. Try to put yourself in our position. You were no longer master of your own life.'

As adolescents during the 1930s he and his friends painted posters proclaiming, 'Don't buy from Jews' and 'The Jews are our misfortune', and hung them over the entrance to a Jewish shop. He felt 'proud' as he did this because he had 'warned against the Jew'. He read the propaganda of the Nazi state, particularly the violently anti-Semitic *Der Stürmer*, and found that it fitted perfectly with his own developing world-view. In 1940 he joined the SS 'because the German Reich was at war' and he 'wanted to be there'. He believes that 'there were connections between Jews and Bolshevism – there was sufficient evidence to prove this'. When as a member of the SS he advanced into the Ukraine in the summer of 1941 he believed he wasn't entering a 'civilized' country 'like France', but instead somewhere that was at best 'half civilized' and 'far behind Europe'. Then, when asked to kill Jews, he did it willingly, all the time thinking he was taking revenge for the Jewish traders who had allegedly cheated his family. That these were different Jews altogether – Jews, indeed, from another country – mattered not at all. As he puts it, 'They're all Jews.'

Far from being sorry for having participated in the extermination of the Jews, Hans Friedrich has no regrets of any kind. Although he never said so in these terms, he gives every impression of being proud of what he and his comrades did. The justification for his actions is, in his mind, clear and absolute: the Jews did him and his family harm, and the world is a better place without them. In an unguarded moment Adolf Eichmann remarked that the knowledge of having participated in the murder of millions of Jews gave him such satisfaction that he would 'jump laughingly into his grave'. It is easy to see how Hans Friedrich might feel exactly the same emotion.

However, whilst this expansion in the killing was being implemented on the Eastern Front during the summer of 1941, it is less clear that this was the moment at which the whole of the Nazis' 'Final Solution' – encompassing millions more Jews, including those in Germany, Poland and western Europe – was decided upon. One document does perhaps suggest a connection between the two. On 31 July Heydrich obtained Goering's signature on a paper that stated: 'To supplement the task that was assigned to you on 24 January 1939, which dealt with the solution of the Jewish problem by emigration and evacuation in the most suitable way, I hereby charge you to submit a comprehensive blueprint of the organizational, subject-related and material preparatory measures for the execution of the intended Final Solution of the Jewish question.' The timing of this document, on the face of it, is crucial: Goering signs Heydrich's general authorization for the 'Final Solution' of all the Jews under German control at exactly the moment the killing squads are to be used to shoot Jewish women and children in the East.

However, a recent discovery in the Moscow Special Archive casts doubt on the special significance of the 31 July authorization. This document contains a note from Heydrich dated 26 March 1941, which states: 'With respect to the Jewish question I reported briefly to the Reich Marshal [Goering] and submitted to him my new blueprint, which he authorized with one modification concerning Rosenberg's jurisdiction, and then ordered for resubmission.'[63] Heydrich's 'new blueprint' was most likely a response to the change in the Nazis' anti-Jewish policy caused by the forthcoming invasion of the Soviet Union. The idea of transporting the Jews to Africa had been abandoned, and early in 1941 Hitler had ordered Heydrich to prepare a scheme to deport the Jews somewhere within German control. Since the war with the Soviet Union was expected to last only a few weeks and be over before the onset of the Russian winter, it was reasonable, Heydrich and Hitler must have felt, to plan for the Jews to be pushed further east that autumn in an internal solution to their self-created Jewish problem. In the wasteland of eastern Russia the Jews would suffer grievously.

As the 31 July authorization makes clear, Heydrich was first assigned the task of planning the 'solution of the Jewish problem by emigration and evacuation' at the start of 1939, and so discussions about his jurisdiction and room for manoeuvre within the Nazi state on this issue must have been ongoing since then. Alfred Rosenberg (mentioned in the 26 March document), who was formally appointed Minister of the Occupied Eastern Territories by Hitler on 17 July 1941, was a potential threat to Heydrich's own power in the East, and the 31 July authorization may well have been issued to help Heydrich clarify his own position.

So on balance the new evidence does not support the once prevalent view that there was some conclusive decision taken by Hitler in the spring or summer of 1941 to order the destruction of all the Jews of Europe, of which the 31 July authorization is an important part. The more likely scenario is that as all the leading Nazis focused their attention on the war against the Soviet Union, the decision to kill the women and children in the East was seen as the practical way of solving an immediate and specific problem.

Nonetheless, this particular 'solution' would in turn create further problems, and as a result new killing methods would be devised which would enable Jews and others to be murdered on an even greater scale. A vital moment in that process of transformation occurred on 15 August when Heinrich Himmler visited Minsk and saw at first hand the work of his killing squads. One of those who attended the execution with him was Walter Frentz,[64] an officer in the Luftwaffe who was working as a cameraman at Hitler's headquarters. Not only was Frentz shaken by the killings, it was clear to him that so were some members of the execution squad. 'I went along to the site of the execution,' says Frentz, 'and afterwards the commander of the auxiliary police approached me because I was in the air force. "Lieutenant," he said, "I can't take it any more. Can't you get me out of here?" I said, "Well, I don't have any influence over the police. I'm in the air force, what am I supposed to do?" "Well," he said, "I can't take it any more – it's terrible!"'

It was not just this particular officer who felt traumatized after the Minsk shootings. SS Obergruppenführer (Lieutenant General) von dem Bach-Zelewski, who witnessed the same killings, said to Himmler: 'Reichsführer, those were only a hundred ... Look at the eyes of the men in this Kommando, how deeply shaken they are! These men are finished for the rest of their lives. What kind of followers are we training here? Either neurotics or savages!'[65] Subsequently Bach-Zelewski himself became psychologically ill as a result of the murders, experiencing 'visions' of the killings in which he had participated.

As a result of these protests and what he had personally witnessed, Himmler ordered a search for a method of killing that caused fewer psychological problems for his men. Accordingly, a few weeks later Dr Albert Widmann, an SS Untersturmführer (2nd Lieutenant) from the Technical Institute of the Criminal Police, travelled East to meet Artur Nebe, the commander of Einsatzgruppe B, at his headquarters in Minsk. Previously Widmann had been instrumental in devising the gassing technique used to murder mentally ill patients. Now he would bring his expertise East.

Incredibly, one of the first methods Widmann tried in an attempt to 'improve' the killing process in the Soviet Union was to blow his victims up. Several mentally ill patients were put in a bunker along with packets of explosives. Wilhelm Jaschke, a captain in Einsatzkommando 8, witnessed what happened next: 'The sight was atrocious. The explosion hadn't been powerful enough. Some wounded came out of the dugout crawling and crying ...[66] The bunker had totally collapsed ... Body parts were scattered on the ground and hanging in the trees. On the next day, we collected the body parts and threw them into the bunker. Those parts that were too high in the trees were left there.'[67]

Widmann learnt from this gruesome experiment that murdering by explosion was clearly not the way forward Himmler desired, so he sought another method. The adult euthanasia programme had successfully used bottled carbon monoxide as a killing method, but it was impractical to transport large numbers of such canisters thousands of miles to the East. Maybe, Widmann and his colleagues thought, there was another way of using carbon monoxide to kill. Some weeks earlier Widmann and his boss, Dr Walter Hess, had been sitting in a carriage on the Berlin underground chatting about the fate that had nearly befallen Artur Nebe. He had returned in his car from a party having had too much to drink, parked in his garage without turning off the engine, and fallen asleep; as a result he had nearly died of carbon monoxide poisoning from the exhaust fumes. It seems that the memory of the drunken Nebe emboldened Widmann to attempt a gassing experiment using a car exhaust connected by a pipe to the brick basement of a mental hospital in Mogilev, east of Minsk. A number of hospital patients were locked in the room and the car engine started. Initially the trial was not successful from the Nazis' point of view: not enough carbon monoxide flowed from the car to kill the patients. This was rectified when a truck replaced the car.

The experiment, again from the Nazis' perspective, was a success. Widmann had discovered a cheap, effective way of killing people that minimized the psychological impact of the crime on the killers.

So in the autumn of 1941, in the East, Widmann initiated a significant change in the Nazi killing process – that much is certain. But how and when the decision was taken that Auschwitz should become an integral part of the mass extermination of the Jews is still a matter of controversy. Part of the difficulty lies in the testimony given by Hoess. Not only does he tend to present himself as a victim of both Himmler's demands and his incompetent staff, but also the precision of his dating is often unreliable. Hoess states: 'In the summer of 1941, Himmler called for me and explained: "The Führer has ordered the Final Solution of the Jewish question – and we have to carry out this task. For reasons of transport and isolation, I have picked out Auschwitz for this."'[68] Hoess did indeed visit Himmler in June 1941 to show the Reichsführer SS how the plans for Auschwitz were developing in the light of the I.G. Farben-initiated expansion, but it is not credible that at this same moment he would have been told that Auschwitz was to be a part of the 'Final Solution'. In the first place there is no other evidence that a 'Final Solution', in the sense of the mechanized extermination of the Jews in death camps, had even been planned at this stage. The meeting predates both the initial killings of Jewish men by the Einsatzgruppen in the East and the subsequent expansion of the killing which began at the end of July. Secondly, Hoess contradicts his own dating by adding that 'at that time there were already in the General Government three other extermination camps: Bełżec, Treblinka and Sobibór'. But none of these camps was in existence in the summer of 1941, and all three were not functioning until well into 1942.

Some scholars argue that, despite this internal contradiction in his statement, Hoess may possibly have been ordered in June 1941 to establish some extermination facilities at Auschwitz. But the evidence of the development of the killing capacity at the camp over the summer and early autumn of 1941 scarcely confirms that this was initiated by a June meeting with Himmler. The most likely explanation for Hoess's statement is that he simply misremembered the date. Conversations like the one he described with Himmler could well have happened, but in the following year, not in 1941.

This is not to say, of course, that Auschwitz was uninvolved in the killing process that summer. Indeed, with the expulsion of the sick inmates as part of the 14f13 programme and the shooting of the Soviet commissars in the gravel pits, the authorities at Auschwitz faced a problem not unlike the one the Einsatzgruppen were encountering in the East: the need to find a more effective method of murder. The decisive moment of discovery at Auschwitz appears to have occurred when Hoess was away from the camp, some time in late August or early September. Fritzsch, his deputy, saw a new use for a chemical used to remove the infestations of insects around the camp – crystallized prussic acid (cyanide), sold in tins and marketed under the name Zyklon (for cyclone) Blausäure (for prussic acid), popularly known as Zyklon B. Fritzsch now made the same kind of logical leap at Auschwitz that Widmann was making in the East. If Zyklon B could be used to kill lice, why could it not be used to kill human pests? And since Block 11 was already the place of execution within the camp and its basement could be sealed, was this not the most natural place to conduct an experiment?

Auschwitz at this time was not a camp where such an action could be carried out secretly. There were only a few metres between each block, and gossip was the currency of the place. So Fritzsch's experiments were common knowledge from the first. 'I could see that they were bringing in soil in wheelbarrows to insulate the windows,' says Wilhelm Brasse. 'And one day I saw them take the severely sick out on stretchers from the hospital and they were taken to Block 11.' It was not just the sick who were taken to Block 11. Predictably, so were members of the other target group the Auschwitz authorities had previously demonstrated they wanted to kill: Soviet commissars. 'They gathered Soviet prisoners of war in the basement,' says August Kowalczyk. 'But it turned out the gas didn't work that well and many of the inmates were still alive the next day. So they strengthened the dose. More crystals were poured in.'

On Hoess's return Fritzsch reported the news of the experiments. Hoess attended the next gassings in Block 11: 'Protected by a gas mask, I watched the killing myself. In the crowded cells death came instantaneously the moment the Zyklon B was thrown in. A short, almost smothered cry and it was all over.' Whilst the evidence is that death in Block 11 could be far from 'instantaneous', it was certainly the case that for the Nazis at Auschwitz the use of Zyklon B alleviated the process of murder. No longer would the killers have to look into the eyes of their victims as they murdered them. Hoess wrote that he was 'relieved' that this new method of killing had been found as he would be 'spared' a 'bloodbath'. He was wrong. The real bloodbath was about to begin.

— 2 —

Orders and Initiatives

On 7 April 1946 Rudolf Hoess was questioned during the Nuremberg trials by the American psychologist Dr Gustave Gilbert. 'And it never occurred to you,' Gilbert asked Hoess, 'to refuse the orders that Himmler gave to you regarding the so-called "Final Solution"?'[1] 'No,' replied Hoess, 'from our entire training the thought of refusing an order just didn't enter one's head, regardless of what kind of order it was ... I guess you cannot understand our world. I naturally had to obey orders.'

Hoess thus placed himself squarely in the phalanx of German soldiers who, after the war was lost, wanted the world to think that they had been robots, blindly following whatever commands were given to them regardless of their own personal feelings. But the truth is that Hoess was far from an automaton. During the last six months of 1941 and the first six months of 1942 Hoess was at his most innovative, not just following orders but using his own initiative to help increase the killing capacity of Auschwitz. And it was not just Hoess who was thinking and acting in this way during this crucial period; many other Nazis also played their part. For an important factor in the development of the extermination process was the way different initiatives from lower down the hierarchy contributed to the increasingly radical way forward. Once the war was over, Hoess, in common with hundreds of other Nazis, tried to convince the world that only one man had truly made the decisions: Adolf Hitler. But the 'Final Solution' became the collective will of many – something that can be demonstrated most clearly by unravelling the decision-making process that led to the deportation of the German Jews in the autumn of 1941.

The war against the Soviet Union, begun in June that year, precipitated the most radical solution yet seen to the Nazis' self-created 'Jewish problem': the destruction of Soviet Jewry by the shooting of men, women and children. But, to begin with, the Jews of western Europe and the German Reich remained relatively untouched by this slaughter. The Nazi assumption was still that they would be 'transported East' once the war was over, and in the optimistic minds of Hitler, Himmler and Heydrich that meant some time in the autumn of 1941. What was to happen to these Jews once they went East 'after the war' is unclear, since there were, as yet, no death camps waiting to receive them. Most likely they would have been sent to labour camps in the most inhospitable parts of Nazi-controlled Russia, where genocide would still have taken place, albeit a longer and more protracted one than the swift killing that was to follow in the gas chambers of Poland.

But that August some leading Nazis grew impatient with this plan. They knew that, in the East, Soviet Jews were already being 'dealt with' in the most brutal ways imaginable. Why, they began to suggest, should German Jews not be sent into the epicentre of this killing operation immediately? Joseph Goebbels, the Nazi Propaganda Minister and Gauleiter of Berlin, was one of those who took the lead that summer in pushing for the Jews of Berlin to be forcibly deported East. At a meeting on 15 August Goebbels' state secretary, Leopold Gutterer, pointed out that of the 70,000 Jews in Berlin only 19,000 were working (a situation, of course, that the Nazis had created themselves by enforcing a series of restrictive regulations against German Jews). The rest, argued Gutterer, ought to be 'carted off to Russia ... best of all actually would be to kill them.'[2] And when Goebbels himself met Hitler on 19 August he made a similar case for the swift deportation of the Berlin Jews.

Dominant in Goebbels' mind was the Nazi fantasy of the role that German Jews had played during World War I. While German soldiers had suffered at the front line, the Jews had supposedly been profiting from the bloodshed back in the safety of the big cities (in reality, of course, German Jews had been dying at the front in proportionately the same numbers as their fellow countrymen). But now, in the summer of 1941, it was obvious that Jews remained in Berlin while the Wehrmacht were engaged in their brutal struggle in the East – what else could they do, since the Nazis had forbidden German Jews to join the armed forces? As they did so often, the Nazis had created for themselves the exact circumstances that best fitted their prejudice. But despite Goebbels' entreaties, Hitler was still not willing to allow the Berlin Jews to be deported. He maintained that the war was still the priority and the Jewish question would have to wait. However, Hitler did grant one of Goebbels' requests. In a significant escalation of Nazi anti-Semitic measures, he agreed that the Jews of Germany should be marked with the yellow star. In the ghettos of Poland the Jews had been marked in similar ways from the first months of the war, but their counterparts in Germany had up to now escaped such humiliation.

That summer and early autumn Goebbels was not the only senior Nazi figure to lobby Hitler to permit the deportation of the German Jews. In the immediate aftermath of the British bombing raid on Hamburg on 15 September the Gauleiter of Hamburg, Karl Kaufmann, decided to write to Hitler, asking him to authorize the deportation of the Jews of the city in order to release housing for non-Jewish citizens who had just lost their homes. Hitler was now in receipt of proposals to send the Jews East from a whole variety of sources, including a suggestion from Alfred Rosenberg that Jews from central Europe be deported in retaliation for Stalin's recent action in sending the Volga Germans to Siberia. Now, suddenly, just a few weeks after saying the Reich Jews could not be deported, Hitler changed his mind. That September he decided that the expulsions East could begin after all.

However, it is important not to see in this reversal of policy a picture of an indecisive Hitler somehow bending to the will of his subordinates. He was influenced at least as much by the latest developments in the external military situation as by the pleas of his underlings. Hitler had always said that the Jews could be deported at the end of the war, and in September 1941 it seemed to the Nazi leader that there might be only a matter of a few weeks' difference between deporting the German Jews 'after the war was over' and doing so now. Kiev was about to fall and Moscow seemed wide open to German assault, so Hitler still hoped that the Soviet Union would be defeated before the winter.

There remained, of course, the question of where to send the

Jews. Himmler immediately had one answer – why should the Reich Jews not join the Polish Jews in ghettos? On 18 September Himmler wrote to Arthur Greiser, Nazi Gauleiter of the Warthegau in Poland, and asked him to prepare the Łódź ghetto for the arrival of 60,000 Jews from the 'Old Reich'. However, Himmler knew that at best this could only be a short-term solution since, as the ghetto authorities were swift to point out, the Łódź ghetto was already badly overcrowded.

Seventeen-year-old Lucille Eichengreen[3] was one of the first German Jews to be deported as a consequence of Hitler's change in policy. And at this moment in October 1941, as her mother received a registered letter ordering the family to be ready to leave Hamburg within 24 hours, no one – not even the Nazis who wanted to be rid of her – could have predicted the lengthy and tortuous form her journey to Auschwitz would take. The Eichengreen family were already suffering. Lucille's father, a Polish national, had been arrested and taken to Dachau at the start of the war. Eighteen months later, in February 1941, they heard news of him at last: 'The Gestapo came to our house with hats, leather coats and boots – their typical uniform,' says Lucille Eichengreen. 'They threw a cigar box on the kitchen table and said, "These are the ashes of Benjamin Landau [her father]." Whether they were the ashes of my father or just a handful of ashes from the crematorium at Dachau we will never know. We took the death of my father very hard, all of us, especially my mother and my younger sister; she was very much traumatized by it.' So now, eight months after learning of the death of her father at the hands of the Nazis, Lucille, her sister and her mother left their home for the last time and walked to the railway station past the citizens of Hamburg. On the streets they found no sympathy for their plight. 'They [the non-Jewish population] were just stony-faced,' says Lucille. 'It was either an ugly word or they looked away. It didn't make me feel cross. It made me feel afraid.'

Uwe Storjohann,[4] then 16 years old, was one of the residents of Hamburg who stood and watched the Jews walk by. 'Maybe around twenty per cent of people welcomed this with huge joy,' he says, 'saying, "Thank goodness these useless eaters are vanishing" and "They're only parasites", and they were clapping. But the large majority bypassed what was happening with silence. And this is the great mass of population who later in the post-war years would be saying, "I didn't know anything about it. We didn't see it." They answered by looking away.' One of Uwe Storjohann's friends was partly Jewish, and he had to say goodbye to a favourite aunt and grandmother 'in a heartrending way'. His friend was only a quarter Jewish and therefore allowed to stay; his aunt and grandmother were full Jews and had to leave. As he watched these desperate scenes, one feeling 'obsessed' Uwe Storjohann: 'It was a sense of thank God you weren't born a Jew. Thank God that you don't belong to them. You could equally well have been born a Jew because nobody can choose their parents, and then it would be your turn to be resettled. And then you would run around wearing such a star. I still recall that feeling today ... Immediately,' he continues, 'the thought occurred, "What will happen to these people?" And I knew, of course, after all I'd heard, that it couldn't be anything positive, anything good. They would somehow be sent off into a terrible world.'

The question of what 'ordinary' Germans knew about the fate of the Jews is one that has generated huge controversy. But Uwe Storjohann's admission that he knew the German Jews were being sent into a 'terrible' world is probably close to the state of mind of most Germans at the time. They knew the Jews were not coming back. Street markets were held in Hamburg to sell the household equipment left behind by Jewish families. And equally many 'ordinary Germans' knew that 'bad things' were happening to Jews in the East. A Nazi report by the SD (the intelligence branch of the SS, run by Reinhard Heydrich) from Franconia in southern Germany, dated December 1942, demonstrates that the Nazis themselves were concerned about the effect on the German population of knowledge of the killings in the East: 'One of the strongest causes of unease among those attached to the Church and in the rural population is at the present time formed by the news from Russia in which shooting and extermination of the Jews is spoken about. The news frequently leaves great care, anxiety and worry in those sections of the population. According to widely held opinion in the rural population, it is not at all certain that we will win the war, and if the Jews come again to Germany, they will exact dreadful revenge upon us.'[5]

Despite this level of knowledge amongst the general population, there were few protests at the deportation of the German Jews, and none of any kind in Hamburg in October 1941 at the start of the whole process. So, having walked through the streets, the three Eichengreen women together boarded a third-class train with wooden seats. As the train pulled away, Lucille realized that this 'was a train ride without a destination. It was a train ride into nowhere and we didn't know what to expect.'

They would eventually arrive at Auschwitz, where plans were now under way for a massive expansion of the camp complex. An entirely new camp was to be built 2 miles away from the existing one, on a patch of swampy ground that the Poles called Brzezinka and the Germans called Birkenau. But although Auschwitz–Birkenau was eventually to become the site of the mass murder of Jews, this was not the reason why it was being built. For Birkenau was a camp intended not for Jews, but for prisoners of war.

The current accepted history of the development of Birkenau is that when Himmler visited Auschwitz main camp in March 1941 he ordered Hoess to build a giant new prisoner of war camp, capable of holding 100,000 men. This information is based solely on Hoess's memoirs which, as already shown, can sometimes be unreliable on dating. If the construction of the POW camp was indeed ordered by Himmler in March 1941, it has always been a mystery why the first plans for the site were not initiated until October that year. As a result of research in Russian archives, new evidence has been uncovered which solves that mystery. A document from the Auschwitz construction office dated 12 September 1941 and titled 'Explanatory Report Regarding the Preliminary Draft for the Construction and Expansion of Auschwitz Concentration Camp'[6] contains a detailed description of both the present state and future expansion of Auschwitz 1, the main camp, to a capacity of 30,000 prisoners. But there is no mention anywhere in the document, or in the various attachments, of any planned prisoner of war camp to be built at Birkenau. The strong presumption must therefore be that on 12 September 1941 no detailed plans yet existed for Birkenau.

Another recently uncovered source of archival evidence supports the view that as late as the second week of September the decision had still not been made to build the new camp. The discovery of missing sections of Himmler's desk diary in a Russian archive in the 1990s[7] has facilitated a detailed study of his movements and phone calls during this crucial period. It shows that on 15 September Himmler discussed the issue of '*Kriegsgefangene*' (prisoners of war) with Reinhard Heydrich and Oswald Pohl, the head of the SS Economic and Administrative Department. This was followed by a telephone conversation with Pohl the next day which, according to a note in Himmler's diary, concerned '100,000 Russians' who were to be 'taken over' by the KZ (concentration camp) system. On 25 September the POW department of the OKW (Supreme Command of the German army) ordered that up to '100,000 POWs be transferred to the Reichsführer SS'. On the 26th, Hans Kammler, head of the Central SS Buildings Office, ordered the construction of a new POW camp at Auschwitz.

All of this new evidence therefore points to the final decision to construct Birkenau being taken in September 1941, not March. It remains possible, of course, that Himmler first saw the possibilities of the site when he visited Auschwitz in the spring of that year and may even have mentioned to Hoess that it might one day be a suitable location for expansion. The houses of the small village of Birkenau were cleared by the SS in July 1941and the inhabitants transported elsewhere, which does suggest that the Auschwitz authorities recognized the potential of the site (though they were also clearing other areas nearby as part of the creation of the 'Auschwitz Zone of Interest'). But, as the new evidence reveals, it is highly probable that no concrete decision about Birkenau was taken until September.

The task of designing and building the new camp fell to SS Hauptsturmführer (Captain) Karl Bischoff, newly appointed chief of the Auschwitz construction office, and the architect, SS Rottenführer (Corporal) Fritz Ertl. A study of their plans reveals that from the outset they intended the accommodation to be too overcrowded to sustain human life. Their initial plan was for one barrack block to contain 550 prisoners, which meant that each inmate would have only one third of the total space allocated to a prisoner in 'Old Reich' concentration camps like Dachau. But the plans show that even that level of density turned out to be too low for the needs of the SS planners: in a handwritten alteration, the number 550 was crossed out and replaced with a final figure of

744. Each prisoner at Birkenau would therefore now be expected to exist in a quarter of the total space allocated per inmate in a German concentration camp. Such callousness was perfectly acceptable to the SS because they knew that this was to be a special kind of prisoner of war camp, designed to hold not captured British or French combatants but an enemy they considered subhuman: Soviet POWs.

In the first seven months of the war against the Soviet Union the Germans took 3 million Red Army prisoners. In the course of the war as a whole they took 5.7 million, of whom a staggering 3.3 million lost their lives in captivity. After the war an attempt was made to claim that these appalling losses had occurred because the Germans had never anticipated taking so many prisoners so quickly, and had therefore not made adequate plans to take care of them. But this excuse merely masks a darker truth. As the minutes of the economic planning meetings examined in Chapter 1 demonstrate, mass starvation in the Soviet Union was anticipated as a consequence of the German army feeding itself 'at the expense' of the Soviet population during the war. And the plans for the new camp extension at Auschwitz–Birkenau fit into this pattern of a deliberate attempt to place the Soviet POWs in an environment where it was inevitable that large numbers of them would die.

Following the example of the original Auschwitz camp, it was the inmates themselves who were forced to build Birkenau. To that end 10,000 Soviet prisoners of war were sent to Auschwitz in the autumn of 1941. Polish prisoner Kazimierz Smoleń[8] witnessed their arrival: 'It was already snowing – extraordinary to have snow in October – and they [the Soviet POWs] were unloaded from trains about three kilometres from the camp. They had to give all their clothes away and jump into barrels with disinfectant, and naked they went to Auschwitz [the main camp]. Usually they were completely emaciated.' Once at the main camp, the Soviet prisoners became the first inmates to have their prison number tattooed on their bodies. This was another 'improving' measure initiated at Auschwitz, the only camp in the Nazi state ever to identify prisoners in this way. It seems to have been introduced because of the high mortality rate, and it was easier to identify a corpse from a tattoo than a disc hanging round the neck, which could easily become detached. Initially the tattoos were not placed on the prisoner's arm but punched on to the chest with long needles; the resulting wound was then filled in with ink. As Kazimierz Smoleń witnessed, many of the Soviet prisoners simply could not cope with this brutal admittance procedure: 'They had problems moving, and when they were hit with the tattoo seal they would fall down. They had to be put against the wall so they wouldn't fall over.'

Of the 10,000 Soviet prisoners who began building Birkenau that autumn, only a few hundred were still alive the following spring. One of the survivors who beat the terrible odds was a Red Army soldier called Pavel Stenkin.[9] He was captured by the Germans less than two hours after the war began on 22 June 1941, and was taken first to a giant prisoner of war camp behind the German lines where he and thousands of other Soviet POWs were kept corralled like animals and fed only on thin soup. His comrades started to die of starvation, but he maintains that he survived because he was accustomed to it; he was 'hungry from childhood' as a result of being brought up on a Soviet collective farm in the 1930s. Stenkin arrived at Auschwitz on one of the first transports in October 1941, and was immediately set to work building brick barracks at the new site. 'The average living time for a [Soviet] prisoner at Birkenau was two weeks,' he says. 'If you got something eatable, you must swallow it. Raw potato or not – it doesn't matter. Dirty, not dirty, it's all the same; there is no place to wash it. When it was time to get up in the morning, those who were alive moved, and around them would be two or three dead people. You go to bed and you are alive, and by the morning you are dead. It was death, death, death. Death at night, death in the morning, death in the afternoon. There was death all the time.'

Because these Soviet POWs had been registered into the camp and given a prison number this presented the Auschwitz authorities with a problem – how to explain in the *Totenbuch* (Death Book) the thousands upon thousands of deaths. Their solution was to dream up a variety of diseases from which the Soviet POWs could have perished; for example, 600 alone are recorded as dying of 'heart attacks'.[10] (This was a problem that they were to tackle later, with the arrival of the Jews, through the simple expedient of not registering into the camp the vast majority who were selected for immediate death.)

'They were seen as the lowest category of human beings,' says

Kazimierz Smoleń, who worked alongside the Soviet prisoners of war at Birkenau. 'They were beaten more by the SS and given a harder time. They had to be exterminated. They died like flies.' So appalling were the conditions for the Soviet prisoners that Rudolf Hoess witnessed evidence of cannibalism among them: 'I myself came across a Russian lying between piles of bricks, whose body had been torn open and the liver removed. They would beat each other to death for food.'[11] Hoess documents many examples of such suffering in his memoirs, but nowhere does he address the reason why the Soviet POWs were reduced to this state. The fact that over a six-month period he and his SS comrades were to blame for the death of more than 9000 of the 10,000 Soviet POWs seems to have escaped him. And it is clear why Hoess feels no guilt, because by behaving like 'animals' the Soviet POWs were simply acting as Nazi propaganda had predicted they would. Once again, the Nazis had created a self-fulfilling prophecy.

Pavel Stenkin had one hope while he was labouring at Birkenau, sick and starving, watching his comrades die around him. He knew he was going to die, but to 'die free, that was my dream; let them shoot me dead, but as a free man'. So he and a handful of his comrades planned to escape, in the full knowledge that their chances of success were small. Their plan could scarcely have been simpler. One day in spring 1942 they were sent to fetch the corpse of another Soviet POW that lay just outside the camp perimeter. As they passed the wire that enclosed the camp they shouted 'Hurrah!' and ran off in different directions. The guards in the watchtowers were momentarily confused and so did not turn their machine guns on the Russians until the men had reached the safety of the nearby forest. After a series of adventures over many months Pavel Stenkin finally reached Soviet-occupied territory where, as will be seen in Chapter 6, his suffering did not end.

In October 1941, in addition to planning a new POW camp at Birkenau, the architects at Auschwitz also designed a new crematorium to replace the existing one at the main camp. Recent research[12] suggests that the addition in the plans of a ventilation system that forced out old air and pushed in fresh air, and the recessing of the ventilation ducts, meant that the new crematorium was also designed with the potential to be a gas chamber. This notion is disputed by other scholars, who point out that there is still no facility shown on the plans to allow the delivery of Zyklon B into the building. But even if the SS planners were thinking that the new crematorium should be capable of performing the same function as the old one, which had just a few weeks before been the site of some limited Zyklon B gassing experiments along similar lines to those conducted in Block 11, there is no suggestion that at this stage Auschwitz was preparing any major new extermination capacity.

That October, as the SS architects worked on their plans and the Soviet prisoners began building Birkenau, Lucille Eichengreen and the other Hamburg Jews arrived at Łódź in central Poland, the first stop on their long journey to Auschwitz. What they witnessed that first day in the ghetto shocked them. 'We saw sewage run along the gutters,' says Lucille. 'We saw old dilapidated houses, we saw an area that resembled a slum – except none of us had ever seen a slum before, but we assumed this was it. We saw people within the ghetto and they looked tired, they looked drawn and they paid us no attention. We didn't know what kind of place this was. It just didn't make any sense at all.'

By the time Lucille arrived the Łódź ghetto had been shut off from the outside world for 18 months. Disease and hunger had already ravaged the population; in the course of its existence more than 20 per cent would die within the ghetto walls. Conditions were appalling, with around 164,000 Jews forced into an area of 1.5 square miles.[13]

Initially the Nazis had imprisoned the Łódź Jews in the ghetto and given them no means of earning money to pay for food. Arthur Greiser, in command of the region, wanted the Jews to be forced to give up their valuables under threat of starvation. To survive in such circumstances demanded ingenuity. Jacob Zylberstein,[14] one of the first Łódź Jews to be imprisoned, bargained with Poles who lived just outside the wire fence that enclosed the ghetto. He struck a deal with a man who agreed to throw him a parcel of bread over the wire. Jacob ate half the bread, sold the rest and gave the money he earned back through the wire to the Pole, who thus made a handsome profit: 'He helped us for two months ... He got caught and he got killed for it. But two months was a very long time.' Other Jews sold diamond rings or other jewellery for food. As a result, Poles and ethnic Germans living on the other side of the wire could make a fortune. 'If I got something in my hand for 100 Marks and it was worth 5000 Marks, then I'd be stupid not to buy it,' says Egon Zielke,[15] an ethnic German living in Łódź, who confesses to having made huge profits from his dealings with the inhabitants of the ghetto. 'They [the Jews] couldn't nibble on a ring, but if they could get a piece of bread for it, then they could survive for a day or two. You don't have to be a businessman – that's what life's about.'

By August 1940 it was clear to the Nazis that the Jews trapped in the Łódź ghetto were 'hoarding' no longer, for they had begun to starve. Pursuing typical Nazi short-term thinking, the local German authorities had not prepared for this inevitable crisis. They now faced a moment of decision. Should they let the Jews starve or should they allow them to work? The German Chief of Ghetto Administration, Hans Biebow, favoured employing the Jews, whilst his deputy, Alexander Palfinger, thought – in direct contradiction of the evidence around him – that the Jews might still be hoarding money and should therefore be denied food. If he was wrong and they no longer had the means to pay for their own sustenance, then 'a rapid dying out of the Jews is for us a matter of total indifference'.[16]

Biebow won the argument and workshops were established within the ghetto, eventually nearly a hundred of them, most producing textiles. Those who had jobs were given more food than those who did not, establishing the principle, before it became commonplace amongst Nazi administrators, of a strict delineation between those Jews whom the Germans considered 'productive' and those thought to be 'useless eaters'. The Nazis allowed the Jewish Council of the Łódź ghetto (called the *Ältestenrat* – Council of Elders), under its chairman Mordechai Chaim Rumkowski, considerable latitude in the running of the place. The *Ältestenrat* organized the factories, the food distribution, the ghetto police and a host of other services. In the process they did not make themselves popular with the rest of the Jews in the ghetto. 'They got a special ration,' says Jacob Zylberstein. 'They had special shops to go to and pick up their food, which was very nice. Enough to live quite comfortably. I was very angry that a selective part of people in the ghetto was supplied [that way] and the rest just ignored.'

This, then, was the world that Lucille Eichengreen, her sister and mother walked into in October 1941 – an overcrowded, disease-ridden place where most of the inhabitants were hungry and some lived much better than others. Late and unwanted arrivals as they were, the incoming German Jews were forced to live wherever they could find any space. 'We had to sleep on the floor of a classroom,' says Lucille. 'There were no cots, no straw, nothing. And once a day we would get soup and a little piece of bread.' Jacob Zylberstein remembers the arrival of the German Jews and says, 'They were definitely very depressed. I think because normally they [the German Jews] look down on the Polish Jews – we've been definitely a lower category than them. And all of a sudden it hit them that they've come to the same level or maybe lower than us because they cannot live in the conditions we did.'

The German Jews started to sell their belongings to the Polish Jews in order to acquire extra food or better living conditions. Lucille Eichengreen was fortunate; because her family was of Polish descent, bartering was easier for them. 'My mother traded a silk blouse for some butter and bread, and she was very good at trading because she spoke the language. A few weeks later I traded a leather purse to a young woman who had bread to trade. It was very pathetic looking at the sellers and looking at the buyers. The buyers were ragged. We, by comparison, still looked affluent – we still had a semblance of Western clothing and weren't as hungry as the local people were. For instance, the local people would come into the schoolhouse and say: "I have a spare room, and if you want to sleep a night in a bed I'll charge you either a slice of bread or a certain amount of German money, and you'll get away from the schoolhouse for a night." All kinds of offers were made.'

The German Jews quickly realized that in order to stand the best chance of survival they had to get jobs within the ghetto. But getting employment was difficult, not least because there was an element of friction between the German and Polish Jews. 'The very first [German] transport were very critical of the way things were done in the ghetto,' says Lucille. 'And there were remarks: "This is not official ... this is not correct ... we will teach them." Well, you can't walk into somebody else's house and rearrange the furniture, and this is what they were trying to do.' But the greatest problem the German Jews faced was lack of 'connections' within the ghetto. 'It was basically a fairly corrupt system,' says Lucille. 'You help me, I help you. And outsiders didn't enter into it. When I first tried to get my sister into the hat factory it was almost impossible because the answers I got from the directors of those factories was, "What will I get in return?" In the ghetto everything was paid for one way or another. And payment was high – it was not cheap. But that was what ghetto life had done to human beings. Whether they were the same before the war, I doubt very much. I was seventeen. I was absolutely shocked.'

If resentment was felt by the existing population of the ghetto over the arrival of the German Jews, their presence also caused anger among the Nazi leadership of the Warthegau. Protests had begun as soon as the figure of 60,000 Jews to be deported from the 'Old Reich' to Łódź had been proposed by Himmler. As a result, the number was reduced to 20,000 Jews and 5000 gypsies. But even this influx still presented major difficulties for the Gauleiter, Arthur Greiser. Together with Wilhelm Koppe, the Higher SS and Police Leader for the region, he sought a solution to the problem of overcrowding in the ghetto. And it is hardly surprising, given that ever since the summer of 1941 murder had been the preferred answer in the East to this kind of crisis, that their minds turned to methods of killing. They called upon the services of SS Hauptsturmführer (Captain) Herbert Lange, who had been in command of a special unit charged with murdering the disabled in East Prussia and the surrounding area. For some of the killing he and his team had used a 'gas van' with a hermetically sealed rear compartment into which bottled carbon monoxide gas was pumped, and such vans were now seen by local Nazis as the most appropriate response to the sudden overcrowding in the Łódź ghetto.

According to his SS driver, Walter Burmeister, late that autumn Lange hit upon a suitable site for his gas vans in the Warthegau. 'To make it plain from the start,' Lange told his driver, 'absolute secrecy is crucial. I have orders to form a special commando in Chełmno. Other staff from Posen and from the state police in Litzmannstadt [the German name for Łódź] are going to join us. We have a tough but important job to do.'[17] At the small village of Chełmno, some 50 miles northwest of Łódź, Lange and his team prepared a country house – 'the *Schloss*' – for the 'tough but important job' of mass murder. Chełmno, not Auschwitz, was about to become the first location for the killing of selected Jews from the Łódź ghetto.

But Chełmno was not the only extermination facility under construction towards the end of 1941. On 1 November work began on a camp at Bełżec in the Lublin district in eastern Poland. Most of the personnel for Bełżec, including the first commandant of the camp, SS Hauptsturmführer (Captain) Christian Wirth, were taken from the adult euthanasia programme. Deep in the General Government, Bełżec seems to have been established, like Chełmno, with the intention of creating a place to kill 'unproductive' Jews from the local area. But unlike Chełmno it was the first camp to be planned from the start to contain stationary gas chambers linked to engines producing carbon monoxide gas. As such, it was the logical conclusion of the gassing experiments conducted by Widmann in the East in September 1941.

Meantime, the deportation of Jews from the Old Reich continued. Between October 1941 and February 1942 a total of 58,000 Jews were sent East to a variety of destinations, including the Łódź ghetto. Everywhere they were sent, the local Nazi authorities had to improvise a solution to deal with their arrival, acting sometimes on the authority of Berlin, sometimes on their own initiative. Around 7000 Jews from Hamburg were sent to Minsk, where they were found shelter in a part of the ghetto that had recently been cleared for them by shooting the nearly 12,000 Soviet Jews who lived there. Jews from Munich, Berlin, Frankfurt and other German cities were sent to Kaunas in Lithuania, where around 5000 of them were shot dead by members of Einsatzkommando 3. They were the first German Jews to be murdered on arrival as a result of being transported East. Another transport from Berlin reached Riga in Latvia on 30 November, and all aboard were also killed as soon as they arrived. But this action was against Himmler's wishes; he had previously rung Heydrich with the message: 'Jewish transport from Berlin. No liquidation.' Friedrich Jeckeln, the SS commander who had ordered the execution, was subsequently reprimanded by Himmler.

As these events demonstrate, during the autumn of 1941 there was little consistency of policy regarding the fate of the Reich Jews: Himmler protested at the shootings in Riga, but did not object to those in Kaunas. Nonetheless, despite these confused indicators, there is plenty of evidence that the decision to send the Reich Jews to the East was a watershed moment. In October, talking after dinner, Hitler remarked, 'No one can say to me we can't send them [the Jews] into the swamp! Who then cares about our people? It is good if the fear that we are exterminating the Jews goes before us.'[18] And it is clear that discussions were also taking place amongst the Nazi leadership that autumn to send to the East *all* the Jews under German control. In France, Reinhard Heydrich justified the burning of Paris synagogues by saying that he had given the action his approval 'only at the point where the Jews were identified on the highest authority and most vehemently as being those responsible for setting Europe alight, and who must ultimately disappear from Europe.'[19] That same month, November 1941, Hitler, in a discussion with the Grand Mufti of Jerusalem, who had fled to Berlin, said that he wanted all Jews, even those not under German control, 'to be destroyed'.[20]

By deciding to deport the Reich Jews, Hitler had begun a chain of causation that would eventually lead to their extermination. In the Soviet Union Jewish men, women and children were already being shot by the killing squads. By sending many of the Reich Jews into this exact area, what else did Hitler think would happen to them? The line between killing local Jews to provide room for the arriving Reich Jews, and killing the arriving Reich Jews instead, was a thin one from the first – as Jeckeln's actions in Riga demonstrate. That distinction became even more blurred for the Nazi leadership of the General Government once Galicia, in the far east of Poland and bordering the killing fields of the Soviet Union, came under their control as the war progressed. The Einsatzgruppe had been killing Galician Jews for weeks, and it would be hard for the local authorities to hold to a position that Jews could be shot in one part of the General Government but not in another.

But this does not mean that Hitler and the other leading Nazis took a firm decision in the autumn of 1941 to murder all the Jews under German control. In the first place, there simply was not yet the capacity to commit such a crime. The only killing installations under construction in November 1941 were a gas van facility at Chełmno and a small fixed gas chamber installation at Bełżec. An order was also placed around this time with a German firm for a large 32-chamber furnace crematorium to be built at Mogilev in

Belarussia, which some see as evidence of an intention, never fulfilled, to build another extermination centre far in the East. But all of these initiatives can also be explained by the desire of the local authorities to have the capacity either to kill the indigenous Jews in order to make space for the arriving Reich Jews, or to murder those Jews in their control incapable of work whom they believed were no longer 'useful' to them. Crucially, at Auschwitz in the autumn of 1941 no plans were being made to increase the killing capacity at the camp. A new crematorium was being designed, to be sure, but that was simply to replace the old one in the main camp.

This confused state of affairs was to be clarified, with disastrous consequences for the fate of the Jews, by events that took place halfway round the world. On 7 December 1941 the Japanese bombed Pearl Harbor. On 11 December, as allies of the Japanese, the Germans declared war on the United States. For Hitler all this was 'proof' that international Jewry had orchestrated a world conflict, and in a radio broadcast to the German people immediately after the declaration of war he explicitly stated that 'the Jews' were manipulating President Roosevelt just as they were his other great enemy, Josef Stalin.

Hitler went still further in a speech he gave to the Nazi leadership, both Gauleiter and Reichleiter, the following day. He now linked the outbreak of this 'world war' with his prophecy uttered in the Reichstag on 30 January 1939 in which he had threatened that 'if the Jews succeed in causing world war' the result would be the 'extermination of the Jews of Europe'. On 13 December, Propaganda Minister Joseph Goebbels wrote in his diary: 'As far as the Jewish question is concerned, the Führer is determined to make a clean sweep. He prophesied to the Jews that if they once again brought about a world war they would experience their own extermination. This was not an empty phrase. The world war is here, the extermination of the Jews must be the necessary consequence. This question must be seen without sentimentality.'

Further evidence that the air was thick with talk of 'extermination' that week is provided by a speech that Hans Frank, ruler of the General Government, made to senior Nazi officials in Kraków on 16 December: 'As an old National Socialist, I must state that if the Jewish clan were to survive the war in Europe, while we sacrificed our best blood in the defence of Europe, then this war would only represent a partial success. With respect to the Jews, therefore, I will only operate on the assumption that they will disappear ... We must exterminate the Jews wherever we find them.'[21] Frank, who had been one of those briefed by Hitler on 12 December, also added that 'in Berlin' he had been told that he, and people like him, should 'liquidate the Jews ... themselves'.

The discovery of Himmler's complete desk diary in the 1990s also provides one tantalizing further link with Hitler during this most crucial period. On 18 December, after a one-to-one meeting with Hitler, Himmler notes: 'Jewish question – to be exterminated [*auszurotten*] as partisans.'[22] The reference to 'partisans' is part of the camouflage language that allowed the murder of the Jews to be concealed as necessary security work in the East.

Although no document written by Hitler linking him with a direct order to pursue the 'Final Solution' has ever been found, this body of evidence does demonstrate beyond reasonable doubt that he was encouraging and directing an intensification of anti-Jewish actions that December. It is likely that, even without the catalyst of US entry into the war, the deportations of the Reich Jews to the East, directly ordered by Hitler, would eventually have led to their deaths. The anger and frustration Hitler felt at the launch of the Red Army's counterattack at the gates of Moscow on 5 December had already probably predisposed him to vent his rage further upon the Jews. But what happened at Pearl Harbor brought a murderous clarity to Hitler's thinking. All pretence amongst leading Nazis that the Jews would simply be deported and kept in camps in the East was dropped. One way or another, they now faced 'extermination'.

The day after Pearl Harbor marked another watershed in the practical implementation of the 'Final Solution', for on 8 December the first transports arrived at Chełmno to be gassed. Jews from Koło, Dąbie, Kłodawa and other towns and villages in the immediate area were brought to the camp by truck (later, Jews would arrive by train at Powiercie station nearby). They were taken up to the large house – the *Schloss* – in the centre of the small village and ordered to undress prior to 'disinfection'. Then they were taken down to the basement, forced along a passage and up a wooden ramp until they found themselves in what appeared to be an enclosed dark room. They were in fact locked in the back of a van.

Initially, the gas vans at Chełmno were identical to the ones used in the adult euthanasia actions the previous year, and relied on bottled carbon monoxide to kill the people locked in the sealed rear compartment. But a few weeks into Chełmno's operation new gas vans arrived that used their own exhaust gases to murder those inside. Since the gassing was taking place in the village, with the vans stationary in the courtyard of the *Schloss*, it was impossible to keep knowledge of the murders a secret. Zofia Szałek,[23] who as an 11-year-old girl worked and played just a few metres from the site of the murders, witnessed some of the first arrivals: 'They [the Jews] were terribly beaten. It was winter when they came, they wore wooden clogs ... Here they used to undress. There was an enormous pile of those clothes ... Those who were already undressed were herded into the lorries. What screaming was going on. How terribly they were screaming – it was impossible to bear it. Once they brought children and the children shouted. My mother heard it. She said the children were calling, "Mummy, save me!"'

After the Jews had been gassed at the *Schloss*, the vans drove just under 2 miles into the nearby Rzuchowski forest. 'When I saw it moving I said, "Hell is going!"' says Zofia Szałek. 'I was tending cows by the side of the road – how could I not see it going by?' Once in the forest, the vans were unloaded by Jews who were then forced to bury the bodies. Each evening these Jews were transported back to the *Schloss* and kept locked up overnight. Every few weeks they too were murdered and other Jews selected for this task from the new arrivals.

Physical conditions in the forest soon became appalling, as Zofia learnt first hand from one of the Germans in the Waldkommando (forest commando) charged with supervising the disposal of the bodies: 'He was billeted in our house and he always called me and said, "Clean my shoes!" And then he would say, "Does it stink?" And I would say, "Yes." Because the smell was powerful. Human bodies were decomposing. It stank terribly. They had buried the bodies in pits, but then it got hot and the bodies started to ferment.'

Kurt Moebius was one of the German guards at Chełmno, and was later tried for war crimes. During his interrogation in

Aachen prison in November 1961 he gave an insight into the mentality of the Nazi perpetrators as they participated in the killing process: 'We were told by Captain Lange that the orders for the extermination of the Jews came from Hitler and Himmler. And as police officers we were drilled to regard any order from the government as lawful and correct ... At the time I believed that the Jews were not innocent but guilty. The propaganda had drummed it into us again and again that all Jews are criminals and subhumans who were the cause of Germany's decline after the First World War.'[24]

The main reason for the setting up of Chełmno was to murder the Jews from the Łódź ghetto who were no longer thought productive, and the first transport left the city for the new extermination centre on 16 January 1942. Lucille Eichengreen, who had now lived in the Łódź ghetto for three months, sums up the mood by saying: 'We didn't want to go. We figured the misery we knew was better than the misery we didn't know.' Now, with the added stress and pressure of 'selections' for deportations, life in the ghetto, already bad, was set to become worse.

Chełmno was a landmark along the road to the 'Final Solution', the first centre for the extermination of Jews established anywhere in the Nazi state. But the facility was able to become operational so quickly only because it relied on the hurried conversion of a large house as a base for the killing, and on the existing technology of the gas vans. From the perspective of the Nazi murderers it was therefore inherently inefficient. Secrecy could not be maintained, nor could the bodies be disposed of adequately – 'faults' that would be addressed when the new death camp of Bełżec, already under construction, was eventually finished.

Meantime, on 20 January, four days after the first transport of Łódź ghetto Jews to Chełmno, a meeting was held at an SS villa on the shores of the Wannsee, a lake outside Berlin. This gathering has become infamous as the single most important event in the history of the Nazis' 'Final Solution', an epithet it does not quite merit. The meeting was called by Reinhard Heydrich, who invited the relevant government state secretaries to take part in a discussion about the Jewish question. Included with each invitation was a copy of the authorization that Goering had given Heydrich on 31 July 1941 to pursue the 'Final Solution' (although, as discussed in Chapter 1, it is highly unlikely that the phrase 'Final Solution' had the same meaning in July 1941 that it had acquired by January 1942). Notoriously, because the meeting was due to begin at midday, the invitation also mentioned that 'refreshments' would be provided. The address at which the meeting was held was Am Grossen Wannsee 56–58, a villa once used by Interpol, the organization that coordinated international police activity. It is a useful reminder that the individuals who sat round the table at the Wannsee conference were salaried functionaries from one of Europe's great nations, not back-street terrorists, though their crimes were to be greater than any conventional 'criminal' act in the history of the world. Equally instructive, when today some still refer to an ill-educated 'criminal underclass', is that of the fifteen people around the table eight held academic doctorates.

Invitations had originally been sent in November 1941 and the meeting scheduled for 9 December, but the bombing of Pearl Harbor had resulted in its postponement. One of the unanswered questions of history is therefore what the content of the Wannsee meeting would have been had events in the Pacific not caused a delay. Certainly the intention would still have been to implement an ultimately genocidal 'solution' to the Nazis' 'Jewish problem', but perhaps the discussion would have focused more on an eventual post-war solution or a real attempt to set up work camps for Jews deported to the East. We can only speculate. What is certain is that, whether the USA had entered the war or not, Wannsee was always going to be an important meeting for Heinrich Himmler and Reinhard Heydrich. During the autumn of 1941 a variety of killing initiatives had emerged from a number of sources within the Nazi state. For Himmler and Heydrich, Wannsee was necessary above all else to coordinate them and to establish beyond doubt that the SS were the ones in control of the whole deportation process.

The issues discussed at the Wannsee conference are known primarily because a copy of the minutes, taken by SS Obersturmbannführer (Lieutenant Colonol) Adolf Eichmann, Heydrich's 'Jewish expert', survived the war. Eichmann's record of the meeting is of great historical importance, since it is one of the few documents that shine a light directly on the thinking process behind the 'Final Solution'.

At the start of the meeting Heydrich made reference to the administrative authority given him by Goering that allowed him to preside. Then he announced the formal change in Nazi policy that, no doubt, all the delegates would already have known. Instead of the 'emigration' of the Jews to countries outside Nazi control, there would now be 'evacuation ... to the East' within the Nazi sphere of influence. In total 11 million Jews, a figure that included several million in countries such as Ireland and Britain that were not yet under Nazi domination, would eventually be subject to such 'evacuation'. On arrival in the East these Jews would be separated by sex, and those who were fit and healthy employed in building roads (Heydrich was almost certainly thinking of projects such as the Durchgangsstrasse IV, a road and rail link from the Reich to the Eastern Front already under construction). Those Jews who were not selected for this work would, the implication is clear, be murdered immediately, whilst the rest faced only a stay of execution since large numbers were expected to die as a result of harsh manual labour. Heydrich went on to express particular concern about any Jews who might survive the attempt to work them into the ground: these were the very Jews that natural selection would have determined were the most dangerous to the Nazis. They, said Heydrich, must also be 'treated accordingly'. There could have been no doubt in the minds of the other delegates just what Heydrich meant by this.

Significantly, there was no dissent at the meeting over the broad principle of killing the Jews. Instead, the greatest area of debate focused around the exact legal definition of 'Jew', and thus precisely who would be subject to deportation and who would not. The question of what to do with 'half Jews' stimulated a lively exchange of views. There was a suggestion that such people should be sterilized, or offered a choice between that operation and deportation. Alternatively they might be sent to a special ghetto – Theresienstadt, the Czech town of Terezin – where they would be housed alongside the elderly and those Jews with a high profile whose deportation directly to the East would have caused disquiet amongst the ordinary German population.

The discussion then passed to the more immediate 'problem' of the Jews of the General Government and the occupied Soviet Union. In the latter the Jews were being murdered by shooting, whilst in the former the death camp at Bełżec was already under construction. But millions of Jews were still alive in these areas, so Eichmann recorded in the minutes that 'various possible solutions' were mentioned in this context, an innocuous phrase that masked a discussion of specific methods of extermination.

The minutes of the Wannsee conference are deliberately opaque. Eichmann's draft of them was worked on several times by Heydrich and Heinrich Müller, the head of the Gestapo, to create that exact effect. Since they were intended for wider distribution, it was necessary for them to be written in camouflage language: those who understood the context would realize exactly what was intended, whilst the lack of crude terminology meant they would not shock the uninitiated should they catch sight of them. Nonetheless, they remain the clearest evidence of the planning process behind the Nazis' 'Final Solution' and the strongest evidence of widespread state complicity in the murders that were to follow.

But does that mean that the Wannsee conference deserves its place in popular culture as the most significant meeting in the history of the crime? The answer must be no. The misconception in the popular consciousness rests on the belief that this was the meeting at which the Nazis decided to embark upon their 'Final Solution'. This is simply not the case. Certainly Wannsee was important, but it was a second-tier implementation meeting, part of a process of widening out knowledge of an extermination process that had already been decided upon somewhere else. Much more important than the conversations at Wannsee were the discussions Hitler held in December 1941. If proper minutes were available of the Führer's meetings with Himmler during that period we would truly see the bleak landscape of the mind that made all this suffering enter the world.

The discussions at Wannsee had no immediate effect upon Auschwitz. The Birkenau building plans were not suddenly altered to allow for new gas chambers, and there were no apparent differences that January in the overall operation of the camp. Since the early autumn of 1941 there had, however, been a change in the location of the gassing experiments with Zyklon B. They had ceased to be conducted in Block 11 and now took place in the camp crematorium, just metres from Hoess's own office and the main SS administration block. This solved one problem for the camp authorities – the bodies from Block 11 would no longer have to be wheeled the length of the camp on *Rollwagen* (handcarts) to the crematorium to be burnt – but it created another, since the location of the murders was in a more exposed area above ground in the mortuary next to the crematorium ovens, rather than in the secluded basement of the prison block.

At the start of 1942 Jerzy Bielecki witnessed the arrival of Soviet prisoners of war to be gassed in this new location: 'At night [when he was in his barracks] I heard some kind of movement outside. And I said, "Boys, what's happening? Let's take a look." We came to the window and we heard yells and moaning and you could see a group of people running, completely naked, towards the crematorium. SS men were running as well, with machine guns. We could see all this in the light of the lamps by the wire. Snow was falling and it was frosty, maybe minus fifteen or twenty. Everyone was moaning and yelling because of the cold. It was an incredible sound. I never heard it before. Naked, they entered the gassing chamber. It was a devilish, hellish image.'

But it was not just Soviet prisoners of war and those in the camp who could no longer work who were put to death in this horrific manner. Small numbers of Jews from the surrounding area in Upper Silesia who were unable to do hard manual labour were taken to the camp crematorium to be killed. There are no camp records showing the exact dates when these killings took place, but eye-witness evidence does suggest that it is likely some murders were carried out in the autumn of 1941. Hans Stark, a member of the SS who worked in Auschwitz, gave this testimony: 'At another, later gassing, also in autumn 1941, Grabner [Maximilian Grabner, head of the Political Department at Auschwitz] ordered me to pour Zyklon B into the opening because only one medical orderly had shown up. During a gassing Zyklon B had to be poured through both openings of the gas chamber room at the same time ... As the Zyklon B was in granular form, it trickled down over the people as it was being poured in. They then started to cry out terribly, for they now knew what was happening to them. I did not look through the opening because it had to be closed as soon as the Zyklon B had been poured in. After a few minutes, the gas chamber was opened. The dead lay higgledypiggedly all over the place. It was a dreadful sight.'[25]

The gassing of 'unproductive' Jews from the area around Auschwitz continued in the weeks following the Wannsee conference. Józef Paczyński,[26] an Auschwitz inmate who worked in the SS administrative building next to the crematorium, witnessed the arrival of a group of male Jews who had been sent to the camp to be murdered. He climbed to the attic of the SS building, lifted a roof tile and had a clear view of the scene directly outside the crematorium. 'They [the SS] were very polite with these people,' says Paczyński. '"Please take your clothes, pack your things." And these people undressed, and then they made them go in [to the crematorium] and then the doors were locked behind them. Then an SS man crawled up on to the flat roof of the building. He put on a gas mask, he opened a hatch [in the roof] and he dropped the powder in and he shut the hatch. When he did this, in spite of the fact that these walls were thick, you could hear a great scream.' Having suffered in the camp himself for nearly two years, Paczyński felt no great emotion as he saw these people go to their deaths: 'One becomes indifferent. Today you go, tomorrow I will go. You become indifferent. A human being can get used to anything.'

Crucial to this new way of killing was the lulling of the Jews by reassuring words. The camp authorities realized that prisoners from outside Auschwitz need not be driven by kicking and beating into the gas chamber. The procedure now was to convince new arrivals that walking into the improvised gas chamber in the crematorium was a normal part of the camp admittance procedure – they were not going to be killed, merely 'disinfected' by taking a shower. This was a breakthrough for the Nazis, which solved a number of difficulties that the earlier killing squads had faced. Not only did it prove easier to get people into the gas chamber by deception rather than outright force, it was also less stressful for the killers themselves. And it was also the answer to another practical difficulty the Nazis had faced in exploiting the belongings of their victims. Many of the earliest murders by gassing had been conducted on prisoners who had died with their clothes on, and it had proved difficult to remove them after death. This way, those about to die removed their clothes voluntarily; they even folded them up neatly and tied the laces of their shoes together.

Perry Broad,[27] a member of the SS at Auschwitz, described in detail how the compliant atmosphere surrounding the murders was achieved. He recounts how Maximilian Grabner stood on the roof of the crematorium and told the Jews gathered below: 'You will now bathe and be disinfected. We don't want any epidemics in the camp. Then you will be brought to your barracks where you'll get some hot soup. You will be employed in accordance with your professional qualifications. Now undress and put your clothes in front of you on the ground.'[28] Then the members of the SS would gently encourage the new arrivals into the crematorium, 'full of jokes and small talk'. According to Broad, one of the SS then shouted through the door once it was screwed shut: 'Don't get burnt while you take your bath!'[29]

Despite the advantages gained by this sinister duplicity, Hoess and his colleagues soon realized that using the camp crematorium as a place of murder created difficulties for them. The biggest problem they faced was the level of noise caused by their murders: 'In order to stifle the screams there were motors,' recalls Józef Paczyński. 'Two motorcycles were revving so that no one would hear the cries. People were yelling and then becoming weaker and weaker. They had those motorcycles to conceal the yelling, but they failed. They gave it a try but it didn't work.' The noise of screaming from inside the improvised gas chamber was never adequately masked by the revving engines, and the position of the crematorium so near the other buildings of the camp meant that it was impossible to hide the murders from the other inmates. So during the spring of 1942 Hoess and other senior members of the SS tried to think of another way of conducting the killing. And as they did so, far from merely 'following orders', once again they would attempt to use their own initiative.

Auschwitz was beginning its evolution into a unique institution in the Nazi state. On the one hand, some prisoners were still admitted to the camp, given a number and ordered to work. On the other, there was now a class of people who would be murdered within hours, sometimes minutes, of arrival. No other Nazi camp functioned in quite this way. There were extermination centres like Chełmno, and concentration camps like Dachau; but there was only ever one Auschwitz.[30]

The development of this dual function meant that many inmates of Auschwitz now lived and worked, sometimes for years, in an institution that also killed others whose knowledge of the camp would be but momentary. For the Jews from the surrounding area found unfit to work, Auschwitz was a place of instant murder; for the Poles who had survived in the camp since its inception, Auschwitz had become a warped kind of home. By now Józef Paczyński, who witnessed the murders in the camp crematorium, had been a prisoner in Auschwitz for 20 months. Few of those who had arrived in the summer of 1940 had survived this long unless they had succeeded in getting work indoors, 'under a roof', and Paczyński was no exception. He had managed to get a job in the barber's shop, cutting the hair of SS staff. This was a position of relative privilege, so much so that he was one of the few inmates who came into direct contact with the commandant himself: 'The under-officer took me to Hoess's villa and at the gate his wife was there. I was so much afraid. I went up one flight to the bathroom and there was a chair. Hoess came in and sat down. I stood at attention. He had a cigar in his mouth and was reading a paper. I did the same haircut I had seen done on him before. It wasn't a great piece of art. Hoess didn't say a word to me, and I didn't say a word. I was afraid, and he despised inmates. I had a razor in my hand. I could have cut his throat – it could have happened. But I'm a thinking being, and you know what would have happened? My whole family would have been destroyed; half of the camp would be destroyed. In his place someone else would have come.'

Whilst committing the crime of murder would have had catastrophic consequences for Józef Paczyński and his family, he knew that the act of theft, 'organizing', was a necessity if he was to survive. In his barracks Paczyński slept next to a friend, Stanisław (Staszek) Dubiel, who worked as a gardener at Hoess's house. 'And as I was lying next to Staszek I said, "Couldn't we get some tomatoes from his [Hoess's] garden?" And he said, "It's possible."' Hoess's garden backed on to the crematorium and there was a loose plank in the fence. 'Just enter the garden through there,' Staszek told Paczyński, 'and you will have onions and tomatoes.'

On the prearranged day Paczyński entered Hoess's garden via the loose plank and found pails of onions and tomatoes waiting for him, as promised: 'I took them, and I was about to leave when Hoess's wife came in with another woman. So I moved back and hid in the undergrowth. When I thought they'd left I walked out, but they were still standing on a path and talking. I bowed, and I walked past them carrying the tomatoes and onions. And I was all wet [with perspiration]. I thought, "That's the end of me. I've been caught stealing tomatoes and that's the end of me." That evening I'm waiting for them to take me to Block 11, but no one called me. Staszek came back from work and he said, "Don't worry. Hoess's wife told me everything, and I told her I gave it all to you."'

The adventure of Józef Paczyński and his friend in Hoess's garden is instructive, not least because it demonstrates important aspects of the developing relationship between the Germans and favoured Polish inmates. When Paczyński's friend Staszek explained to Hoess's wife that he himself had authorized the taking of the pails of tomatoes and onions, he put himself forward as the person to be punished for the theft. After all, if gardeners like him were allowed to help themselves to vegetables, why was it necessary to plan the secret journey into Hoess's garden at all? But Staszek knew that Hoess's wife was very likely to forgive him, because they had a working relationship. Of course, it was a relationship that the Nazis would have defined as one between a superior 'Aryan' and an inferior 'Slav', but it was a relationship nonetheless. By reporting Staszek, Hoess's wife would not be calling for the punishment of a nameless inmate she had caught stealing – something that it would have been easy for her to do – but ordering the suffering of someone with whom she had worked closely for some time.

Over the life of the camp this kind of dynamic occurred again and again. Inmates describe how the best way to try to ensure survival (after gaining a job 'under a roof') was to become useful to a specific German. If that German came to depend on you, you would be looked after – even prevented from being punished or, in certain cases, killed. It was not so much that genuine affection existed, though that was possible; more that a major inconvenience would be caused to the German if a new prisoner had to found and trained as a replacement.

The search for a relationship with a powerful figure as a means of survival was not confined to Auschwitz; it was also a common factor of life in the ghetto. Only here the individual with the power of life and death could be Jewish as well as German. As the months went by in the Łódź ghetto, Lucille Eichengreen saw her own condition, and that of her mother and sister, steadily deteriorate. 'The food was not enough to sustain life,' she says. 'There was no milk, there was no meat, and there was no fruit – there was nothing.' The only way to improve their situation was for her to try to find a job, since that meant 'an additional soup at lunchtime'. So she trudged around the streets of the ghetto from factory to factory looking for work.

By May 1942 Lucille still had not managed to find work, and she and her family were placed on the list to be deported: 'They were all unemployed [on the list], and about ninety per cent of them were the new arrivals.' But Lucille knew she possessed one advantage that the other German Jews on the list lacked. She and her family had, through their father's ancestry, connections with Poland. 'I went with our Polish passports from office to office trying to get a deletion from the list, and I finally succeeded. I don't know how, but I did. And we stayed.' Lucille is certain in her own mind that it was her Polish roots that saved her and her family. 'They wanted all the German Jews on that transport out of the ghetto,' she says. 'And I could prove that, though we had come from Germany, we were not German. It shouldn't have been crucial because we were all Jews. It shouldn't have made a difference, but it did.' Between January and May 1942 a total of 55,000 Jews were deported from the Łódź ghetto and murdered at Chełmno. The Germans ordered these deportations, but, through another cynical and divisive measure that the Nazis introduced, the Jewish leadership of the ghetto was forced to collaborate in deciding who went.

The strain of ghetto life had a profound effect on Lucille's mother, who 'really lost all interest. She didn't do much any more. She was blown up with hunger, which meant all the water had accumulated. She couldn't walk properly. She died on 13 July 1942 in the ghetto. The ghetto had a little black wagon with a grey horse that came through every morning and picked up the dead, and they picked up my mother. And more than a week passed, which is not Jewish custom because you bury the next day, and my sister and I walked out and we found a vacant spot and we dug a grave and we carried her out. There were no coffins; there were just two boards and a string around them. And we had to find them in a big house adjacent to the cemetery that had nothing but dead bodies, unburied bodies. And we buried her and we put a little wooden marker on the grave, which of course disappeared very shortly thereafter. I tried to locate the grave fifty years later, and it couldn't be located.'

Lucille and her younger sister were now alone in the ghetto; two orphans who had to cope as best they could. 'We didn't feel anything,' she says. 'We didn't say a prayer, we didn't cry – we were numb, there was no feeling left. We went back to that room, to that furnished room with the other occupants, and my sister essentially just stopped talking. She didn't talk any more. She was very bright, she was tall and was very pretty, but there was nothing left to say. She was totally deserted, and my mother made me promise that I would take care of her – and I couldn't do anything. I tried, and I couldn't.'

Two months later the Germans entered the ghetto themselves to conduct selections, searching for those who were not fit for work: the elderly, the sick and the young. Mordechai Rumkowski, the leader of the ghetto, asked mothers in the ghetto to cooperate and give up their children to the Germans. '"Hand over your children so the rest of us may live," [he said]. I was seventeen when I heard that speech,' says Lucille. 'I could not comprehend how somebody could ask parents for their children. I still cannot comprehend that. People were crying out, "How can you ask this? How can we do this?" But he said, "If we don't, it'll be worse."'

Lucille did all she could to try to ensure her younger sister was spared: she put make-up on her, and encouraged her to appear fit and healthy. Lucille did have some hope; she thought her sister might be safe because she was 12 years old and the cut-off age for selection was 11. But when the Germans arrived they still carried her away: 'They took my sister. They were not supposed to. I tried to get up on the truck with her. The end of a gun hit my arms and I couldn't get on the truck, and those people disappeared.' Even as she watched in despair as her young sister was taken away, Lucille had no idea that she was being transported directly to be murdered. 'It never dawned on us to reason what they would do with a young person, or a very old person, who would not be able to work. We were never rational enough to figure that one out. We just assumed they would be alive.'

Utterly alone and emotionally devastated, Lucille still forced herself to go looking for work in the ghetto. Significantly, when she eventually found her first job it was through one of the few 'connections' she had – a fellow German Jew from Hamburg. He had convinced Rumkowski that the ghetto needed 'improvements', like parks and open spaces, and Lucille worked with him on the plans. After a few months Rumkowski closed the department, but Lucille had made useful contacts. A new acquaintance from Vienna worked in one of the administrative departments in the same building, and through her she managed to get another job, filling out applications to be sent to the Germans for coal rations for the following winter. Life in the ghetto so far had taught Lucille a hard lesson: 'You really couldn't trust anybody, because if I would tell a co-worker something, she would use it for her advantage. You had to be very careful. There was a lot of back-stabbing, and you can understand why – it was a matter of life and death.'

One day Rumkowski arrived at the office to select workers for a new factory within the ghetto. Lucille was 'terrified' of meeting him because this 66-year-old, who looked like everyone's grandfather, had a bad reputation. 'I had heard rumours. I knew he had a vile temper. If he got angry, he would take his cane and hit you. He was an absolute dictator within limits, which came from the German side. I think most people were afraid of him.' She hid in the hallway and tried to escape notice, but her name was on a list and eventually she was called in to see Rumkowski. 'He sat on a chair. He had white hair and darkened glasses. He held his cane in his right hand and for a moment he appeared to me like the king on a throne. He asked me where I was from, what languages I spoke, what my father did, where my family was, if I had any family left. I answered the questions and his last words were, "Oh, you'll hear from me." I didn't pay much attention to it.'

After Rumkowski's visit, Lucille's boss moved her to the statistical department: 'I don't know why they transferred me. It could have been to hide me away because it was a very quiet, secret office.' But then came a phone call from Rumkowski's secretary – he wanted Lucille. When she reported to the main administrative building she found a number of other women of her own age already there. Rumkowski gave them all jobs working in a kitchen he was starting for 'deserving workers'. Some of the young women would be waitresses in the dining room and some, like Lucille, would work in the adjacent office. 'He said he would take me and I would figure out, if we had fifty kilo of red beets, how many portions it would make.' As a reward for working in the new kitchen Lucille would get an extra meal each day. 'It was very meaningful,' she says. 'As you would say today, it was a very big deal.' When she left to go to work in the kitchen her boss gave her one final word of warning about Rumkowski: 'I think he used the word "pig" in Polish.' Her boss was right. In almost every ghetto that the Nazis established the Jewish leader behaved responsibly – but not in Łódź. Rumkowski was known to put people on the deportation list because he himself wanted to be rid of them, and he committed still more personal offences, as Lucille was about to discover.

Lucille started work in the kitchen, and quickly realized that this was one of Rumkowski's pet projects. Almost every evening he would pay a visit, something she came to dread: 'You could hear him arrive with a horse-drawn carriage. He would go into the kitchen and look at the waitress, and if an apron wasn't tied correctly he would hit her with a cane. He looked at the food but he would not eat it – this was below his dignity. And then he would come into the office and you could hear his uneven steps, a sort of slight limp, in the hallway. And I was alone in the office and he would pull up a chair and we had a couple of conversations. He talked and I would listen, and he molested me. He took my hand and placed it on his penis and he said, "Make it work" ... I kept moving away and he kept moving close, and it was a frightening relationship – to me it was shocking. He wanted me to move into a private apartment to which only he would have access, and I started to cry – I didn't want to move. I couldn't understand why anyone would want to do that ... But sex in the ghetto was a very valuable commodity – it was traded like you would trade anything else.' Lucille was most definitely not a willing participant in this 'trade', but she was certain that if she did not let Rumkowski abuse her, then her 'life was at stake'. 'If I would have run away, he would have had me deported. I mean that was very clear.'

'Rumkowski did take advantage of young women,' confirms Jacob Zylberstein, who witnessed how the leader of the ghetto behaved when he saw another young woman whom he fancied. 'We were all in the dining room and he just comes in, took a hand around her and just walks out with her. I saw that. Not anybody told me, but I saw that.' Zylberstein also believes that a woman's life might very well have been 'in danger' if she did not consent to Rumkowski's wishes. 'Personally I didn't like the man,' he adds. 'I didn't like what he represents.'

After some weeks the kitchen closed and Lucille was sent to a leather factory within the ghetto to sew belts for the German army. She never saw Rumkowski again. All that was left was the damage he had done: 'I felt disgusted and I felt angry and I felt abused.' In 1944 both Lucille and Rumkowski were amongst the Jews from Łódź who were transported to Auschwitz when the ghetto was finally closed. Rumkowski and his family died in the gas chambers of Birkenau. Lucille, as a young woman, was selected not for immediate death but for work, and was saved by the defeat of the Nazis in May 1945.

It was nearly three years after she had first been deported from Germany that Lucille Eichengreen eventually arrived at Auschwitz. But the first Jews from outside Poland were sent there as early as the spring of 1942, and the story of how they came to be on trains to the camp is one of the most shocking and surprising in the history of the Nazis' 'Final Solution'. They came from Slovakia, a country whose northern border was less than 50 miles from Auschwitz. Slovakia had a troubled history; as an independent state it was just three years old, created in March 1939 after the Nazis had annexed the adjoining Czech lands of Bohemia and Moravia. Prior to 1939 Slovakia had been part of Czechoslovakia, and before 1918 it had been incorporated into Hungary. The president of Slovakia was Josef Tiso, a Catholic priest, leader of the fiercely nationalistic Slovak People's Party of Hlinka. Tiso allied Slovakia with the Nazis, and a Treaty of Protection allowed Germany to control Slovak foreign policy. The Slovakian government enthusiastically adopted anti-Semitic measures against the 90,000 Slovak Jews. In rapid succession regulations were introduced to seize Jewish businesses, encourage Jewish emigration, exclude Jews from public life and make them wear a yellow star. The effect of these measures on the Slovakian Jewish community was swift and brutal.

'I realized I was an outcast,' says Eva Votavová,[31] who was then a 14-year-old schoolgirl. 'I was not a "decent person" any more. I was kicked out of secondary school. Jews were forbidden to possess certain things; we were not allowed to possess properties. Before that happened I'd lived in a village where we had all grown up together and been equal.' A striking feature of the persecution of the Slovakian Jews was the speed with which friend became foe. There was no gradual transformation. It was as if a switch had suddenly been turned on. 'The young German boys [ethnic Germans living in Slovakia] were starting to act like Nazis,' says Otto Pressburger,[32] a Slovakian Jew who was 15 years old in 1939. 'Before that they were our friends. There used to be no difference between us – Jewish and Christian youth. As children we always used to play together. Then the signs were put up: "No Jews and dogs allowed." We could not walk on the pavement. It was horrible. I was not allowed to go to a school or cinema or watch a soccer game. I had to sit at home with my parents; before, I used to be out with my friends.' It was obvious to Otto Pressburger that the primary motivation for this change in attitude towards the Jews was greed. 'There were posters on the walls taken from German newspapers showing a Jew with a big nose and a bag full of money over his shoulder. Then there was a Hlinka guard kicking him in his buttocks and making his money fall out. The city was full of posters like this.'

The Slovakian Hlinka guards were the shock troops in the anti-Jewish actions, moving against the Jews like Nazi stormtroopers, and like their Nazi counterparts they dripped anti-Semitism from every pore. 'Slovaks were happy to take the [Jewish] stores and become rich,' says Michal Kabáč,[33] one of the Hlinka guards. 'They [the Jews] used to have stores and do the monkey business. They never worked but only wanted to have an easy life. It was in their blood. It was a kind of politics all around the world that the Jews were not willing to work. Even Hitler was afraid of them becoming the royalty of Europe, so he killed them. It was all politics.' It is a striking feature of the inherent illogicality of anti-Semitic prejudice that Michal Kabáč, like Hans Friedrich in Chapter 1, sees no contradiction in simultaneously blaming the Jews for being both lazy and industrious – jealous that they built up powerful and successful businesses while claiming that they never worked. In so far as there is any coherence to Friedrich's and Kabáč's position, it is that they maintain the Jews did not do 'real' work, such as farming, but chose to be dealers or shopkeepers – areas of activity, of course, that the Jews had concentrated on precisely because for centuries they had been banned in many European countries from owning land.

For the Nazis, Auschwitz was now suddenly a tempting place to send the Slovakian Jews. Himmler realized that no more Soviet POWs would be sent to Auschwitz. The stalemate between the Germans and the Soviets close to Moscow made it obvious that the War in the East would not be over as swiftly as had been anticipated. Captured Red Army soldiers were now thought to be too valuable a source of forced labour to be squandered in a camp like Auschwitz, and Goering would soon formally confirm that all available Soviet POWs must work in armaments factories. As a result, Birkenau could no longer be used for the purpose originally contemplated. And who could fill the gap left by the Soviet POWs? Himmler, ever adept at swift policy shifts, had the answer immediately: the Jews.

And the Jews were exactly the people the Slovak authorities now wanted to deport. As far back as the autumn of 1941, the Nazis had asked the Slovaks to provide forced labourers to work in the Reich. Now, in February 1942, the Slovaks offered up whole families – 20,000 Jews in total. Tiso and the rest of the Slovak government had no more desire to retain women and children after their breadwinners had gone than did the Nazis on the Eastern Front. It was much easier for the Slovak authorities if everyone went. But what was easier for the Slovaks was not easier for the Nazis. Lacking the necessary extermination capacity, they had no desire at this time to accept Jews who could not work. To resolve this issue a meeting was held in February 1942 in Bratislava, the Slovak capital, between the Prime Minister of Slovakia, Vojtech Tuka, the chief of his office Dr Izidor Koso, and Eichmann's agent in Slovakia, SS Sturmbannführer (Major) Dieter Wisliceny. Both Wisliceny and Tuka gave evidence after the war about the content of the discussions, and by comparing their testimonies it is possible to reach a judgment about what was said.[34] The Slovakians put forward the view that to separate the breadwinner from the rest of the family was 'unChristian', since after the resettling of the Jewish workers in the Reich the families would have 'no one to look after them'. Wisliceny's recollection of the meeting is that, rather than 'Christian concerns', the Slovaks were primarily worried about the 'financial considerations' that would result from the Nazis receiving the workforce while the families were left behind with no means of support. Finally, the Slovaks suggested they might in some way compensate the Germans for the 'expenses' incurred if the families were taken along with the breadwinners.

The matter was resolved in Berlin. The Slovak government agreed to pay the Germans 500 Reichsmarks for every Jew deported, on condition that they never came back to Slovakia and that no claim was made by the Germans on the property or other assets they had left behind. The Slovaks, whose head of state was a Catholic priest, therefore paid the Germans to take their Jews away.

The forcible deportation of Slovak Jews began in March 1942. For most of them their journey began with imprisonment in a holding camp in Slovakia. Silvia Veselá[35] was one of those held in a temporary camp in the town of Poprad that spring. 'Some of those Slovak soldiers behaved in a really silly way,' she recalls. 'For example, they deliberately crapped on the floor and we had to clean the dirt manually. They called us "Jewish whores" and they kicked us. They behaved really badly. They also told us, "We will teach you Jews how to work." But all of us were poor women that were used to work ... It's a really humiliating feeling when your personality is being taken away. I don't know whether you can understand it. You suddenly mean nothing. We were treated like animals.'

There were rich pickings for the Hlinka guards who worked in the holding camps. 'When Jews were coming to the camps,' says Michal Kabáč, 'we used to take their belongings and clothes. The deputy commander always called us to go and choose the clothes we wanted. Everybody took what he or she could. I took a pair of shoes. I wrapped it up with string and took it home. The guards were doing fine.' And it was not just the Slovakians who robbed the Jews before they left. 'One day a heavy SS officer came,' says Silvia Veselá, 'and started to shout at us. We had no idea why he was shouting. Then we saw big baskets – three big baskets – into which we had to give our gold, silver, money and all our valuables. We were told we were going to work and didn't need these valuables. I was very poor. I had just one watch that was given to me by my aunt, and so I gave them it.'

The holding camp was a place not just of theft but of casual brutality. 'Our guards used to beat them [the Jews],' says Michal Kabáč. 'There was a special kind of unit who used to punish the guilty ones. They used to take them to a special room and punish them by beating them on their feet with a wooden stick.' It was, of course, the Hlinka guards themselves who arbitrarily decided who was 'guilty' and who was not.

The stay in the holding camp could vary from a few days to a few weeks, but eventually the Slovakian Jews were taken to a nearby railway station to be transported out of the country. Silvia Veselá vividly remembers the walk to the station and her last memories of Slovakia: 'They spat at us and shouted, "Jewish whores, it serves you right! You'll finally work!" They also threw stones at us. They used every possibility to humiliate us. There were also some people who just stood still and just witnessed the humiliation. Some of those people cried. However, the majority, older and younger generation, humiliated us. I wouldn't wish this kind of experience on anyone. It is a horrible feeling.'

The Slovakian Jews were escorted to the railway station by the Hlinka guards. 'I was ordered to load the Jewish women on the train and watch them,' says Michal Kabáč. 'I was telling myself: "You did not want to work, you Jewish swine!"' Within months members of the Hlinka guards like Kabáč realized that the Slovakian Jews were being sent to their deaths – news that did not fill them with compassion: 'I was feeling sorry for them, but on the other hand I was not sorry for them considering they were stealing from the Slovaks. We were not very sorry. We thought it was good that they were taken away. That way they could not cheat us any more. They were not going to get rich at the expense of the working class any more.'

Kabáč had little direct contact with Slovakian Jews before knowingly sending them to their deaths. There were no Jews living in his village, and he admits that he himself never had any 'problem' with the Jews in Slovakia. He enthusiastically embraced anti-Semitism not because of any personal experience but because he was a fervent nationalist, proud that Slovakia was now an independent country, and he was told by the Slovakian leadership that 'the Jews were liars and were robbing the Slovaks'. His story is a telling reminder of how quickly prejudice can take root when presented as part of a package of values, the majority of which are more immediately attractive. Michal Kabáč adopted violent anti-Semitism in order to demonstrate that he was a committed and patriotic Slovakian nationalist, and in the process he gained financially, since he now stole from the Jews and dressed the crime up as some kind of 'rightful vengeance'. Silvia Veselá witnessed first hand how quickly the prevailing morality changed in Slovakia: 'I thought about it several times. Human material is very bendable. You can do anything with it. When money and life are involved, you seldom meet a person that is willing to sacrifice for you. It hurt, it really hurt when I, for example, saw my schoolmate shouting with her fist raised, "It serves you right!" Since that time I do not expect anything of people.'

Meantime at Auschwitz attempts continued to improve the killing facility of the camp. On 27 February 1942 Rudolf Hoess, the SS architect Karl Bischoff and Hans Kammler, head of the Central SS Buildings Office,[36] held a meeting at which they decided to move the location of the crematorium that had been planned for Auschwitz 1 to the new camp at Birkenau. The intention was to site the new crematorium in a far corner near a small cottage. This cottage was to be converted quickly into a makeshift killing installation by bricking up the existing doors and windows, gutting the inside and creating two sealed spaces that could be used as gas chambers. New entrances would lead directly into each gas chamber, and a hatch would be placed high in the brickwork of the wall to allow crystals of Zyklon B to be thrown inside. The cottage, known as 'The Little Red House' or 'Bunker 1' was used for the first time as a place of murder at the end of March 1942, when a transport of Jews from the local area who were considered unfit to work in the forced labour programme were sent to Auschwitz. Around 800 people could be murdered in 'The Little Red House' at any one time, crammed tightly into the gas chambers.

Hoess now had at his disposal a murder facility that did not suffer from the disadvantages of the crematorium in Auschwitz 1. No matter how hard those being gassed in 'The Little Red House' screamed, no disturbance was caused to the normal operation of the camp. But Hoess knew it would be many months (in fact it was more than a year) before a crematorium could be built nearby to dispose of the bodies killed in this makeshift gas chamber. So having solved one of his problems (how to kill in relative secret), he had created another (how to dispose of the evidence).

The first transports that arrived from Slovakia in March 1942 were not selected on arrival – everyone was admitted to the camp. But that did not prevent the SS and Kapos immediately terrorizing the new inmates, as Otto Pressburger, who was on one of these transports, experienced first hand: 'From the station we had to run [to Auschwitz 1] in groups of five. They [the SS] shouted, "*Schnell laufen*! *Laufen, laufen, laufen*!" And we ran. They killed on the spot those who could not run. We felt we were less than dogs. We had been told that we were going to work, not that we were going to a concentration camp.'

The next morning, after a night with no food or drink, Otto Pressburger, his father and the rest of the Slovak transport of around 1000 men were made to run from the main camp up to the building site that was Birkenau. He estimates that around 70–80 people were killed on the way. Birkenau, deep in mud and other filth, was an appalling place. As Perry Broad of the SS recalled: 'Conditions in Birkenau were considerably worse than in Auschwitz [main camp]. Feet drop into a sticky bog at every step. There was hardly any water for washing.'[37] Prisoners existed in an environment of utter degradation, covered in dirt and their own faeces.

Once in Birkenau, Otto Pressburger gained an immediate introduction to the brutal regime of the camp. When he saw his father's belt had been stolen by a young Polish boy, he caught the boy and punched him. Another prisoner quickly told him that he had made a potentially fatal mistake. The young boy was a 'pipel' – camp slang for the young servant of a Kapo (and someone with whom the Kapo often had a homosexual relationship). 'We had to run back to the barracks and hide,' says Otto Pressburger. 'The Kapo of the block entered the barracks and ordered us to lie down – head facing towards the aisle. There was the "pipel" coming looking for me. He didn't recognize me. We all looked alike. No hair [all the prisoners had their head shaved on arrival] and the same clothes. I was very lucky, otherwise they would have killed me.'

On that first day at work in Birkenau, Otto Pressburger witnessed another incident that demonstrated in an even more bestial way the desperate situation in which he now found himself: 'We went to work to build roads – Kapos and SS men were supervising us. There was one Jew from our town, a tall and strong man from a rich family. The Kapo spotted his gold teeth and asked him to give them to him. He answered that he could not do that, but the Kapo persisted that he must. He still said he could not give him his gold teeth. The Kapo got angry and said we must all obey his orders. He took the shovel and hit him over the head a couple of times until he fell down. The Kapo turned him upside down and put the shovel on his throat and stood on it. He broke his neck and used the shovel to get the teeth out of his mouth. Not far away stood another Jew who asked the Kapo how he could do this. The Kapo came over and said he'd show him. And he killed him the same way. Then he told us never to ask questions and to mind our own business. That evening we had to carry twelve dead bodies with us back to the barracks. He killed them just for fun. All this happened the first day at work.'

Murderous behaviour by the Kapos had been a feature of Auschwitz from the very beginning, so the experience of these newcomers, though horrific, was nothing out of the ordinary for the camp. But the culture (if one can use such a word in the context of Auschwitz) of the place was nonetheless about to change in two major ways as a result of the arrival of the Slovakians.

The first change occurred because women were now admitted; up to this point Auschwitz had been an exclusively male institution. But the arrival of women did not have the remotest 'civilizing' effect on those in authority at the camp – almost the reverse, as Silvia Veselá witnessed. She arrived at Auschwitz shortly after Otto Pressburger, on a transport containing several hundred women and one man – a Jewish doctor who had been permitted by the Slovak authorities to accompany the women. 'When we came to Auschwitz we were kicked out of the railway trucks,' says Silvia Veselá, 'and the SS officers started to shout at our doctor, trying to find out why he was the only man on the transport. He replied in perfect German: "I am a doctor, and I was assigned here by the central Jewish conference. My role is to accompany the transport and I was told I would then go back to Slovakia." Then an SS officer pulled out a gun and shot him dead. They just simply shot him dead in front of my eyes.

Just because he was the only man amongst so many women. That was the first shock for me.'

The Slovakian women were then marched to Auschwitz main camp. 'We saw high barracks and a gate,' says Silvia Veselá. 'Above the gate was written, "Arbeit macht frei" – "Work sets you free". So we thought we had come there to work.' Several of the blocks in the main camp had been emptied and made ready for the women, who were ordered to strip off their clothes and hand over any valuables they had not already given up. 'Although the Germans hated us so much, they did not hesitate to take our clothes, shoes and jewellery. Explain this to me,' demands Silvia Veselá. 'I always had this question – why didn't they feel an aversion to our belongings?'

As the Slovakian women sat, naked, having their heads shaved, an SS officer entered the room and ordered five of them to go to the doctor's office. 'He wanted to examine Jewish women,' says Silvia Veselá, 'and see if they were real virgins. He also wanted to know if Jewish women were clean. After they carried out the examination they were surprised – but in a negative sense. They couldn't believe we were so clean. Moreover, more than 90 per cent of us were virgins. These were all religious Jewish women. There was no way any of them would allow a man to touch her before the wedding. But in the course of the examination every girl was deprived of her virginity – the doctors used their fingers. They were all deflowered – another way to humiliate them. A friend of mine who was from a religious family told me: "I wanted to keep my virginity for my man, and I lost it this way!"'

Appalling as the experiences of Otto Pressburger and Silvia Veselá were during their first hours in the camp, they do not represent what has come to be seen as the quintessential Auschwitz treatment on arrival. For one of the most infamous procedures associated with Auschwitz was only now about to begin – the initial selection. This was the second of the two important changes to the camp that resulted from the arrival of the Slovakians. Periodic selection of some incoming transports had begun as early as the end of April, but systematic selection did not begin until 4 July 1942 when a transport from Slovakia arrived that was separated at once by the SS into those who were useful for work and would be admitted to the camp, and those who were unfit for work and would be gassed immediately. Only now, two years after the camp received its first prisoners, had the authorities at Auschwitz finally begun the selection process for new inmates that would come to symbolize the cold-hearted terror of the place.

Eva Votavová, along with her father and mother, was on one of the first transports to be subjected to selection on arrival. This wave of Slovakian deportees contained a mix of old people, children and those, like Eva, who were young and fit: 'We arrived at Auschwitz station and had to align in rows of five. The painful scenes began there. They were separating the young from old and children. They separated my father from my mother and myself. From that moment I heard nothing about my father. When I saw him for the last time he looked worried, sad and hopeless.'

By now, some weeks after the completion of 'The Little Red House', another cottage a couple of hundred metres away, known as 'The Little White House' or Bunker 2, had been converted into a killing installation with a capacity of around 1200 people at any one time. Inside Bunker 2, four narrow rooms were constructed as gas chambers. This permitted better ventilation than had been possible in Bunker 1 ('The Little Red House') and allowed the Zyklon B to be cleared more quickly from the cottage once the murders had taken place – another example of the constant small initiatives taken by the Auschwitz authorities to try to 'improve' the killing process.

Otto Pressburger saw the new arrivals from Slovakia who had been selected to die waiting outside the cottages: 'They used to sit there. They must have been eating their food from home. SS men were around them with dogs. They, of course, didn't know what was going to happen to them. We did not want to tell them. It would have been worse for them. We were thinking that the people who brought them here were not humans but some wild jungle creatures.' According to Otto Pressburger, during this period the gassings took place at night: 'They never did it during the day; [because] people were probably shouting or trying to get out. We only saw the bodies next morning piled beside the pits.'

Pressburger was forced to work in a special unit, burying the bodies gassed in the two cottages: 'To kill people with gas is very simple. You only seal the windows and doors to keep the gas inside. They locked the doors and in a couple of minutes they were all dead. They [the SS] brought them [the bodies] to the holes where I used to work. We used to bury them the next morning. We put some powdered lime and soil over them. Just enough to cover the bodies so no one could see them.' It was an inadequate method of body disposal, and when the hot summer arrived, the bodies thrown into pits started to putrify. Pressburger's job, already the stuff of nightmares, became even worse: 'The dead bodies were becoming alive. They were rotting and coming out of the holes. Blood and dirt was everywhere and we had to take them out with our bare hands. It did not look like a dead body any more. It was a rotten mass. We had to dig into that mass and sometimes we took out a head, sometimes a hand or a leg. The smell was unbearable. I had no choice [but to do this work] if I wanted to live. Otherwise they would kill me. I wanted to live. Sometimes I was questioning myself whether this life was worth living.' Once the bodies were disinterred, the SS ordered the prisoners to put them into giant, burning pits. The Auschwitz authorities thus improvised a makeshift crematorium while awaiting the completion of the conventional one nearby. 'We built a big fire,' says Pressburger, 'with wood and petrol. We were throwing them [the bodies] right into it. There were always two of us throwing bodies in – one holding the bodies by the legs and the other by the arms. The stench was terrible. We were never given any extra food for this. The SS men were constantly drinking vodka or cognac or something else from bottles. They could not cope with it, either.'

As he forced himself to carry on with the gruesome work of digging up the bodies and burning them, Pressburger also wrestled with an emotional trauma – the death of his father. The prisoners were kept hungry and thirsty, and his father had drunk rainwater from puddles, a common cause of infection and death. 'The doctor who used to treat me as a child was in Auschwitz as well,' says Pressburger. 'He told me never to drink that water [from the puddles]. Otherwise I would die within 24 hours. People always used to have swollen legs from drinking that rainwater. Water was coming out of their legs.' But his father was not so self-controlled, drank the water and died. After the initial shock and suffering of the loss, Pressburger realized that the only way he could survive was to try to block out what was happening around him – even the death of his own father. 'The longer I wanted to live,' he says, 'the sooner I had to forget.'

In exercising this iron self-control, particularly in dealing with the terrible pains of hunger and thirst, Pressburger was unexpectedly helped by the memory of how he had acted in his childhood: 'When I was a little kid my parents used to give me money to buy sandwiches on the way to school. But I never did. Instead I always got liquorice. So I had no food through the whole day apart from that liquorice until I got home in the afternoon.' This meant that when he was in Birkenau and people around him were 'going insane from hunger' he was able to cope: 'I was used to not eating much. It's the same even now.'

Otto Pressburger is not alone in believing that his ability to draw on the memory of past privation was crucial to his survival. As Jacob Zylberstein pointed out in the context of the Łódź ghetto, many of the arriving German Jews found it hard to cope with ghetto life because of their privileged backgrounds, whilst he and his family, who had come from relative poverty, did not have so far to fall. Silvia Veselá observed a similar phenomenon with rich, middle-class Slovakian women. Even in the transit camps in Slovakia, before they arrived at Auschwitz, they found it much harder to deal with conditions than women like her from poorer backgrounds. And Pavel Stenkin found that as a Soviet prisoner of war in Auschwitz his own harsh upbringing was now an advantage. As a child he had never had much food – or, indeed, much affection – and now the experience was a positive asset.

This form of 'selection' within the ghettos and camps was, of course, precisely the concern Reinhard Heydrich had raised at the Wannsee conference. The Nazis were too wedded to the Darwinian notion of the survival of the fittest to allow the Jews who came through the horrors of forced labour to carry on living. Indeed, Nazi racial theory taught them that they had now isolated the very group they should most fear. This proscriptive insistence on following through their own warped logic to the bitter end is one of the factors that makes the Nazis' 'Final Solution' different from some other genocides, such as Stalin's murderous treatment of minority nationalities within the Soviet Union. Stalin may have persecuted whole nations, but the Soviet system did not seek to eliminate them in their entirety. Yet to fulfil the Nazis' purpose every single Jew had to be removed from German territory one way or the other.

When Otto Pressburger returned recently to visit the burial sites at Birkenau, he remembered the thousands who came with him from Slovakia to Auschwitz and who could not make such a journey today: 'It is terrible. I do remember standing [here] beside my father. The majority of the people working here were from my city. I knew all of them. Every day there were less and less of them. They must be still buried around here somewhere. There were only four of us who survived the three years.'

In the spring and early summer of 1942 thousands of Jews, primarily from Upper Silesia and Slovakia, went to their deaths in 'The Little Red House' and 'The Little White House'. En route to the gas chambers in the cottages, SS officers such as Gerhard Palitzsch would chat with the Jews, asking each what trades or qualifications they possessed. Rudolf Hoess emphasized in his memoirs how the key to successful mass murder on this scale was to conduct the whole process in an atmosphere of great calm. But it could happen, as Hoess recorded, that if one person in the group approaching the gas chambers spoke of suffocation or murder, 'a sort of panic set in at once', making the killing much more difficult. In later transports a careful watch was kept on individuals who were thought likely to cause trouble for the Nazis in this way. At the first sign of any attempt to disrupt the compliant atmosphere the Nazis had created such people were discreetly moved away, taken out of sight of the others and shot with a small-calibre gun that was quiet enough that those nearby would not hear the noise.

The emotional torment of mothers who suspected what was about to happen to them, as they walked with their children to their deaths under, as Hoess puts it, 'the blossom-laden fruit trees of the cottage orchard',[38] is almost impossible to imagine. On one occasion, Hoess records how a woman whispered to him, 'How can you bring yourself to kill such beautiful, darling children? Have you no heart at all?'; on another he saw a woman try to throw her children out of the gas chamber as the door was closing, shouting, 'At least let my precious children live!' These heart-rending sights did cause some emotional disturbance in Hoess, but nothing, according to his memoirs, that either a vigorous gallop on a horse or a few drinks could not chase away.

Concentrating the mass killing in a remote corner of the Birkenau site did mean that the routine of Auschwitz main camp was no longer disrupted by the murders. And whilst life for the prisoners in the main camp remained as harsh as ever, for the SS this had become a place where it was possible after work to relax in some comfort, as Tadeusz Rybacki,[39] who had been arrested by the Gestapo for suspected involvement in the Polish resistance, discovered.

After some months moving between different work kommandos Rybacki finally obtained one of the most sought-after jobs in Auschwitz main camp – working as a waiter in the SS dining room. After women guards affiliated to the SS arrived, at the same time as the Slovakian women in the spring of 1942, he witnessed several riotous evenings. 'It was a gangster feast,' he says, recalling one particular night. 'There was singing, drinking, slapping on the back and all kinds of alcohol. I poured wine in their glasses and there was one SS woman who, when I gave her wine, started pulling my arm. She said to me, "Darling ... ", and everyone started looking at me. The situation for me was very dangerous and I almost spilt the wine, but luckily some SS man yelled at her, "Shut your mouth, you whore!" and she let go.' Later in the evening he noticed another SS woman making advances towards him and the other waiters. 'Some drunk, big woman was walking and swaying, going most probably to the toilet, and she saw us standing and she started making gestures to us suggestive of sexual intercourse. Our faces were stonelike and we were whispering to one another, 'What does she want, that bitch?"'

The contrast between the louche life of the SS and the brutal existence of the prisoners did not escape him: 'Only the prisoners were to die of hunger. The stay at the camp was a slow execution by creating the conditions of hunger, beating and hard labour. But they [the SS] had everything. When we looked at the feast there was everything, there were all kinds of alcohol, even French cognacs, and nothing was lacking. It all looked so hideously like a devilish feast. You cannot imagine what a terrible picture it was.'

Nonetheless, Rybacki knew how lucky he was to be a waiter working in the dining room. The job was not only 'under a roof' – essential, he felt, if he was to survive the winter – but also brought him into direct contact with the single most important commodity in the camp: food. He and the other prisoners who worked as waiters would steal whatever food they could and hide it in the attic of the building. But their actions were not without risk. Once, when several members of the SS were standing at the buffet that adjoined the dining room, he and the other waiters heard a loud noise. They looked back into the dining room and 'our hair stood on end'. 'Suddenly we saw somebody's legs and half the body coming through the ceiling.' They knew at once what must have happened. One of the other waiters, hiding stolen food in the attic, had slipped: 'Up there you had to be careful to step on the beams because otherwise you would fall through.' It was a potentially deadly situation for all of them. But luckily the SS nearby were laughing and drinking so much that they did not turn back to look into the room. The prisoner who had fallen through managed to pull himself back up and the debris was swept away. But that still left the hole in the ceiling. Next morning when they arrived for work they simply bribed one of the SS guards with butter and sausage not to ask too many questions about the damage. Two days later the hole was mended.

Had it not taken place in Auschwitz, Tadeusz Rybacki's recollection of his friend falling through the ceiling, his legs dangling helplessly, would be almost comic; and the knowledge that he and his comrades escaped punishment by bribing a junior member of the SS is reminiscent of the manipulation of German guards in Allied POW camps so beloved of Hollywood producers attached to the semi-romanticization of the prison camp experience in the West. But, set in Auschwitz as it is, his story carries none of these resonances. Instead, it is a telling reminder once again of how, by early summer 1942, Auschwitz had evolved into two separate camps. Not just geographically, with Birkenau emerging from the mud just under 2 miles away from Auschwitz main camp, but philosophically and psychologically as well. In one, prisoners like Tadeusz Rybacki did what they could to survive by scheming to get the best work and 'organizing' additional food; in the other, men, women and children were murdered within hours of arriving.

From Hoess's perspective that summer it was clear that his energy and focus should chiefly be directed on this second camp and killing operation. The gas chambers inside the two converted cottages and the burning of bodies in the open air still represented only interim solutions to the murderous task the Nazis had set themselves, and the killing operation at Auschwitz remained inefficient and improvised. As a centre for mass murder, Auschwitz was still in its infancy, its capacity severely limited. Contrary to the evidence they gave after the war, Hoess and his colleagues had already used their own initiative to help devise temporary methods by which to kill large numbers of people. But they knew their greatest task, the one for which they would become infamous, lay ahead of them: the creation of a killing factory.

— 3 —

Factories of Death

At the start of 1942 the only specialized death camp in operation in the Nazi empire was Chełmno. Despite this, the Nazis still embarked on their orgy of destruction. For unlike those who work in a less radical system, who first plan in detail and only then act, the Nazis launched into the deportation of the Jews before any of the systems they had devised for their destruction were tested or properly in place. It was out of the ensuing disorder that they built their genocide. And the story of how they organized this murderous task, and in the process made 1942 the year of the greatest killing during the 'Final Solution', reveals much about the mentality of the murderers.

Auschwitz was not to play the most prominent part in the mass killings of 1942, but this was to be the year that the camp began for the first time to have an impact on western Europe. Only days after the Slovakian authorities negotiated with the Germans to send their Jews to Auschwitz, another European country sent its first transport to the camp. And the circumstances that led to this and subsequent transports were even more complex and surprising than events in Slovakia, not least because the train that left on 23 March came from a country conquered by the Germans that was permitted great freedom in its own administration: France.

After the swift defeat of June 1940, France was divided into two zones, occupied and unoccupied. Marshal Pétain, a hero from World War I, became head of state, based in Vichy in the unoccupied zone. He was a popular figure in those early years of the war (much more popular than many French people would admit after the war was over), and acted as the focal point of the countrywide desire to restore the dignity of France. As for the Germans, they had apparently contradictory goals – they wanted control of

France, yet desired to have as small a physical presence as possible; fewer than 1500 German officers and officials were based in the whole of the country, occupied and unoccupied. German rule depended to a large degree on the cooperation of the French bureaucrats and on their administrative systems.

For the first year or so of the occupation there was little conflict between the French and Germans. The German military commander, General Otto von Stuelpnagel, operated from the Hotel Majestic in Paris more like a Roman governor presiding over a semi-autonomous province of the Empire than a Nazi trying to reduce the area he ruled to a nation of slaves. Nonetheless, the Jews of France remained vulnerable. There were around 350,000 of them in 1940, and nearly half of that number did not hold French passports. Many had arrived in the 1920s from Eastern Europe, whilst others had fled to France more recently in a fruitless bid to escape the Nazis. It was these foreign Jews who bore the brunt of the early persecution. In October 1940 the new French government proclaimed in the 'Jewish statute' that all Jews were forbidden to work in certain professions, but it was the foreign Jews in the unoccupied zone who were singled out for the additional torment of imprisonment in internment camps.

During this early period of the occupation of France, the Nazis' persecution of the Jews proceeded in their standard way. First the Jews were identified and then registered. Further legislation called for the registration of Jewish property prior to its seizure and the eventual deportation of all Jews from the occupied zone. The Vichy government collaborated placidly throughout this process. But the relative calm of the occupation was to be disturbed in the summer of 1941 by events thousands of miles to the east – the invasion of the Soviet Union. On 21 August 1941 two Germans were shot in Paris – one killed, the other badly wounded. It was quickly established that French Communists were behind the violence. Another killing on 3 September only served to heighten the Germans' concern that their hitherto untroubled life in France was over.

The German authorities reacted to the killings by imprisoning Communists and conducting reprisal shootings – three hostages were shot immediately after the September incident. But this response was considered inadequate by Hitler, who was busy directing the bloodbath that was the War in the East from his headquarters in the forests of East Prussia. Field Marshal Wilhelm Keitel sent word to Paris of Hitler's displeasure: 'The acts of reprisal taken against the three hostages are far too mild! The Führer considers one German soldier to be worth much more than three French Communists. The Führer expects such instances to be responded to with the harshest reprisals. At the next assassination at least 100 shootings for each German [killed] are to take place without delay. Without such draconian retribution, matters cannot be controlled.'[1]

Hitler would have wanted his representative in France to act as decisively, and brutally, as his commander-in-chief in the Ukraine did in December 1941 when faced with a similar threat: 'The fight against the partisans succeeds only if the population realizes that the partisans and their sympathizers sooner or later are killed,' he wrote. 'Death by strangulation inspires fear more particularly.'[2] Hitler himself later remarked: 'Only where the struggle against the partisan nuisance was begun and carried out with ruthless brutality have successes been achieved.'[3]

The German authorities in Paris were in a quandary. If they proceeded with the policy recommended by Hitler, they risked losing the cooperation of the French population – a prediction that seemed to be borne out when there was outrage at the killing of 98 hostages after the shooting of a German officer in Nantes in October. It was obvious to General von Stuelpnagel that such 'Polish methods'[4] simply did not work in France. But he was enough of a political realist to grasp that Hitler would not just change his mind and allow the Germans in France to proceed with discretion on such a subject. The Führer's mind was made up. 'Draconian retribution' was called for. So, in a typical example of the way those in senior positions sought solutions in the Nazi state, the German authorities in France attempted to work round Hitler's dogmatic view by devising other forms of 'draconian retribution' that would damage their relationship with the French far less. Two such alternatives were quickly suggested: fines on whole sections of the population, and deportation. And, since the supposed 'link' between Communists and Jews was engraved in the mind of every Nazi, nothing came more naturally to the German authorities in Paris than the idea of fining and deporting Jews in retaliation for the murder of Germans by Communists. The reprisal killings would continue, but at a reduced level and only as a small part of the overall policy of 'draconian retribution'.

Despite this partial solution to his problem, Stuelpnagel still felt he had to protest once more to his superiors, concluding in January 1942 that he could 'no longer reconcile mass shootings with my conscience, nor answer for them before the bar of history'.[5] Unsurprisingly, shortly after this communication Stuelpnagel left his post, but the principle he had established remained. Jews and Communists would be deported as part of a series of reprisals for any resistance by the French. The first of these transports left France in March 1942 for Auschwitz. German army officers, motivated by a desire not to have to answer 'before the bar of history' for reprisal shootings, had nonetheless still put these people in the greatest possible danger. A combination of starvation, abuse and disease ravaged them. Of the 1112 men who boarded the train at Compiègne, 1008 were dead within five months.[6] Only about 20 of them are thought to have survived the war. Thus more than 98 per cent of this first transport died in Auschwitz.

By this time the deportation of French Jews as a reprisal measure also clearly fitted into another, much larger, vision – the Nazis' 'Final Solution' of their 'Jewish problem' in France. With the long-term strategic vision already spelt out at Wannsee in January 1942, day-to-day responsibility for implementing the policy in France fell to SS Hauptsturmführer (Captain) Theodor Dannecker, who reported to Adolf Eichmann, who in turn reported to Reinhard Heydrich. On 6 May Heydrich himself visited Paris and revealed to a small group that 'just as with the Russian Jews in Kiev, the death sentence has been pronounced on all the Jews of Europe. Even of the Jews of France whose deportations begin in these very weeks.'[7]

The Nazis faced one massive obstacle in obtaining their desired aim of a 'Jew-free' France – the French authorities themselves. There simply was not the German manpower in France to identify, collect and deport the French Jews without the active participation of the French administration and police, especially since the Nazis initially demanded that more Jews be deported from France than from any other country in western Europe. At a meeting in Berlin on 11 June 1942, chaired by Adolf Eichmann, a schedule was announced whereby 10,000 Belgian Jews, 15,000 Dutch Jews and 100,000 French Jews were to be deported to Auschwitz. They were to be between the ages of 16 and 40, and only 10 per cent were permitted to be 'unable to work'. The exact thinking behind these figures and restrictions has never been uncovered, but it is likely that the decision not yet to accept large numbers of children and old people reflects knowledge of the still limited extermination capacity of Auschwitz. Theodor Dannecker, anxious to please, committed himself to delivering every French Jew who fell within the age range decreed. Shortly after the Berlin meeting Dannecker drew up a plan to send 40,000 French Jews to the East within three months.

It was one thing to formulate such an ambitious plan, of course, but quite another to be able to carry it out in a country that still largely administered itself. At a meeting on 2 July between the chief of the Vichy police, René Bousquet, and Nazi officials, the Germans experienced first hand the difference between theory and application. Bousquet stated Vichy's position – in the occupied zone only foreign Jews could be deported, and in the unoccupied zone the French police would not take part in any round-up. Bousquet stated: 'On the French side we have nothing against the arrests themselves. It is only their execution by French police in Paris that would be embarrassing. This was the personal wish of the Marshal [Pétain].'[8] Helmut Knochen, the head of the German security police, who knew that without the collaboration of the French the deportations would be impossible, immediately protested, reminding Bousquet that Hitler would not understand the position of the French on a subject that was so important to him. After this implied threat, Bousquet altered the French position. The French police would carry out arrests in both the occupied and unoccupied zones, but only of foreign, not French, Jews. The French authorities had made a clear political judgment – they would cooperate in handing over foreigners to the Germans in order to protect their own citizens.

At a meeting two days later between the French Premier, Pierre Laval, and Dannecker, Laval offered (according to Dannecker) 'that, during the evacuation of Jewish families from the unoccupied zone, children under sixteen [can] also be taken away. As for the Jewish children in the occupied zone, the question did not interest him.'[9] Historians have described Laval's proposal about the children as meriting his 'everlasting shame'[10] and declared that this moment should 'forever be written in the history of France'.[11] It is impossible to disagree with them, especially given the appalling suffering that was about to follow for these children, much of it inflicted on them by French people on French soil as a result of an offer made by a French politician.

The arrests of foreign Jews by the French police began in Paris on the night of 16 July 1942. At home that night in the family's apartment in the tenth *arrondissement* were Annette Muller, her younger brother Michel, her two elder brothers and their mother. Their father, originally from Poland, had heard rumours that something was in the air and had left the apartment to hide nearby. The rest of the family had remained. The idea that whole families were at risk was inconceivable to them. Annette,[12] nine years old at the time, has a clear memory of what happened that night: 'We were violently woken by knocks on the door and the police came in. My mother begged them to leave us. And the police inspector pushed her back, saying, "Hurry up! Hurry up! Don't make us waste our time!" And that struck me. For years and years I had nightmares because all of a sudden my mother who I had placed on a pedestal [behaved like that]. I didn't understand why she humiliated herself before them.'

Annette's mother hurriedly threw a sheet on the floor and started filling it with clothes and dried food. Minutes later they were out on the stairs on the way down to the street. Annette, finding that she had left her comb behind, was told by the police that she could go and get it as long as she 'came right back'. She returned to the apartment and found the police still there: 'Everything was upside down, and I [also] wanted to take my doll with me, to bring my doll ... and they grabbed my doll from me, they took it out of my arms and threw it violently on the unmade bed. And then I understood that it certainly wasn't going to be something good that was going to happen.'

Once outside on the street in the mêlée of police and Jews, her mother told the two eldest boys, 10 and 11 years old, to run away, and they vanished in the crowd. (Both of them survived the war, hidden by other French families.) Then the police forced the others on to buses and took them to a temporary holding area at the Vélodrôme d'Hiver, an enclosed cycle stadium in the fifteenth *arrondissement*. All the families arrested over the two nights of the raid, including 4115 children out of a total of 12,884 people, were brought here. Just seven years old at the time, Michel Muller[13] remembers what followed in a strong series of 'flash' memories: 'The lights were lit day and night and there were huge skylights and it was very hot. We scarcely saw the cops any more. There were one or two sources of water, and toilets – perhaps two. And what's stayed with me are the smells. After two days the odour became horrible. The children played, because there were a lot of kids that I knew. We slid on the bicycle track – it was a wooden track.'

Annette Muller became sick in the fetid conditions and was taken to the central area inside the cycle track to lie down: 'I saw a man who lived not far from the rue de l'Avenir who was paralysed. And when we'd go to his house he always had a blanket over his legs, and the children of this man were around him speaking with respect. I remember seeing this man, who had impressed me. Now he was lying on the ground, naked – and, by the way, it was the first time I saw a man naked – and he was screaming. His eyes were half open and his body was white and naked. It was a terrifying image.'

After several days at the cycle stadium the families were taken by train to camps in the French countryside, the Mullers to Beaune-la-Rolande. 'It's a pretty village,' says Michel Muller. 'It was very beautiful and hot. There was a big alley of trees and we crossed part of the village and the people looked at us – curious.' The Mullers were amongst the last to arrive at the hastily arranged camp, and there were no beds for them to sleep on, so they lay as best they could on straw on the floor. Even so, Michel was not concerned: 'At the beginning I wasn't worried. I wasn't worried because we were with our mother and that reassured me. And I'd play with my friends.' He had only one anxiety: 'We were all good students and we were concerned – are we going to be in time to get back to school?'

Despite the conditions at the camp, the great consolation for both Annette and Michel remained that they were with their mother. 'Worried as she was at home,' says Annette, 'we couldn't really speak to her any more. In the camp she became very available at first. She played with us, we hugged her. The other women looked at us and laughed to see her play with us in this physical way.' But one memory of those early days in the camp with her mother continues to haunt Annette: 'The first night we were in the barracks it must have been raining, and there was water dripping down on to her, and my brother and I argued with each other not to sleep with her because we didn't want to get the water on us as well. She said something like "You're more afraid of the water than your desire to sleep next to your mum." And when we were separated that tortured me. I didn't jump at the chance to be next to her when we were sleeping.' Days later their mother was able to bribe a *gendarme* (they only ever saw French officials in the camp) to post a letter to her husband, an action that later turned out to be the catalyst that saved the lives of her two youngest children.

After just a few days in the camp, the women were ordered to give up their valuables. But some women preferred to dispose of their most treasured possessions in a way that they hoped would prevent their captors profiting from them. 'In the latrine was a trench,' says Michel Muller, 'a trench with a sort of wooden plank above it, and everybody could see us when we went to the bathroom. It scared me. It was embarrassing to go to the bathroom when everybody could see us. And there were some [women] who actually threw their jewellery into the shit.' Later, Michel saw some of the locals, who had been employed to come into the camp to frisk the Jewish women, searching in the latrine with a stick. 'That really surprised me,' he says.

Whilst the Mullers and thousands of other families suffered in camps such as Beaune-la-Rolande and Pithiviers, a still worse fate was being planned for them. Since the initial German request to the French had been for just adults capable of work to be deported, and the children had been only added as an afterthought to make up the numbers, arrangements had still not been formally agreed in Berlin to deport the families together. But despite the fact that the French authorities knew there would almost certainly be only a few weeks' delay before such arrangements were finalized, they agreed to separate parents from their children and deport the

Above: Heinrich Himmler (left) with Rudolf Hoess, commandant of Auschwitz, during the SS leader's visit to the camp in July 1942.

Above: Adolf Hitler played a decisive role in the creation of the Nazis' 'Final Solution'. Despite his lack of day-to-day involvement in the killing, it was his vision of the destruction of the Jews that his underlings followed.

Right: Reinhard Heydrich, Himmler's deputy: both a man of culture and a mass murderer.

Left: Hans Friedrich of the 1st SS Infantry Brigade. He took part in the shooting of Jews in the Ukraine in 1941.

Below: An execution somewhere in the East. Such a sight was commonplace during the Nazi occupation.

Above: A street scene in the Łódź ghetto in Poland. The vast majority of the people in this picture would be murdered by the autumn of 1944.

Above: Mordechai Chaim Rumkowski (right), the Jewish 'ruler' of the Łódź ghetto: a controversial, even notorious, figure.

Above: Rumkowski, with white hair, talks to Himmler during the SS leader's visit to the ghetto.

Above: Jewish men and women weaving baskets in a makeshift outdoor factory in the Łódź ghetto.

Above: Even children worked in the ghetto – not to have employment was to put oneself at even greater risk.

Above: On a hot day in the summer of 1942 Himmler studies plans for the building of the giant synthetic rubber factory at Monowitz, the largest industrial facility within the Auschwitz complex.

Above: Himmler (second from left) was well pleased with the progress he saw at Auschwitz, subsequently promoting Hoess, the commandant, to SS Lieutenant Colonel.

adults first. Jean Leguay, the Vichy police official, wrote to the prefect of Orléans saying, 'The children should not leave in the same convoys as their parents'; he added, 'While awaiting their departure to rejoin their parents, they will be cared for.'[14] However, Leguay betrayed knowledge that the children themselves would shortly be leaving by stating that 'the children's trains begin to depart in the second half of August'.[15] The French authorities thus made no attempt to avoid the appalling suffering that was to come by suggesting to the Germans that the deportations should be delayed a few weeks until the families could leave together.

Laval had previously stated that his suggestion that children should be included in the deportations was made out of a 'humane' desire not to separate families. That statement, already reeking of the same hypocrisy that informed the Slovakian decision to ask that whole families be deported for 'Christian' reasons, is now shown to be a blatant falsehood. Nothing could be less 'humane' than the policy now outlined by Leguay – that children be snatched from their parents in the camps of Beaune-la-Rolande and Pithiviers. As the historian Serge Klarsfeld wrote: 'Leguay closes his eyes to the real significance of the deportations, which he contributes to making even more atrocious. His principal preoccupation in his sunny office on the Rue de Monceau is to fill the deportation trains scheduled by the Gestapo.'[16]

Rumours circulated at Beaune-la-Rolande in early August that the adults might be taken away. 'I remember she [my mother] sewed money into the shoulder pads of my little suit,' says Michel Muller. 'It was my little Sunday suit, with a vest and some shorts. I think they were like golf shorts, and I was very proud of them. She sewed the money in and told me to be careful. The next day was the round-up.' The French police entered the camp and gathered everyone together. Once they announced that children were to be separated from their parents, there was mayhem. 'There were a lot of children who held on to their mothers,' recalls Michel. 'They were really difficult moments. The children hung on to their mothers, screaming and crying, and the *gendarmes* were overwhelmed.' Annette explains: 'The police very violently beat the women back. The children were holding on to their clothing. They (the *gendarmes*) soaked people with water. They tore the women's clothes. And there was a lot of screaming, crying. It was a lot of noise, and then all of a sudden a big silence.' A machine gun had been placed in front of the women and children and the threat was clear. 'There was a whole row of women in front,' says Annette. 'I can still see it today in front of me. And the children, we were holding on to each other. My mother was in the front row and she made a sign with her eyes and we watched her. I had the impression that her eyes smiled at us, as if she wanted to say that she was going to come back. Michel cried. And that's the last image I have of my mother.'

After their parents left, conditions in the camp for the children quickly deteriorated. Without their mothers to care for them, they became filthy and their clothes were soiled. Because of the diet of weak soup and beans many suffered from diarrhoea. But it was the emotional loss that was hardest to bear. 'The most difficult thing was in the evenings,' remembers Michel Muller. 'It was evening when normally Mother would tell us stories, and then when she was gone we had to do it alone.' Annette adds, 'After her departure, for a few days I didn't want to go out of the barracks because I was so sad. I couldn't stop crying. I stayed sleeping on the straw, and I told myself that it was my fault that my mother left, that I wasn't nice with her. All those sorts of things that I could reproach myself with. And it was Michel that made me go out, because I had dysentery, and he helped wash me and made me eat. And little by little he took me around the camp and we pulled grass and tried to eat it.'

At the age of seven, Michel took on the role of protector of his sister. But he faced huge difficulties. Annette was sick and couldn't queue for soup, and the experiment of eating grass – Michel thought that grass might taste like green salad – was not a success. However, his biggest problem was that at seven years old he was younger and smaller than many of the boys who competed for food at mealtimes. 'I have precise memories of fights at the moment when they served the soup – fights with other kids. Since I was very little I couldn't get into the crowd of people for the soup. Sometimes I'd come back and my can would be empty. I didn't have anything. My sister was always sick, and so we had to go and look in the empty cans where they had gotten the food from and we tried to find food left over. We spoke a lot about eating. We told each other menus of what we would eat, whereas normally at home we weren't big eaters, but at that moment we were really struck by hunger.' Michel realized that he had to change their situation dramatically if they were to survive, since both he and his sister were growing weaker with each succeeding day. So when he saw a sign outside the camp infirmary he decided to act: 'It said children that were younger than five years old could eat at the infirmary. So since I knew how to read and write – I always told my children you need to learn to read and write because it's very useful – I pretended that I was five years old, which worked fine. That way I could eat and [because Michael could smuggle extra food out] so could my sister.'

What marks this episode out as one of particular poignancy in a history that is full of atrocity is not only the snatching of the children from their parents but also the treatment of the children by the French authorities once they were left in their 'care'. The children did not just suffer neglect; they were badly fed and emotionally cast adrift. At this moment in their lives, when they were at their most vulnerable, they were humiliated as well. Despite the hunger, despite the filth, it was the casual humiliation he suffered at Beaune-la-Rolande that affected Michel Muller most: 'Since standards of hygiene were very low and we all had lice, they shaved our heads. I had a lot of curly hair at the time and my mother was very proud of my hair. So when this *gendarme* shaved me, he held me between his legs and said, "Oh, we're going to do Last of the Mohicans." And he shaved a line through the middle of my head. So I had hair on each side and he shaved the part in the middle. I was so ashamed that I stole a beret to cover it.' Michel's appearance was so appalling that it shocked even his nine-year-old sister. 'I remember my mother liked to comb his hair. He had pretty blond hair. She thought he was such a beautiful little boy. Then when they shaved his hair in the middle he became hideous-looking. And I understood why people put Jews apart, because even my own little brother, when I saw him like that with this dirty face and his hair like that, he disgusted me. He inspired disgust in me.' After a few days the *gendarmes* finally finished the job and shaved the sides of Michel's head too. They had enjoyed their fun, and Michel had endured emotional trauma that he remembers to this day.

Meantime, by the middle of August 1942 arrangements had

been put in hand to enable the French to deport these children and make up the numbers they had promised the Germans. The plan was to transfer the children from Beaune-la-Rolande and Pithiviers to Drancy detention and assembly camp in a northeastern suburb of Paris. From there the children would finally be sent to Auschwitz, among convoys of adults. They would thus travel to their deaths in the company of strangers.

On 15 August a forlorn column of children made their way back down the tree-lined streets of the pretty village of Beaune-la-Rolande to the railway station. They looked very different from the relatively healthy boys and girls who had entered the camp with their mothers just over two weeks before. 'I remember that the people of the village looked at us,' says Annette Muller. 'They looked at us with the same disgust that I myself had felt. We must have smelt badly. We were shaved, covered with sores. And I saw the disgusted look of people when they saw us like you see sometimes in the Métro when there's a homeless person and he's dirty and sleeping on a bench. It seemed that we were no longer human.' Nonetheless the children sang as they walked to the station because, as Annette says, 'We were sure that we were on our way to see our parents.' But they were en route not to home but to Drancy, the conduit through which more than 65,000 people were eventually sent to the death camps in the East, more than 60,000 of them to Auschwitz.

Odette Daltroff-Baticle,[17] who was imprisoned in Drancy in August 1942, had volunteered along with two friends to take care of the children from Beaune-la-Rolande and Pithiviers: 'When they arrived they were in really poor shape. The children were surrounded by insects and they were very, very dirty and had dysentery. We tried to give them showers but we didn't have anything to dry them with. Then we tried to give them food – these children hadn't eaten for several days – and we had a hard time giving them any. Furthermore, we tried to make a full list of their names, but many of them didn't know their family names and so they just said things like, "I'm the little brother of Pierre." So we persisted in trying to find out their names; the older ones, yes, of course, but for the smaller ones it was absolutely impossible. Their mothers had tied little pieces of wood on them with their names, but a lot of them had taken off the pieces of wood and played with them amongst themselves.'

Odette and the other helpers, confronted by this pitiable sight, felt they had no option but to try to comfort the children with words they knew to be untrue: 'We lied to them. We told them, "You're going to see your parents again." And, of course, they didn't believe us – curiously, they suspected what was going to happen. A lot of them said to my friends or to me, "*Madame*, adopt me ... adopt me," because they wanted to stay at the camp even though it was bad there. They didn't want to go any further. There was a little boy, a very good-looking little boy, who was three and a half years old. I can still see him in my mind's eye and he didn't stop saying, "Mummy, I'm going to be afraid, Mummy. I'm going to be afraid." It was all he would say. Curiously, he knew that he was going to be even more afraid. They were totally pessimistic. They preferred to stay in the horror of the camp. They understood things much better than we did.'

Odette saw how the children still possessed 'some little objects that were very important to them', such as photos of their parents or small pieces of jewellery. 'There was a little girl who had earrings and who said, "Do you think they'll let me keep little things in gold?"' But the day before the children left, Jewish women from elsewhere in the camp arrived to search them for valuables. 'These women were paid by the day and we knew that about half of what they found they would stick in their own pockets. And I saw that they weren't nice with them at all. They were completely insensitive to the way they treated the children, which seemed curious to me.'

Michel and Annette Muller found life in Drancy, a camp set up in a semi-completed low-cost housing project, 'like walking through a nightmare'. Annette was shocked not just by the living conditions – she and her brother slept on a cement floor surrounded by excrement – but also by the fact that, since the few adults who were trying to look after the children were overwhelmed by the sheer numbers, it meant that 'no one took care of us. We were really left to ourselves. I don't remember an adult looking after us.' Then, just before the transports were due to leave for Auschwitz, she heard her name and that of her brother called out from a list. She and Michel were escorted out of Drancy, past the barbed wire, to a police car that awaited them. 'We thought we were going to be liberated,' says Annette. 'We were sure we were going to see our family again and come back to the rue de l'Avenir. And Michel and I, we made a kind of plan to surprise our parents – to hide under the table and then come out so they would be happy to see us again. And it was at that point that I turned around, and I saw the police officers were crying because they knew very well that we were not going home.'

Annette and Michel were taken to another holding centre for foreign Jews in a house not far from Drancy – a former asylum on the rue Lamarck in Montmartre. They did not know it yet, but this was their first step towards liberation. Their father had received the letter his wife had written from Beaune-la-Rolande. As a result he had made a series of payments, first to an influential French Jew, and through him to the French authorities. This meant that Annette and Michel had been, despite their age, reclassified as 'fur workers' and so transferred out of Drancy. Once they arrived at the new holding centre their father arranged for the children to be taken away by representatives of a Catholic orphanage, where they were hidden for the duration of the war.

The vast majority of the thousands of children sent to Drancy in the summer of 1942 were not so lucky. Between 17 August and the end of the month seven trains were dispatched from the camp to Auschwitz, carrying the children who had been separated from their parents at Beaune-la-Rolande and Pithiviers. 'The morning before the departure we dressed the children as best we could,' says Odette Daltroff-Baticle. 'Most of them couldn't even carry their little suitcase. And their suitcases were mixed up, we didn't know what belonged to whom. They didn't want to go downstairs to the bus and we had to take them. After thousands of them left I remember there were about eighty or so in the infirmary that we thought we were going to be able to save – but not at all. One day they told us that even these eighty were going to leave. And the morning of the deportation when we tried to take them downstairs they screamed and kicked. They absolutely didn't want to go down. The *gendarmes* came upstairs and with a lot of difficulty they made them. One or two of the *gendarmes* seemed a little bit sad to see this horrible show.'

Jo Nisenman,[18] then 18 years old, left Drancy on a transport for Auschwitz on 26 August. On the train were 700 adults and 400 children, including his ten-year-old sister who was 'blonde and very pretty'. Of the 90 or so people in his wagon, around 30 of them were children being deported without their parents. Jo remembers how the children 'stoically' endured life in the freight train during the lengthy journey to Auschwitz. 'We arrived after two or three days – I can't tell you exactly how long – at the station before Auschwitz. And they needed some men who were in good health because there was a work camp nearby. So they stopped the train and took out 250 people.' Jo was one of the adults selected to leave the train: 'They forced us to get out with sticks. They wouldn't have let us stay. I left my sister there ... But in spite of everything we couldn't imagine what was going to happen ... I don't remember them crying. I saw these little ones, some of them very cute, and they were exterminated. It was atrocious.' Sixty years on, Jo Nisenman recalls daily the suffering of his sister and the rest of the children from Drancy: 'Behind where I live there's a nursery school where I see the mothers waiting in line for their kids with little chocolate croissants for them. But these children didn't have their mothers. They didn't have the chocolate croissant ... '

Of all the many terrible incidents from the history of the Nazi extermination of the Jews, the story of the murder of the Jewish children sent from France is one of the most profoundly affecting. At the heart of the story, of course, is the shocking image of the separation of children from their parents. But it is not just the horrific idea of children being ripped from their mothers' arms at camps like Beaune-la-Rolande that is so upsetting. It is rather that some parents, like the mothers who told their sons to run away during the initial round-up, had to act against instinct and abandon their own children so that they might survive. The emotional trauma involved in such actions must have been devastating.

Even Hoess observed how families in Auschwitz wanted to stay together at all costs. And though the selection process separated men from women, husbands from wives, the Nazis soon learnt that it was almost always counter to their own interests to separate mothers forcibly from their children. Even though the Nazis lost valuable labour by sending some young, healthy women to the gas chambers with their offspring, they realized that to wrench boys and girls from their mothers against their will at the initial selection would result in such horrendous scenes that efficient management of the killing process would be almost impossible. Moreover, the upset involved in such separation would be so great as to rival the emotional disturbance caused to the killing squads by shooting women and children at close range – the very trauma that the gas chambers had been designed to diminish.

After the transports of children in the summer of 1942, the French authorities came to the same conclusion. So disturbing was the image of small children fending for themselves, deprived of their mothers, that after the last train containing parentless children left Drancy on 31 August an order was given that such transports were not to be repeated. Never again, as far as the French deportations were concerned, would children be snatched from their mothers; instead, whole families would be sent to Auschwitz together. It is important, however, to draw from this decision the right conclusion, which is not that the French authorities had suddenly developed a sense of compassion but rather that they had realized, just as much as Hoess did at Auschwitz, that it would be easier for them, in pursuit of their own interests, if they avoided separating mothers from their children.

There is another reason that this story sticks in the gullet so badly: the complicity at every stage of the French authorities. As the Nazis knew from the first, it would be impossible to deport the Jews without the collaboration of the French. And the French decision to hand over 'foreign' Jews rather than their 'own' Jews betrays a level of cynicism that is breathtaking even at this distance of time (though this was a decision which, as later chapters will reveal, was to be repeated by several other countries in the years to come). Altogether just under 80,000 Jews were killed as a result of deportation from France during the war, which represents about 20–25 per cent of the total Jewish population in France at the time. That figure, which means that roughly four out of five Jews in France survived the war, is sometimes quoted by apologists as a 'healthy' statistic, showing that the French authorities behaved with relative honour in the face of Nazi occupation. On the contrary, it demonstrates precisely the reverse, since almost certainly little would have happened had the French refused to cooperate in handing over their 'foreign' Jews. Even after the occupation of the whole of France in November 1942, the Nazis did not enforce violent reprisals when the French authorities dragged their feet and the German targets for deportations were subsequently not met.

In the wake of the Paris round-up of July 1942, and the expulsion of the children, there was considerable protest from Church leaders about the actions of the French political leadership. The archbishop of Toulouse ordered a pastoral letter of protest to be read out in his diocese on 23 August, and the archbishop of Lyons told Laval when he met him on 1 September that he supported both protest action and the hiding of Jewish children by Catholics. But all this was too late to affect those taken in the Paris sweep that July. Michel and Annette Muller's mother, snatched from her children at Beaune-la-Rolande, died at Auschwitz. And whilst it was the Nazis who wished her dead, it was the French who put her in harm's way. 'What struck me most,' says Michel, 'was that it was completely gratuitous. People were arrested simply because they were born Jewish. And it was the French who did that – that's still beyond me. Sixty years later, it's still unbelievable to me.'

Every single one of the more than 4000 children deported without their parents from France in the summer of 1942 died at Auschwitz. 'When my two brothers escaped [from the initial round-up],' says Annette, 'there was one of their friends from school whose mother pushed him to escape. And this boy, when he found himself in the street, he didn't want to stay alone. He really wanted to go back and join his mother. So he begged a police officer to [be allowed to] go back to where his mother was, so he was sent off to the gas chambers. These were children with lots of plans. They were full of joy – the joy of life. But because they were Jewish they were condemned like that. And how many of these children had skills, talents, qualities?'

There are witnesses to the separation of the French children from their parents, to their suffering at the various holding camps, even to their 'stoic' attitude on the transports, but until now, once they entered the gates of Auschwitz there was only silence. Trying to imagine this or other similar scenes of selection – still more trying to imagine what it must have been like to participate in the process as a perpetrator – has been almost impossible. The only way to penetrate that darkness would be to find a credible witness who had belonged to the SS and worked at Auschwitz. Exceptionally, and only after many months of research, we obtained an interview with just such a person: Oskar Groening.

In 1942, when he was 21 years old, Groening was posted to Auschwitz. He arrived just weeks after the French children, and almost immediately witnessed a transport arriving at 'the ramp', the platform where the Jews disembarked. 'I was standing at the ramp,' he says,[19] 'and my task was to be part of the group supervising the luggage from an incoming transport.' He watched while SS doctors first separated men from women and children, and then selected who was fit to work and who should be gassed immediately. 'Sick people were lifted on to lorries,' says Groening. 'Red Cross lorries – they always tried to create the impression that people had nothing to fear.' He estimates that between 80 and 90 per cent of those on the first transport he witnessed in September 1942 were selected to be murdered at once. 'This process [of selection] proceeded in a relatively orderly fashion,' he says, 'but when it was over it was just like a fairground. There was a load of rubbish, and next to this rubbish were ill people, unable to walk, perhaps a child that had lost its mother, or perhaps during searching the train somebody had hidden. And these people were simply killed with a shot through the head. The kind of way in which these people were treated brought me doubt and outrage. A child was simply pulled by the leg and thrown on a lorry ... then when it cried like a sick chicken, they chucked it against the edge of the lorry. I couldn't understand that an SS man would take a child and throw its head against the side of a lorry ... or kill them by shooting them and then throw them on a lorry like a sack of wheat.'

Groening, according to his story, was so filled by 'doubt and outrage' that he went to his superior officer and told him: 'It's impossible, I can't work here any more. If it is necessary to exterminate the Jews, then at least it should be done within a certain framework. I told him this and said, "I want to go away from here."' His superior officer calmly listened to Groening's complaints, reminded him of the SS oath of allegiance he had sworn, and said that he should 'forget' any idea of leaving Auschwitz. But he also offered hope – of a kind. He told Groening that the 'excesses' he saw that night were an 'exception', and that he himself agreed that members of the SS should not participate in such 'sadistic' events. Documents confirm that Groening subsequently put in for a transfer to the front, which was refused. So he carried on working at Auschwitz.

Significantly, Groening did not complain to his boss about the *principle* of murdering the Jews, merely its practical implementation. When he saw people in front of him whom he knew were going to die within hours in the gas chambers, he says his feelings were 'very ambiguous'. 'How do you feel,' he says, 'when you're in Russia, here's a machine gun in front of you, and there's a battalion of Russians coming running towards you and you have to pull the trigger and shoot as many as possible? I'm saying it on purpose like this because there's always behind you the fact that the Jews are enemies who come from the inside of Germany. The propaganda had for us such an effect that you assumed that to exterminate them was basically something that happened in war. And to that extent a feeling of sympathy or empathy didn't come up.' When pressed for the reason why children were murdered, Groening replies: 'The children are not the enemy at the moment. The enemy is the blood in them. The enemy is their growing up to become a Jew who could be dangerous. And because of that the children were also affected.'

Clues as to how it was possible that Oskar Groening felt helpless women and children were 'enemies' who had to face 'extermination' can be found in his life before he was posted to Auschwitz. He was born in 1921 in Lower Saxony, son of a skilled textile worker. His father was a traditional conservative, 'proud of what Germany had achieved'. One of Groening's earliest memories is of looking at photographs of his grandfather, who served in an elite regiment of soldiers from the Duchy of Brunswick: 'His position impressed me terribly when I was a boy. He was sitting on his horse and playing his trumpet. It was fascinating.' After Germany's defeat in World War I Groening's father joined the right-wing Stahlhelm (Steel Helmet), one of the many ultra-nationalist organizations that flourished in the wake of what they proclaimed was the humiliating peace of Versailles. His father's anger at the way Germany had been treated grew more intense as his personal circumstances became more strained; lacking capital, his textile business went bankrupt in 1929. In the early 1930s young Oskar joined the Stahlhelm's youth organization, the Scharnhorst: 'I wore a military grey cap, shirt and trousers. We looked rather odd, but we were proud of it. And we also wore black, white and red, the colours of the former flag of Emperor Wilhelm.'

Nothing felt more natural for Oskar Groening, 11 years old when the Nazis came to power in 1933, than to ease from the Stahlhelm's Scharnhorst into the Hitler Youth. He adopted the values of his parents and judged that the Nazis 'were the people who wanted the best for Germany and who did something about it'. As a member of the Hitler Youth, he took part in the burning of books written by 'Jews or others who were degenerate'. And he believed that by doing so he was helping rid Germany of an inappropriate, alien culture. At the same time, he thought National Socialism was demonstrably working on the economic front: 'Within six months [of the Nazis coming to power] the 5 million unemployed had vanished from the streets and so everybody had work. Then [in 1936] Hitler marched into the Rhineland [demilitarized under the terms of the Versailles treaty] and simply occupied it; nobody tried to stop him. We were terribly happy about this – my father opened a bottle of wine.'

In the meantime, young Oskar went to school, and though feeling he was at times 'rather lazy and perhaps a little bit stupid' he eventually finished high in his final class, and at 17 began a traineeship as a bank clerk. Shortly after he started work in the bank war was declared; eight out of the twenty clerks were immediately conscripted into the army and their places taken by young women. This meant that the remaining trainees, such as Groening, could 'get jobs they would have never normally attained. For example, I had to take over the cash till.' But despite this unexpected advance in their banking careers, as they heard news of Germany's quick victories in Poland and France the trainees were filled with 'euphoria' and a feeling that 'you wanted to be part of it' and 'you wanted to help'.

Oskar Groening wanted to join an 'elite' unit of the German army, just as his grandfather had done. And for this young man only one unit fulfilled his dream: 'The Waffen SS was formed from units of the SA [Nazi stormtroopers] when it was important to have a unit that you could absolutely rely on. At the party meetings the last unit to walk by was the black uniform [of the SS] and nobody was less than one metre ninety – it was so uplifting.' So without telling his father, Oskar went along to a hotel where the

Waffen SS were recruiting and joined up. 'And when I came home my father said, "I was hoping that because you were wearing glasses you wouldn't be accepted." And then he said, "I'm sorry, but you'll see what you'll get out of this."'

What Oskar Groening got out of his membership of this elite corps was, initially, a job in SS administration as a book-keeper. He was not at all displeased by this posting: 'I'm a desk person. I wanted to work in a job that had both the soldier's life and also the bureaucratic aspect.' He worked as a book-keeper for a year until September 1942, when the order came through that fit, healthy members of the SS working in salary administration centres were to be transferred to more challenging duties, with the administrative jobs reserved for returning veterans disabled at the front: 'So, under the assumption that we would now enter a fighting unit, about 22 of us went with our luggage and got on a train to Berlin. It was very strange, because generally an order would have come for us to go to a troop-mustering place, but that didn't happen.'

Groening and his comrades reported to one of the SS economic offices, located in a 'beautiful building' in the capital. They were then directed to a conference room where they were addressed by several high-ranking SS officers: 'We had to listen to a lecture where we were told we had to fulfil orders that were given in trust – a task that wouldn't be without difficulties. We were reminded that we had sworn an oath with the motto 'My loyalty is my honour', and that we could prove this loyalty by doing this task which was now given to us, the details of which we would find out later. Then a subordinate SS leader said we were to keep absolutely silent about this task. It was top secret, so that neither our relatives, or friends or comrades or people who were not in the unit were to be told anything about it. So we had to march forward individually and sign a statement to this effect.'

Once in the courtyard of the building, Groening and his comrades were split into smaller groups, given their individual destinations, and then transported to various Berlin stations where they boarded trains. 'We went south,' says Oskar Groening, 'in the direction of Katowice. And our troop leader, who had the papers, said we had to report to the commandant of Auschwitz concentration camp. I'd never heard of Auschwitz before.'

They arrived late in the evening and were directed by military police to the main camp, where they reported to the central administrative building and were allocated 'provisional' bunks in the SS barracks. The other members of the SS they met in the barracks that night were friendly and welcoming. 'We were accepted by the people who were there and they said, "Have you eaten anything yet?" We hadn't, and so they got us something.' Groening was surprised that in addition to the basic SS rations of bread and sausage there was also extra food available, consisting of tins of rollmops and sardines. Their new friends also had rum and vodka, which they put on the table and said, 'Help yourself.' 'We did this, and so we were quite happy. We asked, "What kind of place is this?" and they said we should find out for ourselves – that it's a special kind of concentration camp. Suddenly, the door opened and somebody said, "Transport!", which caused three or four people to jump up and vanish.'

After a good night's sleep Groening reported once more with the other new arrivals to the central SS administrative building. They were quizzed by a number of senior SS officers about their background before the war: 'We had to say what we'd been doing, what kind of job, what level of education. I said that I was a bank clerk and that I wanted to work in administration, and one of the officers said, "Oh, I can use someone like that." So I was taken with him and went to a barracks where the prisoners' money was kept. I was told that when they got their prison number their money was registered here, and when they left they got it back again.'

So far Oskar Groening's personal experience of Auschwitz was that it was a 'normal' concentration camp, albeit one where the rations for the SS were particularly good. But as he began his task of registering the prisoners' money, he learnt for the first time about the additional, 'unusual' function of Auschwitz: 'The people there [working in the barracks] let us know that this money didn't all go back to the prisoners. Jews were taken to the camp who were treated differently. The money was taken off them without them getting it back.' Groening asked, 'Is this to do with the "transport" that arrived during the night?' And his colleagues replied, 'Well, don't you know? That's the way it is here. Jewish transports arrive, and if they're not able to work, they're got rid of.' Groening pressed them on what 'got rid of' actually meant, and, having been told, his reaction was one of astonishment: 'You cannot imagine it really. I could only accept it fully when I was guarding the valuables and the suitcases at the selection. If you ask me about it – it was a shock that you cannot take in at the first moment. But you mustn't forget that not only from 1933 [Hitler's acquisition of power], but even from before that, the propaganda I got as a boy in the press, the media, the general society I lived in made us aware that the Jews were the cause of the First World War, and had also "stabbed Germany in the back" at the end. And that the Jews were actually the cause of the misery in which Germany found herself. We were convinced by our world-view that there was a great conspiracy of Jewishness against us, and that thought was expressed in Auschwitz – that it must be avoided, what happened in the First World War must be avoided, namely that the Jews put us into misery. The enemies who are within Germany are being killed – exterminated if necessary. And between these two fights, openly at the front line and then on the home front, there's absolutely no difference – so we exterminated nothing but enemies.'

To meet Oskar Groening today, and listen to his attempt to explain his time at Auschwitz, is a strange experience. Now in his eighties, he talks almost as if there was another Oskar Groening who worked at Auschwitz 60 years ago, and about that 'other' Groening he can be brutally honest. Crucially, he shields himself from taking full responsibility for playing a part in the extermination process by constantly referring to the power of the propaganda to which he was exposed, and the effect on him of the ultra-nationalistic family atmosphere in which he grew up. Only after the war, once he was exposed to another world-view – one that questioned the Nazis' assumptions about the 'international Jewish conspiracy' and the role of the Jews in World War I – was the 'new' Oskar Groening able to emerge, fit to face life as a useful citizen in the modern, democratic Germany.

This is not to say that Groening attempts to hide behind the 'acting under orders' defence. He does not present himself as a mindless automaton who would have followed any command given to him. When the suggestion is put to him that he would have accepted 'Aryan' children being murdered at Auschwitz, he rejects it absolutely. He gives the lie to the notion, prevalent amongst some historians, that the SS were so brutalized by their training that they would have killed anyone they were asked to. No, Groening's decision-making process operated at a much less simplistic level. Yes, he claims that he was massively influenced by the propaganda of the times, but nonetheless he made a series of personal choices during the war. He carried on working at Auschwitz not just because he was ordered to but because, having weighed the evidence put before him, he thought that the extermination programme was right. Once the war was over he disputed the accuracy of the evidence put before him, but he did not claim that he acted as he did because he was some kind of robot. Throughout his life he believes he did what he thought was 'right'; it's just that what was 'right' then turns out not to be 'right' today.

We should not be unduly cynical about such a coping mechanism. Of course he could have chosen differently. He could have rejected the values of his community and resisted. He could have deserted from Auschwitz (although there is no record of any member of the SS doing so as a result of refusing on moral grounds to work in the camp). But it would have taken an exceptional human being to act in such a way. And the essential, almost frightening, point about Oskar Groening is that he is one of the least exceptional human beings you are ever likely to meet. After a few years as a prisoner of war, he got a job as a personnel manager in a glass-making factory, where he worked quietly until he reached retirement. The only abnormality in Groening's otherwise ultra-normal life is the time he spent working in Auschwitz.

A study of the historical-sociological profile of the SS in Auschwitz, based on statistical records, found that 'the SS camp force was not exceptional in its occupation structure or in its levels of education. The camp staff was very much like the society from which it was drawn.'[20] Oskar Groening perfectly illustrates this conclusion. He was also typical in that he was a rank-and-file member of the SS – the highest rank he attained was Rottenführer (corporal). Around 70 per cent of SS men in Auschwitz fell into this category; 26 per cent were non-commissioned officers (non-commissioned ranks above Rottenführer); and just 4 per cent of the total SS complement were officers. There were around 3000 members of the SS serving in Auschwitz 1 and the related sub-camps at any one time.[21] The SS administration of the camp was divided into five main departments: the headquarters department (personnel, legal and other related functions), the medical unit (doctors and dentists), the political department (the Gestapo and criminal police, the Kripo), the economic administration (including the registration and disposal of property stolen from the murdered prisoners) and the camp administration (responsible for security within the camp). By far the biggest department was the last – around 75 per cent of the SS who worked at Auschwitz performed some kind of security function. Oskar Groening was unusual only in that he had a comparatively 'easy' job as part of the economic administration.

By the summer of 1942 Auschwitz was receiving transports of Jews from all over Europe, including Slovakia, France, Belgium and the Netherlands. The policy that had been in operation since the end of 1941, of sending Jews from the West to holding ghettos such as Łódź where further selection could take place before those Jews 'unfit for work' were murdered, was abolished. Once Auschwitz developed selection on arrival, the whole extermination process was streamlined. The camp's corrosive influence now even reached part of the United Kingdom – the holiday island of Guernsey in the Channel Islands. For those people, and there are still many, who partly define 'Britishness' by the United Kingdom's resistance to Hitler, and who are certain that no one in England, Scotland or Wales would have collaborated with the Nazis had they arrived on these shores, this is a profoundly disturbing story.

The Channel Islands, a small archipelago off the northwest coast of France whose biggest and principal islands are Jersey and Guernsey, were never capable of being defended by the British. Loyal to the British Crown, but fiercely independent of the British government, the islands were occupied by the Germans without a struggle in June and July 1940. Just as in France, the Germans preferred to run their occupation as far as possible through the existing government infrastructure; this was to be a very different kind of occupation from that practised in Poland or the Soviet Union. Nonetheless, the Nazis were, in principle, as intolerant of the presence of Jews in the Channel Islands as they were in Minsk or Warsaw. In October 1941 a notice was published in the *Jersey*

Evening Post calling on Jews to register with Clifford Orange, chief aliens officer in Jersey. That same month a similar notice appeared in the *Guernsey Evening Post*, calling on all Jews to come forward and make themselves known to the police.

Knowing of the imminent arrival of the Germans, the majority of the Jewish population had already escaped to the British mainland. Only a small number of Jews unable, or unwilling, to leave were left behind. As a result, twelve Jews registered on Jersey and four on Guernsey. The registration process, as throughout the Nazi state, was the beginning of systemized persecution. Jewish businesses had first to display a sign in the window announcing 'Jewish undertaking', and then the businesses were 'Aryanized' and compulsorily sold to non-Jews. The Channel Island authorities cooperated in this process; indeed, it was administered by them. A typical, and heartrending, letter from one of the Jersey Jews, Nathan Davidson, to the Attorney General on Jersey dated 23 January 1941 reads: 'In accordance with your instructions I beg to inform you that I have finished the winding up of my business ... the blind on the window pulled down and a notice CLOSED displayed.'[22] Clifford Orange was able in June 1941 to confirm to the Bailiff (the leader of the island's government) on Jersey, and through him to the German authorities, that 'there are no Jews, registered as such, in the island who are carrying on businesses'.[23]

Subsequent orders restricted the hours during which the Jews on the Channel Islands could go shopping and imposed a curfew on them. The only discriminatory order the authorities on Jersey baulked at was one stating that Jews should wear the yellow star. In this one case the Bailiff and Attorney General appealed to the German authorities and asked them to reconsider. But despite their protests, Dr Casper, the German commandant, still requested that special stars be sent to the island with the English word 'Jew' instead of 'Jude' printed in the middle. The stars appear never to have arrived. Subjected to curfew as they were, few Channel Islands Jews could earn a living. Nathan Davidson, having shut down his shop, simply collapsed under the weight of the persecution heaped upon him. He was admitted to a Jersey mental hospital in February 1943 and died the following year. Another Jersey Jew, Victor Emmanuel, committed suicide.

But it was on nearby Guernsey that the actual physical deportation of Jews began. Three women – Auguste Spitz, Marianne Grunfeld and Therese Steiner – were transported from the island in April 1942. All three were foreign nationals, Spitz and Steiner Austrian, Grunfeld Polish. They all therefore knew only too well the Nazis' hatred of Jews. Therese Steiner, for example, had left her native Austria as the country grew ever more anti-Semitic. Eventually she had found work as a nanny, working for an English family who came to the Channel Islands in 1939. They returned to the British mainland in the spring of 1940, but Therese was prevented by the Channel Islands authorities from leaving and, following British Home Office guidelines, was interned as a 'foreign alien'. She thus ended up in the hands of the very people she had come to the United Kingdom to escape. Therese managed to find work as a nurse at a hospital in Guernsey, where Barbara Newman[24] knew her well: 'She was quite good-looking and had very nice curly waving hair and a Jewish nose – that was the only thing. She used to talk very quickly, with an accent of course. She was a bit dogmatic about things, which makes it difficult sometimes. But we were quite good friends, really.' And Barbara Newman was very clear about Therese's attitude to the Nazis: 'I was under the impression that she'd spit on them if she could. That's the way she felt about them.'

In the spring of 1942 the German authorities ordered the Guernsey government to deliver the three foreign Jews for deportation. Sergeant Ernest Plevin of the Guernsey police recalled ordering Therese Steiner to pack her bags and report to the Germans: 'I do remember, well, Therese coming into the office, where I conveyed to her the instructions given to the Guernsey police by the German military authorities. Therese became extremely distressed, bursting into tears, and exclaiming that I would never see her again.'[25]

Barbara Newman accompanied Therese on her last walk on Guernsey, down to St Peter Port on Tuesday, 21 April 1942: 'I've still got a picture in my mind – I think we must have taken her suitcase on a bike. Wheeled it, you know, as one does. And we stood there, saying goodbye and seeing her go through the gateway in the barrier and waving as she went ... Everything was out of our control. You couldn't worry because you couldn't have carried on if you'd worried too much about it. You just had to accept orders and get used to it. And I used to think to myself, "How is everyone going to manage after the war's finished? We won't have anyone telling us what to do."' The idea that Therese was leaving Guernsey to be transported to her death was inconceivable to Barbara Newman: 'It was all outside our experience, really, wasn't it? Things like that don't happen in England.'

Auguste Spitz, Marianne Grunfeld and Therese Steiner all placed themselves in the hands of the Germans at St Peter Port and boarded a boat that took them to the French mainland. Once in France, they registered as Jews and Therese Steiner found temporary employment as a nurse. In July they all became caught up in the mass deportation of foreign Jews from France. On the 20th they were transported to Auschwitz, arriving there three days later. It is not known whether any of the three survived initial selection. What is known with certainty is that none of them survived the war. Therese had been right – the citizens of Guernsey would never see her again.

The remaining Jews on the Channel Islands were deported the following year, in February 1943. But they were sent to an altogether different fate. Their deportation – together with others taken from a broad spectrum of Channel Islanders, including 'Freemasons', 'former officers of the armed forces' and 'suspected Communists'[26] – had been ordered in retaliation for the British commando raid on Sark, one of the smallest of the inhabited Channel Islands, five months before. Only one of the deported Channel Island Jews was singled out by the Germans for 'special treatment' – John Max Finkelstein, originally from Romania, who was eventually sent to Buchenwald concentration camp and then the special ghetto at Theresienstadt. He survived the war.

The other deportees, including the Jews, were sent to internment camps in France and Germany, where their treatment, though extremely unpleasant, was not comparable with the suffering imposed on the inmates of Buchenwald or Auschwitz. Significantly, the Jews (with the exception of John Max Finkelstein) were not separated from the other Channel Islanders. We can only speculate as to why they were treated this way by the Nazis – there were always anomalies in the implementation of the 'Final Solution'. In this case it is perhaps significant both that they were deported along with other categories of people who would have been considered less 'dangerous' by the Germans, and also that they were Jewish nationals from a country that the Nazis considered 'civilized' and perhaps still did not wish to alienate overtly (along the same lines, Jews transported in the autumn of 1943 from Denmark were sent to Theresienstadt and not to Auschwitz).

Of course, whilst the authorities in the Channel Islands helped the Germans deport the Jews, they could not have known for certain what their fate was going to be. But they were aware that the Nazis had singled out the Jews for persecution and that they were almost certainly about to transport their victims to a worse life than the one, already full of suffering, that they had left behind. Yet the authorities did nothing to prevent the deportations. On the contrary, the police and civil servants cooperated promptly with the Germans. It is true that the authorities on Jersey protested at the implementation of the Yellow Star order (though those on Guernsey did not). But it is also hugely significant, as Frederick Cohen points out in his pioneering study of the treatment of Channel Island Jews during the occupation,[27] that much more effort was made by the authorities to protect Masons who were living on the islands. A British intelligence report from August 1945 states: 'When the Germans proposed to put their anti-Jewish measures into force, no protest whatever was raised by any of the Guernsey officials and they hastened to give the Germans every assistance. By contrast, when it was proposed to take steps against the Freemasons, of which there are many in Guernsey, the Bailiff made considerable protests and did everything possible to protect the Masons.'[28]

We can't know for certain what would have happened if the Guernsey authorities had protested vehemently at the deportation of Auguste Spitz, Marianne Grunfeld and Therese Steiner. Probably it would have made little practical difference – though it would remain to this day a proud moment in the history of Guernsey – but there still remains the possibility that speaking out at the time might have saved the lives of these three women who had sought sanctuary in the United Kingdom. That fact on its own is enough to make this incident an indelible stain on the island's past.

The same month that the three deportees from Guernsey arrived at Auschwitz, Heinrich Himmler made another visit to the camp.

On 17 July 1942 the Reichsführer SS drove in through the camp gates, 15 months after his first tour of inspection. Kazimierz Smoleń,[29] one of the Polish political prisoners, remembered Himmler from before: 'He looked not quite a military man. He had glasses with gold rims. He was a bit fat and had a tummy. He looked like – and I'm sorry, I don't want to offend anyone – he looked like a provincial schoolteacher.'

On this visit the ordinary-looking man with glasses and a tummy saw the camp transformed, with a whole new complex under construction at Birkenau. He spent time examining the plans for the future development of the camp and travelled around the 25 square miles of the Auschwitz Zone of Interest (the area under the direct administrative control of the camp). Then he watched the selection of a newly arrived group of prisoners and their subsequent gassing in 'The Little White House'. After witnessing the killings Himmler attended a reception in his honour at the home of Gauleiter Bracht in the nearby city of Katowice. The next day he returned and toured the women's camp in Birkenau. Here he witnessed the flogging of one of the inmates, a punishment he himself authorized. And so pleased was Himmler with what he saw at Auschwitz that he immediately promoted Rudolf Hoess to the rank of SS Obersturmbannführer (Lieutenant Colonel).

Hoess's career was blooming. The visit of the Reichsführer had been a huge success. But there remained at least one problem: his SS bosses were concerned at the number of escapes from Auschwitz. Escapes were not a new phenomenon in the history of the camp: the first recorded one had taken place as early as 6 July 1940. But what led to a warning to be issued to all SS concentration camp commanders in the summer of 1942 were the circumstances of one particularly daring break-out from Auschwitz that had occurred just a few weeks before Himmler's visit.

The plan was masterminded by Kazimierz (Kazik) Piechowski,[30] a Polish political prisoner who had been in Auschwitz for 18 months. He was only too aware of the risks involved: 'There had been all kinds of attempts to escape before, but the majority failed because at roll-call when one person was found missing they [the SS and Kapos] started searching with specially trained dogs and they would find the escapee hidden under some planks or between cement sacks. When they found such a prisoner they would put a sign on his back saying, "Hooray! Hooray! I'm back with you again!" and he would have to beat a big drum and walk up and down the camp and then walk to the gallows. He walked very slowly, as if he wanted to prolong his life.' Another troubling concern for any potential escapee was the terrible consequences for the remaining prisoners if someone was found to have escaped from their block. As with the case of Father Maksymilian Kolbe, ten prisoners from the escapee's block would be selected to starve to death. 'This caused a real paralysis for some prisoners,' says Piechowski, 'but others didn't want to think about what would happen. They wanted to get out of this hell at all costs.'

Before Piechowski faced this double challenge, to escape from the camp and yet prevent reprisals against those who stayed behind, he needed to surmount a more immediate obstacle – simply staying alive. At first he worked outside in the snow in one of the worst commandos of all: 'There was heavy work and the food was hopeless. I was on my way to becoming a "Muselmann"[31] – that's what SS men called prisoners who had lost contact with reality. I felt helpless.' Then he became the beneficiary of a vital piece of luck. He was selected for another work commando: 'I joined this commando and as we walked through the gate I asked my friend next to me, "Where are we going?" My colleague said, "Don't you know? Well, you've won! Because we work in the warehouse. It's a heavy job, but at least you're not outside in the frost. You'll have a roof over your head." I thought I had gone straight to heaven.' Piechowski also found that working inside in the 'heaven' of the warehouse had one extra benefit: 'My comrades taught me that if there's a wagon and we're loading it with flour then I should hit the sack so the flour would come out. The guard would then tell us to get rid of it. But we didn't throw it away. We mixed it with water and made ravioli.' As a result of this change in fortune Piechowski felt that he 'could survive'.

Then one day, shortly after he began work in the warehouse, he had a conversation with a Ukrainian prisoner, Eugeniusz (Genek) Bendera, who worked in the nearby SS garage as a mechanic. 'He [Bendera] walked out to work with us and then returned with us, and one day he confided to me that he'd been told he was on the list of people to be killed – the selections were frequent. He said to me, "Kazik, what am I to do? I'm on the death list!" I told him, "There's nothing I can do." But he persevered and said, "Kazik, why don't we escape from here?" For me this was a shock – how could we escape? And he said, "Well, a car. I could get a car any time." And I started thinking whether it was possible. And I told Genek that we would also need some uniforms to be able to leave – SS uniforms.'

It was at this point that the idea of escape stalled. How could they possibly get their hands on any SS uniforms? Then, once again, they were blessed by good fortune. Piechowski was told by his Kapo to go to the second floor of the warehouse in which they were working and bring down some empty boxes. Walking down the corridor, he saw on one of the doors a sign that read 'Uniforms' in German. He tried the door but it was locked. Then one day shortly afterwards he was sent upstairs on the same mission by his Kapo and this time noticed the door was slightly ajar. 'So the only thing I could think of,' says Piechowski, 'was to enter and see what will happen. I opened the door and this SS man was putting something on the shelf and he started hitting me and kicking me. I fell on the floor. "You swine!" he said. "You Polish swine, you dog, you've no right to be here! Report to the main office, you Polish pig." So I crawled out to the corridor.'

But Piechowski knew that if he reported that he had entered the room it meant transfer to the Penal Commando and almost certain death. So he did nothing and hoped for the best, and the best duly arrived. He escaped punishment altogether as the SS man he had disturbed failed to follow up the incident – another lucky break in a string of accidental good fortune. He had gambled and won, since he had also been able to glimpse just what the room contained: uniforms, grenades, ammunition, helmets, in fact everything he and his comrades needed.

The best day to attempt the escape was a Saturday, since the SS did not work in this area of the camp at the weekend. And Piechowski devised a way to gain access to the warehouse by removing one of the screws on a hatch that was used to enable coal to be poured into storage bins in the basement. From the coal store they could enter the rest of the building. Piechowski was now determined to attempt the break-out, until, lying in his bunk, a 'thunderbolt' struck him. He realized that 'ten people will be killed for every one person who escapes'. 'I couldn't sleep all night – this thought pestered me,' he says, 'until in one split second it came to me. There is one way [to prevent this]: a fictitious work commando.' Piechowski's plan was that four of them would leave the main camp posing as a *Rollwagen* commando, pushing a cart. They would then officially be signed out of the inner security compound, though still be within the outer area where many of the inmates worked. If they subsequently disappeared it was possible that their block Kapo would be held solely responsible, since he would be assumed to have sanctioned the commando.

It was a daring plan, and it required them to find two more prisoners prepared to take the risk since a total of four were now required to make up the *Rollwagen* commando. Bendera immediately recruited one of the priests imprisoned in his block, Jósef Lempart, but then they ran into difficulties. Piechowski approached one of his closest friends but the man said he would take part only if he could, in turn, bring someone else. This was impossible since only four people could be in the commando. The next friend Piechowski approached said, 'There's maybe a chance, but it's minimal,' and so he refused. Finally a youth from Warsaw, a former boy scout, called Stanisław Jaster, agreed to go with them even though he felt the enterprise was 'high risk'.

Jaster immediately spotted the utterly unpredictable element on which the whole escape hinged – whether the SS guards at the outer perimeter gate would let them drive through without asking to see any documents. If the guards did their job properly and stopped the car, they would be finished. In such circumstances, the escapees agreed, rather than shoot at the SS they would turn their guns on themselves. They feared that, if even one SS man died during their escape, the reprisals against the rest of the camp would be horrendous; perhaps 500 or 1000 prisoners would be killed.

Saturday, 20 June 1942 was the date they fixed for their escape attempt. In the morning two of them put on armbands and thus pretended they were Kapos, and then all four pushed a handcart laden with rubbish out through the '*Arbeit macht frei*' gate of Auschwitz 1 towards the camp perimeter beyond. 'By the gate,' says Piechowski, 'I said to the guard in German, 'Prisoner nine hundred and eighteen plus three others with the Rollwagen going to the warehouse.' He [the SS guard] put it down in his book and let us go.' Once past the gate Eugeniusz Bendera made his way to the deserted SS garage to prepare the car while the other three entered the warehouse by the coal hatch. Then they saw that the door to the clothes storage area on the second floor was held fast by a heavy steel rod, but Stanisław, 'full of energy', took a pickaxe and smashed it open. Once inside, they hurriedly selected uniforms for themselves and for Bendera. They also took four machine guns and eight grenades.

The three of them, dressed as SS men, were about to leave the warehouse when they heard two Germans talking outside. 'I didn't know what to do,' says Piechowski. 'What if they enter? But then it was a miracle, if you believe in miracles. These guys conversed and they never came into the warehouse. They just left.'

Through the window of the warehouse they gave Bendera a sign to drive the car the few metres up to the entrance. Then he got out of the car and stood to attention in front of his three friends dressed as SS men. 'There was a watchtower every 60 or 70 metres,' says Piechowski, 'and the guard was looking at us, but we didn't care because we're sure of ourselves. Genek took off his hat, said something to me, and I pointed him to the warehouse and there he changed and dressed as an SS man.'

Now the four of them were ready to embark on the most dangerous phase of their escape: 'Off we went. And after the first bend we saw two SS men. Genek said, "Be careful!" We passed them and they said, "*Heil Hitler*!" and we did the same. We drove about three or four hundred metres and there was another SS man repairing a bicycle. He looked at us and said, "*Heil Hitler*!" and we did the same. Now we were on the way to the main gate and the question was whether they will let us through without any documents – but we believed it was possible. The gate was closed and on the right was an SS man with a machine gun and on the left there was a table with a chair and an SS man sitting down. There's still 80 metres to go and Genek reduced the engine to second gear, then 50 metres to go and the gate was still closed. They can see the car, and all of us in SS uniforms, and still the barrier was in place. About 20 metres away I looked at Genek and I could see the sweat on his forehead and nose. And then maybe 15 metres away I thought, "It's time to kill myself" just as we'd decided. At that moment I was hit in the back by the priest – I knew they're counting on me.

So I yelled at the SS: "How long are we going to be waiting here!" I cursed them. And then the SS man at the watchtower said something and he opened the gate and we went through. That was freedom.'

Exhilarated, the four of them drove off through the Polish countryside and within minutes were several miles from Auschwitz. With the help of friends nearby they then changed out of their SS uniforms, abandoned the car and merged back into the ordinary population of Poland. The first part of their plan – their own successful escape – had been accomplished.

Back at Auschwitz, the second part was also shortly achieved. Kazimierz Piechowski's ruse of the fake work commando did save all but one of the remaining prisoners in his block from reprisal. It was his Kapo alone who was singled out for punishment and sent to the starvation cell in Block 11.

But in a telling reminder of how mere physical removal from Auschwitz did not necessarily end the suffering of those who had been incarcerated there, all three of Piechowski's fellow escapees faced difficulties afterwards. Stanisław Jaster had to deal with the terrible knowledge that his parents were sent to Auschwitz in reprisal and died there. He himself was killed in Warsaw during the occupation.[32] Józef, the priest, was so traumatized by his experiences in Auschwitz that, according to Piechowski, he 'walked around in a trance'. After the war he was killed when a bus ran into him. Eugeniusz Bendera, the man who had first suggested they escape when he found himself on the death list, returned home only to find that his wife had left him. He turned to drink and died. Of the original four, only Kazimierz Piechowski is still alive, and he too says he is still in 'psychological turmoil' as a result of the suffering he endured. In his dreams he is attacked by SS men with dogs and awakes 'completely wet with sweat and dissociated mentally'.

However, despite the tribulations all four faced after their dramatic escape from Auschwitz, none of them ever doubted that they had made the right decision to risk everything on flight. And if they had known what was in Himmler's mind as he made his tour of the camp in July 1942, they would have been doubly sure. For the killing in Poland was about to intensify. On 19 July Himmler announced: 'I herewith order that the resettlement of the entire

Jewish population of the General Government be carried out and completed by December 31.' In this context 'resettlement' was a euphemism for 'murder'. Himmler thus revealed that he had set a target date for the annihilation of several million Polish Jews.

However, Himmler's words were less an order for the future and more a final statement. For they were the end result of a cumulative process of decision-making that stretched back to before the invasion of the Soviet Union, the last link in a chain of causation that we can only see with hindsight. Each of the crucial decisions that preceded his announcement – the decision to ghettoize the Polish Jews, the order behind the pit killings in the East and the subsequent gassing experiments, the decision to deport the German Jews and then find a method to kill 'unproductive' Jews in the ghetto to make room for them – all of these actions and more lay behind Himmler's bland but death-dealing statement of 19 July 1942. The conceptual thinking was over; the fundamental decision had already been made months before. The Nazis were going to murder the Jews. All that remained were the practicalities of implementation. And the SS believed they were good at practicalities.

During 1942 the Nazis were to increase massively the rate at which they killed people in pursuit of their 'Final Solution'. Yet the killing capacity at Auschwitz remained limited to the gas chambers of 'The Little Red House' and 'The Little White House' (regular killings at the crematorium in the main camp having been discontinued as a result of the difficulties discussed in Chapter 2). Therefore Auschwitz, despite its subsequent notoriety, was to play only a minor part in the killing of Polish Jews during 1942.

Himmler felt able to order his men to murder the Poles by the end of 1942 not because he thought Auschwitz would play a leading role, but because he knew that the majority of the killings would be carried out at three new camps already established in the forests of Poland: three places that, unlike Auschwitz, have scarcely seeped into the popular consciousness – Bełżec, Sobibór and Treblinka. That these camps are not mentioned today in the same breath as Auschwitz is something of a black irony, because the Nazis themselves wanted their names erased from history and sought to ensure that every physical trace of them was removed once they had completed their murderous task. Long before the end of the war the Nazis had destroyed the camps, and the land was left to return to forest or ploughed back into farmland. By contrast, no attempt was ever made by the Nazis, even in the last days of the camp's existence, to eliminate Auschwitz as a physical place. It was born of an established pre-war model within the Nazi system – the concentration camp – and no effort was made to hide these camps from the general population. Indeed, a camp such as Dachau was built in the suburbs of an existing town and there were propaganda advantages for the Nazis in making obvious their desire to imprison and 're-educate' those whom they considered malcontents. Only once people started to be murdered en masse at Auschwitz did the schizophrenic nature of its function, already discussed, begin to emerge – a state of mind that led the Nazis to blow up the gas chambers when they left, but to leave the rest of the massive complex largely intact.

Something entirely different was born in Bełżec, Sobibór and Treblinka during 1942. There was no precedent for the existence of these camps in the Nazi state, and arguably no precedent for them in the whole of history. No previous model determined their construction, and in many ways their history and operation more exactly encapsulates the uniqueness of the Nazis' 'Final Solution' than does Auschwitz.

Bełżec, the first to be built, was the only one whose history predates 1942. It was in November 1941 that construction began on a small camp about 500 metres from the railway station in the isolated town of Bełżec in the far southeast of occupied Poland. In the minds of the SS this was to be a local solution to a local problem – the need to kill 'unproductive' Jews from the surrounding area. Just as the Chełmno gas van centre was established primarily to kill Jews from the Łódź ghetto, so Bełżec was built to kill 'unwanted' Jews from the Lublin area.

In December 1941 SS Hauptsturmführer (Captain) Christian Wirth arrived at Bełżec to take up the post of commandant. He was 56 years old. Originally trained as a carpenter, he fought in World War I, was awarded medals for bravery, joined the Nazi party and then, during the 1930s, worked for the Gestapo in Stuttgart. In 1939 he became involved in the euthanasia actions against the mentally ill and helped organize their murder by use of bottled carbon monoxide. By 1941 he was working in the Lublin area, conducting more euthanasia killings. Known by the nickname 'savage Christian', Wirth was a sadist. He was once observed whipping a Jewish woman and chasing her into the gas chamber, and he personally murdered Jews with his own hands. Red faced and sweating, he screamed obscenities while encouraging his men to commit bestial acts.

At Bełżec this loathsome man was able to cram all his previous killing experience into one physical space. He decided to use carbon monoxide gas as the means of murder, not supplied from canisters as in the gas chambers of the euthanasia programme but from a normal combustion engine, just as Widmann had used a few months before in the Soviet Union. The three small gas chambers themselves were incorporated into a brick building that was disguised to resemble a shower room, with the carbon monoxide gas delivered through fake shower heads.

So far, with the use of carbon monoxide from a car engine and the pretend showers, Wirth was adapting previous killing techniques. But now, in supervising the layout of the camp, he entered entirely new territory and broke completely with established concentration camp design. First, he realized that since the vast majority of arrivals would be alive only for a matter of hours, the large complex of buildings that characterized Auschwitz or Dachau could be dispensed with. The death camp, unlike the concentration camp, needed relatively few facilities of any kind, and could be contained in a small space. Thus Bełżec measured less than 300 metres by 300 metres.

Visitors to the sites of Bełżec, Sobibór and Treblinka (of whom there are far, far fewer than travel to Auschwitz) are shocked by how tiny these killing camps were. A total of around 1.7 million people were murdered in these three camps – 600,000 more than the murder toll of Auschwitz – and yet all three could fit into the area of Auschwitz–Birkenau with room to spare. In a murder process that is an affront to human dignity at almost every level, one of the greatest affronts – and this may seem illogical unless you have actually been there – is that so many people were killed in such a small area. Somehow the mind associates an epic tragedy with an epic space – another reason, perhaps, that Auschwitz is so much better known today than these three death camps. The massive scale of Birkenau gives the mind space to try to conceive of the enormity of the crime, something that is utterly denied to visitors at a place like Bełżec. How can the brain conceive of 600,000 people, the estimated death toll here, being murdered in an area less than 300 metres by 300 metres?

But small as it was, Bełżec was not simply one camp. Wirth knew that the key to the smooth functioning of his death factory was concealing the true purpose of the place from the new arrivals for as long as possible. So within the camp he enclosed the gas chambers in a special area known as Camp 2, which was hidden behind trees and wire fences woven through with branches. This area was connected to the rest of the camp only by 'the tube', a passageway through the wire. Camp 1 – the rest of Bełżec – consisted of the arrival area next to the railway, various barracks (in which the new arrivals undressed and where their belongings could be stored before being transported out) and a roll-call square.

Three categories of people worked at Bełżec, and subsequently at the other two death camps. The first consisted of Jews. Wirth realized at once that employing the Jews in the killing process would not just spare his own men psychological suffering but would mean that fewer Germans would be needed to run the camp. No doubt the emotional torment this caused the Jews also appealed to his warped sensibilities. So several hundred fit, able-bodied Jews were selected from the arriving transports and put to work burying the bodies, cleaning the gas chambers and sorting the enormous quantity of clothes and other belongings that rapidly piled high in the camp. Initially these Jews were themselves killed after only a few days' work, but their murder soon caused problems for the Nazis. Not only were the Jews under no illusion as to the fate that awaited them when they were ordered to take a 'shower', but after their deaths more Jews had to be selected and trained. On the other hand, allowing them to live longer created a class of inmate who had nothing to lose, since they knew they were all going to be killed at some stage, whilst giving them collectively time to think about their fate and, perhaps, plot a way to resist. For the Nazis there always remained this dilemma – how do you supervise people who know they will eventually be killed by the very people who are in authority over them?

Ukrainian guards comprised the second category of workers.

Around 100 of them, in two platoons, were assigned to carry out basic supervisory duties at the camp. Famed for their brutality, many of these Ukrainians had previously fought for the Red Army, been retrained by the Germans, and were allowed this opportunity to escape the horrendous conditions of the POW camps. And then, of course, there were the Germans, the third category. But so smoothly had Wirth delegated the mechanics of running his killing machine to other nationalities that only 20 or so German SS needed to be involved at Bełżec in the process of murder. By March 1942, with the arrival of the first transport at Bełżec, Wirth had realized Himmler's dream. He had built a killing factory capable of exterminating hundreds of thousands which could be run by a handful of Germans, all of whom were now relatively protected from the psychological damage that had afflicted the firing squads in the East.

The same month in which Bełżec started operating, March 1942, the Nazis began to construct another death camp: Sobibór, due north of Bełżec but still in the far east of Poland in an area densely populated with Polish Jews. The construction and operation of Sobibór closely followed the Bełżec model. Like Wirth, the majority of the SS involved – including the commandant, Franz Stangl – had experience of the T4 euthanasia programme. And just as at Bełżec, around 100 Ukrainians, many former prisoners of war, were allocated to the camp as guards. The camp was still tiny by comparison with Auschwitz–Birkenau (though at 600 metres by 400 metres it was slightly bigger than Bełżec) and was divided, as was Bełżec, into two internal camps separated by a passageway that linked the reception camp to the gas chambers. But since, unlike at Bełżec,where the SS lived in requisitioned houses nearby, there was no suitable local accommodation, a third internal camp was created as living quarters for the SS and the Ukrainian guards.

The thinking behind the design and construction of Sobibór was identical to that at Bełżec. New arrivals were to be conned into believing they had alighted at a disinfecting stop where they would be treated as a precaution against disease, and were then to be hurried through the camp to their deaths as quickly as possible. Just as at Bełżec, high fences intertwined with branches separated each section of the camp so that it would be hard for new arrivals to grasp exactly what was going on until it was too late. Sobibór accepted its first transport in May 1942, and in little over a year a quarter of a million people were murdered there.

Also in May 1942 building work began on the third and last main death camp, Treblinka. It was no coincidence, since this camp benefited from the Nazis' previous learning experiences at Bełżec and Sobibór, that more people died here than at any of the other dedicated death camps. Indeed the death toll at Treblinka – an estimated 800,000 to 900,000 – very nearly rivals that of Auschwitz. Treblinka was situated northwest of Sobibór, a short railway journey away from Warsaw. The Warsaw ghetto represented one of the largest concentrations of Jews in the Nazi state, and Treblinka's primary purpose was to kill them.

To start with, the killing did not go smoothly at any of the camps. It is worth recalling once again that the Nazis were embarking on something that human beings had never attempted before – the mechanized extermination of millions of men, women and children in a matter of months. Gruesome as the analogy is, the Germans had created three killing factories and, as in any industrial operation, all the various components had to be completely synchronized for the desired end result to be achieved. If the trains failed to send people on schedule, if the gas chambers could not cope with the volume of new arrivals, if there was a bottleneck anywhere in the system, then bloody chaos could result. And in those early days that is exactly what occurred.

At Bełżec it soon transpired that the capacity of the gas chambers was not sufficient to deal with the numbers of people scheduled to be sent there, and so in June the camp shut down for a month or so and new gas chambers were built. At Sobibór the problem was both the size of the gas chambers and the local transport links. The camp ceased operations between August and October while the Nazis sorted out these difficulties. But it was at Treblinka that the greatest problems for the Nazis arose, and truly hellish scenes resulted.

To begin with, Treblinka operated more or less as the Nazis had planned, with around 6000 people arriving to be killed each day. But by August the numbers had doubled and the operation of the camp began to fall apart. Yet still the camp commandant, Dr Irmfried Eberl, kept it open. 'Dr Eberl's ambition,' said August Hingst, another member of the SS at Treblinka, 'was to reach the highest possible numbers and exceed all the other camps. So many transports arrived that the disembarkation and gassing of the people could no longer be handled.'[33] As a result many people were simply shot in the lower camp, but that, of course, destroyed the subterfuge that was the basis of the camp's operation – no one believed they were at a disinfecting station when they saw corpses on the ground. As a result, trains backed up at Treblinka station some 2 miles away, waiting until the camp could be cleared. Conditions on board became so appalling that many died in the freight cars. Oskar Berger arrived at Treblinka on one transport in late August at the height of the chaos: 'As we disembarked, we witnessed a horrible sight: hundreds of bodies lying all around. Piles of bundles, clothes, valises, everything mixed together. SS soldiers and Ukrainians were standing on the roofs of the barracks and firing indiscriminately into the crowd. Men, women and children fell bleeding. The air was filled with screaming and weeping.'[34] In such circumstances it was impossible to keep the reality of the camp's operations from the Poles who lived in the hamlets and villages nearby. 'The smell of the disintegrating corpses was just terrible,' says Eugenia Samuel,[35] then a local schoolgirl. 'You couldn't open a window or go out because of the stench. You cannot imagine such a stench.'

Nonetheless, in the midst of this horror an enormous number of people were killed. In a little over a month, between the end of July and the end of August 1942, an estimated 312,500 people were murdered at Treblinka.[36] This is a phenomenal figure, a killing rate of around 10,000 a day and a death toll not approached at any other camp until the height of the Hungarian action at Auschwitz in 1944 when the four crematoria of Birkenau were functioning at full capacity. But the cost of this incredible rate of destruction was too high for Dr Eberl's superiors to bear. Reports reached them of how Treblinka was degenerating in a spiral of disorganization. Worse still, from the Nazi point of view, the Third Reich appeared to be losing out financially. The belongings of the murdered Jews were left sprawled about the camp, and there were suggestions that some of the valuables were even being pilfered by the Germans and Ukrainians.

Christian Wirth, the creator of Bełżec, was appointed that August to a new job: inspector of the three death camps. And one of his first tasks was to travel with his boss, SS Oberstgruppenführer (General) Odilo Globocnik, to investigate the state of Treblinka. Josef Oberhauser, who worked for Wirth, later gave evidence about what happened once they arrived: 'In Treblinka everything was in chaos ... Dr Eberl would be dismissed immediately ... Globocnik said in the course of this conversation that if Dr Eberl were not his fellow countryman, he would arrest him and bring him before an SS and police court.' Eberl was sacked and transports to Treblinka temporarily ceased. A new commandant, Franz Stangl, who had previously worked with Wirth and was currently at Sobibór, was appointed to sort the mess out.

Eberl had misunderstood what his bosses wanted. He had delivered them an exceptional killing rate, but he had not organized the murders 'properly'. Indeed, one of the most notable aspects of Eberl's sacking is the comment from Globocnik that he would bring him before a 'police court' for the way he had run Treblinka. In the perverted morality of the higher reaches of the SS, Eberl deserved prosecution for not organizing the mass murder of men, women and children in a more effective way. As we look at it today, in the eyes of his superiors Eberl's crime was that he had not committed the crime of mass murder 'well enough'.

A crucial part of the killing process was the delivery of Jews to the new death camps. These factories had to be fed – and in gigantic numbers. As a result, throughout the summer and autumn of 1942 a whole series of resettlement 'actions' were conducted right across occupied Poland. Himmler's blanket instruction of 19 July had deliberately encompassed all the Jews of the General Government. He was concerned that, if local officials on the ground were able to exercise discretion, the whole operation would fail. His fear was that, whilst in theory all Nazis believed in the necessity of dealing with the 'Jewish problem', individuals might still try to save particular Jews whom they thought 'good'. One case in particular highlights the danger that Himmler feared – the impact of the deportation order on a German with a strongly developed sense of humanity.

Oberleutnant (Lieutenant) Albert Battel was a German officer serving in Przemyśl in southern Poland. He was older than most Wehrmacht officers – already over 50 – and had a solid pre-war career as a lawyer behind him. Although a member of the Nazi party, he did not have an unblemished record as a National Socialist since he had been observed treating Jews with civility during the 1930s. In July 1942, a group of Jews was assigned to Battel and the German army in Przemyśl. Many of the Jews worked in the armaments industry and lived in a nearby ghetto; they considered themselves, in comparison to many other Polish Jews, both privileged and protected. There was gossip towards the end of the month that the SS would shortly mount a 'resettlement' action in the town, with the Jews 'resettled' to the death camp of Bełżec. But the Jews working for the German army viewed this news with a certain degree of equanimity for they each possessed an *Ausweis*, a pass from the army that they thought exempted them from any SS action. They also reasoned that, since they were already working for the German war effort, it made no sense to deport them. But they did not reckon with the inflexible ideological theory behind Himmler's order – all Jews were to die, without exception.

On Saturday 25 July, the Jews of Przemyśl heard a rumour that the SS would start the deportations the following Monday, and that in most cases their German passes would be considered worthless. One of the Jews, Samuel Igiel,[37] managed to reach Lieutenant Battel early on the Sunday and warn him about the impending action. Battel rang the head of the local Gestapo to ask him what was going on, only to have the phone put down on him. Furious, Battel consulted his superior officer, Oberstleutnant (Major) Liedtke, and then proceeded to take an army unit and close the bridge across the river San, which ran through the town – an action that prevented access to the ghetto. As a result, the head of the local Gestapo and the Nazi authorities in Kraków made a concession: 2500 of the Jews of Przemyśl could be issued with passes that gave them a temporary stay of deportation. To ensure that those Jews who worked directly for him were saved, Lieutenant Battel sent trucks to the ghetto to pick up them and their families and then installed them in the basement of the German Kommandantur in town. Altogether around 240 Jews were removed from the ghetto in this way.

The SS 'resettlement' action against the Przemyśl Jews went ahead as planned on 27 July and the vast majority were transported to Bełżec, but Albert Battel's actions had saved several thousand of them from immediate deportation. A few weeks later

Battel was transferred from his posting in Przemyśl and a secret investigation launched into his conduct by the SS. The papers finally reached Himmler, who noted that Battel should be held to account for his conduct once the war was over. Battel was subsequently discharged from the army because of ill health, joined the local defence unit in his home town of Breslau and was eventually captured by the Red Army. After his release from a Soviet POW camp he returned home and, because of his previous Nazi party membership, was refused permission to resume his career as a lawyer.

Separating out the various motivations that lay behind Battel's actions in saving the Jews of Przemyśl is not easy. But whilst it is clear that his superiors in the German army supported him primarily out of a desire to prevent the loss of a source of trained labour, it seems Battel was also driven by a sense that the deportations were plain wrong. Thus in 1981, long after his death, Battel's humane actions were recognized when he was awarded the title 'Righteous Among the Nations' at Yad Vashem in Israel.

There were other German officers, like Battel, who protested at the deportation of the Jews during the summer and autumn of 1942, but they represent only a small handful of the Wehrmacht presence in Poland. And their actions did virtually nothing to stop the massive flow of Jews to the death camps. Nonetheless, a small number of Jews *were* saved, and it is important to understand that not all Germans simply adapted to the new reality when asked to participate in the crime.

Oskar Groening, however, was most certainly one of the majority who accepted their part in the process of mass murder during 1942. Once he had been working at Auschwitz for several months, his work, he says, had become 'routine'. He sorted out the various currencies that had been taken from the new arrivals, counted the money and sent it to Berlin. He still attended selections, not to participate in the decision-making process about who should live and who should die – those decisions were taken by SS doctors – but to ensure that the belongings of the Jews were taken away and held securely until they could be sorted. This was done in an area of the camp that came to be called 'Canada', because that country had become a fantasy destination, a land rich in everything.

Groening had thus manufactured for himself what he considered to be a tolerable life at Auschwitz. In his office he was insulated from the brutality, and when he was walking around the camp he could avert his eyes from anything that displeased him. In normal circumstances he had nothing to do with the crude mechanics of the killing process; there was generally no reason for him to visit the remote corner of Birkenau where the murders took place. The only reminder that different nationalities were coming to the camp was the variety of currencies that crossed Groening's desk – one day French francs, another Czech korunas, the next Polish zlotys (and always American dollars) – plus the array of liquor taken from the new arrivals: Greek ouzo, French brandy and Italian sambuca. 'When there was a lot of ouzo,' says Oskar Groening, 'it could only come from Greece. Otherwise there was no reason for us to distinguish where they came from. We didn't feel any empathy or sympathy towards one or other Jewish group from any particular country unless you were keen on getting a particular kind of vodka or schnapps – the Russians had a lovely type of vodka ... We drank a lot of vodka. We didn't get drunk every day, but it did happen. We'd go to bed drunk, and if someone was too lazy to turn off the light, they'd shoot at it. Nobody said anything.'

Although Groening does not exactly use the word 'enjoy' to describe his time at Auschwitz, it is hard to see how that is not an apt description of the life he paints: 'Auschwitz main camp was like a small town. It had its gossip. It even had a vegetable shop. There was a canteen, a cinema, a theatre with regular performances. There was a sports club of which I was a member. There were dances – all fun and entertainment.' And then there was the other 'positive' side of life at Auschwitz for Oskar Groening – his comrades: 'I have to say that many who worked there weren't dull, they were intelligent.' When he eventually left the camp in 1944, he went with some regrets: 'I'd left a circle of friends who I'd got familiar with, I'd got fond of, and that was very difficult. Apart from the fact that there are pigs who fulfil their personal drives – there are such people – the special situation at Auschwitz led to friendships which, I still say today, I think back on with joy.'

But one night, towards the end of 1942, Groening's comfortable life at Auschwitz was disrupted by a sudden glimpse into the nightmare of the actual killing operation. Asleep in his barracks in the SS camp on the perimeter of Birkenau, he and his comrades were woken by the sound of an alarm. They were told that a number of Jews who were being marched to the gas chambers had escaped and run to the nearby woods. 'We were told to take our pistols and go through the forest,' says Groening. 'We found no one.' Then he and his comrades spread out and moved up towards the extermination area of the camp. 'We went in star formation up towards this farmhouse. It was lit from outside in diffused light, and out in the front were seven or eight bodies. These were the ones who had probably tried to escape and they'd been caught and shot. In front of the door of the farmhouse were some SS men who told us: "It's finished, you can go home."'

Overcome by curiosity, Groening and his comrades decided not to 'go home' but to hang about in the shadows instead. They watched as an SS man put on a gas mask and placed Zyklon B pellets through a hatch in the side of the cottage wall. There had been a humming noise coming from inside the cottage that now 'turned to screaming' for a minute, followed by silence: 'Then one man, I don't know whether he was an officer, stood and came to the door where there was a peep-hole, looked in and checked whether everything was OK and the people were dead.' Groening describes his feelings at this moment, when the crude mechanics of murder were placed in front of him, 'as if you see two lorries crashing on the motorway. And you ask yourself, "Must it be that way? Is this necessary?" And of course it's influenced by the fact that you said before, "Yes, well, it's war," and we said, "They were our enemies."'

Later, Groening witnessed the burning of the bodies: 'This comrade said, "Come with me, I'll show you." I was so shocked that I stood at a distance – perhaps 70 metres away from the fires. The fire was flickering up and the Kapo there told me afterwards details of the burning. And it was terribly disgusting – horrendous. He made fun of the fact that when the bodies started burning they obviously developed gases from the lungs or elsewhere and these bodies seemed to jump up, and the sex parts of the men suddenly became erect in a kind of way that he found laughable.' The sight of the gassing installations and the burning cremation pits momentarily shattered the cosy life that Oskar Groening had created for himself at Auschwitz. So much so that he went once more to his boss, an SS Untersturmführer (2nd Lieutenant) who was 'an Austrian and basically an honest bloke' and poured out his feelings. 'He listened to me and said: "My dear Groening, what do you want to do against it? We're all in the same boat. We've given an obligation to accept this – not even to think about it."' With the words of his superior officer ringing in his ears, Groening returned to work. He had sworn an oath of loyalty, he believed the Jews were Germany's enemy, and he knew that he could still manipulate his life at the camp to avoid encountering the worst of the horror. And so he stayed.

As a rank-and-file member of the SS, Oskar Groening lived in a comfortable barracks with several of his comrades. But life for officers was better still. Many stayed with their families in requisitioned houses in the centre of the town of Auschwitz, or in the immediate vicinity of the main camp by the Soła river, and enjoyed a standard of living that far surpassed anything they could have achieved had they been attached to a fighting unit. They lived as conquerors, and as conquerors they needed domestic slaves to cook their meals, clean their houses and look after their children. But this posed a problem. In Nazi racial theory Jewish and Polish prisoners were far too inferior to the Germans to make ideal servants and be allowed intimate access to their comfortable private lives, and in any case they might use the opportunity of work outside the camp wire (albeit still within the guarded sections of the Auschwitz Zone of Interest) to try to escape or, worse still, to attack the German families they served.

Ever ingenious, the Nazis hit on a solution to their servant problem. They would employ a category of prisoners who were for the most part German, and who could be guaranteed never to try to hurt their masters or to flee: Jehovah's Witnesses. Known in Germany as 'Bible Students', in 1933 Jehovah's Witnesses had declared that in broad terms they had little against the Nazi state; ideologically they also opposed Jews and Communists (though not in the overtly hostile way the Nazis did). Serious problems only arose when as pacifists they refused to join the German armed forces, and as a result they were imprisoned in concentration camps.

Else Abt[38] was one of several hundred German Jehovah's

Witnesses sent to Auschwitz. Born in 1914 in Danzig, she was brought up as a Lutheran but introduced to her new faith by friends. She married another Jehovah's Witness, gave birth to a daughter in 1939, and tried to live as peacefully as possible. But their troubles began when her husband refused to employ his engineering skills to help the Nazi war effort. He was arrested, and she escaped imprisonment only because she was nursing their child. But when her daughter was two and a half the Gestapo came for her. In a heartrending scene, with her little girl calling out 'Leave me my mummy! Leave me my mummy!' and grabbing at the trousers of the Gestapo officer, Else Abt was taken away, and her child left in the care of friends.

When she arrived at Auschwitz she noticed a transport in front of her that contained Jewish women: 'They were treated worse than animals, from what we could see. These SS men came and treated us humanely, but the Jewesses weren't treated humanely – that was a shock.' Before Auschwitz, Else Abt had scarcely ever encountered Jews. 'I never went to Jewish shops,' she says, 'and I didn't like it when I heard that my mother was going there because they always had high prices. That's why I never bought anything from a Jewish shop, because they always [charged] higher prices and then they'd give a discount and the stupid people thought they were only paying half-price. That's true, I saw it in Danzig – they'd calculate prices in a certain way. That's personally my opinion. But I don't have anything against the Jews. When we were in the camp, when I was sick a Jewess came and wanted to wash my coat. She wanted to do something good.'

Once at Auschwitz, Else Abt was told that all she had to do to secure immediate release was to renounce her faith. The Jehovah's Witnesses were thus the only category of prisoner in the concentration camp system who simply had to sign a declaration to obtain their freedom. But the majority did not. For many, like Else Abt, believed Auschwitz was a test: 'I'd read in the Bible the story of Abraham. And he was told to sacrifice his son. And the Bible says he was willing to do it. But then our creator Jehovah saw that he was willing to and so he didn't allow it. He just wanted to test his faith. And that's what I thought.'

And so the German Jehovah's Witnesses became the perfect house-servants for SS officers at Auschwitz – much preferred to

Poles, who were used only when there weren't enough Witnesses to go around. Else Abt worked in the home of one of the senior SS members, his wife and their small daughter. She cleaned the house, cooked their meals and looked after their little girl. Her attitude was: 'It wasn't the child's fault [that she was in Auschwitz]. It wasn't the wife's fault.' She performed her duties conscientiously and with compassion, even devotedly nursing the little girl when she fell sick and earning the thanks of her parents.

It was scarcely any wonder, then, that the Jehovah's Witnesses were the prisoners Rudolf Hoess liked best, and not just because of their trouble-free behaviour. He had first come into contact with them in substantial numbers at Sachsenhausen in the late 1930s, when they were sent to the camp for refusing to do military service. Hoess records the extraordinary power of their belief, something that made a huge impression on him. When they were flogged because they did not conform to the rules of the camp he says that, far from begging for mercy, they asked to be thrashed again so that they could suffer more for their faith. He witnessed the execution of two Witnesses by firing squad, and was astonished to see that they held their hands up to the sky with blissful expressions as they awaited their fate. Hoess imagined that the early Christian martyrs must have gone to their deaths the same way.

The behaviour of the Jehovah's Witnesses had a huge impact not just on Hoess, but on his superior officers as well. 'On many occasions,' Hoess records, 'Himmler as well as Eicke offered the fanatical faith of the Jehovah's Witnesses as an example. SS men must have the same fanatical and unshakeable faith in the National Socialist ideal and in Adolf Hitler that the Witnesses had in Jehovah. Only when all SS men believed as fanatically in their own philosophy would Adolf Hitler's state be permanently secure.'[39]

At Auschwitz, Hoess and his wife employed two Jehovah's Witnesses in their own house, and were touched by the care they lavished on their children. Hoess describes many of the Witnesses as 'wonderful beings'.[40] Significantly, Hoess also records that he believes the Witnesses felt it was 'right' that the Jews should be exterminated, as their ancestors had been the ones who had handed Jesus over to be killed; this, however, is an attitude of mind that Else Abt denies. She believed that the SS were doing wrong – serving a 'demon' – by murdering the Jews. However, she thought she should show her own faith by her 'attitude'. This created an odd situation. She was faithfully, almost lovingly, looking after the daughter of an SS officer at Auschwitz, whilst the Nazis denied her access to her own little girl. She explains how she attempted to rationalize her circumstances by saying she felt she had to 'do good for any person', including members of the SS. Indeed, she admits that she would have worked dutifully in Hitler's house had she been told to. And to add further to this complex emotional mix, she could walk away from the camp and return to her own daughter at any moment she chose, just by signing a paper that stated she had renounced her faith. But Else Abt never signed: 'That would have meant compromising. I never did it.'

In a further twist to this strange story, when Else Abt was eventually able to return home after the war she discovered that her little girl had been looked after by one of the few Jehovah's Witnesses who had renounced their faith in order to gain freedom. 'We came to visit him and his wife because they had brought up our daughter, and he cried like a little child because he was a coward.' Else Abt was not particularly grateful to him for taking care of her daughter because 'I wouldn't have been worried [about her]. There would always be people who would have helped. We weren't dependent on one person. Our creator knows to send us what we need when we need it and will always intervene.' Her daughter became a Jehovah's Witness herself. As a result, Else Abt says, 'She knew and was happy that I stayed faithful – not to a human being, but to our creator Jehovah, because he looked out for us, as I found out during my time in Auschwitz. He is able to change all people. People that hated us started to think and stopped hating us – quite the opposite, in fact.' To those who lack the certainty of faith expressed by Else Abt, it is hard to see how a creator was 'looking out' for the Jehovah's Witnesses whom Hoess describes as being shot in Sachsenhausen. Nor does he seem to have been 'looking out' for the Poles, Soviet prisoners, the sick, Jews and countless others who lost their lives so cruelly at Auschwitz. But one of the intriguing aspects of the theological position taken by Else Abt is that such atrocities are immediately explicable to her, simply evidence of the will of a higher power whom we cannot fully understand but in whom we must have absolute faith. If God permits this to happen, then it is for a reason; it is just that we do not yet fully understand what that reason is.

One must be careful of making an immediate and glib comparison, as Himmler did, between this attitude of mind and the fanaticism of the Nazis; not least because Jehovah's Witnesses, unlike the Nazis, believe in treating people with compassion and kindness. Nonetheless, if one substitutes 'Hitler' for 'Jehovah' in Else Abt's testimony, the words do bear a striking resemblance to the ideological position taken by SS men like Hoess.

As 1942 came to an end, the SS had created a settled environment for themselves at Auschwitz. They had their servants and they had their jobs, and they had for the most part found a successful way of distancing themselves from the killing. And it was not just at Auschwitz that this process of turning mass murder into an ordered profession was taking place; Treblinka was transformed during the same period. Franz Stangl had replaced the incompetent Eberl as commandant in September 1942 and had immediately set about reorganizing the camp. Transports were stopped while the bodies that lay littered around were removed and the camp cleaned up. Both Stangl and Wirth also identified at once the fundamental problem that Eberl had faced in making the killing operation function smoothly – the capacity of the gas chambers. As a result a much larger gassing facility was built straight away – a brick building with a central corridor off which ran eight separate small gas chambers. Each of the individual chambers could also be accessed from outside, which meant that clearing them of corpses would be much easier than before. The new gas chambers had a total capacity of over 3000 people, more than six times greater than the previous complex. Along with the construction of the new gas chambers, which were ready for use by October, Stangl initiated a number of measures that were all calculated to lull the suspicions of the arriving Jews. The hut by the platform where the Jews arrived was painted to look like a normal railway station, with signs for waiting rooms. Flowers were planted in tubs, and the whole reception area was kept as clean and ordered as possible.

Until recently no one knew exactly how many people were killed during 1942 in death camps like Treblinka. The Nazis destroyed any documentation that would have revealed the truth, and as a consequence estimates varied widely. But a few years ago a discovery was made in the Public Record Office in London that raised our level of knowledge.[41] It is the text of a German cable, intercepted and then decoded by the British, which contains the statistics of the killing tally of the Operation Reinhard death camps as at 31 December 1942. (After the assassination of Reinhard Heydrich in June 1942 the killing operation in Poland had been named 'Operation Reinhard' in his 'honour'.)

The German cable reveals that Treblinka, Bełżec, Sobibór and Majdanek (a much smaller-capacity camp in the Lublin district) had so far murdered a total of 1,274,166 people. That figure is further broken down as 24,733 at Majdanek, 101,370 at Sobibór and 434,508 at Bełżec. The figure given in the intercepted cable for Treblinka is 71,355, but that is obviously a typing error, as in order to reach the total of 1,274,166 the number killed at Treblinka has to be 713,555. Treblinka was thus, officially, the largest killing centre in the Nazi state during 1942. Auschwitz was left far behind.

But not for long.

— 4 —

Corruption

In the history of Auschwitz and the Nazis' 'Final Solution', 1943 was a year of transformation. During 1941 the majority of the killing had been committed by special mobile units in the occupied Soviet Union; in 1942 the Operation Reinhard camps dominated the process of mass murder; but now, three years after it was first opened, it was Auschwitz's turn to assume a central role. And like so much about this history, the reasons for the change are complex and multi-faceted.

At some time in early 1943 Himmler toured Treblinka and Sobibór and observed at first hand the work of his killers. The Operation Reinhard camps had so far murdered 1.65 million people (97 per cent of the eventual total of 1.7 million killed in these camps).[1] As a result of this 'success', on 16 February, Himmler ordered the Warsaw ghetto to be liquidated. As Himmler would have perceived it, there was now no need for the ghetto to exist. Then, in April, the unthinkable happened – as far as the Nazis were concerned. The Jews in the Warsaw ghetto started fighting back. For the first time the Nazis faced coordinated armed resistance from a determined number of Jews; and the conflict could not have occurred in a more exposed place, in the centre of the capital of Poland.[2]

The initial deportations from the Warsaw ghetto, the largest the Nazis had established, had proceeded without incident during the summer of 1942. Around 300,000 Jews had been deported to Treblinka, leaving a ghetto population of around 60,000. In the knowledge that the Nazis intended to murder them all, more and more of those Jews who remained joined the Jewish Fighting Organization (Żydowska Organizacja Bojowa), which had been established in the ghetto in July 1942. Together with members of the Jewish Military Union (Żydowski Związek Wojskowy) they planned to resist any further attempts at deportation.

There was some resistance to the Nazis' apparent attempt to clear the ghetto in January 1943, but several thousand Jews were still taken. The Jewish leadership believed that their opposition had prevented the total liquidation of the ghetto, but it is now known that the Nazis' action at this time was always intended to reduce the Jewish population by no more than some 8000. Nonetheless, this act of resistance convinced the Jews that they were capable of frustrating the Germans' intentions. They now prepared to defend themselves against the Nazis' attempt to destroy the ghetto completely, which they knew must come soon.

Ahron Karmi,[3] then 21 years old, was one of the Warsaw ghetto Jews planning to resist. He had already experienced one miraculous escape from death the previous year when he had managed to leap from the train that was carrying his father and himself to Treblinka: 'My father said, "Go! Because if I save you it is as though I have saved an entire universe." And then he added: "If any of you survive, he should take revenge for our blood." Then we had to say goodbye. And we knew what kind of a goodbye that was – a different kind of goodbye. A kind of goodbye that there has never been before.'

Karmi and the other resistance fighters sought out what weapons they could and gathered furniture together to construct makeshift defensive positions; others in the ghetto population dug underground bunkers as hide-outs. But despite all this extensive preparation, no one was under any illusion that the Germans could be defeated. 'We never thought of being victorious,' says Karmi. 'This was all only not to get on the trains when they said we should. If we succeeded for one day, then we would try another day.'

Karmi took up position along with half a dozen or so of his comrades on the third floor of a house that overlooked the ghetto wall. He clasped a German P38 pistol in his hand and waited for the Nazis. The rumour was that the Germans had promised to clear the ghetto by 20 April, Hitler's birthday, as a present for their Führer. And it was on Hitler's birthday that Karmi's unit first went into action: 'We heard the sound of three hundred Germans marching towards us – as if they were marching to the front, to Stalingrad or somewhere. They came exactly in front of our position.'

At that moment the leader of his group threw two grenades in quick succession towards the Germans as a signal for Karmi and the others to start firing: 'Immediately I shot with my pistol into the mass [of Germans] that was passing by. The Germans yelled, "Help!" and took shelter behind a wall. It was the first time we saw Germans running away. We were used to being the ones who ran away from the Germans. They had no expectation of Jews fighting like that. There was blood and I couldn't take my eyes off it. I said, "German blood." It reminded me of what my father had told me: "If any of you survive, you should take revenge for our blood." Then the [German] commander of the unit started yelling at his soldiers, "What! Are you hiding? Get away from the wall!" When they moved back they saw where the fire was coming from and they began to shoot back. But it was not like our fire – we only had grenades and a few pistols. When they fired, all the window panes were broken and there was a mixture of smoke and glass.'

The Germans, under the command of SS Oberstgruppenführer (General) Jürgen Stroop, quickly realized that they were facing tougher resistance than they had initially expected. Tens of thousands of Jews were in hiding, the vast majority underground. The streets of the ghetto were all but deserted, and there were scarcely any Jews available to deport. So the Germans decided on a simple and brutal solution to their problem: they would burn the Jews out. Street by street, block by block, they set fire to the ghetto. Faced with overwhelming force in front of them, and flaming buildings all around, Ahron Karmi and his comrades retreated to the sewers. From there he managed to crawl out, under the ghetto wire, and reach the outskirts of Warsaw, where his life scarcely became much safer: 'After two years, from this group of eighty people who went out to the forest only eleven people were left.'

According to Stroop's report of the action, which is the major contemporary written source of information on the ghetto uprising, 56,065 Jews were eventually captured. Stroop further claimed that around 7000 Jews were killed in the fighting inside the ghetto for the loss of fewer than 20 German soldiers – figures that clearly minimize the German losses whilst exaggerating the Jewish dead.

Regardless of how Stroop tried to spin events in the Warsaw

ghetto, the reality of the action did not escape Himmler. The uprising represented a dangerous precedent, evidence for the first time of large-scale, coordinated resistance by the Jewish population. It would have confirmed Himmler in his view that the ghettos were potentially uncontrollable. They were, to him, part of a necessary solution to a problem that was past. For Himmler the future 'management' of the 'Final Solution' lay elsewhere – specifically at Auschwitz.

In March 1943, just a few weeks before the Warsaw ghetto uprising, an event of huge significance took place at Auschwitz: the first crematorium opened at Birkenau. This installation had a long and chequered history. Originally conceived in October 1941, it had been intended to replace the old crematorium in the main camp but its proposed location was subsequently moved to Birkenau. During 1942 the crucial turning point in the planning stage came when its function was changed by SS architect Walter Dejaco. The basement rooms, designed originally as mortuaries, were adapted to perform two separate functions. One underground room would be a large undressing area, and the second, at right-angles to the first, would be a gas chamber. Zyklon B canisters would be introduced into the gas chamber from above by means of hatches on the roof. On the ground floor was a large crematorium with five large ovens, each with three furnace doors. Bodies were to be transferred from the gas chamber in the basement to the crematorium by means of a small lift.

No one knows the exact date on which the SS leadership ordered the transformation of the building. But the subsequent shift in function can be traced via a variety of orders from the Auschwitz construction office; for example, the alteration of the doors to the gas chamber so that they contained a 'spy hole' and opened outwards rather than, as originally planned, inwards (a change necessitated by the knowledge that the doors would be blocked by dead bodies after the gassing had taken place). Other changes included the removal of a corpse chute and the insertion of additional stairs down to the basement, an obvious reference to the fact that more people would now walk, rather than be carried, into what had been originally designed as a mortuary.

At the outset just one crematorium had been planned, but in parallel with this change in function came the decision to order several more similar installations. By early summer 1943 a total of four combined crematoria/gas chambers were in operation at Auschwitz–Birkenau. Two (crematoria 2 and 3) were built according to the modified original plan with the gas chambers in the basement, and they were situated less than 100 metres from what was planned as the new arrival area or 'ramp' within Birkenau (which was not finally completed until late spring 1944). Two more (crematoria 4 and 5) were placed in a remote area of Birkenau near the original improvised gas chambers of 'The Little Red House' and 'The Little White House'. They had their gas chambers not in the basement but on the same level as the cremation ovens on the ground floor. For the Nazi planners this represented an obvious design 'improvement', since it meant that bodies no longer needed to be transported from the basement to the ground floor. Crematoria 4 and 5 each had one large oven with eight separate furnace doors. In total, these four crematoria had the capacity to murder around 4700 people every day and then dispose of the bodies. Thus, if all the new killing installations were working, 150,000 people a month could be murdered at Auschwitz.

The solid brick buildings of the Auschwitz crematoria represent in physical terms the particular horror of the Nazi's 'Final Solution'. No longer was the killing to take place in adapted cottages; now it would be conducted in factory-like installations that were capable of extermination on an industrial scale. The massacre in hot blood of women and children has occurred at various times throughout history, but this seems something entirely new – the careful creation of places where human beings were to be murdered in entirely cold blood. The calm, dispassionate, systematic nature of the process finds tangible expression in the neat red brick of the crematoria of Birkenau.

But in one respect the emphasis placed on the Auschwitz–Birkenau crematoria, though understandable, is misleading – for the crematoria, which did not commence operation until spring 1943, were not the first solid killing installations of the Nazis' 'Final Solution'. Much more improvised gas chambers were in use at the Operation Reinhard death camps the previous year. Indeed, by December 1942, the original gas chamber complex at Treblinka had already been replaced by a much more robust, larger one. Furthermore, the crematoria of Auschwitz came into operation well after the peak of the killing. Around 2.7 million Jews were murdered in 1942 (about 200,000 of them in Auschwitz, 1.65 million in the Operation Reinhard camps, and 850,000 shot by mobile killing squads in the East); whilst in 1943 a total of approximately 500,000 Jews were killed, around half of this number at Auschwitz.

Nonetheless, Auschwitz was of growing importance in the Nazi state. For years there had been tensions between those Nazis who believed that the Jews should be made to work for the Reich and those who believed that they should be murdered. At the January 1942 Wannsee conference, Reinhard Heydrich articulated how these two seemingly contradictory notions could be combined by a policy of working the Jews to death. But in practice, especially following Himmler's order that the Jews of the General Government were to be murdered, the two policies were often in conflict. As Lieutenant Battel witnessed at Przemyśl, Jews capable of work were still ordered to be sent to their deaths at Bełżec.

By spring 1943 it was obvious to men like Himmler that the only installation in the Nazi empire capable of satisfactorily uniting the twin goals of work and murder was Auschwitz. Thus the crematoria/gas chambers of Birkenau were to be the hub of a huge semi-industrial complex. Here selected Jews could first be sent to work at one of a large number of sub-camps nearby, and then, when they were deemed no longer fit to work after months of appalling mistreatment, they could be transported a few miles to the extermination facilities of Auschwitz–Birkenau.

Both ideologically and practically, Auschwitz fitted perfectly into Himmler's plans. He would have perceived flexibility within the system – depending on the need for labour, the standard used to judge 'fitness for work' could be altered. And, perhaps more importantly to him in the light of events in Warsaw, he would have realized that the SS could exercise a level of security within the Auschwitz complex that was impossible within the ghettos.

Eventually there were 28 Auschwitz sub-camps[4] in operation close to various industrial facilities throughout Upper Silesia, from the Goleszów cement works to the Eintrachthütte armaments factory, and from the Energie-Versorgung Oberschlesien power plant to the giant camp at Monowitz built to service the I.G. Farben Buna works. Around 10,000 Auschwitz prisoners (including the

Italian scientist and writer Primo Levi, whose post-war books sought to comprehend the brutality of the Nazi regime) would eventually be based at Monowitz. By 1944 a total of more than 40,000 inmates[5] were working as slave labour at the various industrial plants around Upper Silesia. It is estimated that Auschwitz eventually generated around 30 million Marks[6] of pure profit for the Nazi state by selling this forced labour to private concerns.

Conditions in these sub-camps could be just as bad as at Auschwitz main camp or Auschwitz–Birkenau. One of the most notorious was Fürstengrube, built near a coal mine, and it was to Fürstengrube that Benjamin Jacobs[7] was sent in the early autumn of 1943. Normally this was tantamount to a sentence of death. Life expectancy in the coal mines around Auschwitz could be measured in weeks. But Jacobs had a skill that saved him: he had some training as a dentist. And his experience demonstrates the level of cynicism the Nazis had reached in their desire to exploit the Jews before, and even after, death.

As a result of his knowledge of dentistry, he began to look after first the inmates, and then the Nazis in authority at the camp: 'I was taking care of the SS people and the upper echelon of the concentration camp, doctors and so forth, and they were rather helpful to me because when they came and they needed a dentist they were very nice. They usually brought me some bread or some vodka and just left it. Didn't give it to me per se, but just by "mistake" they left it on the chairs and that's how I got better food ... I felt I was regarded as someone who they really treated better. I was very proud of that. You felt you were in a better position and were getting better treatment.' The 'only time' that Benjamin Jacobs 'regretted' his role as a dentist at the work camp was when he was ordered to extract gold teeth from the mouths of those inmates who had died. He had to walk into the room that contained the corpses of prisoners who had been shot at work or died in the mines. He thought 'the people looked grotesque' and he 'saw things' that he 'could never believe'. He had to kneel close to the bodies and 'open the mouth forcibly by an instrument' that separated the upper jaw from the lower jaw. As it did so it made 'the sound of cracking'. Once the mouth of the dead body was held open Jacobs extracted the gold teeth: 'It wasn't something that I can be proud of. I was emotionless at the time. I wanted to survive.

Even so this life wasn't very acceptable, but life is still something that you want to hang on to.'

The gold taken from the mouths of the dead workers was melted down so that it could be used to fashion jewellery, in a process that exemplified the overall Nazi vision for the whole of the Auschwitz complex. Nothing, no matter how intimate, that belonged to the inmates was to be wasted. This was an attitude that found further expression both in Auschwitz main camp and Auschwitz–Birkenau in the sorting areas known as 'Canada'. Linda Breder[8], 19 when she began working in 'Canada' in the main camp in 1943, had arrived in Auschwitz the year before on one of the first women's transports from Slovakia. After an initial period in a tough commando working in the fields, she had been selected for the comparatively less strenuous task of sorting the belongings stolen from the arriving prisoners: 'Actually, working in "Canada" saved my life because we had food, we got water and we could take a shower there.' The work that Linda Breder was forced to do may have been less gruesome than that done by Benjamin Jacobs, but it was conceptually similar: ensuring that the Nazis obtained the greatest possible economic benefit from those whom they destroyed. 'Those goodies which came in from the murdered people, they were all stored in Auschwitz, and besides folding the clothing, we had to search for valuables. Every piece had to be searched – underwear, everything. And we found lots of diamonds, gold, coins, dollars – foreign currency from all over Europe. And when we found something we had to put it in a wooden box with a slit in that was in the middle of the barrack ... Nobody else was aware of all the wealth and clothes arriving. Only us. Some 600 girls who used to work there.'

The policy of the Auschwitz authorities – indeed, that of the SS throughout the Nazi state – was clear: all valuables taken from the new arrivals were the property of the Reich. But whilst the theory may have been clear, the practice was very different. The temptations of 'Canada' were irresistible, both for the prisoners working there and for the SS. As a result, stealing from 'Canada' was commonplace: 'We always managed to smuggle some clothes,' says Linda Breder. 'We smuggled shoes, panties, underwear – we gave away all those clothes because we didn't need them.' And since Breder and the others who worked in 'Canada' also found food hidden amongst the belongings, they had a better diet than almost any other group of Jewish inmates at Auschwitz. 'Yes, we ate that food. It was a rescue for us. Even animals eat each other when they feel hunger ... We wanted to live. We wanted to survive. Should we have thrown it away? We didn't kill anyone. We ate only their food. They were already dead at that time ... To have food, water and enough sleep – those were the things we cared about. We had all of that in "Canada".'

But not surprisingly, it was individual members of the SS who personally benefited far more from 'Canada'. 'The Germans kept accumulating wealth,' says Linda Breder. 'Death was the only thing that was left for us ... All of them [the SS] used to steal. They came there because there was no other place like that, where they got everything.' Rudolf Hoess admitted that 'the treasures brought in by the Jews gave rise to unavoidable difficulties for the camp itself' because the SS who worked for him 'were not always strong enough to resist the temptation provided by these valuables which lay within such easy reach'.[9] Oskar Groening confirms his commandant's view: 'There was a danger [of theft] because if a lot of stuff is heaped together you can easily steal something and profit from it, which was absolutely common in Auschwitz.' Because he worked in the Economic Agency he was aware that 'many people touched' the valuables in the chain that led from the luggage deposited on the arrival ramp via the sorting barracks of 'Canada' to the placing of the wooden boxes filled with valuables in his office: 'And it's surely been the case that a whole lot of this stuff was carried into channels that it wasn't meant to go.'

Surprisingly, as Groening confirms, the supervision of the SS in Auschwitz was 'actually very loose'. He himself admits that he was an active participant in the corruption and theft that were rife amongst the SS in the camp, stealing from the cash that surrounded him in order to buy goods on the flourishing Auschwitz black market. When, for example, he grew tired of having to draw a revolver from the camp armoury and then return it at the end of his shift, he approached 'people who had connections' and said, 'Dear friend, I need a gun with ammunition.' And since Groening was known as the 'King of the Dollars' because of his job counting and sorting the stolen money, a fee of 30 US dollars was agreed. It was a simple matter for Groening to steal this amount from the money that passed by him every day. So he handed over the 30 dollars and received his revolver.

Groening's transaction was mirrored by thousands of other similar illegal deals every week at Auschwitz. So much wealth was flooding into the camp with so little supervision and so many casual opportunities to steal that it is hard to imagine that any of the SS were free from involvement in this crime. From the SS private who wanted a new radio to the SS officer who dealt in stolen jewellery, corruption at the camp was endemic.

Himmler referred to the ultra-sensitive question of corruption in the SS during his infamous Posen speech of October 1943, delivered to an audience that included 50 senior SS figures.'I want to speak frankly with you about a very grave matter,' said Himmler. 'We can talk about it amongst ourselves, yet we will never speak about it in public ... I am referring to the evacuation of the Jews, the extermination of the Jewish people. Most of you will know what it means when a hundred bodies lie together, when five hundred lie there, or when there lie a thousand. And ... to have seen this through, with just a few exceptions of human weakness ... to have remained decent, that has made us tough. It is a page of glory in our history that has never been written and is never to be written. We have taken away the riches that they had, and ... I have given a strict order, which Obergruppenführer [Lieutenant General] Pohl has carried out: we have delivered all of these riches to the Reich, to the State. We have taken nothing for ourselves. We have the moral right, we had the duty to our people to do it, to destroy the people who wanted to destroy us. We have carried out this most difficult task for the love of our people. And our heart, our soul, our character have suffered no harm from it.'

Himmler thus attempted to draw a clear line between the murders, which were justified and necessary for the good of the Reich, and individual profit, which remained a crime. He did so in an attempt to preserve the image of the SS as both 'hard' and 'incorruptible'. And it is easy to understand why he tried to make this distinction. He had observed first hand, two years before, the psychological damage that shooting Jews at close range had caused his teams of killers. And so he had overseen the development of a system of murder via the gas chambers that to an extent distanced them from emotional trauma. Now he sought to provide intellectual comfort to his men by distinguishing between the moral but hard defender of the Reich and the louche opportunist out for personal profit. In order for them to live with themselves, in order perhaps even to enable them to 'forgive' themselves for their part in the 'Final Solution', Himmler recognized that he had to paint a picture of the SS as killers of women and children, yes, but murderers who had still retained their honour. And his method of doing that was to remind them that they had not profited personally from the killings.

It was all a lie, of course. And not just at the most obvious level – that the SS were massively implicated in corruption and theft at Auschwitz; it was a fundamental lie through and through because no distinction was ever possible during the Nazis' 'Final Solution' between the 'honourable' murder of helpless civilians and pure bestiality. This truth is illustrated most obviously by the actions of the SS doctors at Auschwitz. These medical professionals were involved at every level of the killing process, from the initial selection at the ramp to the murder of certain selected prisoners. Their involvement was symbolized by the fact that the Zyklon B was transported to the gas chambers in a pseudo-ambulance marked with a red cross. As a result of their total complicity, the Auschwitz doctors faced a dilemma more stark than any of the other Nazi perpetrators, best expressed in the question: how can you take part in mass murder and yet still retain a sense that what you are doing is morally compatible with the Hippocratic oath that compels doctors to try to heal the sick?

Crucial in any attempt to understand how the Nazi doctors felt able to answer that question is the realization that for them Auschwitz was not a sudden introduction to the idea that trained medical staff should be involved in murder. From the moment of their accession to power in 1933 the Nazi leadership had been committed to the concept that certain 'races', and indeed certain individuals, were more 'worthy' of life than others. The first indication of the practical implication of this vision was the introduction during the 1930s of compulsory sterilization for those with severe mental disease. Altogether, around 300,000 Germans were forcibly subjected to such sterilization.

The close links between the Nazis' adult euthanasia programme, which originated in the autumn of 1939, and the staff of the

Operation Reinhard death camps have already been described. Those pioneers of the death camps, Wirth and Stangl, both began their careers in killing by helping to murder the disabled. But what is important to note here is the fact that the selection process for the adult euthanasia programme was controlled by doctors, not by police – a practice that was perpetuated in Auschwitz. This intimate link was the necessary consequence of a pre-history of killing that elevated the removal of what the Nazis called '*lebensunwertes Leben*' ('life unworthy of life') to the highest duty of medicine. It was this perverse logic that made it unsurprising to the killers that a medical practitioner, Dr Eberl, could become the commandant of the death camp of Treblinka.

By the time Eberl took up his job at Treblinka this concept of 'life unworthy of life' had of course been extended from the mentally and physically disabled to the Jews. And in attempting to justify the killing of the Jews, the SS doctors fell back on the early Nazi propaganda lie of the Jews as a corrupting influence on the body politic. 'Of course I am a doctor and I want to preserve life,' said Fritz Klein, one Nazi doctor. 'Out of respect for human life, I would remove a gangrenous appendix from a diseased body. The Jew is the gangrenous appendix in the body of mankind.'[10]

Therefore, from the purist Nazi point of view, Auschwitz and the other death camps were an exercise in health management – facilitating the removal of people who were a burden or threat to the wellbeing of the state. Thus some of the earliest killings at Auschwitz of those found unfit to work were carried out at Block 10, the hospital block, by means of injections with phenol. It was an exact inversion of normal medical ethics – a visit to the hospital not to be cured, but to be killed.

Once the system of selection on arrival was introduced in 1942, Nazi doctors played a vital part in the process of mass murder. It was doctors who made the decision that was fundamental to the operation of Auschwitz – who, from the arriving transports, should live and who should die. The active participation of doctors in this selection was essential to the Nazis for two reasons, one practical and the other philosophical. The practical reason was clear: doctors were thought to be best capable of sizing up at a glance a human being's capability to work (each selection took only a matter of seconds). But the philosophical reason is both less obvious and more significant. By involving doctors so intimately in the selection, a sense was created that the killing was not an arbitrary act of prejudice, but a scientific necessity. Auschwitz was not a place of indiscriminate slaughter, but a measured and calm contribution to the health of the state.

It was, however, in the area of medical experiments that the doctors of Auschwitz were to become especially infamous. That prisoners were used for this purpose fitted into the Nazi ideal that enemies of the state ought to provide a 'service' to the Reich, if not by working as forced labour then by dying in the pursuit of 'medical knowledge'. For the doctor ambitious to pursue a career in research and unencumbered by humanity or compassion, Auschwitz was a laboratory without parallel. Dr Clauberg and Dr Schumann both conducted 'medical research' into sterilization at Auschwitz. Significantly, Schumann had previous experience of murder – he had been one of the doctors involved in the adult euthanasia programme, working at the killing centre at Sonnenstein where Auschwitz prisoners had been sent in July 1941.

Silvia Veselá,[11] one of the first Slovakian women to arrive at Auschwitz, was forced to assist Clauberg and Schumann, working as a nurse in Block 10 in the main camp where many of the experiments took place: 'I was told that one part of the block was where the X-rays were kept. There were huge X-ray machines with big cylinders. Dr Schumann carried out these sterilizations. The second part of the building belonged to Dr Clauberg. He carried out sterilizations by means of chemical substances. He injected the chemical substance into the women's womb and ovary to make them stick together. The main aim of these experiments was to find out how much of that substance was necessary to carry out the sterilization correctly.'

Himmler took a particular interest in the sterilization experiments conducted at Auschwitz. Sterilization had, of course, been one of the 'solutions' considered by the Nazis to their self-created 'Jewish problem' that pre-dated the development of the gas chambers; it had even been raised at Wannsee as a possible alternative to deportation for some German Jews of mixed ancestry. But, despite promises from leading medical figures, such as Dr Clauberg, Himmler had yet to be delivered the cheap, efficient sterilization technique he wanted.

As she cared for the women who were the subject of these painful experiments, Silvia Veselá 'tried not to get involved too much – the best thing you could have done was not to think. The impact of X-ray intensity on the small intestine was tested on them. It was more than awful. These women were throwing up all the time. It was really terrible.' X-rays were used either as an attempt to sterilize on their own or to check the progress of chemicals injected into the womb: 'The women were put on the X-ray table in the gynaecological position. As their legs were spread open the doctor opened their wombs and injected the substance. From a console he was able to see whether he got the injection right. And I used to expose the X-rays after every examination and injection to see whether the woman was sterilized and her ovary finally stuck together ... To them we were not humans. We were animals. Can't you understand that? We were not humans. We were just numbers and experimental animals.'

Silvia Veselá herself did not escape the attentions of Dr Clauberg in Block 10: 'I was ill and they carried out some experiments on me ... Unfortunately, after the war when I got married, in spite of those experiments I got pregnant. I had to undertake a very loathsome abortion. Doctors told me, "That's enough! Don't dare to be pregnant anymore."'

In Block 10 not only did Schumann and Clauberg conduct sterilization experiments, but Dr Wirths, Auschwitz's chief medical officer, medically abused women in pursuit of 'research' into the functioning of the cervix. Medical experiments were also carried out on men in Block 28 of the main camp. A particular speciality here was to cover prisoners' skin with a variety of poisonous substances in an attempt to mimic possible tricks that might be used by those trying to escape service in the army.

Auschwitz prisoners were even 'sold' to the Bayer company, part of I.G. Farben, as human guinea pigs for the testing of new drugs. One of the communications from Bayer to the Auschwitz authorities states that: 'The transport of 150 women arrived in good condition. However, we were unable to obtain conclusive results because they died during the experiments. We would kindly request that you send us another group of women to the same number and at the same price.'[12] These women, who had died in testing an experimental anaesthetic, cost the Bayer company 170 Reichsmarks each.

But, terrible as the suffering inflicted was, it is not Clauberg or Schumann or Wirths or even the Bayer company that has invaded the popular consciousness as the most infamous name associated with medical experiments at Auschwitz, but that of a handsome, 32-year-old combat veteran, holder of the Iron Cross, sent to Auschwitz in March 1943 – Dr Josef Mengele. More than any other individual, Mengele has become synonymous with Auschwitz. The reason is a combination of character and circumstance: character because Mengele revelled in the power he possessed at Auschwitz and the opportunities for heartless research the place offered, and circumstance because he arrived at the camp just as the Birkenau crematoria were completed and Auschwitz was about to enter its most destructive period.

The schizophrenic nature of Mengele's character as demonstrated at Auschwitz is remarked on by a number of former prisoners. As he stood before them, immaculately dressed in his SS uniform, Mengele could smile and be charming – or he could be unspeakably cruel. Witnesses saw him shoot a mother and child on the ramp when they caused him trouble, but others remember how he offered them only kind words. Vera Alexander,[13] a Czechoslovakian inmate, saw this duality at close range when she was Kapo of a block that contained gypsy and Polish children: 'Mengele used to come to the camp every day – he used to bring chocolate ... When I shouted and told the children off, they usually reacted, "We will tell Uncle you are bad." Mengele was the "Good Uncle".' But, of course, Mengele behaved in this way for a reason: these children were nothing to him but the raw material for his experiments. Vera Alexander witnessed how children could be returned to the block screaming with pain after a visit to their 'Good Uncle'.

One of Mengele's chief areas of 'interest' was the study of twins – he had previously specialized in 'hereditary biology'. The rumour at the camp was that he was trying to understand the exact circumstances in which multiple births occur, and therefore wanted to undertake research that might eventually allow women in the Reich to have more children more quickly. But it is more likely he was chiefly motivated by the desire to understand the role of genetic inheritance in development and behaviour, a topic that obsessed many Nazi scientists.

Eva Mozes Kor[14] was 10 years old in 1944 and, together with her twin sister, Miriam, she was subject to Mengele's attentions: 'Mengele came in every day after roll call – he wanted to see how many guinea pigs he had. Three times a week both of my arms would be tied to restrict the blood flow, and they took a lot of blood from my left arm, on occasion enough blood until we fainted. At the same time they were taking blood, they would give me a minimum of five injections into my right arm. After one of these injections I became extremely ill and Dr Mengele came in next morning with four other doctors. He looked at my fever chart and he said, laughing sarcastically, "Too bad, she is so young. She has only two weeks to live." I would fade in and out of consciousness, and in a semi-conscious state of mind I would keep telling myself, "I must survive, I must survive." They were waiting for me to die. If I had died my twin sister, Miriam, would have been rushed immediately to Mengele's lab, killed with an injection to the heart and then Mengele would have done the comparative autopsies.'

As Myklos Nyiszli,[15] a prison doctor who observed Mengele closely, remarked: 'This phenomenon was unique in world medical history. Two brothers died together, and it was possible to perform autopsies on both. Where, under normal circumstances, can one find twin brothers who die at the same place at the same time?'

Eva Moses Kor managed to fight her fever and saved not just her own life, but that of her twin sister: 'I was asked by somebody, "You're very strong?" And I said, "I had no choice. I overcame or I would have perished."' Her story is not just an horrific one, it illustrates the truth at the heart of Mengele's life in Auschwitz – he could do to human beings whatever he liked. There was no restriction on the scope or extent of what he called his 'medical experiments'. His power to torture and murder in pursuit of his own sadistic curiosity was endless. He experimented not just on twins, but also on dwarves and inmates with the form of gangrene of the face known as noma, which was common in the gypsy camp in Birkenau because of the appalling conditions that existed there. But Mengele could just as easily have decided to take an interest in three, or thirty, other areas of research. Before he arrived at Auschwitz he showed no signs of becoming a sadist; by all accounts he demonstrated bravery fighting in the East, rescuing two soldiers from a blazing tank, and before that he had led a relatively unexceptional life in the medical profession after studying at Frankfurt University. It was the circumstances of Auschwitz that brought forth the Mengele the world was to know – a reminder of how hard it is to predict who, in exceptional situations, will become a monster.

Mengele was, in many respects, the archetypal Nazi officer in Auschwitz. Perfectly turned out on every occasion, he had utter contempt for the inmates. The idea of any form of intimate relationship with prisoners would have been anathema to him, the thought of sexual contact inconceivable. In this he was entirely consistent with the Nazi ideal. Since in Nazi racial theory those imprisoned in the camp represented a danger to the physical well-being of the Reich, sexual relationships between members of the SS and camp inmates were expressly forbidden. Such acts constituted a 'race crime' for the Germans. Indeed, one of the differences between the atrocities committed by the Nazis who were carrying out the 'Final Solution' and many other war crimes of the twentieth century is the overt insistence by the Nazis that their troops refrain from sexual violence, not out of humanity but out of ideology. In many other instances – for example, the Turkish massacre of the Armenians during World War I, the Japanese war of colonization in China that began in the 1930s, and the more recent Serbian attempt to conquer Bosnia in the 1990s – sexual violence against the womenfolk of the 'enemy' was widespread. From the Bosnian rape camps to the selling of Christian Armenian women into harems and the 'bonding' gang rape of Chinese women by soldiers of the Imperial Japanese army, the conflicts of the twentieth century are redolent with instances of male sexual violence. But for the Nazis the conflict in the East was a different kind of war. Whilst on the Channel Islands or in France it was perfectly possible for German soldiers to have relationships with local women, the Jews and the Slavic population of the East represented, to the Nazis, racially dangerous peoples. Nazi propaganda trumpeted that one of the most sacred tasks for each soldier of the Reich was to ensure the 'purity of German blood'. Slav and Jewish women (especially the latter) were absolutely out of bounds. A law had even been passed in pre-war Germany explicitly forbidding marriage between Jews and non-Jews.

All of this meant that there ought to have been no instances of sexual relationships at Auschwitz between members of the SS and Jewish prisoners. Killing Jewish women was, it seems, a sacred ideological duty for the SS, but having sex with them was a crime. Nonetheless, as Oskar Groening points out, 'If private interests are bigger than the feeling for the Jewish community as a whole – well, these things happen. If one is in a routine where one is looking after twenty young girls and one is a favourite and making coffee and God knows what, then these things, these propagandistic things, they aren't important any more ... ' And so, when the SS were in charge of women prisoners, Groening did not find it surprising that 'they stroked or kissed one another or had forced sexual relations'.

The women who worked in 'Canada' were the most obvious targets for members of the SS willing to set aside their ideological convictions and commit rape. The majority of women in Auschwitz had their heads shaved, were malnourished and were easily susceptible to disease. By contrast, the women working in 'Canada' had access to food that they could take from goods as they sorted them, and they were allowed to grow their hair. In addition, the SS mingled freely with the women who worked in 'Canada', not just to oversee their work but to pilfer goods for themselves. As a result, rape in 'Canada' was not unknown, as Linda Breder confirms: 'When we came to "Canada" there was no running water. However, the commandant [SS officer in charge] of "Canada" ordered showers to be built. These showers were behind the building. Although the running water was ice cold, I took regular showers. Once, a girl from Bratislava was taking a shower. She was a pretty woman, not skinny. An SS officer came to her and misused her in the shower – he raped her.' The SS man responsible was subsequently transferred out of 'Canada' but escaped further punishment. Another SS man known to have had sexual relationships with Jewish prisoners in camp was also dealt with leniently. One of the report officers at Birkenau, Gerhard Palitzsch,[16] was arrested but, almost certainly thanks to the influence of Hoess, he was punished merely by being transferred to a sub-camp away from Birkenau.

Rape also took place in an area of Birkenau in which, as in 'Canada', women were allowed to keep their own clothes and have their hair unshaved. This was the so-called 'family camp', a separate, fenced-in area that from September 1943 held Jews who had been deported from the ghetto-camp of Theresienstadt in Czechoslovakia. Around 18,000 men, women and children were imprisoned here until the camp was finally liquidated in July 1944. For these Jews there had been no selection on arrival: the Nazis planned to use them for 'propaganda' purposes. They were instructed to write postcards home explaining how well they were being treated, in an attempt to dispel rumours that Auschwitz was a place of extermination. Unlike the gypsy camp (the only other location in Birkenau where families lived together), in the family camp men and boys lived in separate barracks from women and girls.

Ruth Elias[17] was one of the inmates living in the women-only barracks of the family camp. She twice witnessed drunken SS men visiting the barracks and selecting women to take away: 'The girls came back crying – they had been raped. They were in a terrible state.'

The fact that members of the SS raped Jewish women in Auschwitz, though appalling, may not on reflection be so surprising. The SS had these women in their power and believed they were ultimately destined to be murdered. A combination of alcohol and the knowledge that the crime could be concealed served to overcome any ideological strictures. That such crimes have not received attention in most of the conventional literature on Auschwitz is perhaps not so strange either. This is an immensely delicate subject, and those who suffered at the hands of the SS might understandably wish to keep silent. As criminologists have long noted, the 'dark' figure for rape – the difference between the number of offences reported and the number of offences that have actually taken place – is one of the highest for any crime.

But if the knowledge that the SS raped women in Auschwitz fits the pattern of behaviour of many soldiers towards 'enemy' women, the fact that at least one SS man fell in love with a Jewish woman who worked in the camp surely destroys our preconceptions completely. Indeed, the story of Helena Citrónová[18]and her relationship with Franz Wunsch is one of the most extraordinary in the history of Auschwitz. Helena arrived at Auschwitz in March 1942 on one of the first transports from Slovakia. Her initial experience of the camp was nothing out of the ordinary – a story of

Above: Auschwitz prisoners employed in one of the many workshops within the Auschwitz Zone of Interest.

Above: Auschwitz prisoners digging drainage ditches at Birkenau – one of the most life-sapping tasks in the camp.

Above: 'Canada', the collection area at Birkenau, where prisoners sorted through belongings taken from new arrivals.

Left: Oskar Groening, who arrived at Auschwitz in the autumn of 1942.

Below: Kazimierz Piechowski, a Polish political prisoner, who took part in one of the most daring escapes from Auschwitz.

Above: Therese Steiner (third from left), a Jewish refugee from Austria, who was subsequently deported from Guernsey, first to France and then to Auschwitz.

Left: Helena Citrónová, a Slovak Jew, who was befriended by SS guard Franz Wunsch on her first day at work in'Canada'.

Above: A transport of Hungarian Jews arrives at Auschwitz–Birkenau in the spring/early summer of 1944. The twin chimneys of crematoria 2 and 3 can just be seen in the background to the left and right of the train.

Above: On arrival the Hungarian Jews are first separated by sex: women sent to one side, men to another.

Above: The separation of the sexes has been completed. Now the infamous selection will begin.

Above: This line of male Jews is being assessed by a Nazi doctor. In just a few moments he will decide who is to live and who is to die.

Above: A family of Hungarian Jews who have been selected to die wait in the grove of trees by crematoria 4 and 5.

Above: The ovens in the Auschwitz crematoria, each capable of holding several bodies.

Above: Crematorium 4. The gas chambers were above ground; the Zyklon B was pushed into them through hatches in the walls.

Above: Crematorium 3, situated near the arrival ramp in Birkenau. Here the gas chamber was in the basement of the building.

Above: Rudolf Hoess in captivity. Responsible for the murder of more than a million people, to his last breath he felt the reasons for the extermination of the Jews were 'right'.

hunger and physical abuse. During her first few months she worked in an outside commando destroying buildings and carrying rubble. She slept on flea-infested straw and watched in terror as the other women around her began to give up hope and die. One of her closest friends was the first to lose her life. She 'saw everything around her' and said, 'I don't want to live one minute more.' She started to scream hysterically and was then taken away and murdered by the SS.

Helena realized, in common with others, that in order to survive she needed to find work in a less physically strenuous commando. Another Slovakian woman she knew already worked in 'Canada' and offered Helena some advice: if she was prepared to put on a white headscarf and striped dress taken from one of the women who had worked in the 'Canada' commando and had just died, she could join them and come to work inside the barracks where the clothes were sorted the next day. Helena did exactly that, but unfortunately for her the Kapo noticed that she was an 'infiltrator' and told her that on her return to the main camp she would be transferred to the Penal Commando. Helena knew that this was a sentence of death, 'But I didn't care, because I thought, "Well, at least one day under a roof."'

Coincidentally, Helena's first (and potentially last) day at work in 'Canada' coincided with the birthday of one of the SS men who supervised work in the sorting barrack: Franz Wunsch. 'During the lunch break,' says Helena, 'she [the Kapo] asked who can sing or recite nicely, because today is the SS man's birthday. One girl, Olga, was from Greece, and she said she knew how to dance, and so she could dance on the big tables where we folded clothes. And I had a very beautiful voice. So the Kapo said, "Is it true you can sing in German?" and I said, "No" as I didn't want to sing there. But they forced me to sing. So I sang for Wunsch with my head down – I couldn't look at his uniform. I wept as I sang, and all of a sudden, when I finished the song, I heard him say, "*Bitte.*" Quietly he asked me to sing it again ... And the girls said, "Sing, sing – maybe he'll let you stay here." So I sang the song again, a song in German that I had learnt [at school]. So that's how he noticed me, and from that moment I think he also fell in love with me. That's what saved me, the singing.'

Wunsch asked the Kapo to ensure that the girl who had sung so memorably for him returned to work in 'Canada' the following day, and by making this request he saved her life. Helena was spared from the Penal Commando and became a fixture in 'Canada'. But whilst Wunsch looked kindly on her from that first meeting, initially Helena 'hated' him. She had learnt he might be violent: she heard rumours from other inmates of how he had killed a prisoner for dealing in contraband. But over the next days and weeks Helena watched as he continued to treat her with kindness. When he went on leave he sent her boxes of 'cookies', which were delivered to her through the intermediary of a 'pipel' – the boys who were the servants of the Kapos. And on his return Wunsch took to doing something even more daring – sending her notes: 'When he came into the barracks where I worked he passed by me and threw me a note and I had to destroy it right away, but I saw the words "Love – I fell in love with you." I was miserable. I thought I'd rather be dead than be with an SS man.'

Wunsch had his own office within 'Canada', and he tried to think of excuses to get Helena to come and see him. Once he asked her to manicure his nails. 'We were alone,' says Helena, 'and he said, "Do my nails so that I can look at you for one minute." And I said, "Absolutely not – I heard that you killed someone, a young man, by the fence." He always said that it was not true ... And I said, "Don't bring me into this room ... no manicure, nothing. I don't do manicures." And I turned around and said, "Now I'm leaving, I can't look at you any more." So he screamed at me – all of a sudden he became SS: "If you go through that door you will not live!" And he took out his pistol and threatened me. He loved me, but his honour, his pride was hurt. "What do you mean you're leaving without my permission?" So I said, "Shoot me! Shoot! I prefer death to playing this double game." So of course he didn't shoot me, and I walked out.'

But over time Helena came to realize that, incredible as it had at first seemed to her, she could depend on Wunsch. Knowing Wunsch's feelings for her gave her a 'sense of security. I thought, "This person won't allow anything to happen to me."' This emotion was compounded when one day Helena learnt from a fellow Slovakian that her sister, Róžinka, and her two young children had been seen in the camp, and that they were being taken to the crematorium. Helena heard this devastating news when she was in her barracks at Birkenau after work. Despite the curfew, she left the barracks and ran to the crematorium nearby. Shortly afterwards Wunsch learnt about Helena's actions, and he caught up with her as she neared the crematorium. He first shouted to the other SS that she was 'an excellent worker in his warehouse'. Then he threw her down on the ground and started beating her for breaking the curfew, so that any SS watching would not be aware of the relationship between them. Wunsch had already been told that Helena had run to the crematorium because her sister had been taken there and so he asked her: 'Quickly, tell me your sister's name before it's too late.' Helena told him, 'Różinka', and also said that she had arrived with her two small children. 'Children can't live here!' said Wunsch as he ran down into the crematorium.

He managed to find Różinka inside the crematorium and dragged her out, saying she was another of his workers. But her children died in the gas chamber. Wunsch subsequently managed to arrange for Różinka to work alongside Helena in 'Canada': 'My sister couldn't understand where she was,' says Helena. 'She was told she would work and the children had gone to a kindergarten – the same stories they sold all of us. She asked me, "Where are the children?" And I said, "On the other side of these buildings there's a children's home." And so she said, "Can I visit?" And I said, "There are days you can."'

The other women working in 'Canada' saw how upset Helena was by the constant questioning from her sister about the fate of her children. So one day they told Różinka, 'Stop pestering! The children are gone. You see the fire? That's where they burn children!' Różinka went into shock. She became apathetic and 'didn't want to live'. Only Helena's constant care and attention secured her sister's survival over the next months.

Emotionally distraught as Różinka was by the terrible realization that her children had been taken from her and murdered, she was still fortunate – she remained alive herself. And, protected by her sister, she did survive the war. The other women in 'Canada' looked on them both with mixed feelings. 'My sister was alive and their sisters were not,' says Helena. 'The fact was my sister came and he [Wunsch] saved her life. Why didn't such a miracle happen to them, who had lost their entire world – brothers, parents, sisters? Even those who were happy for me were not so happy for me. I couldn't share my emotions with my friends. I was afraid of them. And they were all envious – they envied me. One of them, a very beautiful woman, said to me, "If Wunsch had seen me before you, then he would have fallen in love with me."'

Primarily as a result of Wunsch saving her sister's life, Helena's feelings for him changed radically: 'Eventually, as time went by, I really did love him. He risked his life [for me] more than once.' But this relationship was never consummated, unlike some others between the sexes in Auschwitz: 'The Jewish [male] prisoners fell in love with all kinds of women as they worked. They disappeared once in a while into the barracks where the clothes were folded and they had sex there. They would have a guard so that if an SS came they could be warned. I couldn't because he [Wunsch] was SS.' Their relationship was conducted by glances, hurried words and scribbled notes: 'He would turn right and left, and when he saw no one was listening he'd say, "I love you." It made me feel good in that hell. It encouraged me. They were just words that showed a crazy kind of love that could never be realized. There are no plans that could be realized there. It wasn't realistic. But there were moments when I forgot that I was a Jew and that he was not a Jew. Really. And I loved him. But it could not be realistic. Things happened there, love and death – mostly death.' But inevitably, since over time 'all Auschwitz' knew about their feelings for each other, someone informed on them. Whether it was a prisoner or an SS man no one knows. But, as Helena puts it, 'someone ratted'.

One day, as she was being marched back to the camp after work, a Kapo ordered Helena out of the line. She was taken to the punishment bunker in Block 11. 'Every day they took me out and threatened me that if I didn't tell them what had gone on with this SS soldier, then at that very moment they would kill me. I stood there and insisted that nothing had been going on.' Wunsch had been arrested at the same time and, like Helena, under questioning he denied that any relationship existed. So eventually, after five days of interrogation, both of them were released. Helena was further 'punished' by being made to work on her own in a section of the 'Canada' barracks, away from the other women, and Wunsch was careful to be more circumspect in his dealings with her. Nonetheless, as will be seen in Chapter 6, Wunsch went on protecting Helena and her sister until Auschwitz was no more.

The story of the relationship between Helena and Wunsch is a profoundly important one. For tales of the rawness of emotion at the brutal end of the human spectrum – murder, theft and betrayal – are commonplace in Auschwitz. How much rarer is a story of love. And the fact that love could blossom in such circumstances, between a Jewish woman and an SS guard, is nothing short of astounding. Like so much that happened in Auschwitz, were the facts to be imagined in a work of fiction they would be dismissed as unbelievable.

But it is also worth noting that circumstances played a decisive role in permitting the relationship to flourish. It is virtually impossible to believe that Wunsch would have fallen in love with Helena had she still been working in the Demolition Commando. There would have been neither the opportunity for them to come into close contact, nor the chance of Wunsch protecting her once they did. And, not least, she would never have had the chance of captivating him by singing a song in German for his birthday. But in 'Canada' not only was there contact between the SS and Jewish women, there was also the chance that long-term relationships could develop. It is not surprising that proportionately more women survived Auschwitz as a result of working in 'Canada' than almost anywhere else.

The relationship between Wunsch and Helena is also, of course, symptomatic of how far the reality of Auschwitz had strayed from Himmler's aspirations for the camp. He would have seen Wunsch's actions as part of a wider pattern of 'corruption' at Auschwitz, and in the autumn of 1943, with the arrival of SS Obersturmführer (1st Lieutenant) Konrad Morgen, an attempt was made to put the overall situation, as far as the SS leadership was concerned, 'right'. Morgen's visit was to have dramatic consequences, for he was no ordinary SS officer but a judge of the SS reserve and an examining magistrate of the State Criminal Police Office. He had been sent to Auschwitz as part of a concerted effort by higher SS authorities to investigate corruption in the camps – in direct contradiction, of course, of Himmler's pious statement at Posen that 'we have taken nothing from them [i.e. the Jews] ourselves.'

Oskar Groening and his comrades were well aware of the reasons for Morgen's arrival: 'I guess that the ever-increasing corruption became so obvious that they said, "We have to stem that – stem the tide of corruption."' But the actual timing of Morgen's raid on the non-commissioned officers' barracks at Birkenau came as a complete surprise. Groening returned from a trip to Berlin to find 'two of my comrades in jail. In one locker they had found fountain pens and a tin of sardines, and in the other guy's locker I don't know what they found, but he later hanged himself. And my locker was sealed.'

Morgen and his colleagues had not yet opened Groening's locker because they insisted on carrying out their investigation with the owner present. As Groening saw it, this was his great good fortune. The front door of the locker was sealed so that it would be obvious if the locker was opened, but Morgen had not reckoned with the ingenuity of Groening and his comrades: 'We moved the locker forward and took the back wall out – that's pretty easy with plywood – and we removed suspicious soap and toothpaste that didn't belong there and put the wall back and fixed it with nails. Then I went to the Gestapo and said, "Excuse me, what sort of nonsense are you doing? I can't get to my locker." "OK," they said, "we've just got to check first." Then they came, took the three seals off, opened the locker, found nothing, patted me on the shoulder and said, "It's OK – carry on."'

Groening may have escaped sanction himself, but Morgen found plenty of evidence from others that pointed to only one conclusion: corruption at Auschwitz was widespread. 'The conduct of the SS staff was beyond any of the standards that you'd expect from soldiers,' Morgen later testified. 'They made the impression of demoralized and brutal parasites. An examination of the lockers yielded a fortune of gold, pearls, rings, and money in all kinds of currencies. One or two lockers even contained genitals of freshly slaughtered bulls, which were supposed to enhance sexual potency. I'd never seen anything like that.'[19]

And perhaps even more worryingly for those at SS headquarters, he uncovered evidence not only of financial corruption but also of sexual wrongdoing. Most shocking of all was that one of those implicated was the commandant himself, Rudolf Hoess. Morgen was nothing if not a tenacious investigator, and he pursued the allegations against Hoess for more than a year. He eventually interviewed his key witness, a former Auschwitz prisoner called Eleonore Hodys, in a prison hospital in Munich in October 1944.

Hodys had been an Austrian political prisoner at Auschwitz, arriving in one of the first women's transports in March 1942. Classified as *Reichsdeutsche* [citizen of the German Reich], she was immediately placed in a privileged position in the camp and was selected to work as a servant in Hoess's own house. In May 1942, with his wife away, Hoess made a pass at Hodys and tried to kiss her. Frightened, she ran off and hid in the lavatory. According to her testimony she was then summoned to the house some weeks later, when Hoess was in hospital recovering from a riding accident, and dismissed by Frau Hoess. It is reasonable to assume that Hoess's wife was suspicious of the developing relationship between Hodys and her husband. Subsequently Hodys was imprisoned; not in Block 11, but in the special jail in the basement of the main administration building, which was chiefly reserved for SS soldiers guilty of serious transgressions. This was a strange place for an Auschwitz prisoner to be held. But Hodys was no ordinary Auschwitz prisoner, and she had been transferred to the SS jail for a reason.

'One night,' Hodys told Morgen, 'I was already sleeping and he [Hoess] stood suddenly in my cell. I heard him say something like 'Hush!' and a torchlight was switched on and I saw the face of the commandant. He sat down on the edge of the bed. And then he moved closer and closer to me and tried to kiss me. When I resisted, he wanted to know why I was so reserved. "Because he was the commandant and a married man," I replied. Finally he left.'[20] After Morgen interrogated her further, Hodys confessed that Hoess had returned to her cell on several different nights and that 'eventually we had intercourse'. In order to avoid the SS guards, Hoess had entered the jail not by the normal route – straight down from his office above – but via his own garden and through an underground air raid shelter that adjoined the basement. Having found a secret way to Hodys's cell, and convinced her to be compliant, Hoess had sex with her on several different nights. Hodys even recounts how on one occasion the naked commandant was in bed with her when an alarm went off and he was reduced to hiding in a corner of the cell.

After several weeks in the SS jail she was transferred to Block

11. But her condition had changed – she was now pregnant. She recounts how Hoess, to protect himself, made her sign a note confessing that she had slept with another prisoner in the camp. She then spent several months imprisoned in Block 11 and tried, but failed, to give herself an abortion. Released back into the women's camp at Birkenau, she says she finally managed to obtain 'something' to abort the foetus.

Hodys's account of her affair with Hoess is fraught with difficulty. The first problem is that she is the only source for virtually everything she says. But Morgen seems to have believed her, and he was trained as a lawyer. Furthermore, Hodys appeared to have had little to gain from fantasizing a relationship with Hoess, especially since by the time Morgen interviewed her she had already been released from Auschwitz. Hoess never admitted to an affair with Hodys, but his own account of his relationship with his wife is contradictory. He confessed to the American officer Dr Gilbert during his interrogation after the war at Nuremberg that he and his wife rarely had sex once she was aware of just what he was doing at Auschwitz. Yet in his memoirs he speaks in glowing terms about his relationship with her, the woman he had always 'dreamed of'.

Nothing came of Morgen's investigation into Hoess's possible relationship with Hodys. By the time the interview took place, October 1944, it was obvious, with the Red Army closing in, that Auschwitz would not exist for much longer and, indeed, the whole Nazi state was under threat. In any event, Morgen's initial investigation into the running of the camp, held the previous year, had already had a devastating effect. Not only were individual SS soldiers prosecuted for corruption, but – in one of the most bizarre aspects of the history of Auschwitz – the man who controlled the horror of Block 11, Maximilian Grabner, was held to account for not seeking the correct 'permission' from Berlin before executing prisoners. It seems ludicrous that Morgen pushed forward with charges against Grabner when he ignored the killings in the gas chambers of Birkenau – presumably such mass extermination was thought to have 'permission' from higher authority. In any event, Grabner was put on trial and his defence was that Hoess had given him permission to 'clear out' Block 11 by shooting prisoners. Hoess, almost certainly protected by supporters above him in the

Nazi leadership, was never himself charged with any offence. But Grabner lacked protectors and was brought before an SS court, where the case eventually collapsed. He was subsequently tried once more by the Allies and executed – not for breaching SS regulations but for war crimes.

Unravelling the complex motivation behind the whole Morgen investigation is a difficult task. All the leading figures who gave evidence about it – Hoess, Grabner and Morgen himself – had particular agendas they wished to pursue when they finally came to give their account of the episode after the war. For Grabner it was that his actions were entirely authorized by Hoess; for Morgen that he was a crusader for the truth; and for Hoess that whilst he had willingly participated in the extermination programme at Auschwitz, he had always been true to Himmler's dictum and had never 'taken anything' for himself. What does seem plain is that there were internal SS political reasons behind a number of the consequences of the Morgen investigation, not least the decision to remove Hoess from the post of commandant, which was taken in the autumn of 1943. Hoess's dismissal was dressed up as a 'promotion' to a more senior role in concentration camp administration back in Berlin, but it is clear that he did not want to go. Not only did he leave his family behind in his house at Auschwitz, but letters between Martin Bormann (Hitler's powerful party secretary) and Himmler demonstrate that the former was trying to save Hoess's job on his behalf. But Himmler was unrelenting: Hoess was to be moved from the camp.[21]

One of Hoess's last major initiatives at Auschwitz seemed to be one of his strangest – the creation of an institution that seems utterly incongruous in the context of the previous history of the camp: a brothel. The location of this facility for selected prisoners could scarcely have been more prominent: Block 24, immediately next to the main '*Arbeit macht frei*' gate in the main camp. But Auschwitz was not the only camp to have a brothel; in fact it was the fifth camp within the Nazi state to offer such a 'service'. Himmler had decided that providing brothels across the concentration camp network would increase productivity by offering 'hard-working' prisoners (excluding Jews) an incentive to work even harder. He had ordered brothels to be constructed at Mauthausen and Gusen camps in Austria after an inspection as far back as May 1941 (they were finally opened in the summer of 1942). Then, in March 1943, he visited Buchenwald and demanded that another brothel be established there and at other camps. His faithful factotum Oswald Pohl issued the necessary orders to concentration camp commandants in May 1943.[22]

Józef Paczyński,[23] one of the Polish political prisoners who lived in Block 24 in the summer of 1943, laughed when he first heard the news. But it was not a joke. He and the other inmates were transferred out of Block 24 and saw how over the next few days 'brigades of carpenters and bricklayers' began to fashion small rooms out of the large empty space of the barracks on the first floor: 'Then they started painting it elegant colours, brought in beds and even put curtains in there. And one day we came back from work and we noticed that we could see female faces behind the curtains. But they're not allowed too close to the windows and we're not really allowed to look.'

A few days later came the official opening of the 'house of pleasure'. And Paczyński was there: 'Because I was an old inmate, and my Kapo was given two tickets [to the brothel], he gave me the second ticket. So I made myself look nice and I went along.' Paczyński discovered that the first part of the process, in an operation of military efficiency, was for each prospective 'client' to be examined by an SS doctor. If they passed this intimate examination, their hand was stamped and they were taken to another room on the ground floor of Block 24. Here they participated in a 'ballot' to see to which room upstairs (and thus to which prostitute) they were to be allocated, and also in which order they would see her. Paczyński recalls that he was 'second, into room number nine'. A bell was rung every 15 minutes as a sign for each prostitute to change customers. And so anxious was Paczyński for his turn that when the bell rang he rushed into room number nine only to see the previous inmate still trying to put on his trousers. Unfortunately, from his point of view, Paczyński was subsequently 'unable to perform', so he sat chatting on the bed to an 'elegant, good-looking girl' for his allotted time.

Ryszard Dacko[24] was another prisoner who experienced the 'delights' of the brothel. He was 25 years old in 1943 and a fireman at the main camp – a prized job, since firemen could travel relatively freely around Auschwitz and thus 'organize' plenty of contraband for themselves. The Germans also valued the fireman because, Dacko believes, back in their homeland firemen were 'respected'. As a result, the members of the Auschwitz fire brigade received a number of vouchers for the camp brothel and Dacko duly attended. He spent time with a girl called Alinka: 'I wanted to be as close as possible to her, to embrace her. It was three and a half years since I was arrested; three and a half years without a woman.' Alinka, according to Dacko, was a 'very nice girl – she's not ashamed of anything. She gave one what one wanted.'

The rooms where the women conducted their business still exist today and are used to store archival documents. One of the striking features of the doors are the large peepholes set into each of them. 'They [the SS] wanted to maintain order,' says Ryszard Dacko, 'if a prisoner were to strangle a girl or something. So they just looked through the peephole. It was [also] just male voyeurism. Most men like to look when someone's making love.' The visual supervision of prisoners having intercourse was also designed to ensure that 'perverted' sex acts were avoided (according to Józef Paczyński, prisoners had to have sex in the missionary position only) and to prevent close relationships developing between couples (in other brothels in the concentration camp system prisoners were even forbidden to talk to the women).

But the SS did not supervise the brothel so stringently in the early hours of the morning, and that was when real trouble started. Dacko recalls how one of the prisoners managed to duplicate the key to the brothel in order to visit his favourite girl at night. The trouble was that other prisoners had the same idea, and so fights broke out in the corridor on the first floor.

The idea that at Auschwitz prisoners could be found brawling in an SS-sponsored brothel seems, at first hearing, inexplicable. But it is actually a story that illustrates the sophisticated hierarchy of prisoners that had by now developed at the camp. As Józef Paczyński points out, the idea that Jews could use the brothel was inconceivable. They were considered a lower class of inmate, subject to a level of ill-treatment that some of the Polish or German non-Jewish prisoners escaped.

The Nazis could see that one of the keys to the smooth running of the camp was the attitude of the inmates who had managed to gain relatively privileged jobs, many of whom were political prisoners who had entered the camp years before. This class of prisoner was not subjected, as a rule, to the ruthless and regular selections that other inmates endured. But the Germans wanted a better way of motivating them. A brothel, with entrance dependent on vouchers issued by the Nazis, was a reward for good behaviour for around 100 of these key inmates and a clear incentive to behave even better in the future. Another possible reason for the establishment of the brothel, one subscribed to by Józef Paczyński, relates to the prevalence of homosexuality in the camp. He recalls how a number of 'prominent' prisoners took adolescent boys as their personal servants, and how a sexual relationship often developed between them. He therefore believes that it was 'because the Nazis wanted to eliminate such homosexual behaviour' that they set up the brothel.

The whole question of the Auschwitz brothel is, not surprisingly, an extremely sensitive one. And one of the most sensitive aspects of all relates to the attitude of the prisoners who used the brothel. For the most part they seem to have had no problem with the morality of it all. Most of the women who worked there were selected from the inmates of Birkenau (unlike other brothels in the concentration camp system, women were not sent there from Ravensbrück) and then forced to have sex with around six men every day. Their experience in the Auschwitz brothel is one of the hidden stories of suffering in the camp, and bears some comparison with the ordeal of the Korean 'comfort women' who endured so much as a result of the sexual abuse meted out to them by soldiers of the Japanese army. But in Auschwitz the women who worked in the brothel seem not to have been not so much pitied as envied. 'The girls were treated very well,' says Ryszard Dacko. 'They had good food. They took walks. They just had to do their job.'

Nothing demonstrates more effectively the immense power of context in human relations than Dacko's apparently callous statement that they 'just had to do their job'. For in the context of Auschwitz, where torture and murder were commonplace, it was possible for him to see the life of a woman in the brothel as a 'good' life. And, with so much other suffering around him, it clearly never occurred to him to ask, 'Ought I to be having sex with this woman?' Instead, it is clear what was on his mind – that he had endured 'three and a half years without a woman' and here was his opportunity to put that situation right.

There is another difficulty with the existence of the brothel at Auschwitz. Holocaust deniers and other apologists for the Nazis seize upon its presence as evidence that Auschwitz was a very different place from that painted in conventional historiography. This problem is especially stark when combined with knowledge of the so-called 'swimming pool' at Auschwitz main camp. In reality this was a water storage tank over which the firemen had fixed a makeshift diving board, but selected inmates were certainly able to bathe in it. 'There was a swimming pool in Auschwitz for the fire brigade,' confirms Ryszard Dacko. 'I could even swim there.' This facility has become one of the totems of the Holocaust deniers' case. 'This is supposed to be a death camp?' they say. 'With a swimming pool for the inmates? Come off it!' But in reality its existence fits into the same pattern as that of the brothel. Instead of showing how Auschwitz was not a centre for mass murder, which it undeniably was, the presence of these two institutions demonstrates once again the complex make-up of the various camps that together constituted 'Auschwitz'.

The many different hierarchical structures and purposes of the various camps within the Auschwitz complex have allowed the Holocaust deniers to focus on so-called anomalies such as these. There were myriad variations – from the 'swimming pool' and brothel at one end of the spectrum to the crematoria and murder of children at the other. It was the very complexity of Auschwitz as an institution that made the place so appealing to Himmler in 1943, and makes it such a focus of the Holocaust deniers' attentions today.

While Auschwitz was growing and developing during 1943, the Operation Reinhard camps were in decline. And in the autumn of 1943 an act of resistance occurred at the death camp of Sobibór, in eastern Poland, that must surely have confirmed Himmler in his belief that the future of the Nazis' extermination programme lay at Auschwitz. Significantly, it was an act of resistance made possible only because of the pervasive corruption that existed amongst the guards at the camp. Sobibór began its killing operations in May 1942, and by September 1943 around 250,000 Jews, the majority from the General Government, had been murdered in its gas chambers. Toivi Blatt was one of those who had been transported there to be murdered from the small town of Izbica in eastern Poland. And the story of how he came to be still alive today, and his part in the Sobibór revolt, is terrifying and inspiring in equal measure.

Before the war, his home town had contained around 3600 Jews. There was little overt anti-Semitism, especially for Toivi as he grew up. His father had fought in the Polish army and been wounded, and that gave the family a certain status in the town. But once the German army arrived, Toivi witnessed an immediate change: 'The [Polish] population noticed that the Jews are second class and you can do with them whatever you want ... In the end I was more afraid of my neighbours – Christian people – than of the Germans, because the Germans didn't recognize [that I was Jewish] and my neighbours did.'

The Germans did not remove the Jews of Izbica in one single raid, but in a series of 'actions' spread over several years. Typically, the Nazis would arrive at dawn and take a certain number of Jews away – initially to work as slave labour, and then, from the spring of 1942, straight to the gas chambers of Sobibór. In between actions the remaining Jews could live relatively openly. But eventually, in April 1943, the Germans arrived to clear the entire town of Jews. Toivi, a strong and fit 15-year-old, tried his best to run from them. As he dashed through the streets he saw an old schoolfriend, Janek, a Catholic Pole. Toivi shouted, 'Janek! Please save me!'[25] 'Sure!' Janek replied. 'Run to the barn not far past our house.' So Toivi rushed to the barn, only to discover that the door was padlocked. 'So I walked around the barn and then a little Polish woman started to yell at me, "Run, Toivi, run! Janek is coming!" So if Janek is coming why should I run? He will open the gate. But why is she so panicky? And when I turned around I saw Janek coming with a Nazi – the rifle pointed at me. And Janek said to the Nazi, "This is the Jew." I said, "Janek, tell him that you are joking!" And Janek says, "He's a Jew. Take him." Janek then said goodbye to me in a way which is difficult even now for me to repeat ... he said, "Goodbye, Toivi. I will see you on a shelf in a soap store." And this was his goodbye – the rumours were that the Nazis were making soap from human bodies.' As he stood staring in disbelief at his friend who had betrayed him, Toivi was 'scared that this was the last day of my life. When you are young, you are fifteen years old ... you see the trees, you see the flowers and you want to live.'

Toivi was taken back down to the town square where his mother, father and younger brother were waiting under armed guard with several hundred other Jews. They knew that they were to be transported to their deaths; the rumours of a place called Sobibór and of what went on there had been circulating for months. Yet a little later, as they climbed into the railway trucks at three o'clock on a beautiful spring afternoon, they still had hope: 'When everything is gone, and you don't have anything, what is left is hope – hope will be with you until the end ... There was talk in the dark truck: "The German army won't kill us – they'll take us to a concentration camp."' But as the train carried on, past the turn that would have taken them to the work camp of Trawniki, always travelling in the direction of what they knew was Sobibór, the talk turned to resistance: 'I heard the voices of people [saying], "Let's fight them back!" And I heard the voices of people like my father saying, "No – either way we will die."'

After a few hours they reached Sobibór, and Toivi had his first shock: 'I imagined Sobibór as a place where they burn people, where they gas people, so it must look like a hell. And now what I see is actually nice houses, plus the commandant's villa, painted green with a little fence and flowers. On the other side was a platform pretending to be a railway station, but this was for the Jews from Holland or France – they didn't know where they are when they arrive or what's happening to them ... But we Polish Jews did know.'

Immediately after leaving the trains the new arrivals were separated: one group containing mothers and children, the other adult men. At 15, Toivi was exactly at the borderline between the two groups, but because he was a solid, well-built adolescent he went with the men: 'I was with my mother, and I said goodbye to my mother in a way that hurt me until now – probably will to the end of my days. Instead of taking her arm like other people were doing, saying goodbye to their wives and children, I told my mother, "Ma, you told me I shouldn't drink the milk [but] to save it for another day." Like in a way accusing her. Anyway, she said, "Is this what you have to say to me now?" ... What had happened was that the day before they took us to Sobibór I was thirsty, so I told my Ma, "Could I have a little bit of milk?" So she said, "Yes." So when I started to drink I probably drank too much, because she said, "Toivi, leave it for tomorrow." And that's what I reminded my mother of when she was ready to go to the gas chamber.'

As a general rule, in the Operation Reinhard camps such as Sobibór, there was no selection on arrival. Everyone, without exception, was sent to the gas chambers. But very occasionally the Germans needed to select a small number of Jews from the new arrivals to work in the camp. Toivi was fortunate. He was from just such a transport. As they lined up, Toivi realized that the Germans might spare some of them, perhaps cobblers or tailors: 'I didn't have a trade at all, but I wanted to live and I prayed to God – at that time I was still praying. And I prayed to this German, "Please take me" ... and I still believe that my strong will somehow reached him while he was pacing back and forward in front of the group. And I felt he looked at me and I said to myself, "God help me!" And he said, "Come out, you little one!" My luck was that at that time they did need people. So they took out forty people. In this way I started to hope in Sobibór.'

Toivi's father was led off with the other men in the direction of the gas chamber. As he went, Toivi shouted to the Germans, 'He's a tanner!' but 'they needed carpenters, they needed maybe tailors, but they didn't need him'. As he watched his father go to his death, Toivi confesses that he 'didn't feel anything. I'm still thinking about this. You see, if one of my parents had died earlier – two days earlier – it would have been a terrible tragedy. I would cry day and night. And now in the same hour and the same minute I lost my father, my mother, my ten-year-old brother and I didn't cry. I didn't even think about this. Later, when I was looking at people [in the camp], nobody cried. I thought, "Maybe there's something wrong with me", and after the war when I met survivors I asked them, "Did you cry?" "No, I didn't," [they reply]. It's like nature protects us – took us away from the reality of our feelings. Because imagine, if I ever thought, "My dad – my parents – are now in the gas chamber", I would collapse and be killed ... If I show any sign that I weep, I would be killed.'

Within an hour of being selected Toivi met a friend of his, Józek, who had arrived at Sobibór on an earlier transport. His own father had been chosen from the new arrivals because he was a dentist, and Józek had been allowed to accompany him as a 'helper'. 'We were walking behind the barracks and here I saw people with a fiddle, a harmonica and a couple dancing. So I said, "Jozek, I don't understand. You are in a death camp. How can you do that? How can you be dancing?" He said, "Toivi, we are living on borrowed time. We will die anyway. This is the end. You see the smoke? Your father, your brother, your mother went through the smoke. We will also go through the smoke. So what's the difference? Should we put on a black armband? We wouldn't last a day here!"'

The life Toivi now led in Sobibór was in many ways akin to that of the workers in 'Canada' at Auschwitz. Food was available – much of it taken from the belongings of the Jews who had been gassed – and workers at Sobibór were allowed to keep their hair and wear everyday clothes. But unlike those who laboured in 'Canada', those at Sobibór had a close, almost intimate, relationship with the murderous function of the camp.

Toivi Blatt soon learnt his place in the process: 'A Dutch transport of about three thousand Jews arrived at Sobibór. The train was divided into sections, about eight to ten wagons, and pushed into Sobibór up a special side-track. There a group of Jews called the Bahnhof Commando opened the doors of the wagons and held the heavy luggage. I was with other young men standing, yelling in the Dutch language. I asked them to leave their luggage. Women still had their handbags – now they were told to throw them on the side. At that point I noticed in their eyes some kind of special anxiety. They were afraid. Some women didn't want to leave them and a German hit them with a whip. Then they went straight to a big yard and there a German we called 'the angel of death' talked to them so nicely. He apologized for the three-day journey from Holland but now he said they're in a beautiful place, because Sobibór was always beautiful. And he said, "For sanitary reasons you need to have a shower, and later you will get orders to leave here." Then people clapped, "Bravo!", and they undressed themselves nicely, and they went straight through a whole room, maybe 60 metres long, to a barrack. And there I was again. I was waiting for them. Then the women started coming, completely nude. Young kids, young girls, old ladies. I was a shy boy and I didn't know where to look. They gave me long scissors. I didn't know what to do with these shears. So my friend, who'd been there many times, said, "Cut the hair – you need to cut it very close." But I'm asked to leave a little, especially by the young girls, and not to cut so much. They didn't know that they will die in a few minutes. Then they were told to go on from the barracks just a few [steps] to the gas chamber. This trap was so perfect that I'm sure that when they were in the gas chambers and gas came out instead of water, probably they were thinking that this was some kind of malfunction.'

The process that Toivi Blatt participated in was so efficient, so well designed to pre-empt disruption, that 3000 people could arrive, be stripped of their goods and clothes, and be murdered within less than two hours. 'When the job was finished, when they were already taken out of the gas chambers to be burnt, I remember thinking to myself that it was a beautiful night [with] the stars – really quiet ... Three thousand people died. Nothing happened. The stars are in the same place.'

The Dutch Jews, who arrived at Sobibór in ignorance of the camp's true function, could be conned into entering the gas chambers without protest; not so the Polish Jews. The majority of them were not fooled by any pretence that this was a 'hygiene stop'. 'How can you do this?' demanded one middle-aged Polish woman as Toivi Blatt cut her hair. 'They will kill you too. Your time will come!' He said nothing in reply and remembers her words 'like a curse'. 'My whole orientation, my thoughts, were how to survive – how. Because I will die, but right now I am alive and I don't want to die today. And then the next day would come and I don't want to die today either.'

Toivi was all too well aware, of course, that he was, however unwillingly, helping the Nazis to operate the camp. Indeed, it was obvious to him that the work of cutting hair, sorting clothes, taking baggage from the trains, cleaning the camp – most of the practical duties involved in maintaining the operational capacity of Sobibór – was carried out by Jews: 'Yes,' he says, 'I thought about this. But nobody did anything. [I was] fifteen years old and had people with grown-up experience all around and nobody was doing anything. People change under some conditions. People asked me, "What did you learn?" and I think I'm only sure of one thing – nobody knows themselves. The nice person on the street, you ask him, "Where is North Street?" and he goes with you half a block and shows you, and is nice and kind. That same person in a different situation could be the worst sadist. Nobody knows themselves. All of us could be good people or bad people in these [different] situations. Sometimes, when somebody is really nice to me, I find myself thinking, "How will he be in Sobibór?"'

Toivi Blatt's view that people change depending on the situation is one that is shared by many who went through the horrors of the camps. And it is more than just the seemingly banal comment that human beings alter their behaviour according to circumstance, as we all clearly do in our own lives. Obviously, one behaves differently at a rock concert from how one would at a funeral. But Toivi Blatt points to a fundamental change in extreme circumstances that is less a change in behaviour – though that occurs as well – and more a change in essential character. It is as if, for people like Toivi Blatt, the realization came in the camps that human beings resemble elements that are changeable according to temperature. Just as water exists as water only in a certain temperature range and is steam or ice in others, so human beings can become different people according to extremes of circumstance.

One of the most disturbing aspects of this analysis is that, in my experience, it is one shared by many perpetrators. I remember one former dedicated member of the Nazi party saying to me in an exasperated manner, after I pressed him on why so many went along with the horrors of the regime, 'The trouble with the world today is that people who have never been tested go around making judgements about people who have.' A view that Toivi Blatt would no doubt echo.

This is not to imply, of course, that the significant change in character that could occur in the camps was necessarily a negative one. Choice exists in all circumstances, and it was possible for people to behave admirably, as Toivi Blatt witnessed when he was told to rake the sandy path that led from the lower camp to the gas chambers: 'I noticed that no matter what you do with the rake, little pieces were still [left] in the sand. I asked my friend, "What is this?" and he said, "This is money." And I remember wondering, here are people knowing they are going to their deaths and they have these few dollars or roubles in their hands. Finally they realize it's the end and they take the time to [tear] all the pieces so the enemy shouldn't have any use [of them]. I think this is heroism – spiritual heroism.'

In contemplating acts of greater resistance – actually fighting back against the Germans – Toivi Blatt had to overcome a feeling of what he calls 'reverse' racism. For when he first saw German soldiers dressed in steel helmets and smart uniforms he felt they were 'better' people. 'And at the other side of the spectrum I've seen Jews or Poles afraid, running and hiding.' This attitude, of course, is precisely the one the Germans hoped to create amongst those they wanted to oppress. It is one of the reasons Dr Mengele appeared on the ramp at Auschwitz immaculately dressed in his SS uniform, his boots shining like mirrors. For, just as the Germans wanted to create a self-fulfilling prophecy that those whom they fought were inferior, so by dressing and acting as if they were members of a master-race they wanted to force their enemies to subscribe to the belief that the Nazis were indeed their superiors.

In such circumstances it is hardly surprising that the catalyst for radical change at Sobibór came with the arrival of people who had been less exposed to the kind of 'reverse racism' Toivi Blatt describes – Jews who were former Red Army soldiers. 'We arrived at Sobibór on 21 or 22 September 1943,' says Arkadiy Vajspapir,[26] one of the Soviet prisoners of war who came to the camp on a transport from Minsk. 'We'd been trapped for three days in locked carriages – carriages for cattle. Three days without food or light.' As luck would have it, the Nazis decided to select slave labour from this particular transport. 'They asked whether there are carpenters or builders,' says Vajspapir, 'and we were asked whether there are any people who can lift 75 kilos.' At the moment of their selection, the Soviet POWs had no idea of the function of the camp: 'We didn't know what was going on – we thought it was a labour camp. But in the evening the old prisoners came to us and said, "Your friends are burning." Then we understood what kind of a camp this was.'

Amongst the 80 or so Soviet POWs selected to act as labourers was a charismatic lieutenant in the Red Army called Alexander ('Sasha') Pechersky. 'He was a very handsome, good-looking man,' says Vajspapir, 'tall and solidly built. He was respected – his every word was law for us.' Pechersky made an immediate impact on the camp, and soon became the focal point of an underground resistance movement. Before the arrival of the Soviet POWs there had been several attempts by prisoners to escape, mostly by running from work details that operated outside the wire. But the vast majority of such attempts failed. 'Where will you go when you escape finally in the forest?' asks Toivi Blatt. 'Practically every day farmers who lived nearby came with Jews they caught hiding some place in the fields' and handed them in for 'five pounds of sugar and a bottle of vodka'. But Pechersky and his comrades managed to change the fatalistic attitude that prevailed in the camp. They worked with Leon Feldhendler, who had led the small Sobibór underground before the arrival of the Soviet POWs, and tried to think of ways of organizing a mass escape.

Just two weeks after their arrival at Sobibór an attempt was made to dig an escape tunnel, a project that was abandoned a few days later when the tunnel became flooded. In any case, as Pechersky knew, it would scarcely be possible to enable all the inmates of Sobibór – more than 600 of them – to crawl out during one night without incident. He quickly realized that if there were to be a successful mass escape, it would have to come through armed resistance. Pechersky also recognized that the prisoners had better act quickly. The first snowfalls, expected in only a few weeks, would make it easy for the Germans to track any escapees through the forest. So over the next few days, with the cooperation of some of the key Kapos, a plan began to take shape. 'The first phase,' says Toivi Blatt, 'was to collect weapons – knives and axes – because a lot of carpenters had tools in their workshops.' The second phase was to 'lure' the Germans to secluded places in the camp, kill them and steal their firearms. The third, and final, phase was open revolt.

In the second week of October the underground learnt that several of the most important Germans at Sobibór – including Wagner, one of the leading NCOs – had gone on leave to Germany. The German presence in the camp was thus weaker than it had been for some time. The remaining Germans were to be enticed to the tailors' or cobblers' workshop by the promise of personal gain; the success of the revolt thus depended upon the corruptibility of the guards. Vajspapir was ordered by Pechersky to hide in the cobblers' shop in the camp and use an axe to kill a German guard when he arrived for a fitting for his new shoes. 'I was very excited,' says Vajspapir. 'We understood that our destiny was at stake.' Elsewhere, other Germans would be lured by the promise of a new leather coat to the tailors' shop, where they too would be killed. The next stage was for the inmates to escape through the main gate, gambling that the Ukrainian guards, who were very much dominated by the Germans, lacked both the ammunition and the will to offer much resistance.

The revolt began on 14 October. At half past three in the afternoon, Vajspapir, together with Yehuda Lerner, a fellow Jew from the Minsk transport, concealed himself at the back of the cobblers' hut: 'The German came in for a shoe fitting. He sat down just in front of me. So I stepped out and hit him. I didn't know that you should do it with the flat side of the axe. I hit him with the blade. We took him away and put a cloth over him. And then another German came in. So he came up to the corpse and kicked him with his leg and said, "What is this? What does this disorder mean?" And then when he understood [what was happening] I also hit him with the axe. So then we took the pistols and ran away. Afterwards I was shivering. I couldn't calm down for a long time. I was sick. I was splashed with blood.'

Lerner and Vajspapir had killed two Germans in the cobblers' workshop. Three more SS men were murdered in the tailors' shop, and others who could not be enticed out were murdered in their offices. By five o'clock in the afternoon most of the SS in the camp, a total of nine, had been killed; but, worryingly, the commandant still remained alive. The prisoners began to assemble for roll-call as usual. 'But then at about fifteen minutes before six,' says Toivi Blatt, 'Sasha [Pechersky] jumped on a table and made a speech – I still remember it. He talked about his motherland, the Soviet Union, and how a time will come when everything will change and there will be peace, and if somebody survives, his duty is to tell the world what's happened here.'

Next, as planned, the prisoners began marching towards the main gate, but suddenly they came under fire from the watchtowers and from the commandant, Frenzel, who emerged from a barrack and started shooting. It was immediately clear that escape through the main gate was impossible. An attempt was now made to breach the barbed wire at the back of the camp, even though the area beyond was mined. As Toivi Blatt wrestled with the wire, under fire from the guards in the watchtowers, he felt the whole weight of the fence collapse, pinning him down. 'My first thought was, "This is the end!" People were stepping over me, and the barbed wire points went into my coat. But finally I had a stroke of genius. I left the leather coat in the barbed wire and just slid out. I started to run. I fell down about two or three times; each time I thought I was hit, but I got up, nothing happened to me, and finally [I reached] the forest.' In front of him, as he ran, Toivi Blatt saw 'flying bodies' torn apart by the exploding mines, and so came to realize that it was his 'luck' to have been one of the last to leave the camp.

Altogether around half of the 600 prisoners at Sobibór managed to escape from the camp that day. As Toivi Blatt sees it, this success was made possible by one major factor: 'They [the Germans] didn't consider us as people, being capable of doing something. They considered us trash. They didn't expect that Jews were going to [be prepared to] die, because they had seen thousands going to die for nothing.' As far as Arkadiy Vajspapir is concerned, another necessary precondition for the escape was the arrival of the Soviet POWs, who faced every privation in the camp with solidarity. Significantly, these POWs had been in the camp for less than a month before making their move. Although they had suffered in previous German camps, they had experienced nothing like the horror of Sobibór before, and they therefore had the opportunity to react quickly against the appalling sights they saw. Their military discipline, together with the singular personality of Sasha Pechersky, was crucial to the success of the revolt.

The majority of the 300 Sobibór prisoners who escaped from the camp did not survive the war. Many wandered around, lost in the woods, and were captured within hours; others were later betrayed by Poles and handed over to the Germans. Sasha Pechersky and a handful of his comrades managed to reach partisans sympathetic to the Red Army, and eventually met up with the advancing Soviet forces. Toivi Blatt had a series of adventures and narrow escapes, helped by some Poles, hindered to the point of betrayal by others. After the war he decided to make a new life for himself in America.

Himmler was acutely concerned by the revolt at Sobibór, and in its wake he ordered the murder of Jews at Trawniki, Poniatowa and Majdanek camps. These killings, carried out from 3 November, were among the bloodiest of the Nazis' 'Final

Solution'. Some 43,000 people were murdered in the action, codenamed by the Nazis 'Harvest Festival'. In a telling reminder that technologically advanced methods are not ultimately necessary to kill people in large numbers, 17,000 Jews were shot at Majdanek in just one day.

The 'Harvest Festival' killings of November 1943 came at a time when the *raison d'être* behind the Nazis' 'Final Solution' had shifted. During autumn 1941 and spring 1942 the extermination programme had been at least in part motivated by a desire to create 'space' for a new German empire in the East. But by the winter of 1943 it was clear that the Nazis were losing the war, and another motivation came to the fore: vengeance. The Nazi murder of the Jews would now be primarily driven by the desire to ensure that their greatest enemies would not profit from the war, no matter how it ended. Of course, the desire to murder Jews for ideological reasons had always been present behind the planning and implementation of the Nazis' 'Final Solution'. The inclusion of the Jews of western Europe in the Nazis' plan for mass extermination showed that economic measures and the creation of 'space' were never exclusively the motivation for the crime. But not until now, with the dream of the new 'Nazi Order' in the East collapsing around them, had the leaders of the Third Reich sought solace in the mass murder of Jews out of pure, unadulterated hatred.

However, the Germans faced increasing difficulty enforcing the 'Final Solution' outside their area of direct rule. While the Bulgarian authorities had previously given up 11,000 Jews from occupied Thrace and Macedonia who had then been murdered in Treblinka, there had been protests in 1943 at proposals to deport Jews from Bulgaria itself. And the Romanian leader Ion Antonescu, having participated in the destruction of Jewish communities in Bessarabia, Transnistria and Bukovina, was now refusing to send the remainder of the Jewish population of Romania to the gas chambers of Bełżec. In Italy, too, though Mussolini had implemented various anti-Semitic measures, he had so far refused to hand over Italian Jews.[27] Many allies of the Nazis were no longer of the opinion that they were backing the winning side. They had helped the Nazis persecute Jews when they felt it was in their own interests; now that it was not, they started to distance themselves from the whole policy. For the most part, their change of heart was motivated less by moral awakening and more by cynical pragmatism.

Of the European countries occupied by the Germans, only one emerges untainted by the moral corrosiveness of the 'Final Solution': Denmark. A concerted effort by the Danish population enabled 95 per cent of the Jews in the country to be spirited away from the Germans. And the story of how the Danes saved their Jews is not just an inspiring and an intriguing one, it is also laced with an intricacy that at first sight it seems to lack.

Germany occupied Denmark on 9 April 1940, and from the very beginning it was clear that the Danes would experience a very different kind of occupation from that endured by other European countries. The major Danish institutions – including the monarchy, parliament and police – remained largely untouched. And the Danes were not asked by the Nazis to enforce any of the anti-Semitic legislation that was commonplace elsewhere in the Nazi state. As far as the Danish authorities were concerned, the 8000 Danish Jews were full citizens of the country and would remain so. 'We didn't have any discrimination whatsoever,' says Knud Dyby,[28] a Danish policeman at the time. 'The Jews were absolutely assimilated. They had their businesses and their houses like everyone else. I'm sure in Denmark there was a lot of intermarriage. One of my family members married a Jewish showgirl.' Even those Jews who chose actively to practise their religion under the Nazi occupation faced little problem. Bent Melchior,[29] then a schoolboy, was initially concerned when the Germans arrived since his father, a rabbi, had been outspoken against the Nazis. But nothing untoward happened: 'We went to school, the synagogue, cultural activities – it all continued to function.'

One exceptional story, recalled by Bent Melchior, illustrates the extent to which tolerance was embedded in Danish society. His father wrote a short book of commentaries to the five books of Moses, and since the King of Denmark was the focus of patriotism for all Danes, he decided to have one copy of the book specially bound as a gift for his monarch. On New Year's Eve 1941, Bent's elder sister was given the task of delivering the book to the palace in Copenhagen. As she approached the gates, by coincidence the Queen walked out, saw her and asked, 'Is this for my husband?' His sister said, 'Yes, Your Grace', and the Queen took the book. That night King Christian X of Denmark sat up and wrote a personal thank-you note to Bent's father, sending greetings to him and to the Jewish community. 'It [the letter] arrived on 1 January 1942,' says Bent Melchior, 'and it made a very great impression on the whole community – how he answered a little rabbi who sends him a book.'

It seems incredible, in the context of the anti-Semitic persecution the Nazis inflicted on the rest of Europe, that the Germans permitted such tolerance to exist. But they faced a delicate situation in Denmark. In the first place they wanted to ensure that food supplies from that country to Germany were unaffected. They also recognized the propaganda value in this 'ideal' occupation of a fellow 'Aryan' state, and knew the added benefit that would come from a peaceful Denmark that required few Germans soldiers to be stationed on Danish soil. This attitude was, however, to change over the summer and autumn of 1943. In the wake of the defeat at Stalingrad, and the retreat of the German army, there were a number of acts of resistance in Denmark, culminating in a series of strikes. The Germans insisted that repressive measures must be introduced to counter such actions, but the Danish authorities refused to do as they were ordered. On 29 August, therefore, the Germans assumed power in Denmark.

The German plenipotentiary in Denmark, Dr Werner Best, now faced a dilemma: what should be done with the Danish Jews? Little in Best's background suggested he was likely to take a sympathetic line. Trained as a lawyer, he had joined the Nazi party in 1930 and the SS the following year. He had been legal adviser to the Gestapo and worked directly for Reinhard Heydrich. While at the Reich Security Main Office he was complicit in the murder of Polish intellectuals, and he had then worked in France, directly involved in the oppression of French Jews. Yet now this committed Nazi was prepared to do something completely out of character. Through intermediaries, he was about to warn the Danish Jews of their impending arrest.

The round-up was planned for the night and early morning of 1–2 October 1943. But just days before Best had a meeting with the German naval attaché, Georg Duckwitz, and informed him about the forthcoming raids. Best did this knowing that it was almost certain that Duckwitz, who had known sympathy with the Danes, would leak the information to Danish politicians, who would in turn warn leading members of the Jewish community. This chain of causation duly occurred.

'It was on a Tuesday night [28 September],' says Bent Melchior, 'that a woman came to our apartment, asked to speak to my father and said that this coming Friday night the action would take place.' Next morning, because it was a Jewish holiday, there were more people in the synagogue than usual when Bent's father rose to speak: 'My father stopped the service and told the community that this was serious, and he repeated the message he had received. "Don't be at home on Friday night." He also said that the services at the synagogue the following day would be cancelled. But we could not rely on this being enough. It was up to everyone present to go out and tell family, friends, people you thought of as lonely – try and get in contact with as many as possible.'

The exodus began later that day, 29 September, and Rudy Bier[30] and his family were part of it. They travelled about ten miles out of Copenhagen to stay with some business friends of Rudy's father: 'They were a very nice family with three daughters, a bit older than us. They lived in a villa and there was a garden, which we didn't have because we lived in a flat. They took extremely good care of us.'

As the Bier family settled into their new home outside Copenhagen, the Danish police learnt of the impending deportations. 'I was at the police station when I heard the news,' says Knud Dyby, 'and a police comrade of mine said he had been contacted by a Jewish neighbour of his, a merchant by the name of Jacobson. He and his family were very, very nervous and needed help.' It is remarkable, of course, given the previous actions of police in other Nazi-occupied countries, such as France and Slovakia, that the immediate reaction of Dyby and his colleagues was to offer assistance to the Danish Jews. In this case, Dyby offered to help the Jacobsons himself, and organized their escape across the narrow strait between Denmark and neutral Sweden: 'We had to tell them to use either streetcars or a local train to get into the port station in the east of Copenhagen. From there we took several taxicabs down to the harbour. The taxi drivers knew what was happening and were very, very helpful, and in some cases didn't even charge for the transport. At the harbour we hid ourselves in the sheds the Germans normally used for nets and tools.'

Once the Jewish families were concealed, Knud Dyby went out in search of fishermen prepared to take the risk and carry them through the night across the strait: 'I would tell the fishermen how many I had, and we would have to beg and borrow enough money to pay them – as much as we could to get everyone on board.' It was a journey fraught with difficulties: 'I was once with three Jewish men and all of a sudden a German patrol started coming our way. We jumped deep into a trench. And we stayed there until we could hear the Germans pass by. That's one time I had my pistol ready because I would have defended the four of us ... I didn't want to be caught and sent to a concentration camp.'

It was not just the Danish police who helped the Jews escape; many members of other institutions made their contribution, from the Danish coastguard who looked the other way when countless small boats left the harbours at night, to the Danish clergy who helped support the fleeing Jews. A statement from the bishop of Copenhagen registering the Church's forthright position was read in Danish churches on 3 October: 'Wherever Jews are persecuted for racial or religious reasons, it is the duty of the Christian Church to protest against such persecution ... Irrespective of diverging religious opinions, we shall fight for the right of our Jewish brothers and sisters to keep the freedom that we ourselves value more highly than life.'[31]

Meanwhile, Rudy Bier's family felt that it was no longer safe for them to continue living with friends in the country, and they too began the journey to Sweden: 'We had to pass through the centre of Copenhagen, and there we had this unpleasant event. Our driver made a wrong turn and stopped just in front of the German headquarters building. That was a bit frightening for a moment, but then he turned round, found his way again and off we went.' The Biers were driven on past Copenhagen, 25 miles south to the point at which Sweden is farthest from Denmark. This was thought by their protectors to be the safest place to make the crossing. Here two ships, each capable of taking 200 passengers, lay a little way off the coast. The Biers were rowed out to one of the ships and began their voyage at about 11 o'clock at night: 'We were on deck,' recalls Rudy, 'and my smallest brothers and sisters were given some light medication not to cry and they slept their way over the crossing.' After several uneventful hours they reached

Sweden: 'Once we were on Swedish shores it was very different. In Denmark we had a blackout but in Sweden there were lots of lights on in the streets. And we were received in a very friendly way by the population. There were songs – the Swedish and Danish national anthems were sung – and people were just extremely happy that now they were out of immediate danger.' The Swedes could scarcely have been more helpful. They sent out lighted boats to ensure the refugees made it safely to shore, having previously announced on the radio on 2 October that they would welcome all incoming Danish Jews.

Rudy Bier's experience was not unusual, and the vast majority of Danish Jews successfully fled to Sweden. During the round-up on the night of 1 October the Germans caught just 284 Jews,[32] and in the following weeks they managed to catch fewer than 200 of those escaping to Sweden. Out of a Danish Jewish population of 8000, fewer than 500 were eventually arrested and deported. Significantly, those that were caught by the Germans were sent not to Auschwitz but to the ghetto of Theresienstadt in Czechoslovakia, where, though they endured a life of privation, they did not face selection and systematic murder. More than four out of five of the deported Danish Jews returned home at the end of the war.

The story of the rescue of the Danish Jews is, of course, an immensely cheering one amidst the catalogue of betrayal and vindictiveness that pervades many of the other stories of deportation. But the ambiguous attitude of the Germans to the arrest and deportation of the Danish Jews shows that whilst this is certainly an admirable story, it is not a simplistic one. And at the heart of its complexity lies the curious attitude of Werner Best, for not only did he warn the Danish Jews through an intermediary, he presided over a distinctly lacklustre attempt to catch them. There were pockets of vigorous work by the German security forces – most infamously the efforts by Hans Juhl ('Gestapo Juhl') to arrest the Jews in Elsinore – but for the most part the Germans do not seem to have been particularly diligent. 'I always maintain,' says Rudy Bier, 'that if the Germans had wanted to stop that operation, they could have done it extremely easily because the whole of the water between Denmark and Sweden is not that wide, nor that long, and with four or five motor torpedo boats the whole operation would have gone flat.' Yet not one of the escaping boats was stopped by German naval patrols.

A clue as to why Werner Best acted as he did is given by a report he sent to Berlin on 5 October: 'As the objective goal of the Judenaktion in Denmark was the de-judaization of the country, and not a successful headhunt, it must be concluded that the Judenaktion has reached its goal.'[33] Thus Best claims credit for making Denmark 'Jew-free' by methods that minimized disruption to the overall Nazi occupation. That the Jews had fled to safety rather than been captured also offered one practical benefit to him – it made it more likely that the Danish authorities would subsequently be cooperative.

There is another area in which recent scholarship challenges the conventional history of the Danish Jews – the question of the 'altruism' of those involved in the rescue. It is clear, for example, that many of the first Jews who fled had to pay considerable sums to the fishermen. 'Unfortunately some of the refugees would flash some money to get on the first boat they could,' says Knud Dyby. 'And the fishermen were actually a rather poor bunch of people – they had made very little money. So I'm sure somebody welcomed an extra income.' But was the position of the Danish fishermen so very unreasonable? They were being asked to risk their livelihood – for all they knew, their lives – in helping the Jews escape. Was it therefore wrong for them to charge what they could? Especially since, during the first nights of the operation, there was no guarantee that German patrol boats were not waiting offshore to intercept them. Indeed, seen from that perspective, the most reprehensible way for the Danish fishermen to behave would have been to refuse to take the risk of crossing at whatever price. And significantly, there is not one case of Danish Jews being left behind because they could not pay.

Of course, the Danes were helped in their rescue action by a number of factors outside their control. Geography clearly played a part – unlike in the Netherlands or Belgium, there was a neutral country nearby. And the relatively lax occupation of Denmark up to the summer of 1943 had meant that key institutions, such as the police and coastguard, were relatively free from Nazi control. Then there was the timing of the Nazi attack on the Danish Jews. As has been noted, it was obvious by the autumn of 1943 that the

Germans were losing the war and the Danes knew that to help the Jews would be to help the aims of the winning side. Another important factor is that the Nazi occupation of Denmark was never as violent as that of, for example, Poland, and we cannot know how the Danish population would have acted had the persecution of the Danish Jews, and reprisals for helping them, been similarly brutal. Nor can we take from this story the notion that the Danes are somehow uniquely caring as a people, not least because Denmark was reticent to accept large numbers of Jewish refugees from Germany during the 1930s. But what those who seek to relativize the Danish experience sometimes forget is that, even when it looked as if the Germans were going to win the war, during 1940 and 1941, the Danes still held steadfast to their moral principles and did not persecute the Jews, as would surely have pleased their Nazi masters.

Nor should the knowledge that Best's Machiavellian mind intended all along to allow large numbers of Danish Jews to escape change our judgment about the moral worth of the actions of the rest of the Danish population. For crucially, when the Danes rose up in solidarity against the deportations, no one knew what was in Best's mind. Everyone who helped the Jews believed at the time that they were acting directly against the wishes of the Germans, and at great personal risk. So it remains hard not to agree with Knud Dyby that 'what the Danish people did, they did out of their own heart and their own friendliness. It was a simple feeling of humanity. It was simply goodness and decency. And that was what everybody, all over Europe, should have done.' There could be no starker contrast with the heroic action of the Danes than what was about to occur in another European country during the spring and summer of 1944, the year of greatest killing in the history of Auschwitz.

— 5 —

FRENZIED KILLING

Auschwitz became the site of the largest mass murder in history as a result of the events of 1944. Up until the spring of that year the death toll at the camp remained several hundred thousand below that of Treblinka. But in the spring and early summer of 1944 Auschwitz was stretched to capacity and beyond by the most horrific and frenzied period of killing the camp would ever see. The majority of the Jews who were to suffer and die during this terrible time came from one country: Hungary.

The reasons why so many Hungarian Jews suddenly found themselves on trains to Auschwitz as the war neared its end are complex. The Hungarians had always tried to play a sophisticated political game with the Nazis, wavering between two powerful and contradictory emotions. On the one hand they had a traditional fear of German power, and on the other they wanted to cooperate with the winning side, especially if it meant gaining territory at the expense of their eastern neighbour, Romania. It was not until October 1940 that the Hungarians finally made their minds up and allied themselves completely with the Axis powers by joining the Tripartite Pact. By then an agreement had been reached, brokered by Ribbentrop, the Nazi Foreign Minister, which transferred northern Transylvania to Hungary from Romania. Bribed by this territory, which they had long coveted, and betting on the Nazis winning the war (which was the 'smart' position to take in the summer and early autumn of 1940), the Hungarians moved politically and strategically closer to their giant neighbour.

In spring 1941 the Hungarians joined Hitler in his invasion of Yugoslavia and then, in June, sent troops to take part in the Nazis' attempted conquest of the Soviet Union. But as the promised Blitzkrieg defeat of Stalin failed to materialize and the war dragged on much longer than expected, the Hungarians began to realize they had backed the wrong side. In January 1943 the Red Army smashed through Hungarian forces on the Eastern Front, causing catastrophic losses – around 150,000 Hungarian troops were killed, wounded or captured. The new 'smart' position, the Hungarian authorities thought, was to distance themselves from the Nazis. Secret talks were held during 1943 with the Western Allies, and an arrangement was reached that the Hungarians would change sides once Hungarian territory was under threat from the Allied advance.

In the spring of 1944 Hitler decided to move on his fair-weather friend. In traditional historiography this decision is characterized as the act of a man driven by considerations of ideology rather than practical strategy. But recent scholarly research[1] shows the opposite. Rather than being motivated by a simple desire to punish his ally for fickleness, Hitler and the Nazis were acting relatively rationally. Hungary was one of the few countries in eastern Europe that they had not yet plundered. It was a place of enormous wealth, and now, judged Hitler, was the time for the Nazis to snatch it.

It was, of course, the Jews who were to be the Nazis' particular target. There were over 760,000 Hungarian Jews – nearly 5 per cent of the population – and although they had suffered the effects of anti-Semitic legislation, the majority of their communities (and much of their wealth) were still largely intact. Hungarian Jews of military age had been sent to work in labour gangs on the Eastern Front where many thousands had died, but there was still hope amongst the rest of the Jewish community that they might escape crippling persecution; hope, that is, until the Nazis occupied their country. The German army drove into Hungary on 19 March 1944, and the very next day SS Obersturmbannführer (Lieutenant Colonel) Adolf Eichmann followed, with the task of expropriating everything possible from the Jewish population of Hungary and then deporting them. Typically, one of the first objects Eichmann expropriated from the Hungarian Jews was something for himself: the luxurious Aschner Villa in the smart Rose Mount area of Budapest.

By now the Nazis' 'Final Solution' had evolved into a new phase. Eichmann was charged not with organizing simple extermination, as his colleagues in the General Government in Poland had been in 1942. Given the dire military situation and the increased need for forced labour, more effort was to be made by the Nazis to separate those Jews who could serve the German war effort through work from those who served no useful purpose for the Third Reich and so were to be killed at once. Auschwitz was therefore, from the Nazi perspective, the perfect destination for the Hungarian Jews, since by now Dr Mengele and his colleagues had considerable experience of exactly this kind of selection. Auschwitz could thus become the conduit – a kind of giant human sieve – through which selected Hungarians could reach the slave labour factories of the Reich.

To begin with, Eichmann's initiatives in Hungary seemed to conform to the all too familiar pattern of Nazi anti-Jewish action. He successfully negotiated the cooperation of the Hungarian police for the impending deportations, and he helped organize the ghettoization of the Jewish population outside Budapest. The Germans had initially demanded that 100,000 Hungarian Jews be sent 'to the Reich', but following the ghettoization of the Jews, the Hungarian authorities volunteered that the rest of the country's Jews could follow. Just as others, notably the Slovakians, had found before them, once the status quo was disturbed and breadwinners removed from Jewish families, the 'easiest' way forward was to encourage the Nazis to take everyone; and this was something Eichmann was all too happy to do.

However, in parallel with these predictable developments, Eichmann was about to pursue another course. On 25 April 1944 Joel Brand, a Hungarian Jew who was a leading figure in the Relief and Rescue Committee, an organization committed to helping Jews escape from Nazi control, went to the Hotel Majestic in Budapest to meet Eichmann. Brand had already attended previous meetings with him and other SS officers in an attempt to bribe them to allow a number of Jews out of Hungary. Now Eichmann said to him: 'You know who I am? I was in charge of the "Actions" in the Reich, in Poland, in Czechoslovakia. And now it's Hungary's turn. I've called you to propose a deal. I am prepared to sell one million Jews to you. Who do you want to have saved? Men and women who can produce children? Old people? Babies? Sit down and tell me.' Brand, not surprisingly, was astonished by Eichmann's offer. He protested that he could not be put into a position of deciding who should live and who should die. But Eichmann replied: 'I can't sell you all the Jews of Europe. But I could let one million go. We are interested in goods, not in money. Travel abroad and liaise directly with your international authorities and with the Allies. And then come back with a concrete offer.'[2]

It was an extraordinary moment in the history of the Nazis' 'Final Solution'. What caused the man whose career had been closely tied to the extermination of the Jews for so many years to make a proposal so seemingly out of character? A clue lies in the confused political situation in which Eichmann found himself, for on his arrival in Budapest he had discovered that he was not the only SS officer charged with special tasks in Hungary; two others, Lieutenant Colonels Gerhard Clages and Kurt Becher, were also in town. Clages was pursuing various 'intelligence' tasks, whilst Becher was trying to blackmail the Weiss family, owners of the biggest industrial conglomerate in Hungary, into giving their shares in the company to the SS in return for safe passage out of the country. It was obvious to Eichmann that the duties of his SS colleagues, who were all of similar rank to him, crossed over into what he had previously considered his exclusive area of control. The riches of Hungary lay like a piece of raw meat in front of all of these jackals, and Eichmann realized he would have to fight to gain the upper hand.

By the time of his meeting with Brand, Eichmann knew that his rival Becher had successfully arranged for shares in the Manfred-Weiss works to be transferred to the Nazis; in return, around 50 members of the Weiss family were allowed to leave for neutral countries. Becher's career seemed to be on the ascendancy, and he had moved into an even grander villa than Eichmann's, left vacant by one of the Weisses. Eichmann, in a typical piece of self-serving testimony, claimed in court during his prosecution for war crimes in 1961 that he had wanted Brand to succeed in negotiating with the Allies, but it seems likely that his motivation for the 25 April offer was more venal and straightforward – he was seeking to regain the initiative from Becher. If his boss, Himmler, was permitting this new development in Jewish policy, then he, Eichmann, would not be left behind, even if it did go against his instincts. Eichmann must also have strongly suspected that the chances of the deal succeeding, and of the Allies actually handing over material to the Nazis that they could use against the Red Army in the East, were never very high. By going along with the Brand mission he could show Himmler he was willing to adapt to changing circumstances, gain ground on Becher and still almost certainly be able to pursue the selection and extermination programme to which he had become committed.

Over the next two meetings between Eichmann and Brand the deal took shape. Brand was to be dispatched to Istanbul, where he would try to arrange for the Allies to hand over 10,000 trucks equipped for winter operations against Soviet forces; in exchange the Nazis would give up 1 million Jews. Brand argued for some Jews to be released in advance to show Eichmann's 'good faith', and made reference to 600 emigration passes that the Relief and Rescue committee had managed to obtain. These were certificates that, in theory at least, allowed the bearer to emigrate to Palestine. Eichmann, however, not only rejected Brand's proposal but insisted that his wife, Hansi, was moved to the Hotel Majestic as a hostage.

At the final meeting at the Hotel Majestic, Clages, Becher and several other Nazis were also present. It seemed that every German agency in town now wanted a piece of this mission. Clages was particularly keen that a mysterious individual called Bandi Grosz accompany Brand to Istanbul. Grosz had been an agent of the Abwehr, the German intelligence agency whose work had recently been wound up in Hungary and superseded by Clages' intelligence operation. Grosz was leaving on an altogether different mission from Brand's, one that would only become clear in the succeeding months. At dusk on 17 May 1944 the two men were driven across the border to Austria to catch a plane to Istanbul. Brand remembers looking across at Grosz, who sat next to him scruffy and unshaven, furtively trying to memorize the contents of a page and a half of typewritten instructions.[3] It was an inauspicious and mysterious beginning to what would turn out to be an inauspicious and mysterious mission.

The possible existence of any 'Jews for trucks' deal made no difference either to Eichmann's immediate timetable to deport the Hungarian Jews or to the special arrangements that were being made at Auschwitz to receive them. In preparation for the massive influx expected at the camp, there were changes in the SS leadership. Arthur Liebehenschel, who had taken over as commandant of the camp in November 1943, was relieved of his command and transferred to the more minor job of commandant of Majdanek in the Lublin district. A new appointment was made as commander of the overall SS garrison at Auschwitz – none other than Rudolf Hoess. The commandants of both Auschwitz 1 and Auschwitz–Birkenau were now answerable to him. Hoess had returned with a vengeance; any of his past alleged misdemeanours were now forgotten by the SS leadership in the face of the huge task that lay ahead.

Just one day after returning to the camp, on 9 May, Hoess ordered preparations for the arrival of the Hungarian Jews to be accelerated. Gossip at Auschwitz had characterized Liebehenschel's reign as one of inefficiency and lack of true SS 'hardness', and Hoess was determined to change all that. It was only now that the railway spur from the main line just over a mile away was finally completed so that transports could be delivered into the heart of Birkenau, arriving at a new ramp 100 metres away from twin crematoria 2 and 3. Hoess also ordered the immediate repair of the furnaces of crematorium 5, and five pits to be dug nearby for the burning of corpses.[4] He knew from his previous experience during 1942 that actually murdering the Jews would present him and his SS colleagues with little difficulty; the hardest task for the Nazis would be disposing of so many hundreds of thousands of bodies at one time.

It is worth noting in passing that Hoess showed every sign of being keen to return to Auschwitz. Indeed, he had refused to sever all his ties with the camp when he left at the end of 1943, and his family had remained in the commandant's house on the edge of Auschwitz main camp while he had been working in Berlin (perhaps conscious of the fact that it was a good deal safer for a German family to live in southern Poland than the Nazi capital, the target of Allied bombing raids). Now he threw himself with great energy into his new, more senior role. One's intuitive position – that running Auschwitz would be almost the worst job in the world – is therefore proved wrong in Hoess's case. Not only did he fight to keep the post before it was taken from him in November 1943, but he relished returning to it six months later. Hoess's memoirs are silent on his true feelings about returning to the camp, but it is not hard to suggest reasons why he would have been happy to be in control of Auschwitz once again. First, he must have felt a strong proprietorial interest in the camp – after all, he had been commandant from the moment of its inception – and second, he would have known how comparatively rich the Hungarian Jews were, and there is a strong possibility that he sought to profit personally from their demise. But perhaps more than all that, this would be a major operation, and Hoess, an absolute believer in the necessity of the 'Final Solution', would have relished the task ahead.

For the majority of Jews in Hungary, this was to be the beginning of a nightmare. The change from relative safety and affluence to imprisonment and despair occurred more swiftly here than in any other country subjected to the Nazis' 'Final Solution'. At the start of March 1944 Alice Lok Cahana[5] had been living happily with her family in the town of Sárvár, close to the Austrian border. She felt they had a joyous life. Their grandfather owned a large carpet-weaving factory and the family was relatively wealthy. But once the Nazis arrived, the factory and their home were sold within weeks to a man named Krüger for one dollar. Shortly afterwards, like hundreds of thousands of other Hungarian Jews, they were forced to board trains to take them to Auschwitz. As Alice, who was then 15, and her sister Edith, two years older, walked under guard with the rest of their family to the railway station, they passed directly in front of their old house and saw Mr Krüger sitting by the window. 'I was so embarrassed,' says Alice Lok Cahana. 'The scene of going out of Egypt came to my mind. And here was Mr Krüger watching us go by, not with compassion but with glee – the owner of our factory, the owner of our house. And at the same moment our dog jumped up and recognized us and started to bark.'

As they neared the railway station Alice experienced an even stronger sense of the sudden, shocking change that was taking place in their lives: 'The train station always had a wonderful memory for me because Father had a business office in Budapest and we would always accompany him to the station on Monday and then wait for him to come back on Thursday, and he would always bring us something.' Yet now, this place that she associated with such happiness had mutated into something entirely different: 'We saw cattle trains! I told my sister, "It's a mistake! They have cattle trains here – they can't mean we should go in cattle trains. Grandfather cannot sit on the floor in a cattle train!"' But, of course, it was no mistake. They boarded the train, the doors were slammed shut, and the only light that entered was what filtered through the narrow wooden slats of the railway truck. In the shadows they could see their grandfather trying to sit on the baggage, their mother next to him. It was very hot. Soon the air became rancid with the smell of sweat and excrement from the bucket in the corner that had to serve as their toilet. It was four days before they reached Auschwitz.

'When we arrived,' says Alice, 'I told Edith that nothing can be so bad as this cattle train. I'm sure they will want us to work, and for the children there will be better food.' Once out of the train and milling around on the ramp inside Birkenau, Alice was told by her sister to go and stand with the children, since they were both convinced that children would be better treated than adults. After all, they reasoned, the Nazis came from a civilized country. So Alice, who was tall for her age, stood with the children and their mothers – the very group, of course, that in the warped logic of the camp the Nazis wished to murder most quickly. Dr Mengele, who was conducting the selection on the ramp that day, saw Alice waiting there and was curious about her – was she an exceptionally tall child or a very young mother? '*Haben Sie Kinder*?' ('Have you children?') Mengele asked. Alice, who had learnt German at school, replied that she was only 15. Mengele then told her to stand in another line, amongst a group of adults and adolescents not selected for immediate death. Shortly afterwards she was taken to the 'sauna' in Birkenau, where she showered, had her hair shaved and was given ragged clothes three times too big for her.

Alice then found herself allocated to the women's camp in Birkenau. By now she had lost contact with her mother, father, grandfather and sister – her entire family. Desperate for news of them, she started to ask questions of the other women in the block. Insistently she demanded to know where the rest of her family, in particular Edith, had been taken. But then the Block Kapo came over and slapped her face. 'You don't ask questions here!' she screamed. 'Be quiet from now on!'

But Alice was determined not to be quiet. At whatever cost, she meant to find her sister. She seized on the next chance she had to ask more questions when everyone in the block was awoken at four o'clock the next morning and ordered to visit the latrines en masse. Here, in the gloom, amidst the filth and the smell of an open sewer, she asked if anyone knew where the last Hungarian transport might have been taken. Eventually she found one woman who said that she thought they might be in the compound immediately next to them. But Alice still had no idea how to contact her sister. Auschwitz–Birkenau was divided by fences into a series of smaller sub-camps, and it was difficult to pass from one to another. But then another inmate told her that every morning the same person delivered putrid ersatz coffee to both camps. If Alice could write a message, maybe she could persuade the woman who delivered the coffee to take it. Then, if Edith could be found, she might be able to obtain permission to move barracks.

Alice soon learnt that favours had to be bought in Auschwitz, and she gave up her ration of bread for a scrap of paper and a pencil. She wrote a note to Edith saying, 'I am in Block 12 Camp C', and managed to bribe the woman who made the coffee deliveries to take it. Then, by what Alice describes as 'some miracle', a few days later her note was returned and scrawled on it were the words 'I am coming – Edith.' One morning shortly afterwards Edith herself was among the women bringing back the empty coffee cups. 'I just held her hand,' says Alice, 'and we were together. And we swore to each other that we will never be parted again.'

Alice Lok Cahana and her sister Edith were just two of the more than 400,000 Hungarian Jews transported to Auschwitz. The percentage on each transport selected for forced labour varied – sometimes it was as low as 10 per cent, sometimes around 30 per cent. But the majority of people on board each train were always sent to the gas chambers. The camp had never seen a killing spree like it, with over 320,000 murdered in less than eight weeks; indeed, for sustained killing within the Nazi state the only comparable event was the scale of the initial murders in Treblinka, which resulted in the sacking of Dr Eberl.

In order to keep up with the pace of the arriving transports, the Nazis increased the number of Sonderkommando working in the four crematoria at Auschwitz from just over 200 to nearly 900. These Sonderkommando were the people who had the most gruesome job in the camp: they helped guide and reassure the new arrivals as they walked into the gas chambers, and cleaned up after the murders.

Dario Gabbai[6] and Morris Venezia[7], cousins from Thessalonika in Greece, were two prisoners unwittingly caught in the Nazis' Sonderkommando recruitment drive. Having arrived at Auschwitz in April 1944, they volunteered when the Germans asked if anyone had experience as a barber. Morris's father had owned a hairdresser's and, even though Dario knew nothing of the craft, Morris told him to put his hand up. Like so many relatives in Auschwitz, they took comfort in knowing that whatever they had to face they would face together.

Morris and Dario were taken to one of the crematoria in Birkenau, given huge scissors, which they thought more suitable for shearing sheep than cutting human hair, and led into a room that was packed with naked human bodies. 'We couldn't believe it,' says Morris. 'They looked like sardines in a can!' The Kapo who accompanied them started clambering over the bodies, cutting off the women's hair at a frantic rate, demonstrating what he wanted Morris and Dario to do. But when the two of them both tried to cut the hair of the dead women they were wary of standing on the bodies and moved carefully around them. This angered the Kapo, who beat them with his cane. So they cut more quickly, moving amongst the corpses, but as Dario stood on the stomach of one dead woman he pushed gas out through her mouth and the body emitted a groaning noise. 'Dario was so scared,' says Morris, 'that he jumped from the top of the dead bodies.' There had been no explanation from the Kapo or the Germans about the nature of the job they were now expected to do, no preparation, just immediate immersion in a world of horror. 'Unbelievable!' says Morris. 'How could I feel? Nobody can imagine what really happened and what the Germans were doing to us.' What they did not know at the time was that the authorities at Auschwitz and other concentration camps had been ordered by the SS economic division in August 1942 to collect any human hair longer than a couple of centimetres, in order for it to be spun into thread to make 'felt socks for submarine crews and felt hose for railways'.[8]

Dario and Morris learnt that in order to survive they needed to adapt – and quickly. So, as transport after transport was brought down into the basement of the crematorium, they swiftly mastered the routine of their job. The new arrivals would be forced into the long underground undressing room and then, as the Germans shouted, '*Schnell! Schnell!*', told to take their clothes off and to remember where they had placed them, since the Germans also said they would need to recover them after their shower. Many of the women shouted, 'Shame! Shame!' as they were forced to rush naked towards the gas chamber that lay beyond. 'There were people who were starting to understand that something funny was going on,' says Dario Gabbai, 'but nobody could do anything. The process had to go [on], you know. Everything was done from the Germans' point of view. They'd been organizing this for many, many years, so everything was going through well.'

The gas chambers of crematoria 2 and 3 were below ground, so the delivery of the Zyklon B, once the chamber was crammed with people and the door secured, was relatively straightforward. Standing outside on the gas chamber roof, members of the SS would take off hatches that gave them access to special wire columns in the gas chamber below. They would then place canisters of Zyklon B inside the columns and lower them, sealing the hatch again once the gas had reached the bottom. From the other side of the locked door, Dario Gabbai and Morris Venezia heard children and their mothers crying and scratching the walls. Morris remembers how, when the gas chamber was crammed with around a thousand people, he heard voices calling out, 'God! God!' 'Like a voice from the catacombs. I still hear this kind of voice in my head.' After the noise ceased, powerful fans were turned on to remove the gas, and then it was time for Morris, Dario and the other Sonderkommando to go to work. 'When they opened the door,' says Dario, 'I see these people that half an hour before were going [into the gas chamber], I see them all standing up, some black and blue from the gas. No place where to go. Dead. If I close my eyes, the only thing I see is standing up, women with children in their hands.' The Sonderkommando had to remove the bodies from the gas chamber and transport them via a small corpse lift up to the crematorium ovens on the ground floor above them. Then they had to re-enter the gas chamber wielding powerful hoses and clean up the blood and excrement that lay on the walls and floor.

This whole horrific operation was often supervised by as few as two SS men. Even when the killing process was stretched to the limit there were only ever a handful of SS around. This, of course, limited to a minimum the number of Germans who might be subjected to the kind of psychological damage that members of the killing squads in the East had suffered. But far from there being reports of psychological breakdowns amongst the few SS who oversaw the actual killings, there were instances where the Germans seem to have taken sadistic pleasure in what they did. Dario Gabbai remembers one member of the SS who would occasionally visit the crematorium, select seven or eight beautiful girls and tell them to get undressed in front of the Sonderkommando. Then he would shoot them in their breasts or their private parts so that they died right in front of them. 'There are no feelings at that time,' says Dario. 'We knew our days were numbered too, that we could never survive in such an environment. But everything becomes a habit.'

Morris Venezia remembers one night during the height of the Hungarian action when three young women, two sisters and a friend, approached one of the SS and asked to be killed together. The SS man was 'very happy' to do as they asked, so he arranged them in one line, took out his revolver and shot all three of them with one bullet. 'Right away we took them,' says Morris Venezia, 'and threw them in the flames. And then we heard some kind of screaming – the first one didn't get a bullet, but fell down unconscious ... And that German officer was so happy because he killed two of them at least with one shot. These animals ... No human brain can believe that or understand it. It's impossible to believe it. But we saw it.'

In a striking example of how testimony from survivors today can chime accurately with contemporary records, Morris and Dario's experiences tally closely with letters written by other Sonderkommando, which were buried in containers around the site of the crematoria. These fragments, recovered after the war, contain some of the most moving material in the history of Auschwitz, not least because every one of those who recorded their experiences was subsequently murdered. Fragments of one letter by a Sonderkommando, discovered in the ground near the remains of crematorium 3 in 1952, give examples of sexual sadism similar to the acts recalled by Dario and Morris: '... or Scharführer (Staff Sergeant) Forst. This one stood at the gate of the undressing room in the case of many transports and felt the sexual organ of each young woman that was passing naked to the gas chamber. There were also cases when German SS men of all ranks put fingers into the sexual organs of pretty girls.'[9] This Sonderkommando also recorded the remonstrations of other Jews at the assistance they were giving the Germans – in one case a small boy of seven or eight spoke out: 'Why, you are a Jew and you lead such dear children to the gas – only in order to live? Is your life among the band of murderers really dearer to you than the lives of so many Jewish victims?'[10]

Perhaps the most poignant letter of all written by a Sonderkommando is the one that Chaim Hermann addressed to his wife and daughter, which was recovered from underneath a heap of human ashes near one of the crematoria in February 1945. He cannot have known for certain if his family were alive or dead, but still he asks forgiveness of his wife: 'If there have been, at various times, trifling misunderstandings in our life, now I see how one was unable to value the passing time'.[11] He describes his life in Auschwitz as 'an entirely different world, this one here, if you like, it is simply hell, but Dante's hell is incomparably ridiculous in comparison with this real one here, and we are its eye-witnesses and we cannot leave it alive ... '[12] And with great pathos he seeks to reassure her about his mental state: 'I am taking this opportunity of assuring you that I am leaving calmly and perhaps heroically (this will depend on circumstances).'[13] Alas, no eye-witnesses survived to tell us if Chaim Hermann kept his promise to his wife when his time finally came to die shortly after he finished this remarkable letter in November 1944.

Many of the Sonderkommando, including Dario and Morris, knew that their close relations had already perished in the crematoria, and they were all aware that they were now easing the process by which the Nazis killed thousands more. Each of them had to develop his own strategy for coping. With Dario it was simple – he 'closed' his mind to what was happening around him and became 'numb' like a 'robot': 'After a while you don't know nothing. Nothing bothers you. That's why your conscience gets inside of you and stays there until today. What happened? Why did we do such a thing?' But in his heart he knows why he carried on working in the Sonderkommando. Because no matter how bad it got 'you always find the strength to live for the next day' since the desire for life is so 'powerful'. Morris Venezia feels an even greater level of responsibility for his actions, saying, 'We became animals too ... every day is burning dead bodies, every day, every day, every day. You get used to it.' As he heard the screams from inside the gas chamber 'we feel that we should kill ourselves and not work for the Germans. But even to kill yourself is not so easy.'

As both the testimony from witnesses today and the buried letters make clear, the Sonderkommando were involved in the killing process at almost every stage; but that involvement was at its greatest when smaller numbers of people were delivered to the crematorium to be murdered. In such cases, the gas chambers were too large to kill 'efficiently', so a more traditional method was used. 'There were times when the transports were fifty people,' says Dario, 'and we had to take them, bring them one by one by the ears, and the SS will shoot them in the back.' He remembers there would be 'a lot of blood' when this happened.

Paradoxically, while the Sonderkommando were forced to witness such appalling events during their working day, their accommodation was, in the context of how the other prisoners lived in Auschwitz, comparatively good. Morris and Dario slept at the top of the crematorium in beds that were less dirty and lice-ridden than those in the normal barracks. Here, in the evening, they would sit and talk about their past lives, and sometimes even sing Greek songs. The food was better than elsewhere in the camp, and even vodka was occasionally available. This life was possible because the Sonderkommando had access to valuables in just the same way as did the prisoners who worked in 'Canada'. There were several opportunities during the killing process to 'organize' goods for themselves. They were charged with gathering up the clothes left in the undressing room, and often found hidden food or valuables – shoes were a favourite hiding place for diamonds or gold. In addition, in a shameful searching procedure to find jewellery, they were ordered to examine all the orifices of the people who had been gassed.

All these valuables were supposed to be handed over to the

Kapos, who would then in turn deliver them to the SS. But, just as with the other prisoners in 'Canada', it was possible for the Sonderkommando to conceal some of the stolen goods and trade them on the thriving Auschwitz black market, either by negotiating with the prisoners who came, for a variety of reasons, into the crematorium compound as part of their duties – such as the Auschwitz firemen – or by dealing with the SS direct. In this way the Sonderkommando could supplement the meagre rations they officially received with delicacies such as salami or cigarettes or alcohol. Miklos Nyiszli, a forensic pathologist who was a prisoner at Auschwitz, recalled the sight of the food available: 'The table was piled high with choice and varied dishes, everything a deported people could carry with them into the uncertain future: all sorts of preserves, jellies, several kinds of salami, cakes and chocolate.'[14] He remembered that 'the table awaiting us was covered with a heavy silk brocade tablecloth; fine initialled porcelain dishes; and place settings of silver: more objects that had once belonged to the deportees.'

Of course, eating like this did virtually nothing to compensate for the horror of the Sonderkommando's life. And it would be easy to imagine – especially after hearing Dario Gabbai talk of how he closed his mind and acted like 'a robot' – that the emotions of the Sonderkommando were utterly deadened by their sickening routine. But one revealing incident in the lives of Morris and Dario shows that this was not the case, and that there was always a spark of human spirit that the Nazis could not extinguish. One day, in the summer of 1944, they saw one of their cousins amongst a group of sick prisoners arriving at the crematorium to be shot. They knew there was nothing they could do to save him – the crematoria were surrounded by high fences – but Morris wanted to do something to make his last moments easier: 'I ran up to him and asked, "Are you hungry?" Of course everybody was hungry. Everybody was dying for food. So he says to me, "I'm very, very hungry."' And as he saw his cousin in front of him, weak through starvation, he decided to take a risk. When the Kapo was not looking he ran upstairs to his room, took a can of meat, opened it and rushed back down to give it to his cousin: 'And in one minute he swallowed it – he was so hungry. And then he got killed.' Rushing off to get a relative a last meal on this earth may not sound like a heroic act, but in the context of the lives of the Sonderkommando, who endured lives of the utmost emotional stress – lives of horror equal to anything history has to offer – it surely deserves to be considered as such.

Meantime, by the end of the first week in July 1944, nearly 440,000 people had been sent to Auschwitz from Hungary, the vast majority murdered on arrival. The story Eichmann told after the war that he had been keen to see the Brand mission succeed is totally discredited by this damning statistic. For the trains started rolling to Auschwitz before Brand had left Budapest, and they carried on relentlessly as he tried to interest the Allies in the Nazis' proposal.

When his plane landed in Turkey on 19 May, Brand immediately contacted the Turkish branch of the Jewish Agency, representatives of the Jewish leadership in Palestine, at the Pera Palace Hotel in Istanbul. There he hurriedly explained to them Eichmann's proposal, and revealed that in his opinion it was unlikely that the British would ever deliver trucks to the Germans. But Brand thought that scarcely mattered as long as the Allies came up with some kind of counter-proposal in order to keep the Nazis talking. However, Brand was distressed to find that no one senior in the Jewish movement was available to meet him and that sending a cable to Jerusalem was considered impossible – messengers would have to deliver the news personally to Palestine. It was to be the beginning of a lengthy process of disillusionment for Joel Brand.

It was not until 26 May that the head of the Jewish Agency in Palestine notified a British diplomat, Sir Harold MacMichael, of the Nazis' proposals. But it took the British only a matter of moments to reject the Brand mission, seeing it as an attempt to split the Western Allies from the Soviets. The British War Cabinet Committee on the Reception and Accommodation of Refugees met on 30 May and reached the conclusion that Eichmann's proposal was simply crude blackmail and could not be accepted. The Americans just as quickly came to the same view, and, keen that Stalin be informed as soon as possible, notified Moscow of the Nazis' proposal on 9 June. The Soviet Deputy Foreign Minister duly responded on the 19th that his government did not consider it 'permissible'[15] to carry on any discussions with the Germans on this subject.

In the meantime, Brand and his companion Bandi Grosz found themselves in the custody of the British, and it was the unappetizing figure of Grosz that now attracted greatest attention. In mid-June he was interrogated in Cairo by British intelligence officers, and the story he told was a surprising one. He claimed that Brand's mission was only a camouflage for his own. He had been sent on the direct orders of Himmler to facilitate a meeting in a neutral country between high-ranking British and American officers and two or three senior figures from the SD, Himmler's own intelligence service. The purpose of the assignation was to discuss a separate peace treaty with the Western Allies so that they could all fight together against the Soviet Union.

It is impossible in the murky world that Grosz moved in – it transpired that he was at least a 'triple' agent working for, and betraying, anyone who paid him – to be absolutely certain about the motivations behind the offer he laid before the British in Cairo. But the proposal did come from Himmler,[16] and the Reichsführer SS clearly felt it in his interests to fly this particular kite. There was enough of a buffer, in the form of Clages and others, between him and Grosz for the offer to be deniable should it become public. Equally, if the Western Allies did make any attempt to proceed with the proposal, then Himmler had the intriguing option of either leaking the information himself in order to sow discontent between Britain, the USA and the Soviet Union, or actually trying to pursue the deal to fruition.

Of course, the British and Americans never gave serious consideration to Grosz's offer, and from today's perspective it seems incredible that it was ever made. But it does reveal the mentality of leading figures in the Nazi party, particularly Himmler, at this crucial time in the conflict. He obviously knew the war was going badly for Germany, and that must have formed a large part of his thinking in suggesting this deal, but a strong ideological component was involved too. Simply put, Himmler, in common with virtually all the members of the Nazi party, had almost certainly never understood why Britain and the United States had tied themselves to Stalin. The Nazi dream had been for an alliance with Britain against the Soviet Union. Hitler's vision had been for Germany to be the dominant power on mainland Europe, and Britain to be the world's dominant seapower, via the British

Empire. But in 1940 Winston Churchill had smashed any possibility of an Anglo–Nazi partnership. So deeply felt was the sense of outrage at this upset in foreign policy that it still rankled with former Nazis after the war. Some years ago one former member of the SS greeted me, when I arrived to interview him, with the words: 'How could it ever have happened?' Thinking that he was referring to the extermination of the Jews, I replied that I was glad he felt so badly about the crime. 'I don't mean that,' he said. 'I mean how could it have ever happened that Britain and Germany ended up fighting each other? It's a tragedy. You lost your Empire, my country was devastated, and Stalin conquered eastern Europe.'

This was no doubt a sentiment shared by Himmler in the late spring of 1944. Part of him would still have expected the Western Allies to act 'rationally' and join forces with the Nazis to fight Stalin. This was to be a consistent train of thought amongst leading Nazis right through to the last moments of the war when, even after Hitler's suicide, German generals attempted to surrender only to the Western Allies, not to the Red Army. But nothing suggests that Hitler shared Himmler's desire for a separate peace with the Allies in the spring of 1944, and there is no evidence that he knew anything about Bandi Grosz's mission. Hitler was enough of a political realist to understand that any peace treaty concluded from a position of great weakness would be untenable. The Brand mission thus marks the beginning of a split between Hitler and his 'loyal' Heinrich – one that was to become more pronounced as the war drew to a close.

The Brand–Grosz mission may have been rejected by the Allies, but they were careful never to communicate their negative response directly to the Nazis, so as to allow space for further local negotiation inside Hungary. In the face of silence from the British and Americans, Brand's wife, aided by another member of the Relief and Rescue Committee, Rudolf Kasztner, tried to persuade Eichmann once again that he should demonstrate his own commitment to the 'Jews for trucks' proposal by releasing some Hungarian Jews before any response was heard from the Allies. But as they tried to negotiate with Eichmann, both Hansi Brand and Rudolf Kasztner were arrested by the Hungarian authorities, who were anxious to know what was going on, and beaten by them in custody before the Germans intervened to have them released. They revealed nothing, and still carried on trying to convince Eichmann to make a gesture to the Allies.

Eventually Eichmann and his SS colleagues agreed to allow a small number of Hungarian Jews to board a train that was supposedly to take them out of the Reich. The primary motivation behind the SS's action was straightforward – avarice. The price of a seat on the train started at 200 American dollars (from Eichmann), rose to 2000 dollars (a demand from Becher) and was eventually settled at 1000 dollars. A committee, on which Kasztner sat, selected who should go on the train. The idea was, according to Éva Speter,[17] a Hungarian Jew who knew Kasztner, that this should be a 'Noah's Ark – everything and everyone should be represented: youth organizations, illegal refugees, Orthodox people, scientists, Zionists'. But this was in many ways a strange 'Noah's Ark', one where personal connection could play a part in gaining admittance, for another class of people who were let on to the train in their hundreds were Kasztner's own friends and family from his home town, Cluj. And Éva Speter's own father was on the committee that decided she, her husband, son, uncle and grandfather should get on the list.

Since many of those allowed on to the train could not pay the exorbitant fee demanded by the Nazis, some of the seats were sold off to wealthy Hungarians who subsidized the rest. This led to some seemingly arbitrary distinctions within families. For example, Éva Speter, her husband and her son were not asked to pay for their seats, but her uncle and grandfather were. This decision appears all the more illogical since Éva's husband (who was not paying for his place himself) was the one who stumped up the cash for the others: 'My husband was pretty rich at the time and he gave the money to my uncle and my grandfather, and whatever money he had he gave it to Kasztner.' László Devecseri[18] was another Hungarian Jew who managed to get a seat on the train, and he was allowed on board because he helped organize the collection camp on Columbus Street in Budapest, where those selected for the train stayed pending its departure: 'Naturally everybody heard about it [the train] and wanted to get on the list, but many people could not because you're talking about six hundred thousand Jews and only sixteen hundred could be taken by the train. Those who stayed made Kasztner a scapegoat.'

Kasztner was indeed to be heavily criticized after the war for his actions, not just in placing his own family on the train, but by not warning other Hungarian Jews of their impending fate. In Israel in 1954 Kasztner sued for libel a man named Malkiel Gruenwald, who had accused him of being a 'traitor' to the Jews, but the case quickly became an examination of Kasztner's own behaviour and the judge eventually declared that he was guilty of 'selling his soul to Satan'. It was a judgment that seemed harsh, given the pressures of the spring and summer of 1944, for Kasztner had previously demonstrated that he was committed to saving Jews by helping many escape from Slovakia. And as for not warning the other Hungarian Jews, to attempt to do so would most likely have jeopardized any future negotiations with Eichmann and, according to one leading scholar of the period, Kasztner 'was in no position to warn anyone'.[19] However, this man was by no means a perfect human being. He was not helped in his defence by his brash personality, nor by the fact that he had conducted an affair with Hansi Brand while her husband was out of the country. He became a hate figure for some on the nationalist right in Israel, and was murdered in 1957, just before the Israeli Supreme Court reversed much of the damning verdict against him pronounced at the original libel trial.

The train full of refugees finally pulled away from Budapest on 30 June 1944, after huge sums of money and other valuables had been handed over in suitcases to the SS; by now Becher, Clages and Eichmann were all involved in the extortion. There was, of course, still no guarantee that the 1684 passengers were not going to travel the well-worn route to Auschwitz. 'We were always afraid,' says Éva Speter, 'and, of course, in the train we were afraid. We never knew what will be our future, but you don't ever know your future, whether in five minutes there will be an earthquake. And that's good.' But the train headed west, not north, and crossed into Austria, eventually reaching Linz. Here they stopped because, the Nazis said, there was an opportunity for the Hungarian Jews to be medically examined and 'disinfected'. This announcement spread enormous fear amongst everyone on the train, since they suspected this was the ruse that the Nazis used to send Jews to the gas chambers. 'I remember I was standing naked before the doctor,' says Éva Speter, 'and still looking very proud, into his eyes, and I thought he should see how a proud Jewish woman is going to die.' She walked into the shower rooms, and from the taps came 'fine warm water'. 'It was a very relieving experience after we were ready to die there.'

Although the Kasztner train was not en route to a death camp, neither was it travelling out of the Reich as had been promised. Instead it was heading for Germany, for the concentration camp of Bergen–Belsen in Lower Saxony. Bergen–Belsen was to become infamous when the Allies liberated the camp in April 1945 and pictures of the appalling condition of the surviving prisoners were transmitted around the world. But the Bergen–Belsen the Hungarian Jews arrived at was very different, for the camp had been opened in April 1943 charged with an unusual task: it was to house prisoners whom the Nazis thought at some later stage they might wish to deport from the Reich.

The situation at Bergen–Belsen was further complicated by the fragmentation of the camp into several sub-camps, with markedly different conditions existing between them. In the so-called 'prisoners' camp', built for the 500 'ordinary' inmates who had originally constructed the camp, conditions were appalling, whilst in the 'star camp' for *Austauschjuden* (exchange Jews) life – though still full of privation – was comparatively better. Here families were able to stay together and prisoners were allowed to wear their own clothes. As a small boy, Shmuel Huppert[20] was sent to Bergen–Belsen with his mother as a potential *Austauschjuden*. Because they were among the few Jews who held certificates from Palestine authorizing them to emigrate there, the Nazis considered them prime subjects for possible hostage exchange. 'The life was in a way reasonable,' says Shmuel. 'Reasonable in a sense that we got three blankets so we weren't cold, and we got something to eat. It wasn't plenty, but we could survive. We didn't work. I learned to play chess in Bergen–Belsen and I play chess still today. But what was most important was the fact that we were together, that I was never separated from my mother.'

The idea that the Nazis were considering releasing Jews to the West seems, at first sight, completely at odds with the policy of extermination. But it must be remembered that before the Nazis had developed the 'Final Solution' their preferred method of dealing with their self-styled 'Jewish problem' was to rob the Jews and then expel them, a policy practised assiduously by Adolf Eichmann in the wake of the annexation of Austria in 1938. It was therefore in line with Hitler's policy of 'getting rid' of the Jews to try to ransom the richer ones for foreign currency. Whilst nothing on the scale of the 'million Jews for 10,000 trucks' deal had ever been attempted before, as far back as December 1942 Himmler had gained permission in principle from Hitler that individual Jews might be expelled from the Reich for money.

In July 1944 the 1684 Hungarian Jews from the Kasztner train discovered for themselves that Bergen–Belsen was not the place of horror they had first feared. Éva Speter remembers the camp as offering a certain degree of 'cultural life', as lectures and musical recitals were organized by the prisoners. But the constant fear was that the Nazis would not keep their promise and the Hungarians would never be released; this fear grew in intensity as the months went by and conditions in Bergen–Belsen began to worsen. But the vast majority of them were eventually released, and they owed their freedom to the negotiations that continued, chiefly via Becher, with Jewish representatives in Switzerland. In December 1944 Éva Speter and her family boarded a train from Bergen–Belsen that took them, at last, out of the control of the Nazis. 'The moment I knew we are in Switzerland,' she says, 'a big stone fell from my heart, I must tell you. The Swiss behaved beautifully to us – Turkish towels, warm water and soap. It was heaven.'

Kasztner and Hansi Brand could not have predicted the fate of the train that had left Budapest on 30 June, nor could they have guessed the dramatic turn of events that would lead, in a matter of days, to the cessation of deportations from Hungary. For, just over a week before the train departed, the Allies received certain and detailed knowledge of the horrors of Auschwitz. Information about the extermination of the Jews had been known and publicized in the West since the killings of 1941 – Churchill himself had spoken openly about the Nazis' policy of mass murder, and the Polish government in exile in London had informed the Allied governments in May 1941 about the existence of Auschwitz as a concentration camp for Poles and about the executions that had taken place there. In July 1942[21] the *Polish Fortnightly* review, published in London, printed a list of 22 camps, including Auschwitz, where Nazi atrocities were taking place. And on 17 December Anthony

Eden, the British Foreign Secretary, read a statement to Parliament condemning Nazi atrocities, including the murder of the Jews. After he had finished, MPs stood for a minute's silence. A message sent by the Polish resistance in March 1943 also mentioned Auschwitz as one of the places where Jews were being killed, and on 1 June that year[22] the London *Times* published an article about 'Nazi Brutality to Jews' at Auschwitz.

The next most significant event that increased the Allied level of knowledge about Auschwitz occurred when a report from a Polish agent codenamed Wanda[23] arrived in London in January 1944. It stated that 'children and women are put into cars and lorries and taken to the gas chambers in [Auschwitz–Birkenau]. There they are suffocated with the most horrible suffering lasting ten to fifteen minutes.'[24] The report went on to state that 'ten thousand people daily' were being murdered in 'three large crematoria' and that nearly 650,000 Jews had already been murdered at the camp. Since many of the documents relating to this subject are still classified, we can only speculate as to why Wanda's report made such little impact. Part of the reason could have been that the very complexity of Auschwitz – its multiple functions as concentration and death camp – made it harder to interpret. But it is also possible, given the short debate that was about to occur over the question of whether or not to bomb the camp, that for the Allies the existence of Auschwitz was almost a distraction from the main task, as they saw it, of defeating the Germans.

Information about Auschwitz was about to reach a new level of detail because of the actions of four prisoners, the first two of whom, Rudolf Vrba and Alfred Wetzler, managed to escape from Auschwitz in April 1944, and the next two, Arnošt Rosin and Czesław Mordowicz, in May. When they reached nearby Slovakia the information they gave was collated to form what became known as the Auschwitz Protocols. Kasztner himself was given an early copy of the report based on the first two prisoners' evidence when he visited Slovakia on 28 April, but he chose not to publicize its contents, presumably fearful of the effect on his negotiations with Eichmann. It was only in June that the Auschwitz Protocols finally reached the West. On 18 June the BBC broadcast news about Auschwitz, and on the 20th the *New York Times* published the first of three stories about the camp, reporting the existence of 'gas chambers in the notorious German concentration camps at Birkenau and Oświęcim [Auschwitz].'[25]

But, in June–July 1944 knowledge of the mass murders taking place at Auschwitz did undoubtedly produce one change in policy – on the Axis side. In the wake of the mass deportation of Hungarian Jews numerous protests had been made to Admiral Horthy, the Hungarian head of state. Even Pope Pius XII, whose failure during the war publicly to denounce the extermination of the Jews has been much criticized, appealed to Horthy to stop the deportations; the Vatican had received reports of the horrors of Auschwitz in May via the escapees' reports. President Roosevelt and the King of Sweden also lobbied Horthy in close succession. Finally, on 26 June, Richard Lichtheim, a member of the Jewish Agency in Geneva, transmitted a telegram to England containing information about the Auschwitz Protocols, and called on the Allies to hold individual members of the Hungarian government responsible for the crime. This cable was intercepted by the Hungarian authorities and shown to the Prime Minister, Dome Sztojay, in early July and the contents were then communicated to Horthy.

It was all too much for the 76-year-old Hungarian leader. In 1940, thinking the Germans would win the war, he had supported them; in 1943, thinking they would lose, he had tried to sidle up to the Allies; in March 1944 he had cooperated with Hitler and stayed in office after German troops occupied his country; now, in the wake of threats of personal retribution, this weathervane of a man changed direction once again and informed the Germans that the deportation of the Hungarian Jews must stop. With Hungarian troops protecting him in the capital, Horthy enforced his order, and on 9 July the official deportations ceased.

Horthy was challenging the Germans at a time when they were at their weakest, for June 1944 had been a catastrophic month in the fortunes of Nazi Germany. On 6 June Allied forces had landed on the Normandy beaches, and by early July it was clear that they were not going to be pushed back into the sea as Hitler had foretold. In between, on 22 June the Soviets had launched Operation Bagration, a massive push against German Army Group Centre in Belorussia. This latter action, which unlike D-Day has not entered the public consciousness in the West, was of much greater moment to Horthy who ruled a country in the centre of Europe. Whilst the Germans fielded 30 divisions in an attempt to deal with the D-Day landings, they had a massive 165 divisions facing the Red Army, and yet they were still being pushed back. It could only be a matter of a few months before the Soviets were at the gates of Budapest. Horthy, like Werner Best in Denmark before him, knew it was time to construct an alibi.

There was another consequence of detailed information about the true nature of Auschwitz reaching the West, a controversial question that still simmers on in debate today – the call for the bombing of the camp. In June 1944 the War Refugee Board in Washington received a plea from Jacob Rosenheim of the Agudas Israel World Organization that the Allies bomb the railway lines to Auschwitz. This request was forwarded six days later by John Pehle, head of the War Refugee Board, to the Assistant Secretary of War, John McCloy, though Pehle added that he had 'several doubts'[26] about the feasibility of this idea. The suggestion was rejected by McCloy on 26 June both as impractical and because it would cause the diversion of bombers that were engaged in 'decisive operations'[27] elsewhere.

Another telegram had arrived in Washington on 24 June, this one from the World Jewish Congress in Geneva via the War Refugee Board in Switzerland. It called, amongst other measures, for the gas chambers themselves to be bombed. On 4 July this call too was rejected by McCloy, who cited the same reasons he had outlined in his 26 June letter. Significantly, an inter-office memorandum at this time addressed to McCloy from a member of his staff, Colonel Gerhardt, contains the phrase: 'I know you told me to "kill" this ... '[28] suggesting, at the very least, that the idea of bombing was dismissed without considered judgment.

Requests to bomb Auschwitz were also reaching London. When Churchill heard about them on 7 July, he famously wrote to his Foreign Secretary, Anthony Eden: 'Get anything out of the Air Force you can and invoke me if necessary.'[29] The Air Ministry examined the various possibilities and Sir Archibald Sinclair, the Secretary of State for Air, replied on 15 July in a broadly negative manner. He pointed out to Eden that it was impossible for British Bomber Command to cover such a great distance during one night – and the British specialized in night-time bombing. Only the

Americans bombed by day, and so he proposed laying the matter before them. He did suggest that one way forward might be for the Americans to drop weapons at the same time as they attempted to bomb the killing installations, in the hope of instigating a mass breakout. In any event, as his letter makes clear, he was passing responsibility for the whole business over to the US Air Force. American General Spaatz was questioned about the proposal when he visited the Air Ministry shortly afterwards. He suggested aerial reconnaissance of the camp as a possible way forward, and the request was passed on to the Foreign Office, where it never surfaced again.

The overall question of bombing Auschwitz rumbled on through the summer, with John McCloy in the US War Department dismissing further pleas for action from the World Jewish Congress in August. In Britain a Foreign Office official suggested in an internal memorandum that, regardless of any practical difficulties, there were also 'political'[30] reasons not to pursue the bombing – almost certainly the 'flood' of displaced Jews who would after the war seek sanctuary in Palestine, a territory currently governed by the British.

So the decision was taken on both sides of the Atlantic not to bomb Auschwitz. But, crucially, the decision was also taken not even to *consider* the bombing of Auschwitz. No proper aerial reconnaissance of the camp was undertaken, no feasibility study drawn up, no detailed attempt of any sort made to evaluate the various options. The overwhelming sense is of both governments' attention being focused elsewhere (with the possible exception of Winston Churchill, though even he dropped the matter after his initial 'get anything out of the Air Force you can' note). Of course, the British and Americans had a great deal on their minds in July 1944: the progress of Allied troops through Normandy demanded huge attention; the Red Army were at the gates of Warsaw and the Polish 'Home Army' was calling for support; and on 20 July an assassination attempt was made on Adolf Hitler at his headquarters in East Prussia. There were clearly a large number of competing priorities for Allied air resources, and it is easy to see how the prevailing wisdom in London and Washington became that Auschwitz would best be destroyed by ignoring the camp directly and putting every effort into winning the war as swiftly as possible on the ground. All that is true, and yet the motivation behind the rejection of the calls for bombing the camp appears to possess a less savoury dimension: the lack of proper consideration, the dismissive tone in some of the documents, all give off the lingering sense that no one was bothered enough to make bombing Auschwitz a priority.

The officials who so swiftly dismissed the calls for bombing would no doubt be astonished by the veritable academic industry that has grown up around the question today. So deeply has the issue penetrated the popular consciousness that one academic, when talking to Jewish audiences, finds 'that many people are convinced that bombing the camps would have saved many of the six million Jewish victims'.[31] The bombing question has become much bigger than a debate about practicalities and has taken on a symbolic dimension – proof that the Allies could have prevented Jewish deaths but chose not to. This is why the issue has to be examined carefully and calmly, to prevent the emergence and growth of a new myth that 'many of the six million' could indeed have been saved by the bombing.

The problem, of course, with examining the practicality of any Allied bombing of Auschwitz is simple: it did not happen. We are thus in the realms of counter-factual history, a land where little can ever be finally resolved. Although there seems general expert agreement that nothing would have been achieved by bombing the railway to the camp, since the Nazis would have diverted the Auschwitz trains on to another route and swiftly repaired the track, there is no such consensus on the question of actually bombing the gas chambers. Hence impassioned articles are written detailing the immense difficulties of a bombing raid either by USAF B17s or B24s or by the lightly armed British Mosquitoes,[32] whilst other publications fiercely question the alleged technical obstacles and suggest that bombing could well have destroyed the crematoria.[33] As with much counter-factual history, there is no conclusive answer.

But luckily there is a way through the maze – at least if one considers the moment when the most impassioned and insistent pleas were made to the Allied authorities for the bombing of the camp. Given the timing of the delivery of the Auschwitz Protocols to the Allies, and the decision by Horthy to cease deporting the

Hungarian Jews to Auschwitz, it is possible to say conclusively that there is no possibility that the bombing of the camp or the railway lines would have prevented the Hungarian Jews dying. The detailed information simply reached the Allies too late (for example, the Hungarian deportations officially ceased on 9 July and the British Air Minister replied negatively to Eden about the proposed bombing on the 15th).

The next area of this complex issue that one can approach with almost the same level of certainty is the effect of any bombing on the extermination capacity of the camp. The Auschwitz Protocols contain detailed descriptions of the location of the four main crematoria. But even if a daring daylight bombing raid had been mounted against them with pinpoint accuracy, and even if these killing installations had been completely destroyed, the Nazis would still have been able to carry on gassing elsewhere at Auschwitz. Crucially, the location of 'The Little White House' and 'The Little Red House' were not disclosed in the Auschwitz Protocols, and they offered all the extermination capacity the Nazis now required. After the Hungarian action was discontinued, Auschwitz was operating with massive excess killing potential. Instead of a maximum of 10,000 people being killed daily, the number dropped to an overall daily average of fewer than 1500,[34] and continued at around that level until November and the closing of the crematoria. Therefore the conclusion has to be that, far from saving 'many' of the 'six million', any bombing of the camp initiated by the requests in the summer of 1944 would, almost certainly, have saved no one. In fact, because of collateral damage to the barracks only metres from the crematoria it would probably have killed hundreds of the very prisoners the raid was designed to save.

This is, of course, an intellectual conclusion and not an emotional one. And since so much of the debate around this issue is conducted at an emotional level it will prove unsatisfactory to many who want to think that the Allies could have done much more to prevent the killings. Perhaps they could have. Maybe, for example, dropping guns into the camp would have precipitated a revolt, though it seems unlikely in the extreme that prisoners weakened by hunger could have suddenly and without preparation staged a revolt against SS men in watchtowers armed with machine guns and protected behind electrified fences. We shall never know, since by posing that question we are back in the downward-spiralling land of the counter-factual.

The debate about the possible bombing of Auschwitz is so passionate because it masks a wider ranging and less specific question: shouldn't more have been done to try to save the Jews? The British government, for example, knew for certain of the existence of the Nazis' systematic campaign of destruction against the Jews – even knew the names of the Operation Reinhard camps and the death toll in each – by the beginning of 1943. Yet despite pleas from MPs such as Eleanor Rathbone that immigration restrictions should be loosened so that large numbers of Jews from Bulgaria, Hungary and Romania could be offered the right to emigrate to countries of safety, the British government remained steadfastly opposed. In February 1943, Anthony Eden, in reply to a similar plea from William Brown MP, stated: 'The only truly effective means of succouring the tortured Jewish, and I may add the other suffering peoples of Europe, lies in Allied victory.'[35] A few weeks later, during discussions in Washington in March 1943, Eden said that it was important 'to move very cautiously about offering to take all the Jews out of a country', adding 'if we do that, then the Jews of the world will be wanting us to make similar efforts in Poland and Germany. Hitler might well take us up on any such offer, and there simply are not enough ships and means of transportation in the world to handle them.'[36] (This despite the fact that during the last three years of the war, means were found to ship more than 400,000 German and Italian POWs across the Atlantic)[37]. Eleanor Rathbone was bitter in her criticism of the inaction of the Allies in her speech during a House of Commons debate on 19 May 1943: 'If the blood of those who have perished unnecessarily during this war were to flow down Whitehall, the flood would rise so high that it would drown everyone within these gloomy buildings which house our rulers.'[38] Whilst we can never know for certain what would have happened if the Allies had dropped immigration restrictions for Jews under threat, it is hard not to agree with Ms Rathbone that more could have been done by the Allies to try to help. It is possible, therefore, that the current debate would be more fruitful if it focused less on the bombing of Auschwitz, and more on the admittedly more complex question of Allied wartime immigration policy.

Meanwhile, the ending of the deportation of the Hungarian Jews had consequences both in Budapest, where Eichmann fumed, and at Auschwitz, where the spare capacity in the gas chambers meant that plans were now made to liquidate the population of one whole section of Birkenau: the gypsy camp. This special section of Birkenau had been used since February 1943 to accommodate (at its peak) around 23,000 gypsy men and women. They were allowed to live as families and wear their own clothes, and did not have their hair shaved. But conditions in the gypsy camp soon became amongst the worst in Auschwitz. Overcrowding combined with lack of food and water meant that disease was rife, particularly typhus and the skin disease called noma, and many thousands died. Altogether, 21,000 of the 23,000 gypsies sent to Auschwitz died there, whether of disease, starvation or in the gas chambers when the gypsy camp was eventually liquidated.

The Nazis considered the gypsies racially dangerous and 'asocial'. They wanted to be rid of them, and, proportionate to their population numbers, they suffered more than any other group under the Third Reich apart from the Jews. There is no accurate statistic for the number of gypsies killed by the Nazis, but around a quarter to half a million are thought to have perished. However, the implementation of the Nazis' anti-gypsy policy was inconsistent; in the Soviet Union, Nazi killing squads murdered gypsies along with Jews; in Romania the extensive gypsy population was not targeted en masse (though thousands still died as a result of mistreatment); in Poland the majority of gypsies were sent to concentration camps; whilst in Slovakia the policy of persecution was enforced unevenly; within Germany itself many gypsies were deported first to ghettos in Poland – 5000 were sent to Łódź and were amongst the first to die in the gas vans of Chełmno in January 1942.

In Germany the Nazis saw one of the greatest 'dangers' as the transference of gypsy racial characteristics into the 'Aryan' population through so-called *Mischlinge* (mixed blood) gypsies, and nothing illustrates more clearly the warped sensibilities of the Nazis in this regard than the story of how one eight-year-old girl called Else Baker[39] found herself in the gypsy camp at Birkenau in the summer of 1944. At the start of the year she had been living happily with her family in Hamburg. Even though disturbed by war, she had a secure place in a normal family unit – or so she thought. Suddenly, one night early in 1944, there was a knock at the front door and several strangers entered, announcing themselves as members of the Gestapo. They said they had come to take Else away, back to her 'real' mother. Under the eyes of her devastated parents she was dragged away, out of the house and into the darkness. She was taken to a warehouse down by the port that was full of gypsies, many of whom she remembers as being very dishevelled. Else, dressed by her mother in her best clothes, stood and looked at them and gradually went into shock. Only later did she discover that she had been adopted and that her 'real' mother was a half gypsy. The man and woman whom she had always known as her mother and father were in fact her adoptive parents, who had brought her up since she was ten months old.

Else was put on board a freight train with the other gypsies and transported to Auschwitz. She remembers being taken to the 'sauna' at Birkenau and told to undress and take a shower. Afterwards she tried to find her clothes amongst the pile in front of her, but she could not see them. And, being a well brought up little girl, she did not want to take anything that was not hers. So she stood, naked and alone, while the gypsy families around her dressed themselves as best they could. Eventually, when only half a dozen pieces of clothing lay on the cement floor in front of her, one of the women next to her said, 'You have to just grab anything.' So, having arrived in her Sunday best, with layers of clothing to protect her from the cold, she left wearing one pair of knickers and wearing a thin summer dress.

In the gloom of a crowded barracks, and surrounded by gypsy families, this eight-year-old girl gradually became immobile with shock. Not saying anything, not crying out – for there was no one to heed her cries – just standing in the middle of this morass of people who were all, as she saw it, looking out 'for number one'. Then she was the beneficiary of a piece of luck that almost certainly saved her life. One of the block Kapos, called Wanda, took pity on her and led her to a nearby barracks. Here Wanda allowed Else to share her own small room and sleep next to her on a table covered with a rug, where 'it was about a hundred times better than being in the barrack'. For most of the time Else's life in the camp was one of enforced idleness. Every day she would walk up to the top end of the gypsy camp, where the wires abutted the railway, and watch the new transports arrive. She saw columns of people 'most of them nicely dressed' walking in the direction of what she later learnt was the crematorium. These were the Hungarian Jews selected to die, though she did not know that at the time. When there was no incoming transport to watch through the wire she would 'play' with the one toy she had – a lens from a pair of glasses, which she had found on the ground. She would pile up dry grass and then focus the sun's rays through the lens until the grass started to burn.

After several weeks, Wanda said to Else, 'You cannot stay with me any more,' and disappeared. 'I was so shocked,' says Else, 'being completely on my own again that not many things penetrated my shocked mind ... things started to go really topsy-turvy, haywire – you name it.' Else remembers being placed back in one of the main barrack blocks again, but this one was not so crowded as before. There had been a selection, and many of the gypsies were now held elsewhere in the camp. Then the water was turned off and everyone was told to go back inside the barracks. That night there was a 'massive noise – loud screams. I'd never heard screams of that nature.' The nature of the atrocity that was being committed outside is impossible to establish. It could have been occasioned by any number of actions within the camp, possibly the SS preparations for the liquidation of the gypsy camp that was shortly to occur. Else was one of the 1400 gypsies selected to be spared that particular horror and transferred to another concentration camp. Auschwitz records confirm that Else, registered as gypsy number 10,540, left Auschwitz on 1 August 1944.

Else's experience could scarcely have been dreamt up by the most creative writer of fiction. Think of it. An eight-year-old girl raised as a German is snatched from her loving parents, learns she was adopted and is part gypsy, is transferred to Auschwitz where she is left to fend for herself until being adopted by a Kapo, is abandoned once more, and then finds herself in dark barracks surrounded by strangers while terrible atrocities are taking place outside, only to be shipped off to another concentration camp the very next day. No wonder Else feels that this cumulative experience 'buggers up your mind for the rest of your life. I can say that with total authority. It does.'

The day after Else left Auschwitz, on the night of 2 August 1944, the gypsy camp was liquidated. Many people attest to the terrible scenes as the Nazis tried to clear the camp. Władysław Szmyt[40] was one of those who witnessed it. A gypsy himself, he had been misclassified by the Nazis as a Polish political prisoner and imprisoned in a section of Birkenau next to the gypsy camp, where many of his own relatives were incarcerated. On the night of 2 August he watched as gypsy children were smashed against the side of trucks and he heard automatic machine-gun fire and pistol shots. He saw the gypsies fight back with whatever makeshift weapons they could find, often spoons or knives, but soon they were overwhelmed. 'I started yelling,' he says, 'I knew they were taken to be destroyed. That's the end. Must be the worst feeling in the world.' That night 2897 gypsies were taken to the crematoria and gassed. Many of their bodies were burnt in open pits nearby.

In the meantime, Else had been taken to Ravensbrück concentration camp north of Berlin. Here she stayed for several weeks, suffered more appalling privation and fell into a near-comatose state. Salvation came one morning in September 1944 when her block Kapo, a Polish woman, called out her name. Else was escorted to the administration block and suddenly told, 'You're going to be released.' She was ordered to take a shower, the first since the day she arrived in Auschwitz, and was then led naked into a room piled high with clothes. She stood there 'too frightened or shocked to do anything – naked, wet and looking around, probably expecting punishment for being there even in the first place, because I'd been beaten before for doing nothing wrong whatsoever'. Only after she failed to emerge from the room for some time did a woman come in and help her dress. Then Else waited in an office of the administration block until her adoptive father was brought in. On seeing him, Else felt 'numb': 'Too numb to feel anything. If they had said, "God Almighty is coming to see you", it wouldn't have had any effect then.' Before Else was released she was made to sign a document – standard practice for prisoners leaving concentration camps – agreeing that she would not divulge where she had been or what she had experienced. 'I didn't have to make crosses because I could write,' she says. 'And I think that was the first signature I ever gave in my life.'

Else then boarded a train with her stepfather to take her back to

Hamburg. In their carriage was a German army officer, and Else remembers how her father told him about his adopted daughter's arrest and imprisonment, all because her grandmother was a gypsy: 'And he lifted my skirt and exposed my legs, which were covered in big sores and he said, "This is what you're fighting for at the front."' She has no recollection of the officer's response. She does remember, though, that on her return home her eldest sister made her a cake out of mashed potatoes, since sugar was rationed, and boiled some carrots to stick in it like candles. And then, after a six-month absence, Else returned to school; pretending to be a normal eight-year-old German girl once more.

No one knows for sure why she was released. Any records that might reveal the truth were destroyed by the Gestapo at the end of the war. Perhaps her adoptive father's protests that Else had been completely assimilated into German society finally registered with the local Nazi authorities. He had even joined the Nazi party himself that year in order to show his own loyalty, and it is possible that action tipped the balance. What we do know for certain is the legacy: a human being hugely damaged by living a nightmare for six months. 'The level of human depravity is unfathomable,' says Else Baker. 'And it will always be like that. It's a very cynical view that has been formed in my mind out of my experiences, I'm sorry to say.'

Else Baker's horrific personal story illustrates many of the worst aspects of life at Auschwitz: the sudden brutality, the arbitrariness of human behaviour, the casual cruelty. But perhaps above all it shows how important personal relationships were in order to enhance the chances of survival – in order, indeed, to try to make life worth living. In Else's case, it is hard to see how she could have lived through Auschwitz without Wanda's help. This was something that Alice Lok Cahana, who was in Auschwitz–Birkenau at the same time as Else, also realized all too well. Her love for her sister Edith had already driven her to take huge risks within the camp so that they could be together. But that summer there was a problem. Edith became sick with typhoid and was taken to one of the hospital barracks. This was a potentially deadly turn of events for Edith, not just because of the lack of adequate medical care, but because regular selections were made for the sick to be taken directly from there to the gas chambers. However, Alice was determined that Edith would survive and visited her regularly. In order to gain entrance to the hospital she had to bribe the Kapo with her bread ration, and also agree to help her take out the bodies of prisoners who had died during the night. 'I was fifteen years old,' says Alice, 'and had never seen a dead person. I thought, "These are people who were alive yesterday and could talk and walk, and here I am dumping them in a pile." It was so horrendous, but I had to do it in order to see Edith, to go in for a minute.'

As a visitor in the infirmary, Alice was in great demand – all the sick prisoners wanted news of the outside. They would pull at Alice's clothes as she walked along the barracks to visit her sister and demand, 'What's happening?' Amidst the dark, disease-ridden atmosphere of the hospital, with the smell of bodily waste and decomposition, listening to the moans of the dying, Alice tried to offer some comfort: 'I learnt to make up stories – that soon the war is over. "Hold on," because soon we will go home.' But Alice knew all this was a lie because she witnessed first hand the alarming rate at which people 'disappeared' from the infirmary, either dying in their bunks or selected for the gas chamber. So she decided that, sick as Edith was, she had to get her out. She told her: 'If you can just bear it, I will take you out as a dead person and then we'll go back to our barrack.' The next day Edith pretended to be dead and Alice carried her out of the hospital along with those who had truly expired during the night. Once outside, she helped her stagger across Birkenau and they both returned to their original barracks.

But protecting her sick sister outside the infirmary in an environment that was supposed to be full of 'healthy' women was even harder. 'Every day there were selections,' says Alice, 'and [they] were so severe and so scary.' The women often had to stand for selection in front of the immaculately turned out Dr Josef Mengele. 'By then we were infested with lice,' says Alice, 'and it felt so horrible – horrible. Nothing can be so humiliating as when you feel your whole body is infested. Your head, your clothes – everywhere you look on your body there's an animal crawling. And you cannot wash it off. There's no water.'

One day Alice and her sister were selected, but only to go to another barrack. And it was here, at Birkenau, that Alice had her most unlikely escape. By now it was October 1944, and since the days were getting colder, the block Kapo announced that any teenagers should stand apart in order to receive additional clothes. So Alice decided to join this 'children's' group and go and get warm clothes for Edith to protect her from the forthcoming bitter Polish winter: 'So we went. And we came to a nice building with flowers at the windows. And we went in and an SS woman said, "Everyone put their shoes nicely together, your clothes on the floor." And we were taken into a room – naked.' Alice and the others sat in the room and waited, thinking they were to be given a shower before receiving the promised new clothes: 'It was a large room and grey in colour. And very sober because when they closed the door it was almost dark in there. And we sat there waiting and shivering. Waiting and waiting and waiting.' Then suddenly the door flung open and the SS woman screamed, 'Hurry, get out from here! Get out fast!' and she started to throw clothes back at the teenagers. 'Go!' she shouted. 'Run as fast as you can!' Alice could not find her own clothes again but, dressed in whatever she could, made her way back to the barracks. There she complained to the others that, 'They'd told us we'd get warm clothes and I didn't even get my clothes back!' It was only then, when she was told by other prisoners: 'Stupid child! Don't you know where you were?' that she finally realized she had been waiting inside the gas chamber of crematorium 5.

What is perhaps the strangest aspect of all in Alice's story is that, even after many months in Birkenau, she did not realize where she was being sent. Of course she had been told about the existence of the gas chambers – anyone who lived in Birkenau more than a few days knew about them. But her way of trying to cope with camp life had been to block out this knowledge, and she certainly had no idea of the exact mechanics of the killing process. 'I was so focused on Edith,' says Alice, 'that all the energy I could muster was on how to keep her alive. So that kind of fear didn't occur to me; maybe it was so horrendous you couldn't comprehend. How could a fifteen-year-old from a normal environment comprehend that they will put you in a gas chamber? It's after all the twentieth century! I go to the movies, Father is in an office in Budapest and I never heard of such a thing. In our house you could never utter an ugly word. So how can you imagine something so foul that they kill people this way? And we were always taught that the Germans were a civilized people.'

This is an important insight – the knowledge that even those who lived in the shadow of the crematoria chimneys could erase the existence of such places from their minds. And they were able to do so, not just because the practical function of the killing factories was simply too horrendous to contemplate, but because the daily humiliations of life in the camp – the lice-ridden clothes, the battle to use the latrine, the struggle to find enough to eat, the filth and dirt that pervaded everything – pushed any thoughts away other than the fight to live for the immediate moment. But there is another, still more sinister, reason why Alice did not realize the significance of the room in which she was waiting. Even after 60 years, her strongest memory of approaching the crematorium is of the red flowers, perhaps geraniums, growing in window boxes. Flowers were unheard of in Auschwitz. And to Alice they symbolized the safe and secure life she had left behind: 'I see flowers in a window – reminding you of home. Reminding you that mother went out when the Germans came into Hungary, and instead of being scared or crying or hysterical, she went to the market and bought violets. And it made me so calm. If Mother buys flowers, it can't be so bad. They will not hurt us.' It is touches like this – flowers in the window boxes of the crematorium – that raise the killing process the Nazis devised above mere brutality to a level of cynicism as yet unsurpassed in the so-called 'civilized' world.

Alice survived that day because of a monumentally unlikely piece of luck: she was sitting in the gas chamber on 7 October. This was a unique day in the history of Auschwitz – the day of the Sonderkommando revolt. Some of the Sonderkommando had been planning to rise up against their guards back in June in a revolt organized with the help of an underground resistance movement run by Yaacov Kamiński. But the SS learnt of the plans. It was almost impossible for Jewish prisoners to sustain a secret resistance movement for any length of time at Auschwitz because of the network of Kapos who so closely supervised them and, of course, because of their appalling mortality rate in the camp. Kamiński was informed upon and killed, but the nucleus of his group survived and continued to try to 'organize' whatever weapons they could – knives, pickaxes and the like – and negotiate with others through the wire in the rest of Birkenau to gain access to further supplies.

The Sonderkommando had felt driven to action on 7 October

by an announcement days before asking for 'volunteers' to join Otto Moll, one of the most notorious SS overseers of the crematoria, who had recently left to become commandant of Gliwice sub-camp. They knew this was a ruse, since the last group of Sonderkommando who had been selected to 'go' to Majdanek camp had instead been killed by the SS and their bodies burnt overnight in crematorium 2. The next morning some of the remaining Sonderkommando had recognized the half-burnt corpses of their comrades, and any last illusions they had about the eventual fate the Nazis intended for them were dispelled.

The Sonderkommando were also well aware that their usefulness to the Nazis had tailed off considerably. Only the arrival of around 65,000 people as a result of the liquidation of the Łódź ghetto during August and September had prevented the Nazis from cutting back on the number of Sonderkommando at Auschwitz earlier. Now, after no one had come forward to 'volunteer' for the mythical transfer to Gliwice, the Sonderkommando learnt that the Kapos in crematoria 4 and 5 had been told to come up with the names of 300 Sonderkommando who would be 'transferred to rubber factories' – factories that were just as imaginary as all the previous destinations for the Sonderkommando that the Nazis had promised.

In response to the clear threat of their own immediate execution, at around 1.30 p.m. on Saturday, 7 October the Sonderkommando in crematorium 4 mutinied.[41] Armed with pickaxes and rocks, they attacked the SS guards as they came towards them and then set fire to the crematorium. After a few minutes of hand-to-hand fighting with the SS, some Sonderkommando managed to escape into the nearby woods and reached the village of Rajsko beyond, but they were still trapped as they remained within the secure area of Auschwitz. Meanwhile, the Sonderkommando in crematorium 2 also rose up against the SS and shoved one of their guards, alive, into the lit ovens.

About 250 members of the Sonderkommando were killed during the ensuing struggle in Auschwitz. All of those who escaped were later captured and shot, along with others suspected of involvement in the revolt – a total of 200 more people. Three SS died as a consequence of the Sonderkommando action that day. But the revolt did save some lives. It must have been because of the chaos caused by the Sonderkommando in crematorium 4 that the SS emptied the gas chamber of crematorium 5 next door without killing Alice Lok Cahana and her group.

Eight days after the Sonderkommando revolt at Auschwitz the political situation in Hungary changed once more when Horthy's non-compliant regime was overthrown with the help of the Nazi-backed Hungarian Arrow Cross militia. Eichmann, who had passed the months since the end of the deportations partly by getting drunk, immediately called Kasztner for a meeting and greeted him with the words, 'I'm back!' The Jews of Budapest, who had up to now largely escaped deportation, were his new target. It was impractical, given the nearness of the Red Army and the difficulties in organizing rolling stock, to send them to Auschwitz. So Eichmann determined that they should walk to Vienna, over 120 miles away.

During November tens of thousands of Jews from Budapest were forced out of the city and made to trek west to Austria, marching without food through rain and snow. The sight of this pitiful column appalled even hardened SS officers, and Eichmann was told to halt the deportations. Nonetheless, he worked around the order and carried on, earning the vilification of representatives of neutral countries who observed the suffering. With over 100,000 Jews still in Budapest waiting to become part of Eichmann's sadistic planned march, Kurt Becher, always a more pragmatic Nazi, protested to Himmler at his colleague's action. Becher, and Himmler, realized that the war must end soon, and that with Germany's defeat, ideology needed to be twinned with realism.

Himmler called Becher and Eichmann to a meeting in his private train stationed at Triberg in the Black Forest. According to Becher, Himmler told Eichmann to cease the deportations of the Budapest Jews, saying that 'If until now you have exterminated Jews, from now on, if I order you, you must be a fosterer of Jews.'[42] It was a dramatic about-face for Himmler, the man who had helped mastermind the Nazis' 'Final Solution'. But, as the war entered its last few months, still more surprises were to come from the Reichsführer SS.

— 6 —

Liberation and Retribution

When the end came, it came quickly. One night in January 1945, as ten-year-old Eva Mozes Kor[1] and her twin sister Miriam lay in their bunks at Auschwitz–Birkenau, they were suddenly awoken by a huge explosion. Outside the winter sky was red with flames. The Nazis had blown up the crematoria. Moments later they were forced out of their barracks and marched with other twins, all of whom had been subject to Dr Mengele's experiments, down the road to Auschwitz main camp. It was a nightmarish scene. Above them they saw distant flashes of artillery, and in the darkness the SS harried them on without respite. Any of the children who could not make the journey were shot and their bodies left by the side of the road. In the chaos two of the sets of twins lost their siblings, and never saw them again.

Once in Auschwitz main camp, Eva and Miriam were left largely on their own. The rigid system of supervision by Kapos and guards had suddenly broken down and the prisoners looked after themselves. Eva even managed to break through the perimeter fence and walk to the edge of the Soła river, which ran along one side of the main camp, to try to get water. As she looked up from breaking the ice on the surface of the river, she saw a little girl about her own age on the other side of the bank. She was dressed in beautiful clothes, with carefully braided hair decorated with ribbons, and carried a school bag. It was an 'almost unbelievable' sight to Eva, wearing rags and swarming with lice, who stood and stared at her. 'This was my first realization since we arrived in Auschwitz,' she says, 'that there was a world out there with children who looked like children, and who went to school.'

Eva and Miriam are fortunate to be alive because the Nazi plan was that they should die along with the rest of the several thousand prisoners who were left behind, judged too weak to take part in the mass exodus from Auschwitz. An order for their murder had been sent by SS Obergruppenführer (Lieutenant General) Schmauser,[2] the commander of the local area, on 20 January. During the next seven days special SS units murdered around 700 prisoners at Birkenau and nearby sub-camps. But nearly 8000 other prisoners, including Eva and Miriam, escaped death because the Red Army were closing too rapidly on Auschwitz and the SS were concerned more with saving themselves than with following orders.

Shortly afterwards the guns fell silent, and on 27 January Red Army soldiers from the First Ukrainian Front arrived at the complex. They found around 600 prisoners alive in the Monowitz slave labour camp next to the I.G. Farben Buna works, a little under 6000 at Birkenau, and just over 1000 at Auschwitz main camp, including Eva and her sister Miriam. The first Eva heard that her suffering might be over was when one of the women in the barracks started shouting: 'We're free! We're free! We're free!' Eva ran to the door but could see nothing in the snow. Only after some minutes could she make out Red Army soldiers dressed in white camouflage coats: 'We ran up to them and they gave us hugs, cookies and chocolates. Being so alone, a hug meant more than anybody could imagine because that replaced the human worth we were starving for. We were not only starved for food but we were starved for human kindness, and the Soviet Army did provide some of that. Actually, one of the things that I missed most after the war when we got back was that I desperately needed hugs and kisses and I never got any. And so when I lecture students I tell them, "When you go home this afternoon, please go and give your parents an extra hug and an extra kiss for all of us children who survived the camp and who had no one to hug and kiss."'

Ivan Martynushkin was a lieutenant with a Red Army mortar company who fought his way with his comrades into Auschwitz town. But when he reached Birkenau, just hours after its liberation, there was a strange calm. The former prisoners looked at him 'with gratitude in their eyes' and with 'forced smiles'. 'We had a feeling that we had done something good,' he says, 'a very good deed, that we had somehow fulfilled our duty.' But significantly, though he says he and his comrades had 'feelings of compassion' for the Auschwitz prisoners, they were not hugely affected by what they saw: 'You have to understand the psychology of people who have been at war ... I already had more than a year of direct combat experience behind me, and during that time I had seen camps – not like this one, but they were nevertheless smaller prison camps. I had seen towns being destroyed. I had seen the destruction of villages. I had seen the suffering of our own people. I had seen small children maimed. There was not one village which had not experienced this horror, this tragedy, these sufferings.'

Ivan Martynushkin's words are a useful reminder of the context in which Auschwitz would have been seen initially by many who fought on the Eastern Front. For them it was a horror, true enough, but also just one more terrible sight in a war already overflowing with atrocity. Indeed, the liberation of Auschwitz was not huge news at the time. It was mentioned in the papers – *Pravda* published an account by their correspondent Boris Polevoi on 2 February[3] and the story was picked up a few days later by the *Jewish Chronicle* in Britain – but the liberation was not publicized in the way that the discovery of Majdanek camp had been the previous summer. Majdanek had been the only other Nazi camp to use Zyklon B for killing (but on a much smaller scale than Auschwitz), so it was possible for the press at first to see Auschwitz as 'another Majdanek'. There were also a great deal of other competing stories for the newspapers to report in January 1945, not least the forthcoming meeting of the 'Big Three' war leaders (Churchill, Roosevelt and Stalin)[4] at Yalta in the Crimea. But there was also perhaps one more reason why the liberation of Auschwitz was not a massive immediate news story in the West. The Red Army had discovered the camp, and already some were beginning to question the extent to which the alliance that had won the war would survive victory. Traces of an overtly Marxist interpretation of Auschwitz, as the ultimate capitalist factory where the workers were dispensable, were evident in Polevoi's article in *Pravda*. It was a moment that marked the beginning of a rift in historical interpretation between East and West concerning the operation of the camps that would not be resolved until the fall of Communism in the Soviet Union. One of the least appealing aspects of the Soviet analysis of Auschwitz, now and later, was the downplaying of the scale of the suffering endured by Jews in the camp; the emphasis was on referring to everyone who died as collectively 'victims of Fascism'.

But back in January 1945 Eva Mozes Kor and her sister Miriam rightly considered themselves lucky to have been liberated by the Red Army. For if they had not been left behind, then on the 18th, with the Red Army just a few miles away, the Germans would have included them amongst the other 60,000 so-called 'fit' prisoners drawn from the huge complex of Auschwitz camps and they would have begun the journey west, on foot. These next few weeks would be remembered by many of the prisoners who were forced to take part in the evacuation as the worst experience they suffered while in captivity; worse than the constant selections, worse than the starvation diet in the camps, worse than the disease-ridden, freezing huts they lived in. For the Auschwitz prisoners were embarking on a journey that would become known, with complete accuracy, as a death march.

The concept of the death march was not new to the Nazis. In January 1940, 800 Polish prisoners of war, all Jews, were marched just under 60 miles from Lublin to Biała Podlaska.[5] Only a handful survived the journey through Poland in winter; the majority froze to death or were killed by the SS who accompanied them. In the following years death marches were imposed by the Nazis on Jews after the liquidation of ghettos, and on Soviet prisoners of war as they were marched west to makeshift camps.

But, as discussed in Chapter 5, it was in the autumn of 1944 that the biggest death marches of the war took place. One of the worst occurred in Hungary in November 1944 when, on Eichmann's insistence, nearly 80,000 Jews, including women and children, were forced to march west from Budapest in the direction of Austria. Those who survived that appalling journey – a march so bad that even the Nazis commented on the brutality of it – eventually ended up in camps such as Mauthausen and Dachau. Thus the death march that the Auschwitz inmates were about to embark upon had many bloody precedents.

Prisoners were beaten out of the camp, clad in thin prison garb that offered wholly inadequate protection against the snow and bitter wind of a Polish winter, and assembled on the road to begin the march. And it was at this moment that Franz Wunsch of the SS made his final gesture towards the woman he loved, the Jewish prisoner Helena Citrónová. As she stood with her sister Róžinka by the camp gates, shivering, he brought over 'two pairs of warm shoes – fur-lined boots. Everyone else, poor things, were wearing clogs lined with newspapers. He was really endangering his life [giving them to us].' Wunsch told her that he was being sent to the front, but that his mother in Vienna would look after her and her sister because, as Jews at the end of the war, they would have 'nowhere else to go'. He pressed a piece of paper with his mother's address into Helena's hand. But once he had left them Helena remembered her own father's words to her: 'Don't forget who you are.' He had emphasized to her that she must always remember: 'I am a Jew and I have to remain a Jew.' Consequently she threw away the address of Wunsch's mother.

And so the two women began the march west through the driving snow. Helena describes those first days as 'unbelievably harsh'. She watched as around her other prisoners 'dropped in the snow. They didn't have any strength left and they died. Each person took care of himself. Total chaos. Whoever lived – lived. Whoever died – died.'

Ibi Mann,[6] a 19-year-old who had arrived at Auschwitz the previous year from Czechoslovakia, was also seared by her experience of the death march: 'They gathered us in the middle of the night and we never knew the time, the hour, nothing. We were disconnected from the world.' Despite the noise of a Soviet bombardment nearby, the Nazis still insisted on counting the prisoners and then marching them off in rows of five: 'Anyone who dared even to bend over, who stopped even for a moment, was shot.' Like so many other prisoners who survived, Ibi Mann did not face the journey alone; her sister marched with her, offering constant encouragement. 'I was saying, "This is the end. I can't go any further," [but] she pulled me on by force.' At night they slept in barns, once even in a pigsty, or out in the open, sheltered only by bare trees and hedgerows. Ibi and her sister were two of the last to leave, and as they marched they passed ditches full of corpses. They struggled on as the snow turned to slush, invading their thin shoes and raising blisters and sores. Neither woman felt hunger on the march, just a raging thirst that they could never slake. They knew that if they bent down to eat a handful of slush they would be shot. Against this background of suffering it is almost incredible that the Nazis were marching these inmates out of Auschwitz because they thought they represented a useful resource. At this stage in the war slave labour was of great importance to them – by the end of 1944 around half a million prisoners were working in German factories.

There were two main routes used by the Nazis to march the Auschwitz prisoners towards the Reich. One was northwest through Mikołów, just under 30 miles to the railway junction at Gliwice; the other was due west, about 40 miles to the train station at Wodzisław. But the torment did not end there for those prisoners who survived to board the trains that would take them on to camps in Germany and Austria. Ibi and her sister were herded into railway trucks that contained about 'half a metre of snow'. Prisoners were crammed in so tightly that there was often no room to sit down.

Morris Venezia,[7] who had been a Sonderkommando in Auschwitz, was another who made this terrible train journey. He was one of the rare prisoners who managed to find a place to sit in one of the open trucks. But he still remembers the intense cold, the snow falling and lying on him and his friends, and the constant need to throw dead bodies from the truck as those around him succumbed to the appalling conditions. He also recalls another aspect of his journey that is even more remarkable: committing murder.

In the truck with Morris and the other inmates was a German prisoner who was desperate to sit down, having stood in the snow for so long. He came to what he thought was a deal with Morris: for the price of some cigarettes he would be allowed to sit while Morris stood. Morris got up, took the cigarettes and smoked them whilst the German slumped in the corner of the truck. After ten minutes or so, when Morris had finished the cigarettes, he told the German to stand up. He refused. 'So what I did,' says Morris, 'was me and a couple of friends we sat on him. And [after] about thirty minutes or one hour he was suffocated and we threw him out of the wagon. No problem. We were glad we killed a German.'

Even today Morris has 'no problem' with having killed this German prisoner. It mattered not that the man he murdered had been a fellow inmate of Auschwitz. All that was important was the language he'd been speaking: 'I was happy. They [the Germans] killed all my family, thirty or forty people, and I killed one

German. Phuh! That was nothing. If I could kill a hundred of them I would be glad because they destroyed us completely.' No matter how he is questioned on the subject, Morris is unable to see any difference between the Germans who ran Auschwitz and the German prisoner he killed on the cattle truck on that freezing winter night in Poland. 'Anyway,' he says, 'I wanted to be seated too because I got tired. Why should he live because he gave me two or three cigarettes? He didn't want to get up, so we sat on him and he passed away – easy.' Morris Venezia's lack of concern for the German prisoner he and his comrades killed on their journey west is, of course, a reminder of the debased moral landscape of the camp, and of how each prisoner was often forced to consider his or her own survival above all else.

The destination for around 20,000 of the Auschwitz prisoners was Bergen–Belsen concentration camp in Lower Saxony. As discussed in Chapter 5, Bergen–Belsen is infamous today, primarily because of the heartrending film footage that was shot there in the aftermath of the British liberation of the camp on 15 April 1945. These appalling images of emaciated bodies and walking skeletons rightly shocked the world when they were shown. But they also created an image of the camp that does not reflect the reality of its original conception, and in the process the film adds to the confusion that exists in many people's minds over the difference between a concentration camp and a dedicated death camp.

Whilst at its inception in 1943 Bergen–Belsen had been intended as a place for 'privileged' Jews who were to be held as hostages, in the spring of 1944 it took on another function as prisoners considered unable to do useful work were sent there from other camps. These prisoners suffered appallingly at Bergen–Belsen, where they were particularly brutally treated by the German Kapos. And the preconditions for the transformation of Bergen–Belsen into the scene of horror the Allies liberated in the spring of 1945 were subsequently completed by three additional factors: the appointment of Josef Kramer as camp commandant in December 1944; the decision to remove any 'privileges' that may have existed in the camp for any 'exchange Jews'; and the flood of new arrivals from the death marches in the early months of 1945. An idea of the scale of change at Bergen–Belsen can be gained from simple numbers – at the end of 1944 there were around 15,000 inmates at the camp; when the British arrived in April 1945 there were 60,000. Virtually no effort was made by the Germans to house or feed this massive influx.

However, as always in history, statistics give little insight into individual experience. That can only be gained by listening to stories like that of Alice Lok Cahana and her sister Edith who were at Bergen–Belsen in April 1945. They had thought Auschwitz at the limits of what human beings could endure, but life here was even worse. Alice and Edith arrived at the camp when there was an epidemic of typhoid raging through the huts. Overcrowding meant there were no bunks and scarcely any accommodation of any kind. There was no food and virtually no water. The Auschwitz prisoners had essentially been corralled into this one space and left to die. Over the next few weeks many lost control mentally. 'There's no vocabulary that can tell what was Bergen–Belsen,' says Alice. Every night a Kapo who slept near them 'went berserk' and stamped on Alice and her sister. The barracks were half built, and what had been erected was falling apart: 'When you had to go to the bathroom, you had to step over people. Some people fell into the cracks in the corridor.' Day and night they heard the cry of 'Water, mother! Water, mother!'

Renee Salt[8] was another Auschwitz prisoner who had been transported to Bergen–Belsen. She was 16 years old in 1945. And her first sight of the camp, after being forced down a road littered with dead bodies from previous transports, was a vision from hell: 'We saw skeletons walking, their arms and legs were like matchsticks, the bones protruding through the remains of their skin. The stench that arose from the camp was terribly overpowering. It seemed that, after all we've been through already, this was something new and horribly different.'

All traces of the organization of the camp had broken down. Roll-calls were no longer held – people didn't even have the strength to get up – and without food the prisoners were starving to death. Within three weeks Renee knew that she was dying. Then, as she veered towards unconsciousness, someone pointed out to her a British tank in the distance. She collapsed and did not regain consciousness for ten days. When she awoke she was in a British delousing centre, being washed in disinfectant, utterly weak – but free.

On 15 April 1945, someone shouted, 'Liberated! We are liberated!' says Alice Lok Cahana. She immediately leapt up and said to her sister: 'What is liberation? I have to find liberation before it melts away.' She staggered out of the barrack and saw Allied soldiers in jeeps. But her joy was short-lived because by now Edith was sicker than ever, and shortly after the British arrived she was taken to a Red Cross hospital. Alice wanted to stay with her, but the British soldiers insisted that she was not ill enough to remain with her sister. Alice protested: 'I said, "You don't understand. We can't be separated. I can help you here. I can take out the bedpan."' She tried to lift up the bedpan, but she could barely walk herself. As she reached the door, a soldier picked her up, put her in a jeep and took her back to the barrack.

However, Alice, having protected her sister through the torment of Auschwitz and Bergen–Belsen, was not to be put off so easily. The next day, despite her own frailty, she walked back to the hospital. She arrived just as Edith was being placed in an ambulance. Quickly she climbed on board herself, announcing: 'Here I am. I'm going with you. Wherever they take you.' But the same soldier who had driven her back to the camp the previous day recognized her and said: 'Are you here again? You can't be here. We have to take your sister to another hospital, a military hospital.' Alice was forced to get down from the ambulance and watch as her sister was driven away.

So began Alice's search for her sister – one that lasted for half a century. She tried to trace her through the Red Cross, through any means she could think of, but she heard nothing. Not, that is, until 53 years after her sister's disappearance when she discovered in the records of Bergen–Belsen that an Edith Schwartz had died on 2 June 1945. Schwartz was the maiden name of Alice's mother, and one that Edith had used in the camp so as to pretend not to be Alice's sister. She had been frightened that if the Nazis had known they were related they would have done their best to separate them.

So after a 53-year wait – 53 years in which every time the phone rang, every time a letter was delivered Alice had prayed it was news of Edith – having endured all this emotional suffering, she discovered that her sister had lived for only a few days after they had last parted. Alice had protected her sister through the deportation from Hungary and Auschwitz, on the death march and amidst the starvation and disease of Bergen–Belsen, but in the end the Nazis had still killed her. 'Liberation came too late for you, my beloved sister,' wrote Alice in a poem shortly after she learnt the news of Edith's death. 'How could they do it? How? Why?'

One of the men most responsible for Edith's death, Heinrich Himmler, would, in the early days of the implementation of the 'Final Solution', have had no difficult in answering the two questions posed by Alice Lok Cahana in the most brutal and simplistic way: the Jews were to die because he and his Führer perceived them as a threat. But his actions during the last months of the war were a good deal less straightforward. Himmler's approval of the 'Jews for trucks' scheme in Hungary in 1944, and his use of Bandi Grosz to open a channel through which peace feelers could be explored, have already been discussed. These schemes came to little, but they show the way Himmler's mind was now working. Pragmatism, rather than ideological rigidity, was the way forward as far as the Reichsführer SS was concerned.

In February 1945 Himmler's more flexible attitude found expression in the transportation of 1200 Jews from Theresienstadt to Switzerland. It was a release arranged with the American Union of Orthodox Rabbis via a series of intermediaries, and this time it was not Jews for trucks but Jews for hard currency. Rita Reh[9] was one of the inmates of Theresienstadt who made the journey: 'When we were on the train the SS came and told us to put on some make-up, comb our hair and dress up so we'd look all right when we arrived. They wanted us to make a good impression on the Swiss.'

The first Adolf Hitler learnt of the release of the Theresienstadt Jews was when he saw it reported in a Swiss newspaper. He was beside himself with rage. It was true that as far back as December 1942 Himmler had secured Hitler's agreement in principle that selected Jews might be ransomed for hard currency – the use of prominent Jews as 'hostages' was in line with established Nazi thinking – but the release of the Theresienstadt Jews had occurred without Hitler's knowledge or approval, and, now that the war was clearly in its final stages, must have smacked to the Nazi leader of defeatism. Hitler forbade any more such transfers.

But Himmler was to go against Hitler's instructions once again when he allowed Bergen–Belsen to be captured by the Allies in April. Hitler had ordered that all concentration camps be destroyed before the Allies arrived. Yet Himmler expressly disobeyed. It is likely that he permitted Bergen–Belsen to be taken intact as a 'concession' to the Allies, and that he was ignorant about the true nature of the conditions that existed in the camp. Himmler's actions backfired dramatically as pictures of the appalling conditions flashed around the world. 'The things in this camp are beyond describing,' said one British soldier interviewed for a newsreel. 'When you actually see them for yourselves, you know what you're fighting for. Pictures in the paper can't describe it all. The things they have committed – well, nobody would think they were human at all.'

Despite this disastrous attempt to curry favour with the Allies, Himmler still continued to act against Hitler's wishes. On 20 April he had a meeting with Norbert Masur, an emissary of the World Jewish Congress, and agreed to release 1000 Jewish women from Ravensbrück concentration camp. Himmler's only stipulation was that they be categorized as 'Poles', not Jews; that way he hoped Hitler would never get to hear of his actions. Later that night, after Masur had gone, Himmler confided to Felix Kersten, his masseur: 'If I could have a fresh start, I would do many things differently now. But as a loyal soldier I had to obey, for no state can survive without obedience and discipline.'[10]

It was not just Himmler who was disobeying the German leader during the last moments of the war, but entire SS units. Deep in the Führer's bunker in Berlin, Hitler was woken on 21 April by the noise of artillery. It was the moment he must have believed was inconceivable – the Red Army had reached Berlin. Hitler ordered SS Oberstgruppenführer (General) Felix Steiner to make a counter-attack against the soldiers of Marshal Zhukov's 1st Belorussian Front who were advancing through the capital's northern suburbs. But Steiner refused. 'When the order came in,' says Franz Riedweg,[11] General Steiner's adjutant, 'he said, "I will not launch another attack on this Russian avalanche. I'd be sending men to their death. I won't sacrifice my troops for a senseless command."' When he heard of Steiner's refusal, Hitler shouted and screamed in the worst display of anger that anyone in the bunker had ever seen.

The SS had deserted him. All that was left to do now, he said openly, was for him to take his own life.

On 23 April the news of Hitler's outburst was passed to Himmler, who that day was meeting Count Folke Bernadotte, a representative of the Red Cross. Himmler believed that, since Hitler had announced he was going to commit suicide (and might even be dead already), he was now empowered to act on behalf of the Reich. So he told Bernadotte that he could take this proposal with him to the Western Allies – Germany would surrender unconditionally to Britain and the United States, but not to the Soviet Union.

Himmler's plan for partial surrender was rejected by the Allies, but news of his attempt to end the war in the West was broadcast on BBC Radio and Hitler learnt of it. The German leader was not dead. Far from it. When he heard the news Hitler was still able to feel one of the most powerful emotions of all: betrayal. 'Of course Hitler was outraged in the extreme,' says Bernd Freiherr Freytag von Loringhoven,[12] who, as a member of the General Staff of the German army, was in the bunker at the time. 'Militarily, there was no hope left. And now this move had been made by the man he probably had trusted most. This man had deserted him and approached the Allies. As a result, Hitler took the logical step and dictated his political and personal wills. And within two days he was dead.'

Hitler killed himself just before 3.30 p.m. on 30 April 1945 as Red Army soldiers approached the German parliament building, the Reichstag. He died leaving a political testimony composed the previous night – one that blamed the Jews for causing the war. Hitler died as he had lived, consumed with hatred for all Jewish people, without a hint of remorse. As we have seen through the twists and turns of the development and implementation of the Nazis' 'Final Solution', Hitler could be closely involved in the detail of the policy at one moment, more distant at another. But, as Hitler's last dealings with Himmler demonstrate, it was the Führer who was consistent to the end in his fanatical hatred of the Jews.

Himmler revealed himself to be more malleable to events than the man he served: not just negotiating to hand over Jews for cash, but even trying to arrange a secret peace settlement. For Himmler, unlike Hitler, appears to have believed in the last days of the war that there was a future beyond the conflict. And by acting as he did he caused consternation amongst members of his SS entourage. On 5 May, at Admiral Doenitz's headquarters at the Muerwick Navy School in Flensburg in northern Germany, Himmler held a last meeting with senior figures in the SS, amongst them Rudolf Hoess. 'Destiny has a great new task for me,' announced Himmler. 'I will have to undertake this task alone. So now I give you my last order. Disappear into the Wehrmacht!' Hoess was astonished. He had clearly been expecting some symbolic last act, not this tawdry instruction to run off and hide. 'This was the farewell message from the man to whom I had looked up so much,' wrote Hoess, 'in whom I had had such firm faith, and whose orders, whose every word had been gospel to me.' Nonetheless, Hoess followed Himmler's instructions to 'disappear' in the armed services, picked up a naval uniform and tried to pass himself off as an ordinary member of the German navy, the Kriegsmarine.

But Himmler's confidence that 'destiny' had a great new task for him was, like so many of his beliefs, a fantasy. Just over two weeks after his last meeting with Hoess, on 23 May, he committed suicide, having finally realized that there was no possibility that the Allies would do business with a man responsible for the murder of millions. That he ever did entertain such thoughts reveals much about the man: his capacity for delusion, his inflated sense of self-importance, his crazed optimism. But above all it shows his opportunism – how, despite having being Hitler's loyal creature for so many years, when the situation changed he was prepared to be someone else's.

With Hitler and Himmler dead, and other, lesser perpetrators scurrying for cover, the days immediately after the end of the war ought to have been a time of comfort and recuperation for all those who had suffered in the camps. But they were not.

Helena Citrónová and her sister wandered around the newly liberated Germany in confusion during May and June 1945, mingling on the crowded roads with German refugees trying to escape to the West. They slept in barns or bombed-out houses, and scavenged food wherever they could. It was not long before they encountered soldiers of the Red Army. And as far as Helena and her sister were concerned, these men behaved not as liberators but as conquerors. There were occasions when the Soviet soldiers sought out the refugees wherever they were sheltering overnight. 'They were drunk – totally drunk,' says Helena. 'They were wild animals.' The soldiers entered the places where they slept and 'looked for cute girls and raped them'. Helena hid under her sister as this was happening, hoping that the sight of her sister, ten years older than she was and often mistaken for her mother, would cause the soldiers to look elsewhere. It was a ploy that worked. But she heard everything that the Red Army soldiers did to the other women: 'I heard screaming until they were quiet and had no more strength left. There were cases where they were raped to death. They strangled them. I turned my head because I didn't want to see because I couldn't help them. I was afraid they would rape my sister and me. They were animals. No matter where we hid, they found our hiding places and raped some of my girlfriends. They did horrible things to them. Right up to the last minute we couldn't believe that we were still meant to survive. We thought if we didn't die of the Germans, we'd die of the Russians.'

Helena herself had one especially narrow escape. One morning she went for a bike ride and 'became ecstatic with riding. I loved to ride a bicycle as a child at home – the freedom and the quiet.' She rode off far into the bright spring countryside. Then, when she stopped for a rest by a deserted warehouse, 'a Russian man came along with a motorcycle. He'd seen a young woman – Jewish, not Jewish, it didn't matter. He threw his motorcycle down and a terrible battle began. I don't know how I managed to get away from this cruel Russian soldier, this criminal. He hadn't seen sex in a long time and he could not manage to rape me. I kicked and I bit and I screamed and he asked me all the time if I was German. I said, "No, I am Jewish from the camp." I showed him the number on my arm. And at that moment he recoiled. Maybe he himself was Jewish. I don't know what he was. He turned, stood up and ran.'

The exact number of sexual attacks perpetrated by Soviet soldiers as they advanced through Germany, and then in the immediate aftermath of the war, will never be known, but the figure is certainly in the hundreds of thousands. In recent years much publicity has been given to the suffering of German women in cities like Berlin. But the revelation that women who had already endured so much mistreatment in camps like Auschwitz were then subsequently raped by their liberators adds a level of nausea to the history that did not exist before.

Terrible as the raping of former camp inmates by soldiers of the Red Army undoubtedly was, there remains a special quality to the suffering they inflicted on their own compatriots as they 'liberated' the camps. Stalin had said that there were no Soviet prisoners of war held by the Germans, only 'betrayers of the motherland'. And this attitude could not have been expressed with more clarity than when units of the Red Army arrived at the concentration camp in southern Poland in which Tatiana Nanieva[13] was held. Captured by the Germans in 1942 when the hospital in which she worked as a nurse had been encircled, she had endured two and a half years of imprisonment, and in the process had to witness fellow Soviet women prisoners being raped by the Germans. Then, in January 1945, she heard the soldiers of the Red Army arriving with great 'pomp', singing patriotic songs with their heads held high: 'Our feelings were joyful, elated. We believed that victory was at hand and that a normal life would begin again. I was yearning for my motherland, for my family.' Then, as joy flooded through her at the moment of liberation, two Red Army officers approached her. One of them was drunk and he shouted, 'So how did you live it up here? You whores!' Tatiana felt her world collapse as he stood swaying, reaching for his pistol. She ran and managed to hide until these front-line troops who had liberated the camp had sobered up. But, whether they were drunk or sober, the charge against her was still clear: 'Betrayal of the motherland'. For the 'crime' of allowing herself to be captured by the Germans she was sentenced to six years in a Gulag and lifetime exile in Siberia.

Pavel Stenkin,[14] who had already beaten the odds and survived Auschwitz, had to endure similar treatment at the hands of his fellow countrymen. He had been one of the original 10,000 Soviet prisoners who had been sent in October 1941 to Auschwitz to construct the camp at Birkenau. By the following spring, with only a few hundred of them left alive, he had escaped into the forest and eventually managed to join the advancing Red Army. But instead of being welcomed back and allowed to fight the rest of the war against the Germans as he wished, he was interrogated for weeks, the standard question of the SMERSH investigators being: 'When did you join the German army?' He was sent into internal exile in the closed city of Perm in the Urals, where the questioning did not stop. 'I was called up every second night: "Admit this, agree to that, we know everything – you are a spy." They were tormenting and tormenting me.' After some months working in the day and being interrogated at night, Stenkin was prosecuted on a trumped up charge and sentenced to several years' imprisonment. Demonstrating the level of cynicism that operated in the Soviet legal system, the judges rushed through his case because they had tickets to the theatre that night. Only in 1953, with the death of Stalin, was Stenkin released, one of more than a million Soviet soldiers who were imprisoned twice – once by the Germans and once by their fellow countrymen.

Pavel Stenkin's and Tatiana Nanieva's experiences are particularly important because they so conspicuously lack the redemptive quality that many in the West have come to expect from the history of World War II. For generations of British and Americans, this war has attained the near mythic quality of a fight of 'good' against 'evil'. And of course it is true that Nazism was defeated, and there can be no argument that the world benefited immeasurably from the removal of that scourge. But the history of the aftermath is not as simplistic as the popular myth would have us believe. There were certainly few 'happy endings' for the Soviet prisoners liberated by the Red Army, or indeed for many others in the East.

As the war came to an end Stalin too committed crimes that, in part at least, are reminiscent of aspects of the Nazis' 'Final Solution'. Like Hitler, Stalin persecuted whole groups of people. Nearly 100,000 Kalmyks from the steppe land south of Stalingrad were deported en masse to Siberia for the collective 'crime', in the Soviet dictator's eyes, of not resisting the Germans sufficiently. The Crimean Tartars, the Chechens and many other ethnic minorities within the Soviet Union were to endure the same fate in the last days of the war and its immediate aftermath. No one knows exactly how many Soviet citizens were deported, but the figure is certainly more than a million. And although – unlike the Jews, the majority of whom were murdered once they fell into Nazi hands – a large proportion of the ethnic groups that Stalin persecuted were able to return from Siberia to their homeland after his death, what is certain is that Chechens, Tartars, Kalmyks and others did suffer hugely as a result of Stalin's desire to punish whole groups for the infractions of individuals.

In May 1945 most of eastern Europe swapped one cruel dictator for another, a stark reality that was to impact on many of the Auschwitz survivors as they tried to return home. Initially, Linda Breder's[15] experience of Soviet occupation was immensely positive. These were the people, after all, who had defeated the Nazis, liberated the camps and stopped the mass extermination of the Jews. When, on 5 May, she was finally liberated at the camp north of Berlin to which she had been transferred after two and a half years in Auschwitz, the Red Army soldiers were 'very friendly' to her and the other inmates. They helped them find new clothes so that they could cast aside the hated striped uniforms they had worn for so long, by the simple expedient of taking them to a nearby German house and telling them they could take anything they wanted. The terrified woman who lived there started shouting, 'No SS! No SS!' as Linda and several other Slovak ex-prisoners pushed past her and started searching for clothes. When they opened the wardrobe they found several SS uniforms – clearly this was the wife of an SS man. So they 'looted' the whole place, throwing eiderdowns and other belongings out of the window and taking all the clothes they needed. Linda Breder claims they scarcely touched the woman, though she admits one 'strong girl' did 'grab and yell at her'.

All Linda thought of was returning to Slovakia; others dreamt of a new life in America or Israel, but her only desire was to go home. And so she began her long journey through a Europe devastated by war, with railways smashed and roads destroyed, travelling with some other Slovak ex-prisoners. In Berlin they saw German prisoners of war flattening the ground and repairing giant potholes. The sight of members of the 'master race' forced to do manual labour excited Linda and the other women so much that they asked the Red Army soldier who was supervising the POWs if they could speak to them. He agreed and the women all started to taunt them, shouting, 'Quick! Quick! Move! Move!' and then they 'really shoved them around'. More than the 'looting' of the German house, this was a moment of absolute realization for

Linda Breder that she would never have to be frightened of Germans again. No longer would she feel terror in her heart at selections, desperate that she would be the one chosen to live.

Beyond Berlin they travelled on foot – there was no other means of transport available. Then one day, as they walked the dusty roads of central Germany in the hot summer of 1945, some Red Army soldiers drove up and offered them a lift. Linda and the other women 'were really scared because they often raped girls'. But they longed to have a rest from walking and so, in spite of their fears, they climbed aboard the truck with the Soviet soldiers. But then, after they had travelled only a few miles, the soldiers suddenly stopped and robbed them of almost everything they had. 'They even stole those things we had stolen from the Germans,' says Linda Breder. 'But at least we saved our lives.'

Dumped by the side of the road and now with scarcely any possessions, they walked on again, with only the occasional respite of a short train ride, until at last they reached Prague. Linda and a number of the other women found shelter in the city, but still she was obsessed with a desire to return home to Slovakia as soon as she possibly could. Once one train a day was running between Prague and Bratislava, the Slovak capital, Linda was able to travel to her family home in the eastern Slovakian town of Stropkov. At last, after more than three years away from home, after deportation in freight trucks, after the privations and suffering of Auschwitz and the struggle of the journey home from northern Germany, at last she had attained the goal she had been dreaming of for so long – she stood in front of her own home. But there was one problem: someone else appeared to be living there. She knocked on the door, which was opened moments later by a Russian or Ukrainian man. 'What do you want?' he demanded. 'I've come back home,' she replied. 'Go back to where you came from!' he said as he slammed the door in her face.

Linda was in a state of shock. She wandered off down the main street of her home town, and as she did so the sudden realization came to her that all of the houses that had previously belonged to her friends and relations were now occupied by people from the Soviet Union: 'When I looked into the windows of those houses I had a feeling that all eyes were gazing at me.' Only the non-Jewish population of the town were still in evidence, but many of them had previously been friendly with Linda and her family and she still thought they at least would welcome her. She was wrong. 'I recognized one of them,' says Linda, 'but she didn't come to tell me, "I'm glad to see you." Everybody was keeping their distance as if I was poisoned or something. I left the next day and never went back. Going back was my worst experience. It was really catastrophic.'

Linda Breder's story of her bitter return home is one mirrored by many survivors, not just from Auschwitz, but from other camps as well. In captivity they had been inspired by the thought of home, believing that they could recapture the life they had possessed once the war was over. But it was impossible. Linda Breder eventually left Slovakia and made a new life for herself in California.

Walter Fried[16] was another Slovakian Jew who returned home in the summer of 1945. He was 17 years old and had been imprisoned with his family in a labour camp in Slovakia. Jewish deportations from Slovakia had ceased in October 1942, partly as a result of pressure from a faction within the Slovak government, and a number of Slovakian Jews had subsequently been retained as forced labour within the country rather than handed over to the Nazis. Walter came from a relatively wealthy family; his father owned a restaurant and a taxi in the town of Topolčany, and until 1939 they had all lived happily alongside their neighbours. Now, as they returned home with Fascism defeated, they expected to regain their former lives.

They were part of a small minority who made it home; out of 3200 Jews who had lived in the town before the war, only around 10 per cent ever returned. But when they came back they found something waiting for them that they could never have imagined: hatred. Someone else was in their apartment, and when they tried to recover it the current occupant refused to leave. It was the same with their restaurant. The new proprietor told them that under Soviet occupation the business was now 'nationalized', and since he was the one paying the rent, he was there legitimately.

The Fried family thought they had one salvation. Walter's father had asked some good friends, a Christian family, to hide their gold, jewellery and money before they were deported. Now, full of confidence, they went to collect it. They met their friends over lunch and initially the conversation was stilted. Eventually Walter's father broached the subject that was on all their minds, saying, 'We left a little package with you, and you know exactly what the package contained – there was gold, diamonds and money.' But their friends had a different recollection, replying that whilst the Frieds had indeed left some things with them, they consisted of only a few clothes, which they were now happy to return. 'We gave you gold and diamonds!' said Walter's father in despair. But it was useless; they never recovered their valuables.

The devastation the Frieds felt was caused not just by the outright theft of their money and property, but by the feeling of emotional betrayal. 'We lost our minimum of hope,' says Walter Fried, 'that the good Christian, who used to be a friend of the Jew, someone the Jew supported all the time – who used to be given food when he didn't have any money when he came to our restaurant – would respond. They didn't want us to come back, so they wouldn't have to settle their accounts with us and look us in the eye and say, "We don't owe you anything." Our best friends from before became our worst enemies. In 1945 we were more threatened than in 1942 when we left. That's how much hatred there was.'

The hatred directed against them took physical form one night in the summer of 1945. Walter and his father were walking down a street in Topolčany when they encountered a group of around 30 young people. One of them was an old schoolfriend of Walter's from before the war, called Josho. However, Josho was anything but friendly now. The group rushed towards Walter and his father and started hitting them. 'Jew! You're a Jew!' shouted Josho as he beat them. As Walter lay on the ground, injured, he remembered how before the war he had shared his bread with Josho at school. He said to him: 'Isn't it enough you ate my bread? Now you come and beat me up! Why?' But all Josho replied was, 'Jew! You are a Jew!'

Others in the mob screamed: 'Jews! You take Christian blood!' They beat Walter and his father not just with their fists but with sticks until they were both badly injured. The attack was perpetrated in the open on one of the town's main streets, and Walter observed how not a single person stopped to help them, even though some of those who walked by were acquaintances. 'I had thought that I knew so many people,' says Walter, 'but all of a sudden nobody knew us.' Then the youths dragged them to the local police station and threw them on the steps. 'The police were no better,' says Walter. 'Instead of chasing them away or arresting them, they let them go. Then they gave us another beating.' Walter knew he could remain in Slovakia no longer, and at the first opportunity emigrated to Israel, where he lives today.

There were also reports of post-war pogroms against the Jews in Poland, and no one knows how many more Jews returning from the camps endured similar experiences across eastern Europe. No detailed statistical survey has ever been completed of the extent of the lack of restitution. But such evidence as there is suggests that Walter Fried's and Linda Breder's stories do not represent isolated incidents but are part of a wider pattern. In the chaotic atmosphere of the immediate post-war years, with the population adjusting to living under their new masters, pursuing justice for the Jewish survivors of anti-Semitic persecution was not high on anyone's agenda, if it appeared on the agenda at all.

Toivi Blatt, who had escaped from Sobibór in October 1943, had an even more immediate experience of how life could never return to its relative pre-war calm. As he travelled through Poland after the revolt, hiding from the Germans and seeking help from locals, he found that many Poles refused him aid – not just because they were frightened of the Nazis, but because of outright anti-Semitism. When eventually a farmer did agree to hide him in an underground chamber in one of his farm outbuildings, it was a strictly business transaction – the farmer demanded money for concealing him. And when the war did not end as quickly as expected, one of the farmer's relatives entered Toivi's hiding place and tried to kill him. Only by first pretending to be dead did he miraculously manage to escape.

At the end of the war Toivi Blatt returned to his home in Izbica but discovered, just as Linda Breder and Walter Fried had found, that the Jewish community of his town had been destroyed. He subsequently left Izbica and tried to make a new life elsewhere in Poland, but without finding much happiness. 'Most of my life was in Poland,' he says, '[but] I still felt like I didn't belong there. I wanted to get married and there was a problem – how will she act if I am Jewish? Most of them are negative I must tell you.' Toivi felt sufficiently out of place in the land of his birth that in 1957 he took the opportunity to emigrate, first to Israel and then to America. He thought he had detected anti-Semitism from the Communist Party of Poland, who he believed perceived the Jews as a 'fifth column'.

Toivi Blatt eventually made a successful life for himself in the USA, but he always felt part of him remained Polish, so he returned to visit Izbica in the early 1990s. He walked back into a village that had once been home to nearly 4000 Jews and now contained not one. A Polish Catholic friend of his who lived in the village had always said that Toivi should stay with him if he were ever in town, but now, when Toivi arrived to take up the offer, he was turned away without reason – although Toivi felt he knew the reason all too well: 'He didn't want the neighbours to know that he had a Jew sleeping at his place.'

This reticence to admit to a friendship with, or even to knowing, Toivi Blatt extended to those Poles who had hidden him during the war. As Toivi is the first to acknowledge, there were some gallant Poles who did give him food and shelter on his long journey back from Sobibór (and recent scholarship focused on Warsaw reveals that there were thousands of such brave people),[17] but instead of feeling pride at these actions, some today feel only shame. When Toivi was walking through a nearby village with a Catholic priest he pointed out the house of someone who had helped him during the war, and started to walk up to the front door. But the man hid behind the curtain and would not let them in. Again the reason seemed clear to Toivi: 'Many people that hid Jews didn't want the neighbours to know because they would immediately say, "Oh, he had a lot of money because he hid Jews."'

But the most devastating example of how anti-Semitic beliefs and values still live on occurred when Toivi visited his old family home in Izbica. He knocked on the front door and asked the man who now lived there if he would be happy to let him enter and look round the house in which he had been raised, the house in which he had hidden from the German 'actions', and the house in which his beloved mother and father had spent their last days before being taken to Sobibór. Initially the new owner was reluctant, but when Toivi pressed three American dollars into his hand he was allowed to enter. Toivi immediately noticed a chair in the living room and remarked that it had once belonged to his father. 'Oh, no,' the man replied. 'That's impossible.' So Toivi took the chair, turned it over, and there, written on the base of it, was his family name. At this the man said, 'Mr Blatt, why the whole comedy with the chair? I know why you are here.' Toivi looked at him, bemused. 'You have come for the hidden money,' the man continued. 'We could divide it – 50 per cent for you and 50 per cent for me.' Furious, Toivi Blatt left the house without a backward glance.

There is a fitting postscript to this story, one that deserves a place in a morality tale. When he next returned to Izbica, Toivi passed by his old house and saw the place in ruins. He went to his neighbours and asked them what had happened. 'Oh, Mr Blatt,' they said, 'when you left we were unable to sleep because day and night he was looking for the treasure you were supposed to have hidden. He took the floor apart, the walls apart, everything. And later he found himself in the situation that he couldn't fix it – it would cost too much money. And so now it's a ruin.'

But if the post-war experiences of Toivi Blatt, Linda Breder and Walter Fried illustrate a dark and depressing side of the human condition, then a more comforting story comes from another part of Europe. When the Danish Jews returned home – the majority from exile in Sweden, a few from the Nazi ghetto-camp of Theresienstadt – they enjoyed a heartening reception. 'It was not like places where people had taken over the property of the Jews and made themselves at home,' says Bent Melchior.[18] 'Here nothing was touched.' As soon as the Melchior family returned, their landlord gave notice to the new tenants of their apartment, and within three months they were back living exactly as they had been before the deportation. Their landlord had even carefully packed up and stored their furniture ready for them.

Rudy Bier[19] and his family also came back home to Denmark to discover their apartment 'spotless'. The rent had been paid by their friends during the years they had been away. 'It was a wonderful feeling,' he says, 'that we were expected to come back.' The worst experience he can remember concerns his wife's family. They had left an uncooked duck in their flat, and 18 months later they returned to find the duck still there but in an advanced state of decomposition. From that moment his mother-in-law never ate duck again.

As a general rule, the Danish Jews fared much better on their return than the Polish or Slovak Jews, and the reasons behind this are predominantly situational. Jews attempting to rebuild their lives in countries now occupied by the Soviet Union faced the near impossible task of trying to recover their property in a new political system that preached total nationalization and prevented individuals from owning houses or factories as they had before the war. The non-Jews who had moved into houses or flats left when the Jews had been forcibly deported could now simply say that the state owned the property and they were merely renting it (as was the case when the Frieds tried to recover their restaurant in Slovakia). Nor was it, of course, in the interests of many non-Jews in these countries to open up a discussion on just how they had behaved during the Nazi occupation and persecution of the Jews, and, as a result of the scale of the murders, few Jews actually managed to return in any case to initiate the debate. The Soviet desire to portray the Nazi campaign of genocide as directed merely against those who opposed 'fascism' also played directly into the desire felt by many non-Jews in the East to airbrush the traumatic events of the Nazis' 'Final Solution' out of their history. There were simply too many awkward questions to answer.

Example after example in this history shows how hard it is for the majority of people to go against prevailing cultural mores. Walter Fried's old friend Josho turned against him not because he made that decision in isolation, but because the culture surrounding him had changed as a result of both the arrival of the Soviet forces, and by the presence after the war of the few Jews who did manage to return home and remind everyone of a past many wished to forget. Choice is always possible, but it is much easier to go with the flow. And if that flow happens to lead to anti-Semitism and persecution, then so be it.

The Danes, on the other hand, faced no such difficulties. Because they felt they had behaved admirably in the autumn of 1943 in the face of the Nazis' attempted deportations, the return of the Danish Jews after the war was an event to be celebrated, not ignored. Economically, politically, perhaps even morally, it was easier to be a Dane immediately after the war than a Pole or a Slovak. This is not to say that life for the Jews who returned to their former homes in the countries of Western Europe was always easy – it wasn't. Despite the work of the Joint Distribution Committee and the restitution money paid by the Federal Republic of Germany to Israel via the Luxembourg Agreement during the 1950s, many Jews never received their due. The struggle for proper restitution and compensation continues, of course, even to this day.

Whilst those who had endured Nazi persecution faced distinctly mixed fortunes after the conflict ended, their SS perpetrators knew with certainty from the moment of the German surrender that they were at risk of arrest and prosecution. And just as Rudolf Hoess sought to conceal his past, so a much more minor cog in the Auschwitz machine, Oskar Groening,[20] tried to do the same. In 1944 his application for a transfer to a front-line unit had finally been granted and he had joined an SS unit that was fighting in the Ardennes. After being wounded and sent to a field hospital he rejoined his unit before they eventually gave themselves up to the British on 10 June 1945. Once they were in captivity, the British handed a questionnaire to all of them. Groening then realized, as he puts it, that 'involvement in the concentration camp of Auschwitz would have a negative response', so he 'tried not to draw attention to it'. He put down on the form that he had worked for the SS Economic and Administration office in Berlin. He did this not because he was suddenly overcome with a sense of shame about what had happened at Auschwitz, but because 'the victor's always right and we knew that the things that happened there [in Auschwitz] did not always comply with human rights'. Groening still feels that 'my time as a prisoner of war was the consequence of my membership in the Waffen SS, which retrospectively was made into a criminal organization. So I found out that I had been in a criminal organization without having known I'd joined it'.

Along with the rest of his SS comrades, he was imprisoned in an old Nazi concentration camp, which was 'not very pleasant – that was revenge against the guilty'. But life improved when he was shipped to England in 1946. Here, as a forced labourer, he had 'a very comfortable life'. He ate good food and earned money to spend. He became a member of the YMCA choir and for four months travelled through the Midlands and Scotland giving concerts. He sang German hymns and traditional English folk songs such as 'A Lover and His Lass' to appreciative British audiences, who competed to have one of the Germans stay with them overnight and give them a good night's sleep and breakfast.

When he was finally released and returned to Germany in 1947 he found he could not regain his old job at the bank since he had been a member of the SS, so he got a job in a glass works and began the long climb up the management ladder. He continued his policy of trying not to draw 'undue attention' to his time in Auschwitz, so much so that he insisted that his close family erase their memories as well. Once, shortly after his return to Germany, he was sitting at the dinner table with his father and his parents-in-law and 'they made a silly remark about Auschwitz', implying that he was a 'potential or real murderer'. 'I exploded!' says Groening. 'I banged my fist on the table and said, "This word and this connection are never, ever, to be mentioned again in my presence, otherwise I'll move out!" I was quite loud, and this was respected and it was never mentioned again.' Thus did the Groening family settle back and begin to make a future for themselves in post-war Germany, enjoying the fruits of the German 'economic miracle'.

The post-war years would also see the formation of the state of Israel and, as a consequence, a concerted attempt by a well-funded and well-organized security force to track down Nazi perpetrators. Their most famous success was the capture of Adolf Eichmann in Argentina and his subsequent secret transfer to Israel and trial in Tel Aviv in 1961. Moshe Tavor[21] was one of the members of the Israeli security team that captured Eichmann, but, proud though he is of that action, which was publicized around the world, it is the secret 'revenge' he took in the days and months immediately after the war that he believes accomplished more.

When he was 20 years old, in 1941, Moshe Tavor joined the British army and subsequently served in the Jewish Brigade, a unit of 5000 Jewish soldiers under the command of a Canadian-born Jew, Brigadier Ernest Benjamin. Their emblem was the Star of David, now the flag of the state of Israel. Jews from Palestine had first been incorporated into the British army in 1940, and a Palestine Regiment had subsequently fought in North Africa in 1942. But there had been opposition for many years within the British government, notably from Neville Chamberlain, to the formation of a separate and distinct Jewish unit. Winston Churchill was much more open to the idea, and the Jewish Brigade was finally formed in 1944.

As they fought their way up through northern Italy, and in the immediate aftermath of the end of the war, Moshe Tavor and his comrades learnt more and more about how their fellow Jews had been treated by the Nazis. 'We got angry,' he says simply. 'And many of us felt it wasn't enough that we participated in the war.' So Moshe Tavor and his comrades discussed ways they could take 'revenge' on the Germans. First, he says, they used whatever contacts they had in the intelligence section of the army and through Jewish organizations to obtain a list of names of Germans who were believed to have been involved in the killing of Jews. Then they disguised their vehicles, covering up the Star of David and replacing it with identification marks from non-Jewish units, and put British military police armbands on their sleeves. Once all this preparation was complete, they would drive up to the house of the suspected perpetrator and take him away for an 'interrogation'. 'They weren't too suspicious,' says Tavor, 'because they didn't know we were Jewish Brigade – they thought we were British soldiers. We would take this guy and he wouldn't resist. And from that moment on he no longer saw anything. He never saw his house again.'

Moshe Tavor and other members of the Jewish Brigade drove with their German captive to an isolated spot and there they 'gave him a trial'. They put to him all the allegations against him they had themselves been given, then 'maybe we gave him a chance to say a few words'. And then, in every case, they 'finished him off'. They were anxious not to leave behind any traces of the killing – no blood and no body: 'The method was that one of us would strangle him.' And he confesses that he himself personally strangled one suspected perpetrator: 'Not that I was happy to do it, but I did it. I never had to drink before to make myself enthusiastic. I was always enthusiastic enough. I'm not saying that I was indifferent, but I was calm and quiet and I did my work. You can compare me perhaps even to the Germans themselves who did it, because they also did their work.' After killing the suspected perpetrator, they disposed of the body. 'Then we would drive to an area we had chosen in advance. We would tie something heavy, like a part of an engine, to his feet and then we would drag him into a river.'

Moshe Tavor has no regrets that he personally killed Germans in this way: 'When I did it I felt very good. I mean not at the moment of the killing, but during that [overall] period of time. I can't say that I feel bad about it now. You can tell me I murdered people, but I know who I killed. So I'm not proud and I'm not guilty about it. I don't wake up at night with bad dreams or anything. I sleep well. I eat well. I live.'

Moshe Tavor accepts that his version of 'justice' was far from that of a proper trial with judge and jury, and confesses that 'in my life until then I had done quite a few things which were not exactly straight'. And, of course, the 'evidence' that he and his comrades would have received could on occasion have been little more than suspicions – accusations that were never to be properly tested in a court of law. The possibility, indeed the probability, is therefore that he was involved in the killing of some innocent people. But such was the anger felt by him and his colleagues that this was a risk they were prepared to take. Indeed, he even witnessed members of the Jewish Brigade killing Germans against whom they had no evidence whatsoever: 'There were guys who did things spontaneously. One had a brother or a mother who'd been killed [by the Nazis]. So when we were in Germany or Austria and they'd see a German on a bicycle then the driver would simply run him over.'

Moshe Tavor says that he himself was involved 'about five times' in revenge killings, and claims that altogether his comrades in the Jewish Brigade 'were involved in about twenty executions'. Not surprisingly, given that he and his comrades were acting outside the law, it is hard to substantiate the detail of Tavor's testimony. He is careful not to refer to specific individuals whom he killed or specific places where the murders took place. Equally, it is always possible that the reality was a good deal less dramatic than the concerted campaign he describes – perhaps just the occasional murder of a suspected Nazi (and one must treat his claim that the killings were based on proper 'intelligence' with caution). But other evidence,[22] including eye-witness testimony from Haim Laskov, a former chief of staff of the Israeli army, confirms that members of the Jewish Brigade did take part in 'revenge' killings, and the (ultimately unsuccessful) attempts of other Jewish 'avengers' to poison the water supply of a camp in which SS prisoners were held are well established.[23]

The motivation behind the actions of Moshe Tavor and his comrades in the Jewish Brigade seems clear enough: to avenge the murder of other Jews, some of whom were their own relatives. But it is not quite that simple. There was another element lurking in their minds that drove them to be tough and ruthless – a lingering feeling that the Jews who had suffered at the hands of the Germans had not resisted enough. 'I couldn't understand,' says Tavor, 'how six or eight German soldiers could lead one hundred and fifty people into vehicles and take them away. I think I might have attacked one of those Germans and let them kill me and get it over with. But I'm a different type of person than those Jews who lived in small towns in Poland. As kids we'd pretend we were old Jewish heroes and fight mock wars. I feel very connected to the people who fought here [in Israel] two thousand years ago, and I was less attached to the Jews who went like sheep to the slaughter – this I couldn't understand.'

Moshe Tavor's attitude is not unique. Some survivors of the camps who settled in Israel after the war claim that they faced a latent sense of criticism that they too had not done more to fight back against the Nazis. Never mind that it would have been almost impossible for women and children who had no homeland, who were living in communities in eastern Europe that often even now have little sympathy for them, to do more to resist. There remains the often unspoken belief from others that they should not have been, as Moshe Tavor puts it, 'sheep to the slaughter'. And if there was one single lesson that someone like Tavor took from the Nazis' 'Final Solution' and sought to embed in the psyche of the new state of Israel, it was that the Jews should never again submit to an enemy without resistance.

While Moshe Tavor carried out his distinctly unauthorized retribution against the Germans, the rest of the Allies tried to stay within the law and catch the perpetrators. Initially they did not have much success. Most of the SS who had worked at Auschwitz were not identified in the immediate post-war period. Notable figures like Dr Mengele and Rudolf Hoess were both initially held by the Allies and then released. In Mengele's case the lack of an SS blood group tattoo under his arm meant he was never identified as

SS, and Hoess's disguise as a member of the German navy, the Kriegsmarine, meant that his tattoo was never looked for.

But by the autumn of 1945 the War Crimes Investigation Section of 21 Army Group and the British Intelligence Corps were on the trail of Rudolf Hoess.[24] The British first learnt in detail about the his career as a result of the liberation of Bergen–Belsen. Systematic questioning of the survivors revealed intriguing news – many of them spoke with horror about their time at another camp in Upper Silesia: Auschwitz. Now the British determined to capture the commandant of this murderous place. The Intelligence Corps recognized that often the best way to find perpetrators was through their family. Individual Nazis might have taken a new identity, might even have fled the country, but they remained emotionally attached to their wives and children, and the families were almost always easier to find. So it was with Frau Hedwig Hoess and her children. Traced by British intelligence to a village 6 miles from Belsen, they were immediately put under surveillance. Frau Hoess was finally arrested on 8 March 1946 and imprisoned. For several days she was repeatedly asked where her husband was, and each time she responded: 'He's dead.' Finally the Intelligence Corps officers tricked her into revealing the truth. The rear of the prison abutted a railway line, and a train was noisily shunted into position directly behind her cell. According to Captain William 'Victor' Cross, Officer Commanding 92 Field Security Section: 'We then informed Frau Hoess that the train was there to take her three sons to Siberia unless she told us where her husband was and his aliases. If she did not do this, then she would have two minutes to say goodbye to her sons ... We left her for ten minutes or so with paper and pencil to write down the information we required. Fortunately our bluff worked; she wrote down the information and she and her sons were sent home.'[25]

Frau Hoess revealed that her husband was currently living on a farm at Gottruepel near Flensburg. Intelligence officers immediately left for northern Germany, liaised locally with 93 Field Security Section and moved up to the farm at 11 o'clock on the evening of Monday 11 March. They surprised Hoess in his pyjamas at his bunk in the stable block, which also doubled as a slaughterhouse. A British medical officer quickly prized Hoess's mouth open to search for a poison capsule – they all knew that

Himmler had managed to kill himself in just such a way the previous year. Hoess was hit across the face four times by a British sergeant before he admitted who he was, and was then dragged to one of the slaughterhouse tables where, according to one of the British soldiers who witnessed it, 'the blows and screams were endless'. The medical officer shouted to Captain Cross: 'Call them off unless you want to take back a corpse!' Hoess was then covered in a blanket, yanked over to a car and driven back to Field Security Headquarters at Heide.

Snow was falling as they arrived in the early hours of the morning, but Hoess was made to walk naked through the barrack courtyard to his cell. He was then kept awake for three days – soldiers were detailed to prod him with axe handles if he showed signs of dozing off. According to Hoess, he was also beaten with his own riding crop. Then, on 14 March, he signed an eight-page confession.

There are Holocaust deniers who point to the abuse Hoess suffered at the hands of British soldiers immediately following his arrest and claim that this discredits his confession. But whilst it could be argued that his initial statement was tainted, during his subsequent imprisonment and interrogation, first at 'Tomato' – the codename for No. 2 War Criminals Holding Centre at Simeons Kaserne – and then subsequently both at Nuremberg and at his own trial in Poland, there is no evidence that Hoess was mistreated again. It was during this subsequent period that he wrote his memoirs – indeed, he remarks in them how grateful he is to his captors for giving him the chance to write his personal history – and neither then, nor in the witness box when he had the open opportunity to do so, did he recant any of his original confession, though he did feel secure enough to record that he had initially been beaten by his British captors.

In April 1947 Rudolf Hoess returned to Auschwitz, to the same building in which he used to work. Only this time he was imprisoned in the basement cells of the SS administration offices rather than installed behind his desk in his first-floor office. It had been thought fitting that the man who had presided over the death of more than a million people at Auschwitz should be executed at the site of his crimes. But there were problems on the day originally scheduled for the execution. Several thousand people, many of them former inmates, came to watch. The atmosphere grew ugly and they pushed forward against the wooden fence erected to restrain them. There was a real feeling, according to Stanisław Hantz,[26] a former prisoner who witnessed the gathering, that 'they will lynch Hoess here'. He heard mutterings in the crowd. What would the soldiers who were standing guard do if there was a huge surge forward? Would they shoot? The situation grew so dangerous that Hoess was not taken from his cell as planned. Instead, an elaborate ruse was devised whereby the soldiers marched off and then drove away, escorting a car that everyone thought contained Hoess. But Hoess had not been taken away; he was left in his cell overnight and then taken out the next morning. In front of only a handful of people – not the screaming crowds of the day before – Rudolf Hoess prepared to die. 'I thought as he climbed the gallows, up the stairs, knowing him as a tough Nazi supporter that he would say something,' says Stanisław Hantz, one of the few witnesses to his execution. 'I thought that he would make a statement to the glory of the Nazi ideology that he was dying for. But no. He didn't say a word.'

Hoess's end was quick – the exact opposite of what Hantz, who had been tortured in the camp, wanted: 'I think Hoess should've been put in a cage and been driven all around Europe so that people could see him – so people could spit on him, so that it would get to him what he did.' But the intriguing question is this: would what he had done ever have 'got to' Hoess? All the clues in his autobiography, which he completed just before his execution, point one way: all the humiliation and mistreatment in the world would never have caused Hoess to search into his heart and think that what he did was fundamentally wrong. Of course, he does say in his autobiography that he 'now' sees that the extermination of the Jews was a mistake, but only a tactical one, since it has drawn the hatred of the world upon Germany.

My personal experience of having encountered a number of former Nazi perpetrators makes me believe that one single paragraph in Hoess's memoirs offers the strongest clue as to what he really felt at the end. In it he asks, as he did at Nuremberg, what would have happened to a pilot who had refused to drop bombs on a town that he knew contained mainly women and children. Of course, says Hoess, that pilot would have been court-martialled:

'People say that is no comparison,' writes Hoess. 'But in my opinion the two situations are comparable.'[27]

In essence Hoess justifies his actions by this simplistic comparison: the Allies killed women and children by bombing, the Nazis killed women and children by gassing. This is a line of argument still supported by many former perpetrators (and Nazi apologists) today. One former member of the SS, who refused to be interviewed formally, went so far as to say in a casual conversation with me: 'The children who died in our gas chambers suffered less than the children who died in your fire bombing of German cities.' More openly, and expressing himself more carefully, Oskar Groening says: 'We saw how bombs were dropped on Germany, and women and children died in firestorms. We saw this and said, "This is a war that is being led in this way by both sides", and the Holocaust was part of the fight against the warmongers and part of our battle for freedom.' As he sees it, the fact that the Allies, 'regardless of whether it was militarily necessary or not, murdered women and children by throwing bombs of phosphorus on them', and were not then held accountable for their actions at the end of the war, means that it is hypocritical to focus all the guilt for 'war crimes' on SS perpetrators.

Of course, one instinctively finds such a comparison repellent. And the arguments about the conceptual difference between the two actions – the Allied bombing of cities and the Nazi extermination of the Jews – are easy to rehearse: that the German leadership could have stopped the bombing instantly by surrendering, whilst the extermination of the Jews was a policy determined by ideology; that no individual group of Germans was targeted by the bombing, unlike the Nazis' murder of one specific category of people in their empire; that it was the towns and buildings the bombers primarily sought to destroy, not the people themselves; that the Nazi persecution of the Jews (for example Eichmann's brutal Nisko plan) predated the bombing of German cities, so the notion that the bombing in any way acted as a justification at the time for the Nazis as they committed crimes against the Jews is nonsense; that any comparison between the pragmatic Allied planners and dedicated Jew-haters like Hitler, Heydrich or Eichmann, is ludicrous. And then there is the additional argument, often the first recourse of the non-specialist, that runs simply: 'The Germans started it, as they bombed British cities before the British bombed Berlin.' But this is, in reality, the weakest rationale of all, since it can scarcely be a defence to say of any action that it becomes legitimate if one's enemy commits it first.

But despite all the attempts to differentiate the two methods of killing, the false comparison between them made by Hoess and other Nazis still remains emotionally disturbing. One reason is that it is well known that there was disquiet about the policy of bombing German cities inside the Allied leadership – not least, towards the end of the war, from Churchill himself. And the revelation in recent years that in spring 1945 one Allied criterion used in the process of deciding which German cities and towns to target was their 'burnability', something that helped lead to the targeting of medieval cities like Würzburg, only adds to the sense of unease. And there is another, less obvious, reason why the comparison is unsettling. It is because the development of high-level bombing involved the inevitable 'distancing' of the aircrew from the killing. 'It's not like I was going out and sticking a bayonet in someone's belly, OK?' says Paul Montgomery,[28] a member of an American B29 crew who took part in the fire-bombing of many Japanese cities during the war: 'You still kill them but you kill them from a distance, and it doesn't have the demoralizing effect upon you that it did if I went up and stuck a bayonet in someone's stomach in the course of combat. It's just different. It's kind of like conducting war through a video game.'

Montgomery's testimony is, of course, worryingly reminiscent of the distancing effect the Nazis sought to create for themselves by building the gas chambers. Just as it was easier to kill someone by dropping a bomb on them rather than bayoneting them, so it was easier for the Nazis to kill someone by gassing them rather than shooting them. Twentieth-century technology not only allowed more people to be killed in war than ever before, it allowed those who did the killing to suffer less psychological damage as a result of their actions.

But none of this means that any legitimate comparison is possible between the Allied bombing of Germany and the extermination of more than a million people at Auschwitz. For all the reasons mentioned above, the two actions are conceptually different. But in Hoess's mind, and that of many other Nazis, the comparison did hold: bombing and gassing were simply different methods of killing the enemy. And this meant that no matter how Hoess was treated – even if he had been paraded round 'in a cage' as Stanisław Hantz wanted – he would never have truly regretted what he had done. As it is, he is most likely to have walked up the steps to the gallows with two thoughts in his head: 'I die not because of my crimes, but because we lost the war; and I die a much misunderstood man.' Ultimately, that is why such an outwardly nondescript person as Hoess is such a terrifying figure.

In 1947, as Hoess left this life, the camp complex he created was decaying fast. Poles in the nearby area were dismantling some of the barracks at Birkenau to use the wood to repair their own houses, and an even more disturbing looting of the camp was taking place. When Polish teenager Józefa Zielińska and her family returned to Auschwitz after the war they discovered they had nowhere to live. Their house had been destroyed in the massive Nazi reorganization of the area and they were forced to live in a shed that had once housed chickens. In order to make money Józefa and her friends went down to the site of the crematoria at Birkenau and searched for gold. They dug up the soil, and the fragments of bones that lay within it, placed the mixture in a bowl and sieved it through with water. 'Everyone felt bad doing it,' says Józefa. 'Whether they had family that had died in the camp or not, everyone felt uneasy because they were human bones, after all. It wasn't a pleasure. But it was poverty that forced us to do such a thing.' With the money gained by selling the gold they had prospected from the soil of Birkenau, Józefa Zielińska's family managed to buy a cow.

Jan Piwczyk was another Pole forced by circumstance to live in one of the chicken coops near Birkenau, and he too admits that he searched for valuables near the remains of the crematoria: 'I remember I found a gold tooth and a Jewish coin and a gold bracelet. Now today I wouldn't do it, right? I wouldn't look through human bones because I know this is sacrilege. But at the time the conditions forced us to do it.' When he was not searching for valuables Jan and his friends also bribed the Soviet soldiers who occasionally patrolled nearby so that they could take wood from the barracks of Birkenau in order to build their own houses. 'You know,' says Jan, 'after the war it was tough. You had to start from scratch.'

Immediately after the war Stanisław Hantz, the former Polish political prisoner who had witnessed Rudolf Hoess's execution, got a job guarding the Birkenau site. He tried to protect the camp from locals intent on stealing from the remains of the crematoria by firing warning shots above their heads. 'We called them cemetery hyenas,' he says. 'We couldn't understand how these people could search these tombs.' Away from the site, he had a foolproof way of detecting their presence: 'You could recognize them by the smell – they smelt from afar. It was a stench of fermenting bodies. You could tell such a person walking down the street.'

It would take years for the site of the atrocities at Auschwitz to be appropriately maintained and cared for. Indeed, not until well after the fall of Communism would the signage at the museum finally be changed to reflect in a proper manner the suffering of the Jews.

Meantime, Oskar Groening, who had spent several years in the SS at Auschwitz, steadily rose through the management structure of the glass factory where he now worked, eventually becoming head of personnel. Finally he was made an honorary judge of industrial tribunal cases. Without seeing any sense of irony or inappropriateness in his words, Oskar Groening believes that the experience he gained in the SS and Hitler Youth helped him do his job as a personnel officer better, since 'from the age of twelve onwards I learnt about discipline'.

Even though he had worked at Auschwitz and helped in the extermination process by sorting and counting the foreign money stolen from the arriving transports, he never considered himself 'guilty' of any crime: 'We drew a line between those who were directly involved in the killing and those who were not directly involved.' In addition, he felt he was, using the words of the infamous Nazi post-war defence, acting under orders, and he attempts to defend himself with this analogy: 'The first time a company of soldiers gets a volley of machine-gun fire they don't all get up and say, "We don't agree with this – we're going home."'

This was, perhaps surprisingly, a similar line to the one taken by West German prosecutors after the war as they sought to determine who from Auschwitz should face war crime charges and who should not. If a member of the SS was not either in a senior leadership position or directly involved in killing, he generally escaped prosecution. Thus when Oskar Groening's past was eventually uncovered – inevitably, since he never made any attempt to change his name and hide – the German prosecutors did not press charges against him. His experience therefore demonstrates how it is possible to have been a member of the SS, worked at Auschwitz, witnessed the extermination process, contributed to the 'Final Solution' in a concrete way by sorting the stolen money, and still not be thought 'guilty' by the post-war West German state. Indeed, out of the 6500 or so members of the SS who worked at Auschwitz between 1940 and 1945 and who are thought to have survived the war, only around 750 ever received punishment of any kind.[29] The most notorious legal process was the 'Auschwitz trial' in Frankfurt between December 1963 and August 1965, when, of the 22 defendants, 17 were convicted and only six received the maximum penalty of life imprisonment.

However, it was not only Germany that failed to prosecute in substantial numbers those SS members who had worked at Auschwitz. This was a collective failure of the international community (with the possible exception of the Polish courts, who tried a remarkable 673 out of the 789 Auschwitz staff[30] ever to face justice). Prosecutions were hindered not just by lack of consistency between nations about what conduct constituted a 'crime' in Auschwitz, but also by the division caused by the Cold War and, it must be said, by a clear lack of will. Despite the Nuremberg trials stating that the SS was a 'criminal' organization in its entirety, no attempt was ever made to enforce the view that the mere act of working in the SS at Auschwitz was a war crime – a view that popular opinion would surely have supported. A conviction and sentence, however minimal, for every SS man who was there would have sent a clear message for the future. It did not happen. Around 85 per cent of the SS who served at Auschwitz and survived the war escaped scot-free. When Himmler set in train the development of the gas chambers in order to distance the SS from the psychological 'burden' of shooting people in cold blood, he could scarcely have predicted that it would have this additional benefit for the Nazis; this method of murder meant that the vast majority of the SS who served at Auschwitz could escape punishment after the war by claiming successfully that they had not been directly part of the extermination process.

Nor does Oskar Groening feel a moment's unease that, whilst many of those who were imprisoned in Auschwitz faced further hardship after they were liberated, he enjoyed (and continues to enjoy) a life of comfort. 'It's always like that in the world,' he says. 'Each person has the freedom to make the best of the situation he's in. I did what every normal person tries to do, which is to make the best possible situation for himself and his loved ones, if he has a family. So I succeeded in doing that; others didn't succeed. What happened before is irrelevant.'

Given this attitude of insouciance, it is all the more surprising that towards the end of his life Oskar Groening decided to speak openly about his time in Auschwitz, and the circumstances that led to his change of heart are intriguing. After the war Groening became a keen stamp collector and was a member of his local philately club. At one of the meetings, more than 40 years after the war, he started to chat to the man next to him about politics. 'Isn't it terrible,' said the man, 'that the present government says it's illegal to say anything disputing the killing of millions of Jews in Auschwitz.' He went on to explain to Groening how it was 'inconceivable' for so many bodies to have been burnt, and he also maintained that the volume of gas that was supposed to have been used would, in reality, have killed 'all living beings' in the vicinity.

Groening said nothing to contradict these statements at the philately club, but later obtained one of the Holocaust deniers' pamphlets that his fellow stamp collector had recommended, wrote his own ironic commentary on it and posted it to him. Then he suddenly started to receive odd phone calls at home from strangers who disputed his view that Auschwitz was really the centre of mass killing by gassing. It turned out that his denunciation of the Holocaust deniers' case had been printed in a neo-Nazi magazine. And now '90 per cent' of the calls and anonymous letters he received 'were all from people who tried to prove that what I had seen with my own eyes, what I had experienced in Auschwitz was a big, big mistake, a big hallucination on my part because it hadn't happened'.

Motivated now by a desire to speak out against those who denied the sights he personally had witnessed, Groening wrote down his own personal history for his family and eventually agreed to be interviewed by the BBC. Now well into his eighties,

Groening has one simple message for the Holocaust deniers: 'I would like you to believe me. I saw the gas chambers. I saw the crematoria. I saw the open fires. I was on the ramp when the selections took place. I would like you to believe that these atrocities happened because I was there.'

At the end of this tragic story, what are we left with? For certain with a world in which the majority of those who ran Auschwitz were not punished for any crime, and in which most of the inmates of the camp never received full restitution for the suffering they endured. Far from it, since so many endured the consequences of more prejudice and victimization after the war was over. One naturally revolts against this conclusion. There is a deep human need to feel that life offers an element of justice, the sense that the innocent eventually receive recompense and the guilty are brought down. But this history offers little of that comfort, for the most searing example of lack of redemption rests in the soil of Birkenau, the earth worked over for valuables by locals after the war, in the largest graveyard in the history of the world. This, together with the nearby Vistula river where many ashes were dumped, is the final resting place of more than a million people whose testimony we cannot listen to.

Nor does it appear, as a general rule, that those forced to endure Auschwitz could find solace or a sense of redemption in spiritual comfort. For every Else Abt who, as a Jehovah's Witness, felt that God was with her in the camp, there are many more like Linda Breder who believe that 'there was no God in Auschwitz. There were such horrible conditions that God decided not to go there. We didn't pray because we knew it wouldn't help. Many of us who survived are atheists. They simply don't trust in God.' What a survivor like Linda Breder realizes is that she owes her life to a large extent on luck – and the belief that life can be governed by chance factors wholly outside of one's control is hardly a firm basis for religious doctrine.

The current estimate is that of the 1.3 million people sent to Auschwitz, 1.1 million died there. A staggering 1 million of them were Jews, an important statistic for those few who still seek to follow the Communist line and characterize all those who died there as 'victims of fascism'. It must always be remembered that more than 90 per cent of those who lost their lives at Auschwitz did so because the one 'crime' they had committed in Nazi eyes was to be born Jewish.

The highest number of Jews from any one national group transported to Auschwitz[31] came from Hungary, during the frenzied action of early summer 1944 (438,000). The next highest number were from Poland (300,000), followed by France (69,114), the Netherlands (60,085), Greece (55,000), Czechoslovakia and Moravia (46,099), Slovakia (26,661), Belgium (24,906), Germany and Austria (23,000), Yugoslavia (10,000) and Italy (7422). Of course we must also never forget the non-Jews who perished in the camp: the 70,000 Polish political prisoners; the more than 20,000 gypsies; the 10,000 Soviet prisoners of war; the hundreds of Jehovah's Witnesses; the tens of homosexuals; nor any of the others sent to the camp for myriad warped reasons (and sometimes for no reason at all).

Soon the last survivor and the last perpetrator from Auschwitz will have joined those who were murdered at the camp. There will be no one on this earth left alive who has personal experience of the place. And when that happens there is a danger that this history will merge into the distant past and become just one terrible event amongst many. There have been horrific atrocities before, from Richard the Lionheart's massacre of the Muslims of Acre during the Crusades, to Genghis Khan's genocide in Persia. Maybe future generations will see Auschwitz the same way – as just another bad thing that happened in the past, before living memory. But that should not be allowed to happen. We must judge behaviour by the context of the times. And judged by the context of mid-twentieth-century, sophisticated European culture, Auschwitz and the Nazis' 'Final Solution' represent the lowest act in all history. By their crime the Nazis brought into the world an awareness of what educated, technologically advanced human beings can do, as long as they possess a cold heart. Once allowed into the world, knowledge of what they did must not be unlearnt. It lies there – ugly, inert, waiting to be rediscovered by each new generation. A warning for us, and for those who will come after.

NOTES

INTRODUCTION

[1] This assumption is based partly on a BBC audience survey conducted in 2004 to test public knowledge and perception of Auschwitz, which demonstrated that the vast majority of people who had heard of the camp thought it had been built in order to exterminate the Jews.

[2] I acknowledge my great debt to the production teams with whom I have had the privilege of working on these past projects, in particular the brilliant research conducted by Tilman Remme, Detlef Siebert, Martina Balazova and Sally Ann Kleibal.

[3] See particularly Robert Galletely, *The Gestapo and German Society* (Clarendon Press 1990).

[4] It was fascinating to discover from Jonathan Glover's epic *Humanity – a Moral History of the Twentieth Century* (Pimlico 2000) that, in this regard, this distinguished philosopher had, from a study of written sources, reached the same broad conclusions.

[5] See Laurence Rees, *Selling Politics* (BBC Books 1992) for a detailed examination of Goebbels' work.

[6] Rees, *Selling Politics;* see especially Wilfred von Oven's interview.

[7] An expression first coined by Martin Broszart.

[8] See p. 62.

[9] Quoted in Goetz Aly, *Final Solution: Nazi Population and the Murder of the European Jews* (Hodder Arnold 1999), p. 3.

[10] See p. 211.

[11] Testimony of former prisoners Wanda Szaynok and Edward Blotnicki, quoted by Andrzej Strzelecki in 'Plundering the Victims' Property' in *Auschwitz 1940–1945, Central Issues in the History of the Camp*, Vol. II (Auschwitz–Birkenau State Museum 2000), p. 164.

CHAPTER 1: SURPRISING BEGINNINGS

[1] BBC interview.

[2] It is right to be suspicious of broad psychological explanations for the behaviour of Nazis, but Alice Miller in *For Your Own Good: the Roots of Violence in Child-rearing* (Virago Press 1987) does claim that all the leading Nazis had rigid upbringings similar to those of Hoess and Hitler. However, even if that is so, there were many who had such childhoods who did not go on to become Nazis.

[3] Quoted in *Concentration Camp Dachau 1933–1945* (Comité International de Dachau, Brussels Lipp GmbH, Munich 1978), p. 20.

[4] Rudolf Hoess, *Commandant of Auschwitz* (Phoenix Press 2000), p. 131.

[5] Hoess, *Commandant*, p. 131 (although these page references have been given for ease of reference, the quotes used have, for the most part, been translated from the original manuscript held in the Auschwitz–Birkenau State Museum).

[6] In the previous year, 1933, Hoess had formed a troop of mounted SS on the Sallentin estate in Pomerania – effectively a 'reserve force' that he was involved with while still a farmer.
[7] Hoess, *Commandant*, p. 64.
[8] BBC interview.
[9] Of course, some of these politicians were Jewish. But that was not the reason for their arrest.
[10] Hoess, *Commandant*, p. 81.
[11] Hoess, *Commandant*, pp. 70–1.
[12] BBC interview.
[13] Quoted in Danuta Czech, 'The Auschwitz Prisoner Administration', in Yisreal Gutman and Michael Berenbaum (eds), *The Anatomy of the Auschwitz Death Camp* (Indiana University Press 1998).
[14] Laurence Rees, *The Nazis: a Warning from History* (BBC Books 1997), p. 36.
[15] Quoted in Franciszek Piper, 'The Methods of Mass Murder', in *Auschwitz 1940–1945*, Vol. III, p. 71.
[16] Quoted in Jonathan Glover, *Humanity – a Moral History of the Twentieth Century* (Pimlico 2000), p. 344.
[17] Quoted in Glover, *Humanity*, pp. 361–2.
[18] Hoess, *Commandant*, p. 77.
[19] Quoted in Aly, *Final Solution*, p. 19.
[20] BBC interview.
[21] Aly, *Final Solution*, p. 17.
[22] BBC interview.
[23] Goebbels diary, 24 January 1940.
[24] Quoted in Raul Hilberg, *The Destruction of the European Jews* (Holmes and Meier 1986), p. 50.
[25] Quoted in Aly, *Final Solution*, p. 70.
[26] BBC interview.
[27] BBC interview.
[28] Quoted in J. Noakes and G. Pridham (eds), *Nazism 1919–1945*, Vol. 3 (Exeter University Press 1988), p. 933.
[29] Quoted in Aly, *Final Solution*, p. 3.
[30] German Foreign Office memorandum, 3 July 1940.
[31] BBC interview.
[32] BBC interview.
[33] Hoess, *Commandant*, p. 116.
[34] BBC interview.
[35] Remark by Albert Speer, according to his brother Hermann, quoted in Michael Thad Allen, *The Business of Genocide – the SS, Slave Labor, and the Concentration Camps* (University of North Carolina Press 2002), p. 59.
[36] Allen, *Business*, particularly Ch.2, 'A Political Economy of Misery'.
[37] Hoess, *Commandant*, p. 283.
[38] BBC interview.
[39] Quoted in Irena Strzelecka, 'Punishments and Torture', in *Auschwitz 1940–1945*, Vol. II, p. 389.
[40] *KL Auschwitz as Seen by the SS* (Auschwitz–Birkenau State Museum 1998), p. 117.
[41] BBC interview.
[42] Peter Hayes, *Industry and Ideology – I.G. Farben in the Nazi Era* (Cambridge University Press 1987), pp. 347–64.
[43] Ambros document, quoted in Hayes, *Industry*, p. 349.
[44] Franciszek Piper, 'The Exploitation of Prison Labour', in *Auschwitz 1940–1945*, Vol. II, p. 104.
[45] Hoess, *Commandant*, p. 390 and Hoess interrogation by Jan Sehn, Kraków, 7–8 November 1946, Instytut Pamięci Narodowej, Warsaw NTN 103.
[46] Minutes of founding meeting of I.G. Farben-Auschwitz, 7 April 1941. Quoted in Deborah Dwork and Robert Jan van Pelt, *Auschwitz*

1270 to the Present (Norton 1996), p. 211.
[47] I.G. Farben 'report of meeting with commander of the concentration camp near Auschwitz on 27.3.1941 at 3 p.m.', Nuremberg Trial Files Document 15148. And SS report of the same meeting.
[48] Minutes of meeting on 2 May 1941, Nuremberg Trial Files, Vol. 31, p. 84, Document 2718-PS.
[49] 'Political-economic Guidelines', Nuremberg Trial Files, Vol. 36, pp. 135–7.
[50] Goetz Aly and Susanne Heim, *Architects of Annihilation* (Weidenfeld and Nicolson 2002), pp. 63–4.
[51] Quoted in Aly and Heim, *Annihilation*, p. 237.
[52] Quoted in Ian Kershaw, *Hitler*, Vol. 2 (Penguin Press 2000), p. 127.
[53] Quoted in Ernst Klee, Willi Dressen and Volker Riess, *Those Were the Days* (Hamish Hamilton 1991), p. 179.
[54] Quoted in Henryk Świebocki, 'Escapes from the Camp', *Auschwitz 1940–1945*, Vol. IV, p. 233.
[55] Quoted in Robert Jay Lifton, *The Nazi Doctors* (Basic Books 1986), p. 63.
[56] BBC interview.
[57] For a full discussion of the new evidence for Pavel Sudoplatov's approach see Laurence Rees, *War of the Century* (BBC Books 1999), pp. 53–5.
[58] Quoted in Ulrich Herbert (ed.), *National Socialist Extermination Policies* (Berghahn Books 2000), p. 257.
[59] BBC interview.
[60] In the 1960s Friedrich was the subject of a police investigation about his actions during the war, but a prosecution was not proceeded with. In our interview, though he admitted taking part in the shooting of Jews, he did not name the exact places where he had committed the crime. At such a distance of time, and without personal identification from eyewitnesses, it seems unlikely that a criminal prosecution proving his guilt 'beyond reasonable doubt' would succeed.
[61] BBC interview.
[62] BBC interview.
[63] Quoted in Goetz Aly, 'Jewish Resettlement', in Herbert (ed.), *Extermination Policies*, p. 71.
[64] BBC interview.
[65] Quoted in Glover, *Humanity*, p. 345.
[66] Testimony of Wilhelm Jaschke in Widmann trial, Schwurgericht Stuttgart 1967, pp. 62–3, Staatsarchiv Ludwigsburg EL 317 III, Bu 53.
[67] Testimony of Wilhelm Jaschke, Vilsbiburg, 5 April 1960, Bundesarchiv Ludwigsburg 202 AR-Z 152/159.
[68] Gilbert witness statement in Dwork and van Pelt, *Auschwitz 1270*, p. 278.

CHAPTER 2: ORDERS AND INITIATIVES

[1] Quoted in Gustave Gilbert, *Nuremberg Diary* (Farrar 1947).
[2] Quoted in Christopher Browning, *The Origins of the Final Solution: The Evolution of Nazi Jewish Policy September 1939 – March 1942* (William Heinemann 2004), p. 318.
[3] BBC interview.
[4] BBC interview.
[5] Quoted in Ian Kershaw, 'The Persecution of the Jews and German Public Opinion in the Third Reich', in *Yearbook of the Leo Baeck Institute*, 1981, Vol. 26, p. 284.

[6] Russian State Military Archive 502K/1/218.
[7] Peter Witte et al (eds), *Himmler's Dienstkalender 1941/2* (Hamburg 1999), p. 123, footnote 2, and Sybille Steinbacher, *Musterstadt Auschwitz* (Munich 2000), pp. 238–9.
[8] BBC interview.
[9] BBC interview.
[10] Irena Strzelecka and Piotr Setkiewicz, 'The Construction, Expansion and Development of the Camp and Its Branches', in *Auschwitz 1940–1945, Central Issues in the History of the Camp*, Vol. 1 (Auschwitz–Birkenau State Museum 2000), p. 78.
[11] Rudolf Hoess, *Commandant of Auschwitz* (Phoenix Press 2000), p. 123.
[12] Michael Thad Allen,'The Devil in the Details: the Gas Chambers of Birkenau, October 1941', *Holocaust and Genocide Studies* 16/2 (autumn 2002).
[13] *Encyclopedia of the Holocaust*, Vol. 2 (Macmillan, New York), p. 902.
[14] BBC interview.
[15] BBC interview.
[16] Christopher Browning, *Path to Genocide* (Cambridge University Press 1992), pp. 28–56.
[17] From Burmeister's testimony of 24 January 1961, Bundesarchiv Ludwigsburg, 303 AR-Z 69/59, p. 3.
[18] *Hitler's Table Talk 1941–1944* (Phoenix Press 2000).
[19] Quoted in Peter Longerich, *The Unwritten Order* (Tempus 2001), p. 78.
[20] Gerhard Weinberg, 'The Allies and the Holocaust', in Michael J. Neufeld and Michael Berenbaum (eds), *Allies and the Holocaust in the Bombing of Auschwitz* (St Martin's Press, New York 2000), p. 20.
[21] J. Noakes and G. Pridham (eds), *Nazism 1919–1945*, Vol. 3, p. 1126.
[22] Quoted in Longerich, *Unwritten*, p. 92.
[23] BBC interview.
[24] 8 November 1961 pp. 5–6 2 StL 203 AR-2 69/59 Bd3.
[25] Quoted in Ernst Klee, Willi Dressen and Volker Riess, *Those Were the Days* (Free Press, New York 1988), p. 255.
[26] BBC interview.
[27] NB: Perry Broad arrived at Auschwitz in April 1942.
[28] *KL Auschwitz as Seen by the SS* (Auschwitz–Birkenau State Museum 1998), p. 129.
[29] *KL Auschwitz as Seen by the SS*, p. 130.
[30] Majdanek, established as a camp for Soviet POWs near Lublin in October 1941, later held mostly Jews and Poles and developed a small Zyklon B gassing facility. But it had neither the capacity nor scale to become conceptually the same as Auschwitz, nor did it initially function as a concentration camp.
[31] BBC interview.
[32] BBC interview.
[33] BBC interview.
[34] Based on Wisliceny's post-war testimony in Slovakia of 6 and 7 May 1946 (Statny oblastny archive v Bratislave, Fond Ludovy sud, 10/48) and 12 August 1946 (Statny oblastny archive v Bratislave, Fond Ludovy sud, 13/48), plus Koso's testimony of 11 April 1947 (Statny oblastny archive v Bratislave, Fond Ludovy sud, 13/48).
[35] BBC interview.
[36] Deborah Dwork and Robert Jan van Pelt, *Auschwitz 1270 to the Present* (Norton 1996), p. 302.

[37] *KL Auschwitz as Seen by the SS*, p. 105.
[38] Hoess, *Commandant*, p. 150.
[39] BBC interview.

CHAPTER 3:
FACTORIES OF DEATH

[1] Quoted in Ulrich Herbert, 'The German Military Command in Paris and the Deportation of the French Jews', in *National Socialist Extermination Policies* (Berghahn Books 2000), p. 139. For a full discussion and analysis of this issue see the pioneering research contained in this article.
[2] Wolodymyr Kosyk, *The Third Reich and Ukraine* (Peter Lang 1993), p. 621.
[3] Timothy Patrick Mulligan, *The Politics of Illusion and Empire* (Preager 1988), p. 139.
[4] Quoted in Herbert, 'The German Military Command', p. 140.
[5] Quoted in Herbert, 'The German Military Command', p. 142.
[6] Figures taken from Susan Zuccotti, *The Holocaust, the French and the Jews* (Basic Books 1993), p. 89.
[7] Quoted in Herbert, 'The German Military Command', p. 152. Recollection of meeting by Balz, head of the Justice Division.
[8] Quoted in Serge Klarsfeld, *French Children of the Holocaust* (New York University Press 1996), p. 34.
[9] Quoted in Zuccotti, *Holocaust*, p. 99.
[10] Zuccotti, *Holocaust*, p. 99.
[11] Klarsfeld, *French Children*, p. 35.
[12] BBC interview.
[13] BBC interview.
[14] Quoted in Klarsfeld, *French Children*, p. 45.
[15] Quoted in Klarsfeld, *French Children*, p. 45.
[16] Klarsfeld, *French Children*, p. 45.
[17] BBC interview.
[18] BBC interview.
[19] BBC interview.
[20] Aleksander Lasik, 'Historical-sociological Profile of the SS', in Yisreal Gutman and Michael Berenbaum (eds), *The Anatomy of the Auschwitz Death Camp* (Indiana University Press 1994), p. 278.
[21] These figures taken from Lasik, 'Historical-sociological Profile'.
[22] Quoted in Frederick Cohen, *The Jews in the Channel Islands during the German Occupation 1940–1945* (Jersey Heritage Trust 2000), p. 26.
[23] Quoted in Cohen, *Jews in the Channel Islands*, p. 34.
[24] BBC interview.
[25] Quoted in Cohen, *Jews in the Channel Islands*, p. 52.
[26] See Cohen, *Jews in the Channel Islands*, p. 59 for the complete list.
[27] Cohen, *The Jews in the Channel Islands*.
[28] Cohen, *The Jews in the Channel Islands*, p. 92.
[29] BBC interview.
[30] BBC interview.
[31] 'Muselmann' – German for 'Muslim' – was the slang name given to prisoners who were weak with starvation and believed not to be able to survive for long. It was thought to be derived from the bowed-over appearance of these people, as if they were Muslims at prayer.
[32] For the controversy surrounding Jaster's death see Henryk Świebocki, 'Escapes from the Camp', in *Auschwitz 1940–1945, Central Issues in the History of the Camp*, Vol. IV (Auschwitz–Birkenau State Museum 2000), p. 199, footnote 532.
[33] Quoted in Yitzhak Arad, *Belzec,*

Sobibor, Treblinka – the Operation Reinhard Death Camps (Indiana University Press 1987), p. 87.
[34] Quoted in Arad, *Belzec, Sobibor*, p. 84.
[35] BBC interview.
[36] Figure quoted in Arad, *Belzec, Sobibor*, p. 87.
[37] The chronology that follows is based on Samuel Igiel's report in *I Remember Every Day ... The Fates of the Jews of Przemysl* (Remembrance and Reconciliation Inc., Ann Arbor 2002), pp. 237–40.
[38] BBC interview.
[39] Rudolf Hoess, *Commandant of Auschwitz* (Phoenix Press 2000), p. 91.
[40] Hoess, *Commandant*, p. 136.
[41] Public Record Office file ref. HW 16/10.

CHAPTER 4: CORRUPTION

[1] See Yitzhak Arad, *Belzec, Sobibor, Treblinka – the Operation Reinhard Death Camps* (Indiana University Press 1987), p. 165.
[2] Note, however, that as far as the Nazis were concerned, since Poland no longer existed, Warsaw was no longer the capital.
[3] BBC interview.
[4] *Auschwitz 1940–1945, Central Issues in the History of the Camp*, Vol. I (Auschwitz State Museum 2000), p. 103.
[5] Strzelecka and Setkiewicz, 'The Construction, Expansion and Development of the Camp and Its Branches', in *Auschwitz 1940–1945*, Vol. I, p. 104.
[6] Franciszek Piper, 'The Exploitation of Prisoner Labour', in *Auschwitz 1940–45*, Vol. II, p. 136.
[7] BBC interview.
[8] BBC interview.
[9] Rudolf Hoess, *Commandant of Auschwitz* (Phoenix Press 2000), p. 96.
[10] Quoted in Robert Jay Lifton, *The Nazi Doctors* (Basic Books 1986), p. 16. Response quoted in answer to question posed by the survivor-physician Dr Ella Lingens-Reiner.
[11] BBC interview.
[12] Quoted in Irena Strzelecka, 'Experiments', in *Auschwitz 1940–1945*, Vol. II, p. 363.
[13] BBC interview.
[14] BBC interview.
[15] Miklos Nyiszli, *Auschwitz, a Doctor's Eyewitness Account* (Mayflower Books 1973), p. 53.
[16] Aleksander Lasik, 'The Organizational Structure of Auschwitz Camp', in *Auschwitz 1940–1945*, Vol. I, p. 203.
[17] BBC interview.
[18] BBC interview.
[19] See the testimony of Konrad Morgen in Frankfurt-am-Main on 8 March 1962, and at the Auschwitz trial in Frankfurt, in Hermann Langbein, *Der Auschwitz-Prozess: eine Dokumentation* (Neue Kritik, Frankfurt 1995), pp. 143–5.
[20] See the minutes of the interview of Eleonore Hodys by Konrad Morgen, autumn 1944, Institut für Zeitgeschichte ZS 599.
[21] For further details on the Morgen investigation and Hoess's removal and alleged affair see Jerzy Rawicz, *The Everyday Life of a Mass Murderer* (Dzień Powszedni Ludobójcy) (Czytelnik, Warsaw 1973).
[22] Information from the pioneering research in the forthcoming PhD thesis on this subject by Robert Sommer.
[23] BBC interview.
[24] BBC interview.
[25] BBC interview. But see also

Thomas Toivi Blatt, *From the Ashes of Sobibor* (Northwestern University Press 1997).
[26] BBC interview.
[27] Mussolini was removed by the Italian King as leader of Italy in July 1943. He was then rescued by the Germans from imprisonment in September and placed at the head of a puppet regime. During this period of German occupation (unlike the situation under Mussolini's direct rule) Italian Jews were subject to deportation to Nazi death camps. Around 20 per cent of Italian Jews perished during the war.
[28] BBC interview.
[29] BBC interview.
[30] BBC interview.
[31] Quoted in Michael Mogensen, 'The Rescue of the Danish Jews', in Mette Bastholm Jensen and Steven L.B. Jensen (eds), *Denmark and the Holocaust* (Department for Holocaust and Genocide Studies, Copenhagen 2003), p. 45.
[32] Quoted in Mogensen, 'Rescue', p. 33. See also Leni Yahil, *The Rescue of Danish Jewry: Test of a Democracy* (The Jewish Publication Society of America 1969).
[33] Quoted in Mogensen, 'Rescue', p. 58.

CHAPTER 5:
FRENZIED KILLING

[1] Christian Gerlach and Goetz Aly, *Das letzte Kapitel* (The Last Chapter) (Fischer 2004).
[2] Words taken from SIME report no.1 on the interrogation of Joel Brand, 16–30 June 1944, File no. SIME/P 7769, FO 371/42811, as well as Brand's testimony at the Eichmann trial, session no. 56, 29 June 1961.
[3] See SIME report no. 3 on interrogations of Bandi Grosz 6–22 June 1944. File no. SIME/P 7755, TNA 371/42811 pp. 42–3.
[4] *Auschwitz 1940–1945, Central Issues in the History of the Camp*, Vol. V (Auschwitz–Birkenau State Museum 2000), p. 198.
[5] BBC interview.
[6] BBC interview.
[7] BBC interview.
[8] Quoted in Andrzej Strzelecki, 'Utilization of the Victims' Corpses', in *Auschwitz 1940–1945*, Vol. II, p. 407.
[9] *Amidst a Nightmare of Crime: Manuscripts of Members of Sonderkommando* (Publications of State Museum at Oświęcim 1973), p. 119.
[10] *Amidst a Nightmare*, p. 119.
[11] *Amidst a Nightmare*, p. 182.
[12] *Amidst a Nightmare*, p. 185.
[13] *Amidst a Nightmare*, p. 181.
[14] Miklos Nyiszli, *Auschwitz, a Doctor's Eyewitness Account* (Arcade 1993), p. 4.
[15] Yehuda Bauer, *Jews for Sale?* (Yale University Press 1994), p. 180.
[16] Bauer, *Jews*, p. 167.
[17] BBC interview.
[18] BBC interview.
[19] See Yehuda Bauer's comments in *Encyclopedia of the Holocaust*, Vol. 1 (Macmillan, New York), p. 790.
[20] BBC interview (from *Timewatch: Himmler, Hitler and the End of the Reich*, transmitted 19 January 2000. Producer Detlef Siebert, Executive Producer Laurence Rees).
[21] 'Gathering and Disseminating Evidence of the Crime', in *Auschwitz 1940–1945*, Vol. IV, pp. 307–15.
[22] 'Gathering and Disseminating Evidence', p. 315.
[23] See especially Richard Breitman, *What the British and Americans*

Knew (Allen Lane The Penguin Press 1998), Ch. 7 'Auschwitz Practically Decoded in Official Secrets – What the Nazis Planned'.
[24] Quoted in *What the British and Americans Knew*, p. 120.
[25] Quoted in Robert Jan van Pelt, *The Case for Auschwitz* (Indiana University Press 2002), p. 154.
[26] Quoted in Martin Gilbert's essay 'The Contemporary Case for the Feasibility of Bombing Auschwitz', in Michael J. Neufeld and Michael Berenbaum (eds), *Allies and the Holocaust in the Bombing of Auschwitz* (St Martin's Press, New York 2000), p. 66.
[27] Quoted in Neufeld and Berenbaum (eds), *The Bombing of Auschwitz*, p. 67.
[28] Quoted in Neufeld and Berenbaum (eds), *The Bombing of Auschwitz*, p. 68.
[29] Quoted in Neufeld and Berenbaum (eds), *The Bombing of Auschwitz*, p. 70.
[30] Quoted in Neufeld and Berenbaum (eds), *The Bombing of Auschwitz*, p. 73 (and for a detailed analysis of the documents see Gilbert's full essay pp. 65–75).
[31] Deborah E. Lipstadt, 'The Failure to Rescue and Contemporary American Jewish Historiography of the Holocaust: Judging from a Distance', in Neufeld and Berenbaum (eds), *The Bombing of Auschwitz*, p. 229.
[32] James H. Kitchens III, 'The Bombing of Auschwitz Re-examined', in Neufeld and Berenbaum (eds), *The Bombing of Auschwitz*, pp. 80–100.
[33] Stuart G. Erdheim, 'Could the Allies Have Bombed Auschwitz–Birkenau?', in Neufeld and Berenbaum (eds), *The Bombing of Auschwitz*, pp. 127–56.
[34] Richard Levy, 'The Bombing of Auschwitz Revisited: a Critical Analysis', in Neufeld and Berenbaum (eds), *The Bombing of Auschwitz*, p. 114.
[35] Quoted in Martin Gilbert, *Auschwitz and the Allies* (Pimlico 2001, originally published 1981), p. 121.
[36] Quoted in Gilbert, *Auschwitz and the Allies*, p. 127.
[37] Quoted in Gilbert, *Auschwitz and the Allies*, p. 127.
[38] Quoted in Gilbert, *Auschwitz and the Allies*, p. 139.
[39] BBC interview.
[40] BBC interview.
[41] *Auschwitz 1940–1945*, Vol. V, p. 217.
[42] See the testimony of Kurt Becher, 10 July 1947, cited in Eichmann interrogations, TAE Vol. VIII, pp. 2895–6.

CHAPTER 6:
LIBERATION AND RETRIBUTION

[1] BBC interview.
[2] Andrzej Strzelecki, 'The Liquidation of the Camp', in *Auschwitz 1940–1945, Central Issues in the History of the Camp*, Vol. V (Auschwitz–Birkenau State Museum 2000), p. 45.
[3] Quoted in Robert Jan van Pelt, *The Case for Auschwitz* (Indiana University Press 2000), p. 159. See also pp. 158–65 for an examination of the press treatment of Auschwitz post-liberation.
[4] Van Pelt, *The Case for Auschwitz*, p. 164.
[5] *Encyclopedia of the Holocaust*, Vol. 1 (Macmillan, New York), p. 350, and Yehuda Bauer, 'The Death Marches, January–May 1945', in *Modern Judaism* (February 1983), pp. 1–21.

[6] BBC interview.
[7] BBC interview.
[8] BBC interview.
[9] BBC interview (from *Timewatch: Hitler, Himmler and the End of the Reich*, transmitted 19 January 2000).
[10] Quoted in *Timewatch: Hitler, Himmler*.
[11] BBC interview (from *Timewatch: Hitler, Himmler*).
[12] BBC interview (from *Timewatch: Hitler, Himmler*).
[13] BBC interview.
[14] BBC interview.
[15] BBC interview.
[16] BBC interview.
[17] Gunnar S. Paulsson, *Secret Garden: the Hidden Jews of Warsaw* (Yale University Press 2002). Around 28,000 Polish Jews escaped (or never entered) the Warsaw ghetto, with 11,000 surviving the war; this was often thanks to the help of the non-Jewish Polish population.
[18] BBC interview.
[19] BBC interview.
[20] BBC interview.
[21] BBC interview.
[22] Tom Segev, *The Seventh Million* (Hill and Wang 1994), pp. 147–9.
[23] Segev, *The Seventh Million*, pp. 140–6.
[24] This pioneering research was conducted by David List of the BBC History Unit.
[25] Rupert Butler, *Legions of Death* (Hamlyn paperback 1983), and a letter by Captain Cross to Colonel Felix Robson, curator, Intelligence Corps Museum, now held in the files of the Museum of Military Intelligence, Chicksands.
[26] BBC interview.
[27] Rudolf Hoess, *Commandant of Auschwitz* (Phoenix Press 2000), p. 166.
[28] BBC interview, quoted in Laurence Rees, *Horror in the East* (BBC Books 2001), p. 119.
[29] Lasik, 'The Apprehension and Punishment of the Auschwitz Concentration Camp Staff', in: *Auschwitz 1940–1945*, Vol. V, pp. 99–119.
[30] Lasik, 'Apprehension and Punishment', p. 116.
[31] These figures were supplied by Professor Piper of the Auschwitz–Birkenau State Museum.

ACKNOWLEDGEMENTS

This is a book that developed from a television series I wrote and produced, so there are many people whom I must thank. The television series (and therefore this book) exist because of the initial enthusiasm and commitment of Mark Thompson, then Director of BBC Television. It says a lot about how long it takes to finance, develop and make a project like this that in between Mark's authorizing the series and its eventual transmission he left the BBC, took the job of running Channel 4, then returned to the BBC on being appointed Director General. Many others in BBC Television also supported the series, notably Jane Root, then Controller of BBC2, Glenwyn Benson, Controller of Factual Commissioning, and Emma Swain, Commissioner of Specialist Factual Programmes. In particular my immediate boss, Keith Scholey, Controller of Specialist Factual, was extremely understanding and full of good advice.

Many distinguished academics contributed to the project. The series' historical and script consultant, Professor Sir Ian Kershaw, brought an extraordinary level of insight to the programmes – it is no accident that he is a scholar laden with honours. I owe him a huge debt, both for his scholarship and for his friendship. Professor David Cesarani was also influential in shaping both my views and the television series, as was Professor Christopher Browning. Two more eminent experts on the Nazis' 'Final Solution' it would be hard to find. Professor Robert Jan van Pelt was of enormous assistance in helping us to understand the architecture of the camp, and the scholars and administrative staff at the Auschwitz–Birkenau State Museum in Poland were also hugely helpful. Among those at the museum I need to thank in particular Igor Bartosik, Edyta Chowaniec, Adam Cyra, Jadwiga Dąbrowska, Dorota Grela, Wanda Hutny, Helena Kubica, Mirosław Obstarczyk, Krystyna Oleksy, Józef Orlicki, Dr Franciszek Piper, Wojciech Płosa, Dr Piotr Setkiewicz, Kazimierz Smoleń, Dr Andrzej Strzelecki, Dr

Henryk Świebocki, Jerzy Wróblewski and Roman Zbrzeski. Elsewhere in connection with our Polish research we received great assistance from Kazimierz Albin, Halina Elczewska, Abraham and Ester Frischer, Dr Józef Geresz, Bernadetta Gronek, John Hartman, Józef Koch, Edward Kopówka, Alicja Kościan, Dr Aleksander Lasik, Anna Machcewicz, Mariusz Jerzy Olbromski, Łucja Pawlicka-Nowak, Hubert Rogoziński, Robert Rydzoń, Jacek Szwic, Dr Marian Turski and Michalina Wysocka.

In the Channel Islands Frederick Cohen gave us the benefit of his unique historical knowledge, and in France Serge Klarsfeld and Adeline Suard were of great assistance. At Yad Vashem in Israel, particular mention should be made of the help afforded to us by Dr Gideon Greif. Elsewhere in Israel we benefited greatly from the work of Nava Mizrachi. In Slovakia Ivan Kamenec and Dr Eduard Niznansky helped us, as did the following in Germany: Dr Andrej Angrick, Martin Cueppers, Wolf Gebhardt, Niels Gutschow, Peter Klein, Michaela Lichtenstein, Dr Bogdan Musial, Dr Dieter Pohl, Dr Volker Reiss, Robert Sommer, Dr Frank Stucke and Peter Witte. In Russia, Dr Sergey Sluch was a good friend to the project. In Hungary very useful help was provided by Dr Krisztina Fenyo, and in the Ukraine by Taras Shumeiko. In America Adam Levy did a terrific job for us.

Obviously I owe a huge debt to the production team of the TV series. In particular I need to thank Detlef Siebert, who not only brilliantly directed the drama sequences across the whole series but also offered incisive criticism and advice for the rest of the content. He possesses an exceptional mind. The two documentary directors Martina Balazova and Dominic Sutherland also did a first-rate job, often working with our faithful camera team of Martin Patmore and Brian Biffin. Dominic, a tower of intelligence and good sense during the post-production of the series, also supervised the graphic content with the help of the Moving Picture Company and John Kennedy. Alan Lygo, the best film editor in television, made a substantial contribution in the cutting room. Tanya Batchelor did an excellent job as an Assistant Producer on the series, and Anna Taborska was outstanding as our specialist Polish researcher. Declan Smith gathered the archive for the series, and Rebecca Maidens and Cara

Goold were the Production Coordinators: all of them made an important contribution. Emily Brownridge could not have done a finer job as Production Manager, and Anna Mishcon and Laura Davey were always supportive as Production Executives. My own assistants, first Sarah Hall and subsequently Michelle Gribbon, were also always willing to help.

Special mention has to be made of the excellent guidance I received from our American co-producers, KCET. Karen Hunte, Al Jerome, Mary Mazur and especially Megan Callaway all contributed to this work, as did Coby Atlas at PBS. Sally Potter and Martin Redfern at BBC Books were model and supportive publishers, as were Peter Osnos, Clive Priddle and Kate Darnton at Public Affairs in New York. As usual, Andrew Nurnberg gave fine advice.

My own family – my children, Benedict, Camilla and Oliver, and my wife Helena – helped me more than I can say. It is not necessarily pleasant all the time living with someone whose head is full of information about Auschwitz and the Nazis, and they tolerated that and more besides.

However, my most profound thanks must go to the hundred or so eye-witnesses who allowed themselves to be interviewed for this project. Their memories are priceless. And I hope they will forgive me for expressing my thanks to them collectively here – their names are already elsewhere in this book, as are their insights.

INDEX

Abt, Else 168–72, 301
adult euthanasia programme 59–61, 69–70, 87, 91, 184–5
Africa, Nazi plan to remove Jews to 36, 67
Alexander, Vera 188
Allied powers
and Auschwitz 245–52
bombing compared with Holocaust 295–7
and the Brand-Grosz mission 239–42
and Himmler's plan for partial surrender 274–5
Ambros, Dr Otto 48
anti-Semitism 28–30
in eastern Europe 8–9, 282–5, 286
in Germany 12–16, 20–1, 26, 29–30
and Hitler 1, 9, 12, 13–16, 29, 30, 33, 106
and Hoess 20–1
and Nazi emigration policy 35–6, 48, 67
and Nazi war criminals 11–12
and sexual relationships at Auschwitz 190–2
and Slovakian Jews 106–7, 108–10
Antonescu, Ion 216
Arlt, Dr Fritz 34
Auschwitz
as an agricultural research centre 22, 42–3, 50
beginning and end of 6
and Birkenau 78–82, 119
Block 11 43–6, 59, 71–2, 83, 95, 155, 200
brothel 201–5
call for Allied bombing of 248–52
'Canada' sorting area 181–2, 191, 193–7, 209
death march from 266–8
death toll 301–2
decay of the site after the war 297–8
doctors at 184–90
escapes from 58–9, 150–5
'family camp' 191–2
firemen 202–3, 205, 238
gypsy camp 192
and I.G. Farben 46–52, 70, 179, 187
liberation of 264–6
location of 36–7
release of prisoners from 46–8
sexual relationships at 190–7, 198–200
and the SS 141–5
sub-camps 179–80
'swimming pool' 205
theft and corruption at 12, 38, 99–100, 181–4, 197–201, 238
see also killings at Auschwitz-Birkenau
Auschwitz Protocols 246–7, 250–1

Bach-Zelewski, Erich von dem, SS Obergruppenführer (Lieutenant General) 50, 68
Baker, Else 16, 253–7
Bartoszewski, Wladysław 46–8
Battel, Oberleutnant (Lieutenant) Albert 163–5
Bayer company 187–8
Beaune-la-Rolande camp 127–8, 129–32, 134, 135
Becher, Kurt 227–8, 245, 262
Bełżec 70, 87, 88, 92, 95, 156–60, 161, 164, 173
gas chambers 157–9
workers at 159–60
Bendera, Eugeniusz (Genek) 151–2, 153, 154, 155
Benjamin, Brigadier Ernest 288
Bergen-Belsen 244–5, 269–71, 273
Berger, Oskar 162
Bernadotte, Count Folke 274
Best, Dr Werner 218, 221, 223, 248
Biebow, Hans 84
Bielecki, Jerzy 40, 43–5, 57, 96
Bier, Rudy 220–2, 285
Birkenau 78–82, 95, 105, 107
escapes from 82
gypsy camp 253–6
and Polish death camps 60, 158–9
Soviet POWs and starvation 81–2
women's camp 150, 231–2
see also killings at Auschwitz-Birkenau
Bischoff, Karl, SS Hauptsturmführer (Captain) 79, 110
Blatt, Toivi 17, 205–12, 213, 214–15, 283–5
Bormann, Martin 201
Bousquet, René 125
Brand-Grosz mission 226–8, 239–42
Brasse, Wilhelm 37, 38–9, 40, 60–1, 71
Breder, Linda 181, 191, 279–81, 283, 285, 301
Britain
Battle of (1940) 48
and the Brand-Grosz mission 239–42
and emigration restrictions on Jews 252
and the Soviet Union 53
Broad, Perry 46, 97–8, 111
brothel at Auschwitz 201–5

Buchenwald concentration camp 148, 202
Bulgarian Jews 216

Cahana, Alice Lok 230–2, 257–60, 262, 270, 271–2
Chamberlain, Neville 288–9
Channel Islands 145–9
Chełmno gas vans 86–7, 88, 90–2, 98, 101, 121, 157, 253
children
 French Jewish 125, 126–38
 of Jehovah's Witnesses 169, 171
 in the Łódź ghetto 102
 murder of disabled 60
 murdered at Auschwitz 18, 138, 139
 murders at Chełmo 91
 Polish 34–5
 Soviet Jewish 62–5, 67, 68
Christian X, King of Denmark 217–18
Churchill, Winston 48, 241, 245, 249, 265, 289, 296
Citrónová, Helena 192–7, 267, 275–6
Clages, Gerhard, 227, 228, 240
Clauberg, Dr 186, 187, 188
Cohen, Frederick 149
Communism
 and French Jews 123–4
 and the Nazis 21, 23, 26, 55, 56

Dachau 23–7, 37, 46, 48, 76, 79, 98, 157, 266
Dacko, Ryszard 202–3, 204–5
Daltroff-Baticle, Odette 132–3, 134
Danish Jews 17–18, 149, 217–23, 285–7
Dannecker, Theodor, SS Hauptsturmführer (Captain) 124, 125
Davidson, Nathan 146
death marches 266–8
Dejaco, Walter 177
Devecseri, László 242
doctors at Auschwitz 184–90
 and the adult euthanasia programme 184–5
 and the brothel 202
 and medical experiments 186–90
 and the selection process 185–6
Drancy camp 132–4, 136
Dubiel, Stanisław (Staszek) 99, 100
Duckwitz, Georg 218–19
Dutch Jews, at Sobibór death camp 209–10
Dyby, Knut 217, 219, 222, 223

eastern Europe
 anti-Semitism in 8–9, 282–5, 286
 Soviet occupation of 277–81
Eberl, Dr Irmfried 161–2, 163, 172, 185
Eden, Anthony 246, 248, 251, 252
Eichengreen, Lucille 29–30, 76, 77, 78
 in Auschwitz 105
 in the Łódź ghetto 83, 85, 86, 92, 100–5
Eichmann, Adolf, SS Obersturmbannführer (Lieutenant Colonel) 30, 31, 62, 66, 124, 295
 and the Hungarian Jews 225–8, 239, 242, 243, 262, 266
 and the Wannsee Conference 93–4, 95
Eicke, Theodor 24, 25, 170
Eigi, Irma 32
Elias, Ruth 192
Emmanuel, Victor 146
Epstein, Howard 129
Ertl, Fritz, SS Rottenführer (Corporal) 79
ethnic Germans
 and I.G. Farben 49, 50, 51–2
 movement to Poland 28–9, 31–3, 60
Farben, I.G. 48–52, 70, 179, 187
Felder, Josef 24
Feldhendler, Leon 213
Finkelstein, John Max 148
Frank, Hans, Gauleiter of the General Government 31, 34, 89–90
French Jews 122, 123–38, 218, 302
Frenkiel, Estera 33–4
Frenzl, commandant of Sobibór 214
Fried, Walter 281–3, 285, 286
Friedrich, Hans 11, 63–4, 65–6, 106–7
Fritzsch, Karl, Lagerführer (camp leader) 40, 58–9, 61, 71

Gabbai, Dario 233–7, 238
Gajowniczek, Franciszek 59
German Jehovah's Witnesses 168–72
German Jews 29–31
 deportation of 73–8, 83–6, 87–90
Gilbert, Dr Gustave 73
Globocnik, SS Oberstgruppenführer (General) Odilo 163
Goebbels, Dr Josef 7, 13, 14, 22, 33, 61, 89
 and the deportation of German Jews 74, 75
Goering, Hermann 19, 34, 50, 62, 67, 107
 and the Wannsee Conference 92, 94
Grabner, Maximilian, SS Untersturmführer (2nd Lieutenant) 45, 96, 98, 200–1
Greiser, Arthur 76, 83, 86
Groening, Oskar, SS Rottenführer (Corporal) 138–45, 165–8, 191
 on Allied bombings 285
 background 139–41
 and Holocaust deniers

300–1
and killings at Auschwitz 138–9, 142–4, 165–8, 298–9
post-war life 287–8
recruited to the SS 140–1
and theft and corruption at Auschwitz 182–3, 197–8
Grosz, Bandi 228, 240, 272
see also Brand-Grosz mission
Gruenwald, Malkiel 243
Grunfeld, Marianne 147, 148, 149
Grynszpan, Herschel 30
Guernsey, Jews in 145, 146–8, 149
Gutterer, Leopold 74
gypsy camp at Birkenau 253–6

Halder, Franz, Chief of the Army General Staff 53, 61
Hantz, Stanisław 294, 297, 298
Harris, Whitney 20
'Harvest Festival' killings (1943) 215–16
Hassebroeck, Johannes 26–7
Hermann, Chaim 236
Hess, Dr Walter 69
Heydrich, Reinhard 26, 218
assassination of 173
and Birkenau 79
and the deportation of German Jews 74, 77, 87, 88–9
and the 'Final Solution' 16, 19, 67–8
on ghettos 33
and the invasion of the Soviet Union 56, 57
and the Wannsee Conference 92–4, 95, 179
Himmler, Heinrich 12, 25, 26, 205
and Birkenau 78–9
and the Brand-Grosz mission 228, 240, 241
and brothels 201–2
and the deportation of German Jews 74, 76, 86, 87
and the expulsion of Jews 245
and the 'Final Solution' 16, 19, 27–8, 36, 90, 92
and Hitler 15, 27–8, 272–3, 274–5
and Hoess 22, 201
and the Hungarian Jews 262
and I.G. Farben 48, 49–52, 70
and the invasion of the Soviet Union 54–5
and Jehovah's Witnesses 170, 172
and killings at Auschwitz 70–1
and killings in the Soviet Union 62, 63, 68–9
meeting with Hoess (Nov 1940) 41–3
and Polish Jews 31, 33, 34–6, 160, 163, 164
Posen speech (1943) 183–4, 197
and the revolt at Sobibór 215–16
and Slovak Jews 107
and sterilization experiments 186
suicide 275
visits to Auschwitz 50–2, 149–50, 155–6
and the Wannsee Conference 94, 95
and the Warsaw ghetto uprising 174, 175
Hingst, August 161–2
Hitler, Adolf 8, 10, 63, 175, 249
and anti-Semitism 1, 9, 12, 13–16, 29, 30, 33, 106
and the Brand-Grosz mission 240–1
and concentration camps 23
declares war on the United States 89
and the deportation of German Jews 74, 75, 76, 88
and the 'Final Solution' 15–16, 19, 36, 70, 73, 90, 92, 95
and Himmler 15, 27–8, 272–3, 274–5
and Hoess 20
and Hungary 224, 225
invasion of the Soviet Union 52–3, 55, 122–3
and Jehovah's Witnesses 170, 171, 172
and the murder of disabled children 60
suicide 53, 273–4
and World War I 17
Hodys, Eleanore 199–200
Hoeppner, Rolf-Heinz 62
Hoess, Rudolf, SS Obersturmbannführer (Lieutenant Colonel)
and anti-Semitism 20–2
appearance and character 20
appointed commandant of Auschwitz 19, 27, 36
appointed commander of overall SS garrison at Auschwitz 229–30
and Birkenau 78, 79
capture by the Allies 292–3
and Dachau 23–7
disappearance 275, 287
dismissal from post of commandant 201
and escapes from Auschwitz 58
execution 293–4, 298
and families at Auschwitz 135–6
and Himmler's visits to Auschwitz 50–2
and Jehovah's Witnesses 170, 171, 172
and killings at Auschwitz 70–2, 73, 95–6, 98, 110–11, 117, 119–20
meeting with Himmler (Nov 1940) 41–3
memoirs 293, 294–5, 296–7
and the Nuremberg Trials 20, 73, 293
possible relationship with Eleanore Hodys 198–200
recruited to the SS 22–3
and Soviet POWs 82

and theft at Auschwitz 38, 182
villa of 99–100
Holocaust deniers 205, 293, 300–1
Horror in the East 10
Horthy, Admiral 247–8, 250–1
Hungarian Jews 224–32, 239–47, 250–1, 255, 302
and the Brand-Grosz mission 226–8, 239–42
death march 262, 266
ghettoization of 226
and the Kasztner train 242–5
Hungary, changing political alliances 224–5, 247
Huppert, Shmuel 244

Igiel, Samuel 164
Israel, state of 288
Italian Jews 216

Jacobs, Benjamin 180
Japanese war criminals 11
Jaschke, Wilhelm 69
Jaster, Stanisław 153, 155
Jeckeln, Friedrich 87, 88
Jehovah's Witnesses 168–72, 302
Jersey, Jews in 145–6, 149
Jewish Brigade 288–91
Juhl, Hans 221

Kabáč, Michal 106–7, 108, 109–10
Kamiński, Yaacov 260
Kammler, Hans 79, 110
Kapos
at Auschwitz 37, 38–9, 40, 43, 57, 60–1
at Birkenau 111–12
at Dachau 25
Karmi, Ahron 175–6
Kasztner, Rudolf 241–3, 245, 246, 262
Kaufmann, Karl, Gauleiter of Hamburg 75
Keitel, Field Marshal Wilhelm 123
Kersten, Felix 273
killings at Auschwitz–Birkenau
adult euthanasia programme 60–1
Auschwitz camp crematorium 82–3, 89, 95–6, 98, 110
and body disposals 89, 96, 114–15, 120, 167–8
converted cottages 110–11, 114–15, 117–18, 119–20, 150, 156, 178, 251
crematoria 177–9, 188, 229, 251, 263
gas chambers 177–9, 234–7, 259–60
gassings in Block 11 71–2, 83
German Jews 87
Groening's attitude to 138–9, 142–4, 165–8
and Hoess 70–2, 73
Jehovah's Witnesses 170
selection process 113–14, 135–6, 138, 185–6, 258
shootings at Block 11 45, 46
Slovakian Jews 110–11, 113–15, 117
and the Sonder kommando 232–9
Soviet commissars 57–8, 71
Soviet prisoners of war 96
starvation at Block 11 59, 155
'unproductive' Jews from surrounding areas 96–8, 99
and Zyklon B 71–2, 83, 95, 96–7, 177
killings in the East
adult euthanasia programme 59–61, 69–70, 87, 91
by explosion 69
and the Chełmno gas vans 86–7, 88, 90–2
gassing experiments 86–7
and the German population 77–8
'Harvest Festival' killings (1943) 215–16
Nazi starvation policy 54–5, 63
Soviet Jews 56–7, 62–6, 67, 68–9, 74, 88, 94–5
see also Bełżec; Sobibór; Treblinka
Klein, Dr Fritz 185
Knochen, Helmut 125
Kolbe, Maksymilian 59, 151
Koppe, Wilhelm 86
Kor, Eva Mozes 189, 263–4
Koso, Dr Izidor 107
Kowalczyk, August 71
Kramer, Josef 269
Krankemann, Ernst 40, 61
Küsel, Otto 39

Lange, Herbert, SS Hauptsturmführer (Captain) 86, 92
Laskov, Haim 290
Laval, Pierre 125–6, 129, 137
Leguay, Jean 129
Lerner, Yehuda 214
Levi, Primo 180
Lichtheim, Richard 247
Liedtke, Oberstleutnant (Major) 164
Lithuanian Jews 57
Łódź ghetto 33–4, 83, 85, 86, 92, 100–5, 145, 253, 261
deportation of German Jews to 76, 83–6, 87
food crisis (1941) 14, 62
Jews transported to Auschwitz from 105
killing of Jews from 86–7, 92, 101, 157
Loringhoven, Bernd Freiherr Freytag von 274

McCloy, John 248, 249
MacMichael, Sir Harold 239
Majdane camp 261, 265
Mann, Ibi 267–8
Martynushkin, Ivan 264–5
Masur, Norbert 273
medical experiments 186–90
Meinhold, Helmut 54

Melchior, Bent 217–18, 219, 285
Mengele, Dr Josef 188–90, 212, 226, 231, 258, 263, 291
mental hospitals, Jews in 60
Mildner, Dr, Obersturmbannführer (Lieutenant Colonel) 46
Moebius, Kurt 91–2
Moll, Otto 261
Montgomery, Paul 296
Morgen, Konrad, SS Obersturmführer (1st Lieutenant) 197–201
Müller, head of the Gestapo 95
Mulevych, Oleksiy 64–5
Muller, Annette 126–8, 129–31, 132, 133–4, 137
Muller, Michel 126–8, 129–31, 133–4, 137
Mussolini, Benito 216

Nanieva, Tatiana 277, 278
Nazi war criminals 10 11–13
Nazis: A Warning from History 9–10
Nebe, Artur 69
Newman, Barbara 147–8
Nisenman, Jo 134–5
Nuremberg Trials 20, 73, 293
Nyiszli, Myklos 189, 238

Operation Reinhard camps *see* Bełżec; Sobibór; Treblinka
Orange, Clifford 146
Oven, Wilfred von 7

Paczyński, Józef 43, 98, 99–100, 202, 203, 204
Palfinger, Alexander 84
Palitzsch, Gerhard, Rapportführer (commandant's chief assistant) 40, 117, 191
Pearl Harbor 89, 90, 93
Pehle, John 248
Perchersky, Alexander ('Sasha') 212–13, 214, 215
Pétain, Marshal 121, 125
Pfannmüller, Dr 60
Piechowski, Kazimierz (Kazik) 150–5
Pius XII, Pope 247
Piwczyk, Jan 297
Plevin, Ernest 147
Pohl, Oswald, SS Obergruppenführer (Lieutenant General) 41, 79, 183, 202
Poland
  ethnic Germans moved to 28–9, 31–3
  Nazi policies in 31–6, 63
  Warsaw ghetto uprising (1943) 174, 175
  see also killings in the East
Polevoi, Boris 265
Polish gypsies 253
Polish Jews 28–9, 31, 32–3, 35–6, 156–65, 302
  and death camps in Poland 156–65
  see also Łódź ghetto
Polish political prisoners 37–40, 46–8, 150, 202, 203–4, 302
Polish prisoners of war (POWs) 266
Pressburger, Otto 106, 111–12, 113, 114–16, 117
Przemyśl, Jews of 163–5

Rademacher, Franz 36
rape 190–2, 197, 275–7
Rath, Ernst von 30
Rathbone, Eleanor 252
Rathenau, Walther 21
Red Army
  advance on Nazi-occupied territory 247–8, 249
  in Berlin 273–4
  in eastern Europe 279–80
  and the liberation of Auschwitz 264–6
  raping of women 275–7
Reh, Rita 272
Riedweg, Franz 273
Romanian gypsies 253
Roosevelt, Franklin D. 89, 247, 265
Rosenberg, Alfred 67–8, 75
Rumkowski, Mordechai Chaim 84, 102, 103–5
Rybacki, Tadeusz 118–19

Sachsenhausen concentration camp 27, 37, 61, 170, 171
Saddam Hussein 11
Salt, Renee 270
Samuel, Eugenia 162
Schroeder, Manfred von 22, 23
Schumann, Dr 186, 187, 188
Schwartz, Edith 230–2, 257–8, 259, 270, 271–2
sexual relationships at Auschwitz 190–7, 198–200
  brothel 202–5
  homosexual relationships 204
Sinclair, Sir Archibald 248
Slovakian gypsies 253
Slovakian Hlinka guards 106–7, 108–9
Slovakian Jews 105–10, 111–15, 117, 118, 279–83
Smoleń, Kazimierz 60, 61, 80, 81, 82, 150
Sobibór 70, 156–7, 158, 160–1, 173, 174, 205–15
  escapes from 21–15
  gas chambers 160–1, 206, 207–8, 209–10
Sonderkommando 232–9
  revolt 260–2
Soviet Jews, killing of 56–7, 62–6, 67, 68–9, 74, 88, 94–5
Soviet prisoners of war (POWs) 80–2, 96, 107, 277–8
  escapes from Sobibór 212–15
Soviet Union
  and Auschwitz 265–6
  and ethnic Germans 28–9
  and Hitler 16
  Nazi invasion and war 52–7, 61–2, 75, 122–3, 225

and Stalinism 10–11
see also killings in the East; Red Army
Speer, Albert 41
Speter, Éva 242, 243–4, 245
Spitz, Auguste 147, 148, 149
Stahlecker, Dr Walter, SS Brigadeführer (Brigadier) 56
Stalin, Joseph 8, 10, 11, 12, 29, 51, 53, 75, 265
persecution of ethnic groups 278–9
and Soviet POWs 277–8
Stangl, Franz 160, 172, 185
Stark, Hans 96
Steiner, SS Oberstgruppenführer (General) Felix 273
Steiner, Therese 147–8, 149
Stenkin, Pavel 81, 82, 277
sterilization experiments 186–7
Storjohann, Uwe 76–7
Streicher, Julius 14, 21
Stroop, SS Oberstgruppenführer (General) Jürgen 176
Stuelpnagel, General Otto von 122, 123–4
Sweden, and Danish Jews 220–2
Szałek, Zofia 91
Szmyt, Władysław 256
Sztojay, Dome 247
Tavor, Moshe 288–91
Theresienstadt 94, 149, 192, 221, 272, 285
Tiso, Josef 105, 107
Treblinka 23, 70, 156–7, 158, 161–3, 172–3, 185
death toll 161, 162, 173, 174
Trojanoswki, Roman 37, 39, 58, 59
Tuja, Vojtech 107–8
twin studies 188–9

Ukranian Jews 64–5, 66

Vajspapir, Arkadiy 213–14, 215
Valdeman, Vasyl 64, 65
Venezia, Morris 233–7, 238–9, 268–9
Veselá, Silvia 108, 109, 110, 112–13, 116, 186–7
Votavová, Eva 105–6, 114
Vrba, Rudolf 246

Wannsee Conference 92–5, 97, 179, 186
War of the Century 10
Warsaw ghetto uprising (1943) 174, 175
Wetzler, Alfred 246
Widmann, Dr Albert 69–70, 87, 158
Wirth, Christian, SS Hauptsturmführer (Captain) 87, 157–8, 159, 160, 162–3, 172, 185
Wirths, Dr 187, 188
Wisliceny, Dieter, SS Sturmbannführer (Major) 107–8
women
and the Auschwitz brothel 204–5
deportation of French Jewish 126–30
and rape 190–2, 197, 275–7
and the selection process for the gas chamber 135–6
and sexual relationships at Auschwitz 190–7, 199–200
shooting of Soviet Jewish women and children 62–5, 67, 68, 136
Slovakian Jews at Auschwitz 112–14, 117–18
sterilization experiments on 186–7
World War I 12, 17, 20, 21, 29, 143
Wunsch, Franz 192–7, 266–7

Zbozień, Boleslaw 45
Zielińska, Józefa 297
Zielke, Egon 84
Zylberstein, Jacob 83, 85, 104–5, 116

PICTURE CREDITS

BBC Books would like to thank the following for providing photographs and for permission to reproduce copyright material. While every effort has been made to trace and acknowledge all copyright holders, we would like to apologize should there have been any errors or omissions.

Plate Section 1 1 Yad Vashem; 2t Walter Frentz Archive; 2b Bildarchiv Preussischer Kulturbesitz; 3t Hans Friedrich; 3b Ullstein Bild; 4–5, 6, 7 Jewish Museum, Frankfurt; 8 Yad Vashem.

Plate Section 2 1 Auschwitz Museum, 2t Yad Vashem; 2c Oskar Groening; 2b Kazimierz Piechowski; 3t Wendy Davenport; 3b Helena Citrónóva; 4, 5, 6t Yad Vashem; 6b, 7 Auschwitz Museum; 8 Yad Vashem.